RAS ALULA
AND THE SCRAMBLE FOR AFRICA

Rās Alulā in 1890 (see p. 155)

RAS ALULA
AND THE SCRAMBLE FOR AFRICA

A POLITICAL BIOGRAPHY:
Ethiopia & Eritrea 1875-1897

HAGGAI ERLICH

The Red Sea Press, Inc.
Publishers & Distributors of Third World Books

11-D Princess Road
Lawrenceville, NJ 08648

P. O. Box 48
Asmara, ERITREA

The Red Sea Press, Inc.
Publishers & Distributors of Third World Books

11-D Princess Road	P. O. Box 48
Lawrenceville, NJ 08648	Asmara, ERITREA

Copyright © Haggai Erlich 1996

First Red Sea Press, Inc. Printing 1996

All rights reserved. No part of this publication may be reproduced, stored in a retrieval system or transmitted in any form or by any means electronic, mechanical, photocopying, recording or otherwise without the prior permission of the publisher.

Cover Design: Linda Nickens

Library of Congress Cataloging-in-Publication Data

Erlich, Haggai.
   Ras Alula and the scramble for Africa : a political biography : Ethiopia and Eritrea 1875-1897 / Haggai Erlich.
     p. cm.
   Rev. ed. of : Ethiopia and Eritrea during the scramble for Africa. 1982.
   Includes bibliographical references and index.
   ISBN 1-56902-028-0 (cloth) . -- ISBN 1-56902-029-9 (paper : alk. paper)
   1. Alula Qubi, 1847? - 1897. 2. Generals--Ethiopia--Biography. 3. Politicians--Ethiopia--Biography. 4. Ethiopia--Politics and government. 5. Eritrea--Politics and government. 6. Tigray Kifle Hāger (Ethiopia)--Politics and govenment. I. Erlich, Haggai. Ethiopia and Eritrea during the scramble for Africa. II. Title.
DT386.73.A48E74 1996
963' .04'092--dc20
[B]   96-11511
                                                                  CIP

To my father, Hanoch

CONTENTS

Abbreviations viii
Preface ix
Introduction 1
1. 1872–1876: *Shālaqā* Alulā 9
2. 1877–1879: The King's Man: "Rās Alulā who is a Turk Bāshā" . 16
3. 1880–1882: "Rival od Shoa. Ruler of Massawa" 30
4. 1883: The Brink of a Second Egyptian-Ethiopian War 39
5. 1884: Treaty With Britain 43
6. 1884: Disillusionment 50
7. 1885: "The Year in Which the Dervishes Were Cut Down" 58
8. Asmara 81
9. 1885–1886: The Italians in Massawa:
   From a European Neighbor to a Local Rival 88
10. 1886–1887: Dogali 98
11. 1887: The End of Alulā's Government in
    the Marab Mellāsh (Eritrea) 110
12. 1888–1889: The End of the Tigrean Emperor 127
13. 1889–1890: Alulā's Failure to preserve Tigrean Hegemony 140
14. 1890–1892: Alulā's Failure to Create a
    Tirgrean-Eritrean Front Against Menilek 161
15. 1892–1894: *"Wādi Qubi"* challenges the son of Yohannes 179
16. 1894–1897: A King's Man Again:
    An Acceptance of Shoan Hegemony 186
Conclusion 201
Glossary 207
Bibliography 209
Indexed Maps 213
Genealogy of Alulā and the Tigrean Elite 216
Index 217

Abbreviations

AA Rub. Col.	'Abidīn Archives (Cairo). Egyptian documents available in Rubenson's Collection, IES.
A.S.MAI	Archivio Storico del soppresso Ministero dell'Africa Italiana, Rome.
BM	British Museum.
BN	Bibliothèque Nationale.
Dadj.	Dadjāzmāch.
D.I.	Diarii Informazioni in A.S.MAI.
DN	*The Daily News*
Fit.	Fitāwrāri.
FO	Foreign Office.
H.S.I.U.	Haile Sellassie I University (now Addis Ababa University).
IES	Institute of Ethiopian Studies, Addis Ababa.
Int.	Interview with.
JES	*Journal of Ethiopian Studies*.
LV	*Libro Verde*.
MAE	Ministero degli Affari Esteri, Rome.
MAE(F)	Ministère des Affaires Etrangères, Paris.
M.d.G.	Ministero della Guerra.
MG	*The Manchester Guardian*.
NA	*Nuova Antologia*.
RMI	*Rivista Militare Italiana*.
SOAS	School of Oriental and African Studies, London University.
W.	Wayzaro.
WO	War Office.

Preface

"A Political Biography of Ras Alula" — A Generation Later

In September 1970 I joined the School of Oriental and African Studies (SOAS) of London University as a Ph.D. candidate. I arrived in London with a basic knowledge of Ethiopian history, some tentative Amharic, and a decision to write a dissertation on a period of intensive Ethiopian-Middle Eastern relations. I had, in fact, decided to devote my studies to Emperor Yohannes, but my supervisor at SOAS informed me that Dadjazmach Zawde Gabre-Selassie was already working on this subject in Oxford. "Why don't you write instead on Ras Alula?" he asked. "What a brilliant idea!" I answered. "Let me consider." And I ran home to find out who in the world this "Ras Alula" was. I indeed found out and, for the next three years, Ras Alula was the center of my life.

Coping with the historical figure of Ras Alula was a great challenge. Ras Alula had been actively involved in nearly all the major developments that took place in Ethiopia and Eritrea in the last quarter of the nineteenth century. He led Ethiopia's military struggle against the onslaught of imperialism, winning some ten decisive battles — from the clash with the Egyptians in Gura in 1876 to the Battle of Adwa against the Italians twenty years later. To ward off these invaders, and the Mahdists from the Sudan, Alula fortified Eritrea as Ethiopia's gate, abolishing in the process the autonomous status of local leading families. He built Asmara (beginning in 1884) as a local capital, and around it he tried to modernize the Eritrean economy and control intra-religious relations. Ras Alula was closely involved in the internal developments of Ethiopia in his time and was also a prominent figure in the shaping of much of the diplomatic and foreign policies during that crucial period, especially the so-called Hewett Treaty of 1884 with the Anglo-Egyptians.

Ras Alula was the most trusted aide of Emperor Yohannes (1872-1889) in his effort to maintain the hegemony of the crown (but without imposing centralization of power!) against Negus Menilek of Shoa and Negus Takla-Haimanot of Gojjam. Following the death of Yohannes in 1889, Ras Alula struggled to preserve the autonomy of Tigre as a buffer between the Italians in occupied Eritrea and Emperor Menilek (1889-1913) in Shoa. But, realizing that preserving Ethiopia's unity was the only way to stem imperialism, he brought about a general appeasement. His recognition of Menilek in June of 1894 was indeed a significant step leading to the formative victory over Italian imperialism.

The personal history of Alula, the son of a humble peasant with neither formal education nor inherited position, but only his natural intelligence and abilities, is a strong reflection of the central features of Ethiopia's socio-economic and political culture. The story of his achieving power and remaining influential against such a background is closely interwoven with the other dimensions of the above mentioned history. This was not so very exceptional in itself, for there was considerable flexibility in Ethiopia's sociopolitical mobility. While this flexibility contributed greatly to the country's inherent strength, it also preserved the ideological and political conservatism of its traditional elite.

No less exciting than the factual reconstruction of this multifaceted history was the task of coping with the various ways in which Alula was perceived by his contemporaries. None of them were indifferent to him, and he was the center of controversies which would long outlive him. For the Italians of his time, Alula was simultaneously a barbarian African and an admired adversary, and his victory over their forces at Dogali in January 1887 was a landmark in their imperialist history. The British and the French, too, wavered between respect for the resourceful Ethiopian and unforgiving umbrage for his daring to defeat the armies of white men. Alula was the focus of similar controversy in Egypt — feared and respected, admired and detested. The same is true of the Sudanese Mahdists, who also added radical Islamic terminology to their dual-image of Alula: he was the punishment Allah inflicted upon the Europeans and the Egyptians, as well as their own Christian-devil enemy.

Needless to say, Alula was controversial for the Ethiopians of his own time as well: the Christian elite of Eritrea never forgave Alula for putting an end to their political autonomy and for deposing their regional leader Ras Walda-Mikael; the leading families of Tigre were unable to reconcile themselves to his penetration into the upper sociopolitical echelon, and they never forgave him for the killing in this context of Dabab Araya; and the Shoan elite never forgave Alula for challenging their supremacy and fighting for the autonomy of Tigre. Moreover, since Shoan historiography of the twentieth century dominated the collective written Ethiopian memory, the figure of Alula has been quite marginalized. When I began to collect material on Ras Alula in 1970, I was indeed struck by the fact that while on the one hand very little has been written in Ethiopia about him, he was on the other hand admired to the extent of having become a virtual legend. He was undoubtedly a symbolic figure and national hero, a focus of identification the mere mention of whose name was certain to evoke strong reactions. Despite all the controversies about Alula, he instilled in the Ethiopian soul a legacy of purity and heroism, and of longing for an era of great achievement and international respect.

Writing about Ras Alula was, therefore, a very delicate matter. I endeavored to remain loyal to professional standards, refraining from following the controversies or from magnifying the human myth. I also did my best to reconstruct Alula as a mere mortal, and to analyze the story of his life. He conveys the image, I believe, of a very talented politician, a near genius as a military tactician, and a natural leader with an analytic and flexible mind. Ethiopia indeed, owes some of its major victories and achievements during that formative period to him. But I also reconstructed Alula as an occasionally over-ambitious seeker of power ever in dread of losing his position, a weakness which accounts for some disastrous mistakes, most notably the 1887 victory over the Italians at Dogali. This military victory, it must be admitted, although scored in a justified act of national self-defense, was also an over-reaction on the part of Alula and thus led to full Italian mobilization — and to the ensuing (otherwise easily avoidable) loss of Eritrean territory to the Italians.

My dissertation on Ras Alula was written in 1972-3, over twenty years ago. At that time, the entire perspective was completely different from that of today. Tigre Province was still administered by Ras Mangasha Seyum, and though not entirely happy with Haile Selassie's political and cultural centralism, Tigre was far from being rebellious. I reconstructed Alula's struggle to maintain Tigrean hegemony under Yohannes and then to preserve its autonomy under Shoan dominance, without knowing that the whole issue would soon become so vividly relevant. The same was true of Eritrea, for when I was conducting my research in Asmara in 1971, the local Christian elite, especially the representatives of the old generation whom I interviewed, still identified for the most part with Ethiopianism. Many were already bitter over Addis Ababa (especially after the removal of Ras Asrate and the ensuing intervention of the Ethiopian central army in Eritrea). Alula was perceived by them as a usurper of the local elite of Hamasien no less than as the developer of Asmara and a defender against imperialism. But Alula was still widely regarded by the old guard of Christian Eritreans as an all-Ethiopian hero. I reconstructed Alula's role in building Ethiopian administration in Eritrea (the Mareb Melash) and his policy vis-a-vis the local elite as yet another local version of the all-Ethiopian power game. I believe that this was the true perspective in the early 1970s, and that it is perhaps the right perspective even today.

The emergence of Mangistu Haile Mariam, his usurpation of the inevitable post-Haile Selassie revolution in 1974, and his gross brutalization of Ethiopia's political culture created a historical sequence of major disasters. It also created new perspectives on Ras Alula. My book on Ras Alula, based on the dissertation submitted in 1973, appeared only in 1982. When I attended the International Conference of Ethiopian Studies in Addis Ababa in 1984, I was told that Mangistu "liked it a lot." Efforts to translate it into Amharic by some of Mangistu's associates came to nothing, probably because I refused to make substantial changes in the text. It is not difficult to understand why Mangistu admired Alula — or rather the Alula he fashioned in his own mind. For Mangistu, Alula was a killer of enemies on Eritrean soil. Without really grasping its true meaning, he desired his own Dogali victory. When I was invited to take part in the celebrations marking the 100th anniversary of Dogali in January 1987, I delayed my arrival to avoid meeting Mangistu himself. I felt rewarded, however, when I saw posters all over Ethiopia bearing quotations from Alula which I had unearthed in dusty archives, and was excited to watch the national theater performing the play "Alula Abba Nagga" by Mamo Wudnah, which was based largely on my work. I particularly liked the emphasis made throughout on Alula, the peasant's son, challenging the nobility. This was a dimension in Alula's story which appealed to the new generation everywhere. The name Alula, I was told, became quite popular in the new Ethiopia of the 1980s, given to many newly born of whatever origin — Amhara, Gurages, Oromos.

Mangistu's emphasis, however, was on Dogali. According to his interpretation Dogali had been a decisive military victory in Eritrea over "reaction and imperialism," which meant anyone who opposed his totalitarian rule. He gave the name of Alula to one of the elite divisions of his army as well as to the Maqale Airport from which he sent his bombers to Eritrea. In Dogali's 99th anniversary, in January 1986, Mangistu had a monument erected to Ras Alula dominating over the theater of that battle, and came there personally to inaugurate it.

The photograph of Mangistu saluting the Alula monument was displayed all over the country. However, Mangistu lacked the mental or intellectual capacity to distinguish between foreign invaders and home opposition; for him they were all traitors deserving a Dogali-like slaughter. The Ethiopian intelligentsia, on the other hand, was in no position during Managistu's rule to express their views. I discussed Alula with Addis Ababa University professors and other scholars and authors who, in private over coffee or a beer, all lamented such abuse of history. Mangistu's twisted interpretation of Alula was similar to his misunderstanding of Tewodros as staged by the national theater; he saw him as a xenophobic hater of Europeans rather than as a frustrated modernizer of Ethiopia. Mangistu's Alula was the military conqueror of Eritrea rather than the builder of Asmara as a part of a pluralized Ethiopia and a defender against invaders from beyond the seas.

The Eritrean intelligentsia of the post-1974 period generally ignored Ras Alula. Very little was published during the 1970s and 1980s by the Eritrean liberation fronts that could shed light on the Eritrean young generation's interpretation of Alula and his time. In forming and cementing their new Eritrean identity, they justifiably related rather to the contemporary figures of Haile

Selassie and, mainly, Mangistu. The latter represented an Ethiopia from which they desperately wanted to separate. In 1995, however, when I returned to Asmara, now the capital of a sovereign Eritrea, Alula's image for the new Eritrean generation was easily discernible. The leaders of the new country were at best ready to admit that Alula was a great fighter against the Italians and other foreigners but for them he was a foreigner no less. They read Alula's story as part of colonial history: usurpation of local political leaderships, settling of foreign soldiers, maltreating and overtaxing the population, dividing and ruling. They accused Alula for using local manpower in the effort to stem the invading Europeans but reaping all the glory to himself. They remembered Alula for his ruthless massacre of the Kunama and the Baria tribes of the western province, and quoted popular poems on his cruelty as a governor. When the EPLF fighters in 1989 liberated Dogali from Mangistu's army, a prominent commander, now a prominent minister, was delighted to himself blast Mangistu's monument of Ras Alula. It is quite apparent, indeed, that the formative period of the late 19th century, and the central role of Alula in then shaping the Ethiopian government in the territory, is still seen from the perspective of Mangistu's brutality. I have no doubt, however, that with the forthcoming, perhaps inevitable, Ethiopian-Eritrean appeasement (in one political form or another), Alula's story, with its various interpretations, will be widely readdressed by Eritreans.

The TPLF leadership, the Ethiopian-Tigrean allies of the Eritrean-Tigrean EPLF, developed their own image of Alula. For them he was the national hero of Ethiopia as well as the pride of Tigrean history. He was also the son of a peasant and not a member of the Tigrean aristocracy that had failed throughout the twentieth century to introduce reforms and proved to be incapable of preserving Tigrean autonomy. Moreover, Alula was the heroic warrior who twice led Tigrean armies (1878 and 1882) into Shoa, and the leader of the resistance against Menilek's Shoan supremacy after Yohannes's death in 1889. I was not surprised to learn from the leaders of the TPLF, now the architects of Ethiopia's new political structure, that my book on Alula was studied throughout the 1980s in the caves of Tigre, and that the fighters of the TPLF were inspired by his heroism. It was indeed symbolic that the first elite division to penetrate Addis Ababa in 1991 to liberate the country from the yoke of Mangistu's regime was the "Ras Alula Division."

What, then, should Ras Alula's legacy to Ethiopia of today be? The Alula story should, no doubt, transmit to the new generation the notion of pride in one's history. Alula's period was glorious in the sense that Ethiopia managed to mobilize all its resources, stem Western imperialism, revitalize its political and social institutions, and reunite both as a state and as a nation. Alula reflected the best of that period. He was proud and courageous, confidently aware both of his abilities and of his identity, and fully capable of leading, defending and organizing a society. And while Alula was an Ethiopian to the full, he maintained his Tigrean heritage, but as a cultural dimension within a pluralized Ethiopianism. As such, and as a man with innate self-awareness and creative initiative, he was a fully modern person. If we compare Alula to the contemporaneous national heroes of neighboring countries (see my new book, *Ethiopia and the Middle East,* Lynne Rienner Publishers, Boulder, 1994, in which I compare Alula with Egypt's national hero Ahmad Urabi), Alula is by far the more complete personality, and better equipped to cope on an equal footing with the challenge of the West.

But taking pride in one's history does not suffice. In studying past events with an eye towards building a better future, it is necessary to understand the complex results and aftereffects of historical events. Even a great victory has its price, and there is some blessing in any defeat. The triumphant period of Ras Alula ended with the victorious Ethiopia becoming entrenched in its conservative structures. No new, modern political and social institutions were introduced, as they were in most other African and Oriental societies which were defeated and conquered. As a result, the abilities and the energy of Ras Alula, and of the countless other Alulas with which Ethiopian society is so blessed, were not channeled into modern institutions, but went on to be uselessly exhausted in individual competition for power and in vain military and political adventures. The fact that so little was transformed in Ethiopia's economic and social structures must be attributed mostly to the lack of political modernization.

Paradoxically, it is perhaps unfortunate that Alula and the other leaders of his generation in Ethiopia were not constrained to form political parties, establish social movements, set up new educational institutions and, as was the case, for example, in the defeated Egypt of Ahmad Urabi's generation, to begin publishing an opposition press and literature. Throughout its 2000-year long history, Ethiopia suffered only three major defeats. The first was the 16th-century conquest by the Muslim Ahmad ibn Ibrahim Gragn, which marked the beginning of a 12-year long episode that had far-reaching consequences for Ethiopia. The second was Mussolini's conquest and five years of occupation from 1936 to 1941. This traumatic period was perhaps too short to enable fundamental changes to occur, or for political modernization to develop from popular resistance to the Fascists or surface in a challenge to the political authoritarianism of the returning emperor.

Ethiopia's third and indeed major defeat and longest lasting period of brutal subjugation, lasting 17 years, came from within and was a completely "internal affair." The despotic rule of the *Derg* and Mangistu was a period in which the political culture of Ethiopia was colonized and brutalized by its own government. This period was both sufficiently traumatic and long enough to bring about the beginning of political modernization. The anti-Mangistu struggle was for Ethiopia what the anti-colonial struggles had been for other societies in Asia and Africa — a period of fundamental transformation in its political culture, with both the fortunate and the painful implications that such a transformation entails.

Rereading the Alula story in 1995, I hope that it remains a source of inspiration and edification. With less emphasis on the Dogali message of glorious wars and military achievements, and with less weight given to the Ras Alula-Ras Walda-Mikael-Dabab Araya message of individual, competitive, and fruitless internal political power-seeking, the Alula message could and should be one of Ethiopian unity through cultural pluralism and regional autonomy, of renewal of the shared Ethiopian-Eritrean history, and of the construction of towns, development of commerce, and promotion of intra-religious understanding and tolerance. Ras Alula, the son of a mere peasant, indeed won his fame on the battlefield; the Ethiopia of his time needed him for this task. The Ethiopia of today should be grateful for Ras Alula's military bravery, but must recognize and seek to fulfill his other messages and lessons.

Tel Aviv, August 1995

Introduction

The fall of Emperor Tēwodros II (1855-1868) marked the final collapse of the central Ethiopian highlands (the territories lying around Lake Tana and from there to Wāg, Yadju and northern Wallo) as the political core of the realm. Henceforth Tigre in the north and Shoa in the south, hitherto practically independent, became the real centres of power. The destruction of the political power of the militarily strong Yadju and Wallo Galla, (probably one of the more significant effects of Tēwodros' efforts) turned the central Ethiopia of the 1870s and 1880s into a vast buffer zone between the independent Kingdom of Shoa under *Negus* Menilek II (1865-1889, later emperor of Ethiopia, 1889-1913) and the newly-crowned emperor Yohannes IV (1872-1889) of Tigre.

The accession of a Tigrinya-speaking emperor (for the first time in the second millenium) climaxed a long period of de facto Tigrean independence. It was a Tigrean, *Rās* Mikā'ēl Sehul, who, by becoming the king-maker in Gondar (1769), opened the so-called "Era of the Judges." *Rās* Mikā'ēl was the autonomous master of the north till his death (c. 1780). This role was filled later by a member of another Tigrean family, *Rās* Walda-Sellāssē of Endartā (d. 1818), and then by Sabāgādis (1822-1831), a *dadjāzmāch* from Agāmē.

Like his predecessors, Sabāgādis led a Christian Tigrean-Amhara coalition of provincial chiefs against the Yadju Galla (Oromo) dynasty which ruled as the power behind the throne at the imperial court of Gondar. The Tigreans, who regarded themselves as the true bearers of Christian, Ethiopian nationalism, were the natural leaders of these campaigns. Proud of their Semitic language and cultural inheritance, self-consciously the successors of the Aksumite empire, they had engaged in the fiercest resistance to the *jihād* of the *Imām* Ahmad b. Ibrāhīm "Grānya" (1531-1543). The Takazzē River, forming the southern border of Tigre, later became the natural frontier which the Galla (Oromo) tribes did not dare to cross.

Upon Sabāgādis's death, the north became the power base of *Dadjāzmāch* Webē of Semēn (1835-1855), and later of his cousin Agaw Negussē, who were not, strictly speaking, proper Tigreans (*i.e.* natives of the districts of Adwā or Tigre, Tambēn, Shirē, Agāmē and Endartā). Agaw Negussē was executed by Tēwodros (1861), but the latter, whose reign ended the "Era of the Judges," was never able to impose effective government over the Tigreans. Though he managed to imprison such important figures as *Rās* Ar'āyā Demṣu of Endartā, his appointees in Tigre were often challenged by their local adversaries. They were removed in 1865, when the *Shum* of Wāg, Gobazē, temporarily controlled the province. Competition for the actual rule of Tigre was restricted to the descendents of *Rās* Mikā'ēl Sehul and of *Rās* Walda-Sellāssē and *Dadjāzmāch* Sabāgādis. Their fighting ended only in October 1867, when *Dadjāzmāch* Kāssā (born 1837 to Mircha the *Shum* of Tambēn, a direct descendent of Mikā'ēl Sehul and also related to the other two important families), formerly an appointee of Tēwodros and then of Gobazē, became the "Prince of Tigre," dubbed so by the British who came to fight Emperor Tēwodros. In January 1872, the same Kāssā proclaimed himself Emperor Yohannes IV at Aksum.

Throughout his seventeen years on the throne, Yohannes IV did his best to avoid becoming a parochial Tigrean monarch. Amharic, not Tigrinya, was made the official language at his court, and apparently he tried to recruit (through mass conversion) the warrior Galla (Oromo) of the central highlands in order to strengthen the military base of his monarchy (e.g. *Imām* Muḥammad 'Alī the leader of the Wallo Galla was baptized in 1878 as *Rās* Mikā'ēl and remained loyal to Yohannes until the latter's death). Eschewing the centralizing tendency of Tēwodros, however, Yohannes set out to make of Ethiopia a sort of a loose confederation (in 1878 he recognized Menilek as the *Negus* of Shoa, and in 1881 he crowned *Rās* Adāl of Godjām as Takla-Hāymānot) united by the sentiment of Christian nationalism. However, as a result of the circumstances arising out of the emerging imperialist "Scramble for Africa," Yohannes, despite his own effort to the contrary, is still remembered and frequently regarded as a Tigrean emperor.

For, when the British under General Robert Napier marched in to end Tēwodros' reign, the *Wāgshum* Gobazē was their most likely choice for emperor.[1] But Gobazē was suspicious and avoided meeting the British. Consequently Napier left surplus arms with "the Prince of Tigre." In 1871 Yohannes defeated the *Wāgshum*, who in 1868 had proclaimed himself Emperor Takla-Giyorgis.[2] Thus, the military centre of gravity of the ancient realm, by chance had shifted to Ethiopia's north, to remain there till Yohannes' death in 1889. This shift had an immense historical significance, because with the opening of the Suez Canal (1869), Ethiopia was exposed to European powers competing for supremacy in the Red Sea. An Ethiopia centered around Adwā and Maqalē could hardly co-exist with imperialist presences (first Egyptian, then Italian) on the Eritrean coast.

Furthermore, the simultaneous emergence of the *Jihād*ist-motivated Mahdist state in the Sudan led almost inevitably to a clash with Yohannes' Christian nationalism. In order to confront the challenge in the north, Yohannes therefore terminated the semi-autonomy of the Christian communities of the Eritrean plateau (namely the districts of Hamāsēn, Sarāyē and Akalla-Guzāy), where the main battles with the Egyptians, Mahdists, and the Italians were fought.

At the same time Yohannes' rather loose confederation with his southern vassals proved to be too weak to withstand their desire for his throne fomented by the divisive influence exerted on them by the imperialist powers. When Yohannes died in battle against the Mahdists (9 March 1889), he was an isolated Tigrean monarch, a victim of the "Scramble," which made a northern-centered Ethiopia unfeasible.

Thereafter, Menilek of Shoa who was a patient builder of a strong political hierarchy fed on easy expansion in the south, emerged as emperor. In the south, he was in a better position to come to terms with an Italian-occupied Red Sea coast, while the impoverished and strife-torn Tigreans disunited and deprived of the founder of their political hierarchy, found themselves surrounded by the Italian colony of Eritrea and the might of Menilek II. Their continuous effort to maintain Tigrean independence was a major element in the ensuing Ethiopian-Italian conflict, from which emerged a victorious Menilek. He managed not only to mobilize an all-Ethiopian army to defeat the Italians in the decisive battle of Adwā (1 March 1896), but he also succeeded in building a political entity which proved to be strong enough to participate in the "Scramble." Expanding his empire to the south, the great Menilek II created the boundaries of today's Ethiopia.

While the study of the internal processes and conflicts of the late nineteenth century is crucial for the understanding of later events, another major benefit can be gained from a study of this period. It affords the opportunity to gain a perspective from which Ethiopia's uniqueness in relation to most of the Afro-Asian world can be better appreciated. For in facing the "challenge of the West," this realm was the only African community to emerge triumphant, and consequently, even more self-confident than ever before. Even the sad experience of 1935-1941 can hardly be said to have seriously damaged the national pride which had been instilled in the formative period.

Ethiopia's military victory over the representatives of 19th century Europe had farreaching political consequences. No less important were the implications of this experience on the conceptual approach of Ethiopians in later periods towards westernization and modernization. Indeed, Ethiopia's continuing struggle between traditionalism and modernization, conservatism and westernization, still remains under the shadow of the period of the "Scramble for Africa". A reconstruction of activities of an Ethiopian who played a prominent role in this struggle against westerners, of his motives and concepts as they developed during the period of confrontation, may contribute to our understanding of this cardinal theme in the history of modern Ethiopia.

Nonetheless, the inescapable question remains: why Ethiopia of all Afro-Asian nations? How did it happen that Ethiopia not only managed to preserve its independence but also to gain such a victory? An authoritative an detailed study published recently by S. Rubenson[3] constitutes a major contribution to this subject. By emphasizing the role of Ethiopians in the history of the confrontation, Rubenson established the proper balance in an historiography which tended to treat the phenomenon as an abnormality which could be explained by the mistakes made by the Imperialists. However, Rubenson's book deals essentially with the history of diplomatic relations and underlines such aspects as the diplomatic and political awareness of Ethiopian leaders. Without challenging this most valid argument, the story told below is one of diplomatic failure. (Indeed Yohannes, facing a strategic threat, failed to resort to proper diplomacy, his story ending with the loss of Eritrea, the fall of Tigre and the emergence of the more skillful diplomat Menilek II). It is my contention, however, that it was not so much the political awareness and diplomatic skill of her leaders that enabled Ethiopia to withstand the pressure and emerge victorious; rather it was the ability of its natural leaders to mobilise and organise militarily as well as politically all levels of Ethiopian society. Due to socio-political flexibility, talented individuals, coming from whatever background, were encouraged instead of blocked by traditional values to do their utmost and make their way to the various leading positions. Thus young princes were seldom born into power. They had to compete for positions and titles, ocasionally losing—in what might be considered a free political game—to more talented members of leading families, or less frequently even to ambitious sons of poor peasants. It was this aspect of political mobility to which I shall return below—rather than nationalist awareness and sentiments, that helped Ethiopia realise her military and political potentiality, and especially, almost to the full, in periods of exteral threats. Our story is a biography of such a natural leader.

★ ★ ★

Biographies have always constituted a significant part in Ethiopian historiography,[4] as is seen from the ancient and medieval *gadl*s (i.e. biographies of saints), the royal chronicles which described the emperors' activities from 'Amda-Ṣiyon to Menilek II, and the work of many modern Ethiopian scholars.[5] This fact reflects an important aspect of Ethiopia's political reality. Indeed, no less, and possibly more than in many other societies, it was the great men who were the moving power in Ethiopia's history. In 1914, a British diplomat observed that the Ethiopians:

> accustomed for centuries to their systems of feudal government. . .
> leave the decision in all matters of higher politics to their own chief and
> when the time comes, will probably obey his orders blindly.[6]

In the same vein, scholars like D. Levine and C. Clapham regard Amhara-Tigrean socio-politics as "a system founded on authority, in which vertical lines of communication largely replace horizontal ones. Authority in itself is generally regarded as good. . . Relationships tend to fall into the pattern of authority and subservience, and it has often been noted that at the top of the social hierarchy stands the Big Man or Telek Säw."[7]

★ ★ ★

Rās Alulā (1847-1897) was one of those Big Men who played such a prominent role in the period disussed. He was famous enough to be lamented by a British historian in the following words:

> The greatest leader that Abyssinia has produced since the death of the Emperor Theodore in 1868, was undoubtedly Ras Alula; a chief whose honourable and fearless character often stood out in bold relief against the background of intrigue that fills every picture of Abyssinian political life.[8]

Although Alulā died on 15 February 1897,[9] in 1972 only a few old people in the small village of Mannawē, some fifteen miles south of Abbi-Addi, the capital of Tambēn district in Tigre, could remember his father's name, Engdā Qubi.[10] He and his wife, *Wayzaro* Garada (the daughter of Nagid, a local notable from the neighboring village of Bagā), were simple *bālāgars*, farmers.[11] Alulā reported to a European interviewer[12] that he "was born a soldier because his father was a soldier and also his grandfather," an accurate enough statement, since the self-armed peasantry constituted Tigre's main source of military manpower in that period. When the *nagārit* war-drums sounded every season, the farmers followed their local masters on campaign. The young Alulā must have been stirred and conditioned by the stories of courage, bravery, and heroism which he heard while growing up.

The people of Mannawē recall little about the childhood of the future leader.[13] He was educated in their church by the *Mamher* Walda-Giyorgis and, being an aggressive and dominating youngster, he soon became the leader of the children. A huge rock on the top of the opposite mountain, they say, was his favorite playground, and he would give bread to those of his friends who managed to join him there, while regaling them with fantastic tales.

One day—goes a story well known throughout Tigre—a group of people were going to a wedding ceremony carrying baskets full of bread. On their way they met the children of Mannawē led by the young Alulā. "Where are you going?" demanded the little leader, and the people mockingly replied: "To the Castle of Rās Alulā Wādi Qubi". Thereafter his friends and the people of Mannawē nicknamed him Rās Alulā.[14] It was a good example of humour based on the absurd. In Tigre the leading families for many generations monopolized the political and economic life, a son of a peasant seemed to stand a very remote chance for prominence.

Yet Alulā's career as a son of a deprived Engdā Qubi who managed to become a powerful leader and a policy maker in his country was by no means unique. In line with many similar stories[15] it rather reflected the centrality of a very important aspect in Ethiopia's socio-politics. Ethiopia's long history was characterized not only by the power of the Big Men, but also by a strong element of social and political mobility. Such mobility was the result of a constant power-game in which hereditary rights and honorific titles—titles and positions were not inherited—weighed but marginally. They served mainly to legitimize the outcomes of the struggles for power occuring ceaselessly all along the Ethiopian socio-political ladder. In these competitions strong-charactered sons of peasants, though starting from a very low point, did stand a chance to outclimb weak-charactered sons of *rās*es.

This socio-political flexibility was a main factor in the creation of Ethiopia's historical continuity. For a society enabling ambitious individuals to fulfill themselves enjoys stability of values and institutions. In such a society born leaders pursuing their way to power do not have to politically organize social classes or mobilize new ideologies. (it was also due to this factor that Ethiopia did not experience its first revolution until 1974). It was this factor of social mobility that in periods of external threats, like the one described in this story, contributed to the emergence of a strong and well-tested leadership on various levels. Indeed, not only the hero of this biography but also the majority of the other participants in our story were sons of kings or of peasants, who constantly moved up and down the political ladder throughout the period discussed. Success usually meant power and promotion while a failure, rank and title aside, led to an inevitable personal disaster. In such a society periods of external conflicts and threats usually open options and offer new possibilities for persons of ambition and determination. It was under hierarchies which consisted of such persons—individuals who had withstood strong challenges of equally ambitious contenders for rank and power—that Ethiopian society was mobilised and organised to confront imperialism. In the final analysis, Ethiopia's ability to withstand external threats uniting under the leadership of a determined head of such an hierarchy, rested, and still rests, not so much on a unifying sentiment as on this political mechanism, a product of her socio-political flexibility and her constant, often violent, power game.

* * *

Alulā's story has all the ingredients of a personal drama, which in its vicissitudes reflects some of the major issues in his period. The revival of Tigrean hegemony over Ethiopia; the military victories which guaranteed the survival of Ethiopia's independence; the loss of Eritrea to a foreign power; the decline of Tigrean power; the rise of Menilek and the great national victory near Adwā were all milestones in the rās's life. Simultaneously, the story of this son of a peasant, his successes and failures, his ambitions and weaknesses, his achievements and mistakes, was an important factor in those developments.

The young Alulā "Wādi Qubi" started his colorful career at the bottom of the Tigrean "feudal" ladder. He managed to climb up a few relatively accessible rungs and could well have finished his career as a local administrator, had not Tigre become Ethiopia's center. When his Tigrean patron became Emperor Yohannes IV, the young Alulā was translated from the provincial to the national scene, with its far greater opportunities. Alulā's excellent military services in fighting external enemies and consolidating the emperor's supremacy in Ethiopia established him as a king's man. Since he enjoyed no hereditary or traditional basis of power in Tigre, he was more easily trusted by the emperor. Still, when he was given the government of *Marab Mellāsh* (the future Eritrea), he was quick to capitalize on its revenues to obtain the social position which he lacked in Tigre. The border problems which he had to face in this province also made him a key figure in Ethiopia's relations with its African and European neighbours.

Even when he lost the *Marab Mellāsh* to a foreign power, and even after Yohannes had died, Alulā, without any visible source of authority, managed to continue to play a significant role in Ethiopia's history.

★ ★ ★

This biography is an attempt to study an important chapter in the history of a nation through the experiences of a person who was not the head of the state. While it cannot provide a balanced picture of the period in which he lived,[16] such a study enables us to look closely at important events not in the purview of emperors and kings, and especially to penetrate more deeply into the complexed field of internal politics.

NOTES

1   See for instance: "Memorandum by Dr. Beke, showing the Right of Waagshum Gobazye to the throne of Abyssinia," in *British Parliamentary Papers*, "Further Correspondence Respecting the British Captives in Abyssinia," 1866.
2   For Yohannes's rise to power consult Zewde Gabre-Sellassie, *Yohannes IV of Ethiopia*, Oxford 1975, pp. 21-36; Harold Marcus, *The Life and Times of Menelik II, Ethiopia 1844-1913*, Oxford 1975, pp. 33-36.
3   S. Rubenson, *The Survival of Ethiopian Independence*, London 1976.
4   See also D. Levine *Wax and Gold*, Chicago 1965, pp. 271, 272.
5   Peter Garretson claims implicitly that biographies and autobiographies are among the richest sources of modern Ethiopian history. See his "Some Amharic Sources for Modern Ethiopian History, 1889-1935 (with notes by Richard Pankhurst),"*Bulletin of the School of Oriental and African Studies*, v. XLI, 2 (1978), 283-96.
6   FO 371/1880, Thesiger to Grey, 15 May 1914.
7   C. Clapham, *Haile-Sellassie's Government*, London 1969, p. 5.
8   G.F. Berkeley, *The Campaign of Adowa and the Rise of Menelik*, London 1902; New Edition, London 1935, p. 13.
9   Many sources are unsure about Alulā's date of birth. Hill's suggestion of 1847 is a good a guess as any. R. Hill, *A Biographical Dictionary of the Anglo-Egyptian Sudan*, Oxford 1951 (second Ed., London 1967), p. 53.
10   A collective interview in Mannawē, February 1972. Interview with Fitāwrāri Bayyana Abrehā, a descendant of Alulā; Aksum, February 1972.
11   This fact is agreed by all the written and oral sources, with the exception of G. Puglisi, *Chi e? dell' Eritrea*, Asmara 1952, p. 14. Puglisi suggested that "Abba Gubbi" was a dadjāzmāch.

12 L. Mercatelli, "Nel Paese di Ras Alula," *Corriere di Napoli*, 15.6.1891. On Mercatelli, see below, p. 163.
13 Alulā was given the baptismal name of Gabra-Mikā'ēl. He had three brothers: Kāffā, Tasammā, and Gabra-Māryām and two young sisters, Denqu and Kāssā. Interviews with Alulā's descendants. W. Yashāshwarq, Abbi Addi, Feb. 1972. Fit. Bayyana Abrehā of Aksum, March 1972. According to Puglisi, p. 14, he had another sister named Tamārsā.
14 Interview with Dr. Abbā Gabra-Iyāsus Hāylu, Addis Ababā, Jan. 1972. Also his article "Selarās Alulā" in *Yazāreyitu Ityopyā*, Hedār 6th 1955 E.C. Tesfai Seyoum, *Ras Alula Abba Nega*, unpublished B.A. thesis, HSIU 1970, p. 2.
15 Bairu Tafla, "Three distinguished Ethiopian military leaders." A paper presented at the *Social Science Conference*, Nairobi 1969.
16 For the history of the period consult the recently published: H. Marcus, *The Life and Times of Menelik II*, Oxford 1975; Rubenson, *The Survival*; Zewde Gabre-Sellassie, *Yohannes IV of Ethiopia*, Oxford 1975.

1

1872-1876 *Shālaqā* **Alulā**

A. *1868-1872: Lower Rungs of the Local Ladder*

In 1868, *Rās* Ar'āyā Demṣu was released from Emperor Tēwodros's prison; a true representative of the Tigrean ruling class, he descended from a former governor of the province and was the head of a family with hereditary rights (*Rest*) over vast territories in various parts of Tigre. Young Alulā, whose father's land fell under Ar'āyā's jurisdiction, became Ar'āyā's *ashkar*, i.e., one of his followers.[1] As a member of the *rās*'s household, he probably encountered for the first time two of the main personalities in his future career, Ar'āyā's son Dabbab and his youngest daughter Emlasu.

Before long, Alulā, with the *rās*'s cooperation, took service with Ar'āyā's successful nephew, *Dadjāzmāch* Kāssā, to whom he became an *elfegn kalkāy*, a chamberlain and door keeper. After a few years he was promoted to the rank of *agāfāri*, the organiser of meals in the court and the head of Kāssā's personal guard.[2] On 11 July 1871, the ambitious Kāssā defeated the Emperor Takla-Giyorgis in the battle of the Assam River near Adwā. Oral tradition[3] claims that Alulā captured the pretender and was rewarded with the imperial rank of *shālaqā*, or commander of a thousand troops. To cap this stage of his early career, around 1872, Alulā married his first wife, W. Bitwatā Gabra-Masqal, a daughter of a farmer from Tambēn. During the seven years they lived together, she gave birth to three daughters, Dammaqach, Dinqnash and Ṣahāywarada.[4]

A Ge'ez Ms. asserts that after Kāssā became Emperor Yohannes IV on 21 January 1872, the trusted "Shālaqā Alulā became a ligāba,"[5] i.e. official introducer and master of ceremonies at the court, as well as the official-in-charge of the emperor's personal domain.[6] This administrative rank, however, though superior to his military one of *shālaqā*, was only once, to my knowledge, ever mentioned again.[7]

Alulā's activities during the period 1872-1875 are not known, but he probably followed Yohannes IV from battle to battle during the struggle to consolidate power.[8] The young *shālaqā*-cum-*ligāba* was still overshadowed by the men of reputation and position in his master's court (such as *Rās* Ar'āyā and his sons).

B. *1875-1876: the Egyptian Threat and Alulā's Emergence as a General*

Taking advantage of Yohannes's internal difficulties, the Egyptians captured the country of Bogos in July 1872; occupied Matammā (Al-Qallābāt) in May 1873; and, encouraged by the Swiss adventurer Werner Munzinger and the energetic governor of Massawa, 'Arāqīl Bey, Cairo planned a further invasion deep into Ethiopia for July 1875.[9]

Bearing in mind the details and results of the successful 1868-Napier campaign, the Egyptians hoped that their efforts would be assisted by the Ethiopian domestic situations. Indeed, it may be quite safely assumed that the Egyptians were cooperating with Menilek of Shoa, then an active aspirant to the emperorship.[10] The Egyptians did not seek Ethiopia's total conquest since their interest lay in the countries north of the Marab river, the Red Sea coast, and in the regions neighbouring their Sudanese colony, where Cairo could hope to gain the allegiance of the Muslim population. An Ethiopian monarch from Tigre with his capital quite near the Marab river (and especially a devoted Christian like Emperor Yohannes IV) was potentially an obstacle to Khedive Ismā'īl, who would have preferred to see the center of Ethiopia power shifted to the far south. There Menilek of Shoa, still politically independent of Tigre, was apparently considered by Cairo as a replacement for Yohannes. Thus, the Egyptian campaigns of late 1875 and early 1876 were not aimed at the conquest of Ethiopia but rather at the fall of Emperor Yohannes IV.

During his preparations to meet the Egyptian invaders, the emperor must have felt the despair of a deserted man. None of the important leaders of Ethiopia, among them Menilek of Shoa and *Rās* Adāl of Godjām, joined him to face the threat.[11] When the *nagārit* war-drums were beaten on 2 November 1875, *Shālaqā* Alulā, in charge of a one thousand-man advance guard, his brother *Bāshā* Gabra-Māryām, and *Dadjāzmāch* Hagos,[12] were among the few leaders to accompany the emperor.[13]

The Egyptians on the other hand were more successful than the isolated Yohannes in persuading Ethiopians to join their camp. Having beaten the ruler of the Hamāsēn, *Dadjāzmāch* Gabru, they managed, through the distribution of money, arms and titles, to gain the cooperation of local leaders[14] and awaited the Ethiopian army in Addi Qualla and Gundat.

In order to regain the vital cooperation of Hamāsēn, Yohannes mobilized one of the province's hereditary leaders, *Ledj* Walda-Mikā'ēl Solomon. As far back as 1869, this Hamāsēn nobleman had been justifiably suspected of conspiring against the future emperor and encouraging foreign powers to invade the country.[15] He was imprisoned in the same year, to be released in 1871, but was not then permitted to leave court. Pledging to mobilise his people against the invaders, Walda-Mikā'ēl was made a *dadjāzmāch* and allowed to accompany Yohannes's army,[16] whose advance guard *Shālaqā* Alulā commanded.

On 14 November Alulā crossed the Marab river and immediately engaged forward Egyptian posts. The main Ethiopian army under the emperor crossed the river on the night of 15-16 November. Meanwhile *Shālaqā* Alulā had disengaged his forces; he had completed a flanking action from the west[17] against troops advancing from Addi Quala; and had appeared in the Egyptian rear, blocking their line of retreat. On the morning of 16 November 1875, the Egyptians found themselves surrounded in a steep valley, and the battle soon turned into a massacre from which only a few of the 3,000 Egyptians managed to escape.[18] Two thousand, two hundred Remington rifles and sixteen cannons were captured by the Ethiopians, who lost some 550 dead and 400 wounded, among the latter of whom was Alulā's brother *Bāshā* Tasammā, whose wound remained unhealed for a long period.[19]

Alulā, however, was not the only hero of the day. *Dadjāzmāch* Walda-Mikā'ēl also played a substantial part in the victory and, pursuing the retreating Egyptians, managed to capture some seven hundred rifles.[20] Even so, he was not trusted enough to retain the arms; under imperial orders, he grudgingly transferred the weapons to *Shālaqā* Alulā who had been given command over a new force equipped with the captured Remingtons.[21] Hence, the young Alulā emerged as the leader of the king's fusiliers, a position of obvious importance, which vastly irritated Walda-Mikā'ēl.

He was so peeved that he was willing to betray Yohannes. In early December 1875 a fifteen thousand-man Egyptian punitive mission landed in Massawa and invaded the *Marab Mellāsh*. *Dadjāzmāch* Walda-Mikā'ēl, ostensibly Yohannes' governor of Hamāsēn, appeared in the enemy's camp dressed as a Muslim and successfully offered to provide the Egyptians with over two thousand well-armed men. Walda-Mikā'ēl was given the Egyptian military rank of *farīq* and promoted himself to *rās*.[22] Soon, other discontented leaders from the territories to the north of the Marab river joined the advancing Egyptian camp.[23] Thus, the enemy marched down to the Marab river without firing a single shot, and their confident army occupied Khaya Khur and Gurā, where two strong zaribas were constructed.

Oral tradition and some written sources strongly suggest that *Shālaqā* Alulā, leading the Ethiopian advance guard, outmanoeuvred the Egyptians in the battle of Gurā (7-9 March 1876) which resulted in a decisive Egyptian defeat. "The Abyssinian advance guard," Gordon was told later, "defeated the Egyptian army at Gura. The king's main force never came into action."[24] The tactical move attributed to the *shālaqā* by oral tradition was to penetrate between the two Egyptian zaribas on 7 March, and, by pretending to start a panic retreat, he tempted Rātib Pasha to leave his fortified post.[25] Only 1,900 troops of the 5,200 who left the zariba managed to return from the massacre which followed.[26] "He [Yohannes] did all this with only one Tigrean," wrote an Ethiopian chronicler of the emperor, "no one from his other vassals helped him."[27]

The Ethiopian army, however, experienced its share of bloodshed. The next day, when a direct assault on the Gurā zariba was launched, war losses proved that an Ethiopian army which used traditional tactics was unable to face an entrenched force equipped with artillery. "The Dadjāzmāches, the Afa-Negus, the Turk Bāshā perished, let alone the soldiers. *Abuna* Antanewus was injured by lead [shot] . . . became sick and died."[28] Alulā himself—the Italian Savoiroux heard him say eleven years later—was saved from being shot by a sudden move of his horse.[29] Among the 1,800 dead,[30] *Shālaqā* Alulā found the body of his elder brother *Bāshā* Gabra-Māryām whom he later buried at Mannawē and whose only daughter he adopted.[31]

Despite these losses, the victory at Gurā was without doubt a most important event in modern Ethiopian history.[32] For Yohannes personally, it not only helped preserve his Tigrean hegemony over Ethiopia but also brought him personal security. Alulā, henceforward called "The lion of Gurā,"[33] had proved capable of defending the empire. Alulā's unknown contemporary biographer wrote:

> In the fourth year of the reign of Yohannes, King of Kings, Muslims came and arrived in the land of Hamasen, and when Ras Alula heard the news of their coming, the grace of the holy spirit aroused him and messianic power emboldened him. He took up his spear, and girded his sword, and fought with them. This man Alula returned with much spoil and prizes of war, and did homage to the king. He cried out, and said, 'I am your servant, the son of your maidservant.' The king said to him, 'My son, live for me for a long time' because he saw that the grace of the holy spirit rested on him. He said to his officers. 'Do you not see that favour follows this man, who showed promise from his childhood?' And he [Yohannes] said to him [Alulā], 'I give you this land which flows with milk and honey'.[34]

C. *October '76: Governor of Hamāsēn*

The victory over the invading Egyptians, effective as it was in preventing the fall of Yohannes, was not followed by adequate military measures to regain Bogos. Diplomatic negotiations concerning the question of the Egyptian prisoners of war failed to solve the frontier problems. Indeed, the Egyptian delegation received by Alulā near the Marab and escorted by him to Adwā was soon expelled from the country.[35] Beaten twice, the Egyptians now wanted Walda-Mikā'ēl to regain control of Hamāsēn in order to make it a buffer zone to protect Bogos and Massawa and eventually to serve as a springboard for future initiatives. Aware of his enemy's strategy, Yohannes reacted by appointing *Dadjāzmāch* Haylu Habal, Walda-Mikā'ēl's old rival, as governor of Hamāsēn. The two men headed the two strongest and wealthiest families in Hamāsēn:[36] Haylu's family was centered around the village of Sa'zega, while Walda-Mikā'ēl's dominated Hazagā. For many generations, the two families had shared between themselves the hereditary rulership of Hamāsēn.[37]

Dadjāzmāch Haylu assumed his command in June 1876, and in mid-July marched to Hamāsēn, only to be ambushed there by the newly armed and supplied *Rās* Walda-Mikā'ēl. In the battle of Wokidba, 17 July 1876, Haylu was killed; his supporters, those few who survived the ensuing massacre, fled to Tigre and even Sa'zegā was razed.[38] *Rās* Walda-Mikā'ēl rebuilt the power of Hazagā, recalled his elder son, *Dadjāzmāch* Masfen, from Cairo,[39] and prepared himself for a long period of independence.

When Yohannes heard the news, he expelled the Egyptian envoys, swearing he would never again negotiate with Cairo.[40] Then, in September, he ordered *Shālaqā* Alulā and *Rās* Bāriāu, the governor of Adwā, to march to Hamāsēn through Akalla-Guzāy. On 3 October 1876 *Rās* Walda-Mikā'ēl fled to Bogos,[41] and the emperor entered Hamāsēn to join his generals. Before returning to Tigre on 9th October 1876, Yohannes appointed Alulā ruler over Hamāsēn and Sarāyē and promoted him *rās*.[42] The quick promotion from *shālaqā* to *rās* and the appointment of an inexperienced youngster to a province were indeed rare in Ethiopia's history. Yet Yohannes took this step with good reason: the *Marab Mellāsh* had become so strategically important that only a fully loyal lieutenant would suit.

The Egyptian campaign had revealed Yohannes's shaky domestic position. The emperor consequently had to dedicate his time and energy to the home front without being bothered by developments beyond the Marab. The able young Alulā was apparently the man to do the job there. His ambitions and daring would be tempered by his lack of popular support, and he therefore would be no threat to the emperor. Unlike other men of prominence, Alulā was fully the creation of Yohannes, and consequently a trusted king's man.

NOTES

1 "Epistolario Africano", *Italiani in Africa*, Rome 1887, pp. 247-250: A. Bonacucina, *Due Anni in Massaua*, Fabriano 1887, p. 40; *The Daily News*, 10.2.87; F. Fasolo, *L'Abissinia e le Colonie Italiane*, Caserta, 1887, pp. 204-205.
2 Fasolo, *op.cit.*; Interview *Fitāwrāri* Alamē Tafari, Maqalē, Feb. 1972. According to Puglisi, p. 14, Alula was also a *naggādrās*, i.e. chief of the markets and customs and organiser of caravans.
3 Quoted in Tesfai Seyoum, *Ras Alula Abba Nega: A Biography*, unpublished B.A. thesis, HSIU 1970, p. 4. Also: A. Bartincki, *Historia Etiopii*, Wroclaw 1971, p. 261.
4 W. Yashāshwarq, Fit. Bayyana.
5 A Ge'ez Ms. in the Church of Dabra-Berhan Sellāssē, Adwā. This ms. explains that Yohannes promoted and rewarded only those he trusted completely.
6 Interview, Dr. *Dadjāzmāch* Zawdē Gabra-Sellāssē, Addis Ababa, March 1972.
7 Fasolo, *op.cit.*
8 For Yohannes' history, see: Zewde Gabre-Sellassie, *Yohannes IV of Ethiopia*.
9 For the Egyptian invasion and the battle of Gundat, see G. Douin: *Histoire du Règne du*

Khédive Ismail, Cairo, 1933-1941, III, 3⁰, fasc. A., pp. 583-4, 586 and fasc. B., pp. 713, 715, 717, 718, 720, 722, 732, 735, 752, 894, 804, 812, 921.

10   For Menilek's relations with the Egyptians, consult H. Marcus, *The Life and Times of Menelik II*, pp. 37-39.

11   Douin, *op.cit.*, p. 770. For details, see: Aṣmē Giyorgis, *Yagāllā tārik*, IES Ms. 138, p. 81, and *Alaqā* Lamlam, *Ya' atsē Takla-Giyorgisnā ya' atsē Yohannes tārik*, Ms. Ethiopiens No. 259 (Collection Mondon Vidaillet, No. 72), Bibliothèque Nationale, Paris, f. 20 bis.

12   For Hagos (later *rās*), see Index.

13   Douin, *loc.cit.*

14   C. Conti Rossini, *Italia ed Etiopia*, Rome 1935, p. 110; Zewde, p. 60; J.A. Kolmodin, *Traditions de Tsazzega et Hazzega*, Rome 1912-1916, No. 238.

15   A.B. Wylde, *'83-'87 in the Soudan*, London 1888, Vol. I, pp. 324, 326.

16   Kolmodin, No. 238; R. Perini, *Di Qua dal Mareb*, Firenze 1905, p. 36; Wylde, *'83-'87 in the Soudan*, Vol. I, p. 326; W.M. Dye, *Moslem Egypt and Christian Abyssinia*, N.Y. 1880, p. 285.

17   Takla-Ṣādeq Makuriya, *Yaityopyā tārik*, Addis Ababa 1960 E.C., p. 48.

18   Douin, *op.cit.*; Ilyās al-Ayūbī *Ta' rīkh miṣr fī 'ahd al-khidīw Ismā'īl bāshā*, Cairo 1923, pp. 78-85; Luca dei Sabelli, *Storia d'Abissinia*, Rome 1936, vol. III, p. 247.

19   A. Salimbeni, "Diario d'un pioniere africano", *Nuova Antologia*, 1936, p. 149.

20   *Alaqā* Lamlam, f. 21; Kolmodin, No. 239.

21   BM. Add. Mss. 51294, Gordon to his sister, 28.3.77; FO 407/11, Wylde's memo, 11.11.79; FO 78/3083, Gordon's notes 17.8.79; Douin, *op.cit.*, p. 842.

22   Kolmodin, No. 239; Muḥammad Rif'at Bek, *Jabr al-kasr fī al-khilās min al-asr*, Cairo 1314 H, pp. 14-15; *Ayūbī*, pp. 102-109; BM. Add. Mss. 51294, Gordon to Augusta, 15.3.77.

23   See Amharic MSS., Bibliothèque Nationale, Paris, collection Mondon Vidaillet, Ethiop. 291, Mondon 104, p. 22. Perini, *op.cit.*, pp. 36, 37.

24   BM. Add. Mss. 51304, Gordon's "Notes taken from king's interpreter," 23.9.79.

25   Fit. Bayyana Abrehā. Yet, as described by Dye, *Moslem Egypt*, the American advisors forced the Egyptians to march out in order to catch the Ethiopian army between two fields of fire as they marched through the valley in search of water.

26   FO 78/2631, Vivian to Derby, 23.1.77.

27   Lamlam, *op.cit.*

28   Ibid.

29   E. Perino, *Vita e gesta di Ras Alula*, Rome 1897, p. 103.

30   B.M. Add. Mass., 51294, Gordon to Augusta, 15.3.77.

31   Conti Rossini, *Italia ed Etiopia*, p. 77. Int. people of Mannawē.

32   For the battle of Gurā see also: S. Rubenson, *The Survival*, pp. 318-329; Zewde, pp. 68-72, *Ayūbī*, pp. 87-117; Hesseltine and Wolf, *The Blue and the Gray on the Nile*, Chicago 1961, pp. 194-211.

33   Bonacucina, *op.cit.*, p. 43. See also: P. Matteucci, *In Abissinia*, Milano 1880, p. 230.

34   An anonymous Ge'ez manuscript of ninety-five pages kept in the church of Mannawē. The priests there were kind enough to let me photocopy it in Maqale, February 1972. A few additional pages were found later in Abbi Addi and it was then translated by Mr. Roger Cowley. See H. Erlich, "A contemporary biography of Ras Alula: a Ge'ez manuscript from Manawē, Tamben," *BSOAS*, vol. XXXIX, part 1, 1976, pp. 1-46; part 2, 1976, pp. 287-327.

35 Douin, *op.cit.*, p. 1035.
36 For family ownership of land in Eritrea see S.F. Nadel, "Land Tenure on the Eritrean Plateau," *Africa*, vol. XVI, 1946, pp. 1-21, 99-109; see also below, pp. 81-85.
37 See S.H. Longrigg, *A Short History of Eritrea*, Oxford 1945, p. 101.
38 Kolmodin, Nos. 243-250.
39 Kolmodin, No. 251.
40 FO 78/3003, Gordon's notes on the Sudan 17.8.79.
41 FO 78/2634, Gordon to Vivian; Wylde's report, 23.4.77.
41 Douin, *op.cit.*, p. 1085.

2

1877-1879: The King's Man: "Rās Alulā who is a Turk Bāshā"

A. First Meeting With the Border Problems

With their long tradition of self-government, the people of Hamāsēn could not easily accept the appointment of an outsider, a highlander (*"dog'o"*).[1] Thus, Alulā's nomination stimulated support for *Rās* Walda-Mikā'ēl, and many left for his camp in Halhal, Bogos.[2] From his Egyptian-protected sanctuary, Walda-Mikā'ēl started raiding continuously and intensively into Hamāsēn with the aim of undermining Alulā. By October the rainy season was over, and he could freely move in the territory with which he was so familiar. His most effective raid took place on 25 February 1877, when five villages of the Mansa tribe were pillaged and burnt, their inhabitants fleeing to *Rās* Alulā's headquarters at Addi Taklay.[3]

Though Alulā commanded "more than 10,000 Remingtons"[4] and had the reputation of "a young, warlike man who only likes fighting,"[5] he did not dare to cross to the Bogos and pursue the rebels. Possibly he was restrained by the memory of the third day of the battle of Gurā, when Ethiopian troops had so futilely assaulted Egyptian positions. More likely, however, Yohannes ordered him to move elsewhere.[6] The emperor was then attempting to force the submission of Menilek of Shoa, and he could not afford to have Alulā occupied in the north.

Around the village of Aylēt, *Rās* Walda-Mikā'ēl had gathered 4,000 head of cattle. On 1 February 1877, while Alulā cut the Bogos-Aylēt road, he sent his lieutenant, a certain Gabru, towards Aylēt. Like Alulā, he was an ambitious youngster from Tambēn whom Alulā promoted to the rank of *belāttā*. Gabru "Abbā Chaqun" was to serve as Alulā's devoted follower and chief lieutenant during the following nine years. Leading 1,500 men, Gabru raided Aylēt, pillaged the neighboring villages and captured their cattle. Returning to Addi Taklay, he brought with him some twenty Egyptian prisoners and the American geologist Lebbens H. Mitchell, an Egyptian-employed surveyor.[7]

Subsequent negotiations between *Rās* Alulā and the Egyptian governor of Massawa, 'Uthmān Pasha, did not result in the release of the thirty-three-year-old American. Alulā demanded Ethiopian hostages held by *Rās* Walda-Mikā'ēl, and, responding to 'Uthmān's complaint about the raid on Aylēt, he stated: "Ethiopia goes up to the sea; Egypt begins there."[8] To emphasize this fact and, as a reprisal for the raid on the Mansa, Alulā again raided Aylēt in early March.[9]

B. Europeans

The American geologist stayed in Alulā's camp for twenty days before being sent to the emperor in Adwā. In Mitchell's long and detailed report, Alulā was described as an admirer of European technical achievements and character.[10] The fact that Alulā let Mitchell eat during the Ethiopian fast, and that, two years later, he let Gordon smoke (in spite of the ban issued by the emperor which was strictly followed by Alulā) may indicate that he then regarded Europeans as different. Mitchell recalled his meeting with the naive and curious young *rās*:

> A large number of the pieces of my chemical apparatus had been collected. Alluli summoned me, one day, to an audience. I went to his quarters. He was seated upon his carpet, near a brazier of coals. Spread out before him, was perhaps two-thirds of what had been the contents of my blowpipe apparatus case, but, to a large extent, in a condition bordering on ruin. One by one, he asked me the purposes and uses of the articles. I gave him the necessary explanations, in so far as it was possible, with the assistance of an interpreter who spoke very bad Arabic. I suppose the chief was satisfied with my lecture. I had no fear, however, that he would ever succeed in the use of the apparatus for purposes of chemical manipulation! Other things [sic] equal, he could never do *that*. He had already practised upon my watch for nearly two weeks, and it was still with the greatest difficulty that he could succeed in winding it properly.[11]

Alulā's first direct encounter with a representative of western technology made a strong impression on him. As a man who, for the next two decades, was to become one of the main figures in Ethiopia's relations with foreign powers, this was an important starting point. His admiration for European technology resulted in his constant interest in keeping open the trade route to the Red Sea and in importing as many modern firearms as possible.[12] Simultaneously, Alulā began to use such politically harmless individuals as Mitchell (or later Gordon and Italian engineers). This concern with modernity may have been the source of his future interest in having a European ally as a neighbour, instead of a Muslim one.

A few days after Mitchell had been taken to Yohannes in Adwā, Alulā received a letter from Col. Charles G. Gordon, the newly-appointed governor-general of the Sudan, Darfur and Equatoria. Gordon had been sent by the Khedive Ismā'īl to solve the conflict with Ethiopia without losing Egypt's territorial gains.[13] Traveling from Massawa to Sanhīt in early March 1877, Gordon contacted Walda-Mikā'ēl and was not slow to comprehend his negative role in frontier relations. Reaching Bogos, Gordon drafted a letter to Alulā and despatched it with Hasan

Bāshā, the Egyptian commander of the fort of Sanḥīt.

Gordon offered Alulā, "the Emperor's greatest general," six points as a basis for discussion: an armistice; preservation of the present frontier; free Ethiopian trade with Massawa; permission for the emperor to import annually and free-of-duty 50 boxes of gunpowder and 10 muskets; khedivial sanction of an appointment of an *abun*; and removal of Walda-Mikā'ēl from the Ethiopian frontier.[14] In reply, Alulā mischieviously sought permission to enter Bogos country in order to arrest Walda-Mikā'ēl, and promised to ensure that his soldiers would cause no damage before leaving the country.

Only after Gordon's refusal, did Alulā—according to Wylde—show an interest in negotiations, explaining that he was not authorised to deal with the points raised but promising to go to Adwā to discuss them with Yohannes.[15] Ḥasan Bāshā, the Egyptian envoy, reported to Wylde that Alulā considered Gordon's conditions for settlement "just and fair."

In fact these points were not just and not fair. They included the recognition of Egypt's recent conquest of extensive Ethiopian areas in exchange for fifty boxes of ammunition a year and an *abun*. Indeed, in a letter sent on 18 June 1877, Yohannes strongly protested to Gordon, reminding him that the Ethiopian frontier was well known.[16] Alulā also completely understood his master's conception of the Ethiopian frontier; he had witnessed Yohannes expel the Egyptian envoys from Adwā for suggesting less than his demands and swear never again to negotiate with them. Alulā's response to Gordon and what seems to be his readiness to sacrifice so much to reach an agreement was probably based on his interest, as governor of Hamāsēn, in reopening Massawa trade[17] and restraining Walda-Mikā'ēl.

C. Tigrean Hegemony Challenged

Around 18 March 1877 *Rās* Alulā hastily led a force of some ten thousand soldiers to Adwā,[18] where a worried Yohannes was watching Menilek's advance northwards. The King of Shoa, an energetic claimant to the title of "King of Kings," had penetrated as far as Dabra-Tābor,[19] supposedly on his way to the old capital of Gondar.[20] Meanwhile, Yohannes had suffered a crisis in relations with his influential uncle, *Rās* Ar'āyā Demṣu in Akalla-Guzāy,[21] and he could hardly rely on the other members of the leading Tigrean families. He therefore had to call Alulā from beyond the Marab River to help him on the Ethiopian home front.

For years afterwards, *Rās* Alulā was to be described as the constant champion of Tigrean hegemony over Ethiopia (the more so after the death of Yohannes and Menilek's accession in 1889). The key to this reputation may, however, be found by analysing the relations between Alulā and the emperor. Suspecting the powerful Tigrean nobility, many of whom proved to be his open or secret enemies, Yohannes needed an able and trusted man as a general, an adviser and occasionally (being a kind of lonely, melancholic and depressed person) as a friend.[22] With no ambitions or claims for the throne,[23] Alulā was one of several young men of humble origins who enjoyed the emperor's regard,[24] but he was lucky or strong enough to create more chances for himself in order to remain not merely a *bālamwāl*,[25] or "favourite."

Still Alulā owed absolutely everything to Yohannes. Without the emperor he could not have progressed very far, and he doted on his master in a way that astonished many European visitors. For Alulā, Tigrean hegemony was not only animated in the personality of Yohannes but was undoubtedly identical with him.

D. March 1877: "Rās Alulā Who Is a Turk Bāshā"

According to Alulā's unknown contemporary biographer, in early 1877, the emperor sought a new title for Alulā, one which would emphasize Alulā's superior position at court:

> 'With what name shall I magnify him, and with what name shall I honour him for this man [Alulā] is faithful, after my own heart, and he does all my wishes, and he does not hold back from doing my commands. . .' He [Yohannes] called his father and his counsellor, the great chief of the priests *Echägē* [Tēwoflos] . . . whose sea of knowledge is not depleted. . . The king and the *Echägē* met a second time,[26] in private, not in public, and it was said: 'Behold, we have found an honourable name and a high rank which is fitting for the elect and blessed Ras Alula, and saying this they named him Terkwe Basha, saying 'There is nothing which is greater than this name, and there is nothing which is better than this rank' and they closed the matter with this counsel.[27]

In Ethiopia the title of *turk bāshā* was connected with the introduction of firearms. In previous centuries it had been given to the functionary in charge of the imperial stores of firearms and ammunition and commander of the fusiliers. It seems, however, that during the "Era of the Judges," the title lost its importance and became honorific. For example, Yohannes's former *turk bāshā*, mentioned by Lamlam as killed in the battle of Gurā,[28] was apparently a man of secondary importance. The revival of the title as an addition to Alulā's rank of *rās* was significant, and the future Alulā did his best to emphasize it as a sign of his superiority over other *rās*es. Thereafter, he always signed his letter, "Rās Alulā who is a Turk Bāshā."

> He [Yohannes] adorned him [Alulā] with all adornments. . . He did nothing like this for the other officers.
> When, Yohannes, King of Kings, had completed the ceremony of appointment for the Ras, he said to him: '. . . Let your authority be under me. Do all that you wish, and there will not be found one of the princes or officers who will be honoured more than you. And for me, there is nothing with which I could make you greater, except only the throne of my kingdom'.[29]

E. March 1878: Submission of Menilek

In early April 1877 *Turk Bāshā Rās* Alulā, leading the advance guard of the emperor's army, crossed the Takazzē river en route to Godjām. There, threatened by Menilek, *Rās* Adāl awaited on an *ambā* for the emperor to relieve him. Yohannes, however, marched not only to save *Rās* Adāl but also to fight for the imperial crown, since Menilek still referred to himself as "King of Kings," an open challenge.[30] Menilek was also said to be fomenting religious differences between Shoa and Tigre, that "he has brought a new foreign Bishop . . . [the Italian Guglielmo Massaja, and was] corresponding with foreign powers and importing arms."[31]

Reaching Godjām in the early rainy season, Yohannes found that Menilek already had retreated to Shoa.[32] Along with Alulā, the emperor subsequently marched to Wallo to join up with the forces of Muḥammad 'Alī (later *Rās* Mikā'ēl). Thereafter, Alulā was ordered to camp with his army near the Shoan border for the rainy season.[33] The monarch himself established his court in Dabra-Tābor,[34] from where he sought a mediated solution through the clergy.

Only in February 1878 did Yohannes finally decide to invade the southern province. As Alulā's biographer wrote:

> When the king and rulers of the country of Shoa and all the creatures from man to the animals, heard this news, they trembled and were afraid, and melted like wax, all those who were living there. The land trembled, and the whole of the country of Shoa was troubled because of the majesty of the coming of Yohannes, king of kings, and because of the strength of the power of Ras Alula, chief of the princes, for they greatly feared Ras Alula . . . Ras Alula did in that land great deeds which . . . cannot all be written or told. If all the deeds which were done in the land of Shoa were written down singly, the matter would be too much for us. And it would seem false to the hearers.[35]

Menilek had to ask for peace; his country was too disunited to resist, and the King wanted to avoid an open clash. His main interest was to retain his kingdom and his hold on Wallo, both of which could be achieved by recognising Yohannes as emperor.[36] On 26 March 1878 at Boru Mēdā, Menilek ceremoniously submitted to the emperor of Ethiopia. He approached the throne carrying a stone on his neck, and as he lay before Yohannes, the emperor reportedly ordered Alulā to remove the stone as a gesture of reconciliation.[37]

F. Walda-Mikā'ēl Retakes Hamāsēn

While a great political triumph was being obtained in the south, the situation in the north had deteriorated. Alulā's hasty departure from Hamāsēn in March 1877, had been interpreted there as a victory for Walda-Mikā'ēl. In April 1877 the government of Sa'zegā was assumed by a representative of Walda-Mikā'ēl, who was himself encouraged by the Egyptians, then apparently preparing to march into Tigre.[38] In Adwā the emperor had left *Rās* Bāriāu Gabra-Ṣādeq, the local governor, in charge of the affairs of the northern frontier.[39] In May 1878 *Rās* Bāriāu crossed the Marab and was ambushed and killed by Walda-Mikā'ēl's forces on 20 May 1878 near Bet Meca.[40]

G. *June-July: Alulā Sent to the North*

Even after hearing about the disaster, Emperor Yohannes could not leave his affairs in the south and hasten northwards. He had to confer with Menilek and *Rās* Adāl and Muḥammad 'Alī of Wallo over acute religious and political problems.[41] According to Alulā's biographer, the *rās* successfully appealed to his master to send him back to his lost province:

> When Yohannes, king of kings, had returned from the land of Shoa and was in the land of Wello, messengers came and told him the news of the death of the great Ras Bar'u, prince of the land of Tigre. . . .And again the faithful man Ras Alula said [to Yohannes], 'To me the strength of the power and the glory of the authority of this man [Walda-Mikā'ēl] seem like a reed stem which waves before the face of the wind,'. . . Yohannes . . . having heard this matter from Ras Alulā, was silent for a long time while he thought in his heart, and he said: 'If this Ras Alula is separated from me and goes to where the man . . . [Walda-Mikā'ēl] is, . . . who will uphold for me the house of my kingdom, for there is no one who can order the house of my kingdom like him? But if he stays with me, who can fight this [Walda-Mikā'ēl], for there is not to be found a man faithful like him [Alula], who does my will? . . . [And] he [Yohannes] said to Ras Alula . . . 'Go to the place you mentioned to me yourself, and let it be according to your words'.[42]

H. *"Governor of Tigre"*

Thus empowered, Alulā marched north. As his province beyond the Marab was still occupied by Walda-Mikā'ēl, Alulā was given the government of Adwā, succeeding the late Bāriāu. This temporary shift enabled the *rās* to mobilize Bāriāu's troops, until he had regained the Marab Mellāsh. Yet, for years-to-come, many European visitors regarded Alulā as the governor of Tigre.[43] In fact, Alulā was never governor of that province as it is known today, but only, and temporarily, master of Adwā and environs, the area then usually called Tigre.[44]

According to his biographer, Alulā was enthusiastically received in Aksum and Adwā by a population worried about a possible invasion by Walda-Mikā'ēl.[45] Yet for the Tigrean aristocracy, the rise of the king's *bālamwāl*, the young[46] son of an unknown farmer from a tiny village, was an unpleasant surprise. Bāriāu's son,

Dadjāzmāch Gabra-Madhen, who thought he would inherit his father's domain, was openly hostile to Alulā, whom he nicknamed *arastay*, farmer.[47]

It was at this stage in his career that Alulā divorced his wife Bitwatā, the daughter of a farmer from Tambēn and the mother of his three daughters. He sent her back to her village and married, apparently following the emperor's instructions, the nineteen-year-old *Wayzarit* Emlasu (whose baptismal name was Walatta Takla-Hāymānot), daughter of *Rās* Ar'āyā Demṣu, the most prominent Tigrean chief and Yohannes's uncle. According to later evidence, *Rās* Alulā was deeply in love with this sickly, if noble new wife, who bore him no children.[48] His own humble origin, however, was never forgotten by the leading families, and marriage brought no great social power, nor did it secure allies amongst the notables. Alulā's new brother-in-law, *Fitāwrāri* Dabbab Ar'āyā, was soon to become his most bitter enemy.

1. September-December 1878: The Submission of Walda-Mikā'ēl

Hearing the news of Alulā's arrival in Adwā, *Rās* Walda-Mikā'ēl cancelled his plan to cross the Marab. Instead, he started reconstructing Hazagā, where he built a new fort,[49] intending to make this village the administrative and commercial centre of his territories. But Gordon Pasha, who apparently wanted to avoid troubles with the Ethiopians, strongly disapproved of the Egyptian policy of backing Walda-Mikā'ēl. On a visit to Massawa in late May 1878, just after Bāriyāu's death, he instructed his newly-appointed governor, the devoted 'Alā' ad-Dīn Pasha, to cease supporting the renegade *rās*.[50] Consequently, in the coming rainy July, when Walda-Mikā'ēl marched to Aylēt with his hungry troops, he was denied grain from Massawa. The arrival of a British warship to the port persuaded the outlaw that he had been abandoned.[51]

Meanwhile, *Rās* Alulā had mobilised a 20,000-man army in Tigre and, "on the first Saturday after Masqal [27 Sept.] 1878, "he crossed the Marab and entered Hamāsēn. An advance guard cut the Hamāsēn-Bogos road to block Walda-Mikā'ēl's escape route.[52] Alulā's biographer wrote:

> When there was heard the news of the coming of the man of God, Ras Alula, a man resolute and warlike . . . fear and trembling seized this wicked man Däjjazmach Walda Mikael, and he melted like wax before the fire. . . And after this he sent emissaries to him, to Ras Alula, saying 'Forgive me, Ras Alula, my lord, and do not look on the evil of my deeds, because I will not fail to . . . [bless you]; and you, do not lose the opportunity for mercy'. He said this, not desiring to make peace and love, but because of the fear and trembling which had come on him. After this they made reconciliation and peace.[53]

The meeting between Alulā and Walda-Mikā'ēl took place in Aksum, where the rebel, by now desperate, came in December 1878, accompanied by three hundred hungry followers. Alulā then invited him to come to Yohannes, who was camping at Dabra-Tābor:[54]

> And Ras Alula said to him, 'Come, let us go to where our lord, Yohannes, King of Kings, is, that we may see his face, and bow down to the glory of his kingship, for he is forgiving and not revengeful.'
> When Yohannes, King of Kings, saw Däjjazmach Wäldä-Mikael bowing before him and doing homage to the glory of his kinship, he remembered the word of the Book which says, 'If your brother sins, forgive him seventy times seven'. He gave him authority over the land of Hamāsēn, and granted him a name greater than all names . . . that is to say, Ras Wäldä Mikael. And they returned with joy and gladness, as Ras Wäldä Mikael praised Yohannes . . . and magnified the name of Ras Alula, saying: 'What can I give back to Ras Alula for all he has done for me? For he has made me great, and has lifted me up above the chiefs of Hamāsēn'.[55]

In Dabra-Tābor Yohannes confirmed Walda-Mikā'ēl's title of *rās* and nominated him vice governor of Hamāsēn under Alulā.[56] The conciliation had a dual aim: place an hereditary figure in the Hamāsēn government and to use Walda-Mikā'ēl as a check on Alulā. It was also a demonstration of the emperor's characteristically liberal and moderate policy. Yohannes was far from being the fanatic that Europeans judged him to be. In a traditionally Ethiopian "diplomatic" manner, he sought to unite his country through gaining the good will and cooperation of his vassals. Fully aware of the failure of his great predecessor Tēwodros II, Yohannes was realistic enough to understand that he was not in a position to defeat all the leading families in the various provinces and to redistribute land throughout the empire, thus creating an all-Ethiopian set of loyalties based solely on the monarchy. Instead, he worked to create a federal structure for his empire, thereby compromising with hereditary provincial rulers, such as Menilek or *Rās* Adāl of Godjām, who occasionally opposed his government. Simultaneously, Yohannes sought to encourage the spirit of Ethiopian Christian nationalism, hoping that his vassals would join him to campaign against the Muslim Gallas (Oromo) or to face the external threat.

In forgiving Walda-Mikā'ēl, Yohannes also sought at least to obtain temporary peace beyond the Marab. Yohannes was then planning another march on the Wallo Galla, and he wanted Alulā to accompany him.[57] Thus, when *Rās* Walda-Mikā'ēl returned to Hamāsēn in January 1879, *Rās* Alulā was camping near Menilek's border.[58]

J. March-April 1879: Anglo-Egyptian Envoy

Before leaving for Wallo, Emperor Yohannes, aware of the effect of Egypt's policy towards Walda-Mikā'ēl, sent a letter to colonel Gordon in Khartum. Repeating his declaration of 1876 not to negotiate directly with the Egyptians, Yohannes nevertheless asked Gordon to mediate.[59] The latter, however, reasoned that any cession of coastal territory to Ethiopia might result in its later requisition by other European powers.[60] As an Egyptian official, Gordon therefore adopted a tough approach toward Ethiopian territorial demands, particularly in Bogos. So, in January 1879, when his personal envoy, W. Winstanley, met Yohannes at Dabra-Tābor, he had been authorised only to make the same concessions already offered to Alulā early in 1877 (plus the dubious attraction of the return of Tēwodros's captured crown).[61]

Winstanley defined Alulā's position among the other Ethiopian *rās*es (together with that of *Rās* Ar'āyā) as "very superior" and described Alulā as the king's intimate friend.[62] Members of an Italian geographical mission spoke of Alulā as a "prime minister"[63] and expected him to be made *negus*.[64] They reported that Yohannes had appointed Alulā as protector and supervisor to his only son, the eleven-year-old *Rās* Ar'āyā-Sellāssē.[65] Thus, during the many discussions Winstanley had with the emperor in Dabra-Tābor in late March and early April 1879, Alulā was always present, and often the only other man there. Gordon's agent was well received by Alulā, whose friendly attitude was reflected in the Englishman's reports. Yet the *rās* remained passive, and the emperor's reaction to Gordon's offers was, of course, utterly negative: "I do not want a consul at Massawa," he told the envoy, "I want Massawa."[66]

K. July-September 1879: Alulā's First Offensive on Bogos

It was probably Winstanley's mission which persuaded the emperor to take the initiative against the Egyptians. The Ethiopians now enjoyed an enormous advantage due to the unity achieved in 1878. The Egyptian garrisons in Massawa and Karan together numbered merely 3-4,000 troops,[67] while Alulā was reported in July 1879 to have 25,000-40,000 troops, with as many again under the nominal command of the young *Rās* Ar'āyā-Sellāssē.[68]

In July 1879, with Walda-Mikā'ēl in his camp,[69] Alulā crossed the Marab and camped at Gurā in Akalla-Guzāy. The French Vice-Consul in Massawa, Achille Raffray, telegraphed to his superior in Egypt: "Yohannes's intentions unclear but certainly he had ordered . . . [his men] to take territory up to Kassala and the Red Sea."[70] Alulā himself told the French missionary Duflos, "I have come to retake Massawa from the Egyptians, I will not go away until my horse has drunk from the Red Sea." Raffray commented with alarm: "Coming from Alulā, these are weighty words indeed. Everyone, his enemies foremost, agrees that Ras Alula is frank, determined and steadfast. What he says he is going to do, he does."[71] The French in Massawa were concerned about a possible Ethiopian advance, especially to Bogos, where their Lazzarist missionaries (whose religious activities Yohannes denounced) had also served the Egyptian cause and had harboured Ethiopian outlaws like Walda-Mikā'ēl and Bāhtā Hagos. Moreover, French and Italians in Bogos cultivated tobacco plantations, a plant Yohannes had prohibited. Paris therefore instructed Raffray to demand security from Alulā for the missionaries and other French citizens and protégés. Raffray wrote to Alulā and received a polite and affirmative reply.[72]

Meanwhile, London, which wanted to maintain the status quo in Massawa, became worried, and the British Consul in Cairo asked Alulā not to attack or at least to postpone his advance to enable further diplomatic negotiations to take place.[73] Ominously, a British warship arrived at Massawa. Undeterred, in August 1879, Alulā ordered his deputy Walda-Mikā'ēl to send his troops forward. Commanded by one of Walda-Mikā'ēl's devotées, *Kantibā* Shāwīsh,[74] the Ethiopian army entered Bogos, and taxed the various tribes, European colonists, and missionaries,[75] while the besieged Egyptian garrison at Sanhīt remained passive. Yet, this fort was invincible, and no permanent Ethiopian government could be established in Bogos.

L. December 1879: The fall of Walda-Mikā'ēl

Alulā used the Bogos expedition to engineer Walda-Mikā'ēl's fall. He refrained from sending troops towards Massawa, and thus Walda-Mikā'ēl remained at Gurā surrounded by Alulā's men, while his most loyal followers were raiding Bogos. According to Hamāsēn oral tradition, Alulā falsely accused Walda-Mikā'ēl of concealing arms and of being in secret communication with Massawa and Sanhīt. Formal judicial proceedings were organized in Alulā's court: Walda-Mikā'ēl's nephew, *Kantibā* Haylu, to whom Alulā had promised the governorship of Hazagā, testified against his uncle, while potential witnesses for the defendant were intimidated. Together with his sons, *Dadjāzmāch* Masfen and *Ledj* Hāyla-Malakot, and his son-in-law, *Balāmbarās* Keflē Iyāsus, the *ras* was arrested and sent to Yohannes in Adwā.[76] The emperor was not totally convinced about the plot, and in any case Alulā, as a *ras*, was not superior to Walda-Mikā'ēl, so it was up to the emperor to do justice.

In December 1879, Yohannes rescinded the verdict and ordered Alulā and Walda-Mikā'ēl to Dabra-Tābor for a hearing.[77] Alulā repeated his accusations, and "placed Yohannes in the position of having to choose between his faithful servant and the former rebel."[78] Walda-Mikā'ēl was subsequently condemned and, in January 1880, was put on Ambā Salāmā with his sons.[79] Walda-Mikā'ēl was the last hereditary ruler to hold power in the Marab Mellāsh. People in Eritrea still recall Alulā's name in that connection.[80]

* * *

As an *ashkar* in the court of *Rās* Ar'āyā Demṣu in the late sixties, Alulā "Wadi Qubi" had reached a very high position for a man of humble origin. Having no hereditary land rights, he could never join the Tigrean ruling class which derived its power from a combination of land-ownership and imperial office. Alulā nonetheless fully exploited his opportunities: although his function as a *ligābā* in the emperor's court was relatively minor in the administrative scale, he used the position as the basis of a career. Then, as a military officer, Alulā quickly and brilliantly had managed to reach the top of that ladder, too.

Now, unlike the Tigrean nobles who could mobilise a few hundred followers from their self-armed peasantry, Alulā commanded thousands of imperial troops. This circumstance did not, however, enable him to enter the hereditary élite, nor did he succeed in marrying into it. To support his devoted follower, the emperor provided him with *gult* lands, i.e. territorial fiefs donated as usufruct. Alulā was apparently given a small fief in his birthplace of Mannawē,[81] but Tigre could not provide the emperor with lands which could be donated without depriving the local élite.[82] Moreover, Yohannes's roving court did not develop into a non-feudal, central administrative or military system which could supply the ambitious *turk bāshā* with adequate economic resources to support his imperial rank. Thus, for Yohannes, the need to rid himself of the Marab Mellāsh's unfaithful local élite coincided with the need to install Alulā, an outsider in feudal Tigre, in a province of his own.

NOTES

1   See below, section 8.
2   See an example in: Ishaq Yosef; *Hade eritrawi*, Asmara 1961 E.C., Chapter 5.
3   BM. Add. Mss. 51294, Gordon to Augusta 8.3.77 and 15.3.77. This last raid was apparently a retaliation for Alulā's razzia of 1 Feb. 1877; see below p. 16.
4   MAE (F), Massawah 4, Carbonnel to MAE, 5.3.77. Comparing with Walda-Mikā'ēl's 2,000 followers in the Bogos (see FO 407/11, Gordon's account, 15.9.79). The Egyptians had 700 men in Sanhīt and 2,000 in Massawa (FO 78/2631, Vivian to Derby, 23.1.77.)
5   Carbonnel to MAE, 5.3.77.
6   FO 78/2632, Wylde's Report, 23.4.77.
7   MAE (F) Massauah 4, Carbonnel to MAE, 11.2.77; FO 78/2631, Cherif to Vivian 9.3.77; Vivian to Derby, 6.2.77.
8   MAE (F), Massauah 4, Carbonnel to MAE, 5.3.77.
9   FO 78/2632, Carbonnel to French Agent in Cairo 21.3.77.
10 L.H. Mitchell, *Report on the Seizure by the Abyssinians of the Geological and Mineralogical Reconnaissance Expedition*, Cairo 1878, pp. 25, 40, 41, 42, 54, 55, 56, 58.
11 Ibid., pp. 54, 55.
12 For his economic interest, see below, Section H.
13 FO 78/2632, Vivian to Derby 7.4.77; On Gordon's negotiations see more in Rubenson, *Survival*, pp. 335-347.
14 FO 78/2632, Gordon to Vivian 28.3.77, 2.4.77; Vivian to Derby, 7.4.77.

15 FO 78/2632, Wylde's Report 23.4.77. See also A.B. Wylde, *'83 to '87*, vol. I, pp. 332, 333.
16 Yohannes to Gordon, 18.6.77 in G.B. Hill, *Colonel Gordon in Central Africa 1874-1879*, London 1881, p. 291.
17 For Alulā's interest in that trade, see below, Section H.
18 Mitchell, *op.cit.*, pp. 97, 103.
19 Guébrè Sellassié, *Chronique du règne de Ménélik II, Roi des Rois d'Éthiopie*, Paris 1930-32, Ch. XXIV.
20 IO R/20, Vivian to Derby, 29.3.77.
21 FO 78/2632, Gordon to Vivian, 28.3.77, Vivian to FO, 16.4.77.
22 For Alulā as a friend of Yohannes and the best comparative sketches of their characters, see W. Winstanley, *A Visit to Abyssinia*, London 1881, vol. II, pp. 224, 225, 230, 235.
23 FO 78/3806, Egerton to Salisbury, 26.7.85. He quotes Mason Bey, the Egyptian-employed American governor of Massawa: "The Negus has more confidence in him than in any of his chiefs, for the reason that he is of low birth and has no pretensions of himself with the royal family."
24 According to oral tradition Yohannes visited *Rās* Alulā in Hamāsēn in 1884. Alulā thereupon ordered his young lieutenant *Belāttā* Gabru go on a short trip, because he suspected that if the emperor saw him he might take him to his court. See Kolmodin, No. 271.
25 Heruy Walda-Sellāssē, *Yaheywat tārik*, Addis Ababā 1914 E.C., p. 47.
26 *Echage* Tewoflos was known as a great supporter of Tigrean hegemony in Ethiopia (see below, p. 179). The fact that he supported the nomination of Alula indicates that Tewoflos served the interest of a strong united Tigre rather than those of the Tigrean feudal chiefs who undoubtedly opposed the nomination of Alula. See below, pp. 21, 22).
27 Ms. Mannawē.
28 See above, p. 12.
29 Ms. Mannawē.
30 For background, consult Marcus, *The Life and Times*, pp. 50-54.
31 Aṣmē, p. 83. See also Zewde, pp. 94-100; and FO 78/3633, Vivian to FO, 17.7.77.
32 For Menilek's moves, Feb.-June 1877, see Guébrè Sellassié, *Chronique*, chs. XXIV, XXV.
33 L. Gentile, *L'apostolo dei Galla*, Torino 1916, p. 345.
34 Lamlam, f. 23.
35 Ms. Mannawē.
36 For a detailed analysis, consult Marcus, *Life and Times of Menelik II*, pp. 53-55.
37 Pietro Valle: "Abissinia schizzo storico," *RMI*, June 1887, pp. 495-508. In 1887 Alulā's Italian prisoner, Savoiroux, told a journalist he had heard the *rās* tell his soldiers about ". . . This Menelik from whose neck I myself removed the big stone with which he presented himself to ask pardon for his rebellion." Perino, p. 103.
38 Kolmodin, No. 255; FO 407/11, Gordon's memo, 15.9.79; BM Add. Mss. 51294, Gordon to Augusta, 11.12.77.
39 Mitchell, pp. 70, 103.
40 MAE (F), Massauah 4, Carbonnel to MAE, 25.5.78; Kolmodin, No. 259; B. Hill, pp. 313, 314.
41 See Marcus, *The Life and Times*, pp. 55-58.
42 Mannawē Ms.

43 See, among many, Fasolo, p. 206; G. Bianchi, *Alla terra dei Galla*, Milano 1884, p. 50; A.S. MAI 36/3-23, Ferrari and Nerazzini to MAE, 14.9.85.
44 Int. Dadjāzmāch Zawdē, Addis Ababa, Dec. 1971.
45 Ms. Mannawē.
46 Though then over thirty years old, Alulā looked much younger, *Winstanley*, vol. II, pp. 191, 192.
47 A.S. MAI 3/7-47 Memo. on Bāhtā Hagos, 1.1.95.
48 See below, pp. 39, 40. Also Matteucci, p. 233.
49 Kolmodin, No. 260; G. Simon, *L'Ethiopie*, Paris 1885, p. 58.
50 Wylde, *'83-'87*, I, pp. 334, 335; FO 407/11, Gordon, "Abyssinie 1877-1879," 15.9.79.
51 FO 78/2857, Lascelles to Salisbury, 26.9.78, 17.10.78; Kolmodin, No. 261.
52 MAE (F), Massauah 4, Carbonnel to MAE, 13.9.78, 10.11.78. FO 78/2857, Gordon's memo, 19.10.87.
53 Mannawē MS. Compare with Kolmodin, No. 261.
54 Kolmodin No. 261. According to B. Hill, pp. 328, 329, Yohannes received Walda-Mikā'ēl in Gondar.
55 Mannawē Ms.
56 Kolmodin, No. 261.
57 BM Add. Mss. 51304, Winstanley to Gordon, 20.3.79.
58 Matteucci, p. 95.
59 FO 78/2998, Vivian to Salisbury, 11.1.79.
60 FO 78/3004, Lascelles to Salisbury, 5.10.79: "... I have received from Gordon pasha [a private letter] pointing out that if a port on the Red Sea were to be given to King John, there would be a great risk of his conceding it to French or Italian adventurers."
61 FO 78/2998, Vivian to Salisbury, 7.2.79, quoting Gordon to Vivian, 9.1.79.
62 BM 51304, Winstanley to Gordon, 22.5.79. Winstanley, *op.cit.*, vol. II, pp. 224, 225. Also: Matteucci, *In Abissinia*, p. 231; P. Vigoni, *Abissinia*, Milan 1881, p. 181.
64 Matteucci, 18.5.79; *Cosmos*, vol. V, p. 258: *In Abissinia*, p. 231.
64 Matteucci, 12.3.79; *Cosmos*, vol. V, p. 189.
65 G. Bianchi, *Alla terra*, p. 50.
66 Winstanley, II, p. 244.
67 L. Pennazzi, *Dal Po ai due Nili*, Milano 1882, p. 56.
68 FO 407/11, Wylde to Malet, 18.10.79; Zohrab to Salisbury, 12.9.79.
69 Kolmodin, No. 262.
70 MAE (F), Massauah 4, Raffray to Consul, Egypt 8.9.79.
71 MAE (F), Massauah 4, Raffray to MAE, 13.8.79.
72 MAE (F), Massauah 4, Raffray to Alulā, 8.9.79; Raffray to MAE, 22.9.79; Pennazzi, p. 224; Alame Eshete, *"Evolution et Resolution du Conflit Egypto-Abyssinien ... 1877-1885,"* Doctoral thesis, Aix en Provence, 1965 (Available in IES), p. 93.
73 FO 78/3003, Lascelles to Alula, 28.8.79; Lascelles to Salisbury, 29.8.79.
74 MAE (F), Massauah 4, Raffray to MAE, 13.8.79.
75 MAE (F), Massauah 4, Raffray to Consul, Egypt 8.9.79; Raffray to MAE, 30.9.79.
76 For details, see Kolmodin, Nos. 262-265. MAE (F), Massauah 4, Raffray to MAE, 22.9.79. Also Takla-Ṣādeq Makuriyā, *Ya'itiopyā tārik*, Addis Ababa 1960 E.C., pp. 57, 58.
77 MAE(F), Mass. 4, Raffray to MAE, 14.12.79, 18.12.79. Gordon also heard that

Yohannes was very angry with Alulā and put him under his son *Rās* Ar'āyā-Sellāssē, FO 407/11, Gordon to Malet, 14.12.79.
78 MAE(F), Mass. 4, Raffray to MAE, 27.5.1880. cf. Kolmodin, No. 261, and Perini, p. 123, who claim that Yohannes was a party to the plot against Walda-Mikā'ēl.
79 Walda-Mika'el was then around sixty years old (According to Puglisi he was born around 1823, Puglisi, p. 291.). Yet he survived to be released by Alula eleven years later, see below, p. 142.
80 Kolmodin, No. 261. Interviews, W. Walata Berhan, 98-year-old woman, Asmara, March 1972.
81 See below, p. 194.
82 Alula, later in 1882, was given Agaw Meder probably as *gult*. See below, p. 36.

3

1880-1882:
"Rival of Shoa, Ruler of Massawa"[1]

During 1880-1882, *Rās* Alulā worked untiringly to maintain his dual bases of power: the government of the Marab Mellāsh and his position as *turk bāshā*. As Yohannes's general he campaigned each dry season (October-May) to help his master preserve the throne and to obtain revenues. Alulā returned to his province for the rainy season,[2] to collect taxes because during the dry period:

> the fields have not yet been planted and thus nothing prevents the rural peoples from fleeing into inaccessible mountains or the deserts at the least move to collect taxes; it is for this reason that the Ethiopians are in the habit of waiting until August or September at which time the harvest is ready, the people then prefer to submit and pay the tribute rather than lose their crops by fleeing.[3]

During the three years, the busy Alulā mostly exploited his province as a source for finance and manpower and did very little administration. His major concern was apparently the organization of the profitable caravan route to Massawa,[4] which he started in late 1879.[5] Even when freed from helping Yohannes, Alulā concentrated on his province's border problems. Here, the failure of diplomacy left the Ethiopian-Egyptian frontier, particularly the Bogos country, as an arena of continuous raids and clashes.

A. Rainy Seasons 1879:
The Failure of Diplomacy to Solve
the Border Problems

A few days after Walda-Mikā'ēl's arrest in Gurā in early September 1879, Alulā received a short letter from Gordon announcing his arrival at Massawa to resume negotiations. Having nothing new to offer,[6] the Englishman was delighted to hear from Raffray that Alulā had been authorised to deal with the question of the northern frontier. Correspondence with the *rās* made Gordon even more optimistic:

Alulā asked for secret discussions,[7] giving the erroneous impression that he would conduct a policy independent of Yohannes. According to Gordon's own experience and Winstanley's reports, he thought Alulā's approach would surely be more flexible. The colonel optimistically wrote to his sister: "I think when I see Alula I will avoid discussing the question of the frontier, i.e., the retrocession of Bogos."[8]

On 16 September 1879, Gordon climbed to Alulā's camp on the top of the hill of Gurā, and to his surprise was coolly received:

> Solemn silence prevailed; nearly every one had his robe to his mouth as if something poisonous had arrived. The figure at the end never moved, and I got quite distressed, for he was so muffled up that I felt inclined to feel his pulse. He must be ill, I thought. No, this was my friend Alula. He just saluted me, and motioned me to a very low seat, covered with silk, at his side.

A little later the atmosphere became friendlier, and Alulā, as if to hint that he was capable of conducting quite an independent policy, remarked:

> You may smoke, if you like, though the king has forbidden his people to do so.[9]

Then, before starting to talk business, Alulā tried to gain Gordon's admission that he was a British official:

> I quietly denied the soft impeachment, and said that 'here I could only be looked on as the Envoy of the Khedive, and Mussulman for the time'; adding 'if I were to pretend to be anything else, anything I arranged with him would be useless, if the Khedive knew of my false pretences'. Well, after some time, I took leave of the invalid, and left.[10]

Thus the *rās*, who was fully prepared to negotiate with a British official (even above the head of his master?), found himself facing an Egyptian agent. In such circumstances, Gordon could only obtain Alulā's agreement to postpone any attack on Massawa for a period of four months.[11] Alulā sent Gordon to Dabra-Tābor by the right bank of the Takazzē River, the most difficult route. He reached the imperial camp after more than a month's travel to find Yohannes more inflexible than his *rās*.[12]

A few days after Gordon's departure from Gurā, Alulā received a letter from another Englishman, Augustus Wylde, who asked for an interview.[13] Wylde, a merchant and former British Vice-Consul at Jedda, had been invited to accompany Gordon to Alulā, but was not in time to meet his compatriot at Massawa. Though unauthorised, Wylde, an anxious supporter of the Ethiopian cause,[14] approached *Rās* Alulā as if he were still a British official and as such was warmly welcomed in Addi Taklay. Presenting himself as a channel to Her Majesty's Government,

Wylde heard Alulā complain about Egypt's "continual annexation of... territory, stoppage of intercourse with other countries, religious rights denied ... [to Ethiopia] by the prevention of the Aboona entering Abyssinia, whereby their civil and religious customs were nearly at a stand-still, and a general treatment such that a Christian country could not tolerate."[15]

Alulā told Wylde "that he had no orders to treat with Egyptian representatives" and expressed his sorrow that Gordon had presented himself as such. Alulā rejected the possibility raised by Wylde that Ethiopia would be compensated for Bogos by simply asking: "Whether England would be contented if Russia annexed part of India and paid her over the revenues?" The *rās*, however, was surprisingly moderate about Massawa:

> I explained fully to General Alula the responsibilities they would incur by having a seaport, and how easy it would be for Egypt to prevent them establishing themselves on the coast, and after a little pressing he told me that in reality Abyssinia did not wish one, but that they wished to import arms and ammunition, and the usual munitions of war, that they never claimed the coast, but wished to enforce upon Egypt the necessity of allowing them to trade through Massowah.[16]

Alulā was clearly ready to compromise, but his points: British mediation, cession of the Bogos and a satisfactory commercial arrangement in Massawa, were not even discussed in London. The Foreign Office severely condemned Wylde for his unauthorized discussions. He was deprived of any future official service and had to write to Alulā explaining that he had acted without authority.[17] Simultaneously, the queen wrote to the emperor encouraging him to reach an understanding directly with Egypt.[18] Thus, the small window to Britain was shut, and there were no direct diplomatic relations with Ethiopia for the next four years.

B. "Ruler of Massawa":
The Bogos Arena: Raids and Clashes

Gordon's failure as British mediator and the fall of Walda-Mikā'ēl led to another Egyptian-Ethiopian confrontation. As Alulā was interested, for commercial reasons, in maintaining a *modus vivendi* on the road to Massawa, it was the Egyptian-held Bogos which became the arena of confrontation. Since the *rās* was preoccupied by domestic matters (Yohannes called on him frequently to go on campaigns against the Wallo Gāllā or to restrain disobedient vassals) and the Egyptians refused to leave their strong forts, an open war was avoided. The Ethiopians could raid and tax Bogos and other border areas without needing to establish a permanent government, and they caused an anarchy which attracted outlaws who further added to the general misery.

During the early 1880s Alulā could do little to ameliorate the situation, since he was too busy helping Yohannes on the Ethiopian home front. For example, after imprisoning Walda-Mikā'ēl on Ambā Salāmā in early 1880, Yohannes marched southwards to meet Menilek in Wallo and left Alulā in Adwā. In February 1880 Alulā was ordered to remain in the north because *Dadjāzmāch* Gabra-Madhen, the son of the late *Rās* Bariyāu, was in revolt near Adwā.[19] Only in early March did the *rās* move to Maqalē to stay there, inactive, closer to the emperor's headquarters in Zabul.[20]

Left as ruler over Hamāsēn, Alulā's lieutenant, *Belāttā* Gabru established his headquarters at Daro Caulos.[21] Wylde described him as:

> an ugly, middle-sized man . . . with a reputation for being a good general, a quick mover, and cruel to his enemies, and a great robber. There is no doubt that he does take over and above his tribute and pound of flesh, and reads his instructions as to tribute a hundred cattle from one tribe, as a hundred of the fattest and best milch cows belonging to them.[22]

A native of Tambēn and also the son of a tenant, the tough Gabru was trusted and supported by the busy Alulā, who authorised him to crush opposition in the Marab Mellāsh and to raid the neighboring Egyptian occupied territories. Gabru managed to eliminate some remnants of Walda-Mikā'ēl followers[23] but failed to subdue the chronically rebellious Bāhtā Hagos of Akalla-Guzāy. Bāhtā fled and joined the Egyptians in the fort of Sanhīt (Karan).[24]

In July 1880, Yohannes ordered Alulā to Sa'zegā in Hamāsēn with instructions to convert Muslims and foreign missionaries. Yohannes strove for national spiritual unity and persistently worked for a homogeneous Ethiopian Church.[25] He suspected that religious minorities and "imported" religions served Ethiopia's foreign enemies, and he fought against both.[26] While giving a most liberal interpretation to Yohannes's policy against the Muslim inhabitants,[27] Alulā strictly followed his instructions to eliminate missionary activities and to destroy foreign Ethiopic-language literature.[28] The Swedish mission at Galab, among the Mansa tribes, was the first to be affected. The head of that station was ordered to send his native priests to Dabra-Bizan "to study the true Ethiopian religion," and the mission was subsequently closed.[29]

Moreover, as the Lazzarist mission in Karan was known to be under French auspices, Alulā used Yohannes's policy to attempt to gain European recognition of Ethiopian rights over Bogos. In July 1880, Raffray, alarmed by Alulā's rumored threat to raid Bogos, hurried from Massawa to meet the *rās* at Addi Taklay. The Frenchman's long speech about the friendly relations between France and Ethiopia and his request that Alulā refrain from taxing the mission, was countered by the *rās*'s claim that Bogos was Ethiopian and that he had the right to collect revenues there. The embarrassed Vice-Consul answered that he could not interfere in Ethiopian-Egyptian relations. "In fact," he insisted, "the Egyptians are the masters of that country, where they have a large and modern equipped army which governs the country and we must obey them . . . if you want the revenue of Bogos, go and ask for it from the Egyptians."[30]

The French refusal to recognise Ethiopian rights over Bogos and their support for the missionaries was a source of bitterness for Alulā. Indeed, his relations with the French were in line with the policy of his master. For during the 1880s Ethiopia faced the British-controlled Egypt and later, Italy. France was therefore Ethiopia's natural ally, a relationship later achieved during Menilek's reign. Yet Yohannes alienated the French by his misguided anti-missionary policy, and Alulā himself, underestimating the power of France[31], continued to see Britain as the desired mediator with his neighbors. As for the missionaries, Raffray's posture soon proved to be quite harmful.

Alulā's campaign in Bogos of October 1880, was considered by European observers as a tactical masterpiece.[32] At the end of September he led his 12,000-man army into the Ansabā valley. On 10 October[33] he crossed the river towards Karan, near the Egyptian post of Shabbāb. A detachment was sent to neutralize the fort of Sanhīt (Karan), while the bulk of his army marched to the Hallal high plateau and established a fortified camp on top of a mountain. Here, Alulā stayed for three weeks, despatching strong raiding parties against the Ḥabbābs, Banū 'Āmir, Mansa, Barka and others, also including European colonists and the French missionaries.

Some of the victims, among them the missionaries, who had already paid their annual tax to Egypt, appealed to Rashīd Pasha, the commander of the Sanhīt fort, but he made no immediate effort to protect them. One Italian writer later claimed that Rashīd had written challenging Alulā: "Why do you not come to attack me in the fort of Sanhīt instead of bothering innocent civilians?" *Rās* Alulā mockingly responded, "You, who prohibit these innocent civilians from paying the tribute they owe me, why don't you come out of your fort to defend them?"[34]

Only in late October did the Egyptian commander, together with his superior in Massawa and with the help of Bāhtā Hagos,[35] react by mobilising some seven thousand riflemen to block the exit out of the Ansabā valley. To avoid the trap, Alulā led his army, with more than ten thousand head of cattle, on a most difficult route and arrived safely at Sa'zegā early in November 1880.[36]

Alulā's successful raid of late 1880 failed, however, to re-establish Ethiopian rule over Bogos. Though he had a larger army, the *rās* must have realised that as long as the Egyptians held their fort of Sanhīt, which could be reinforced from Cairo in three weeks,[37] he would not be able to achieve anything better. Unable successfully to assault a fortified position, he could only threaten: "If Egypt would not restore the stolen territories we shall destroy Massaua and Kartum."[38] Yet the raid convinced Alulā that he could tax and raid Bogos every rainy season, which he would do for the next five years.

C. "Ruler of Massawa": Egyptian Supported Outlaws

The lack of a well-defined frontier between Egypt and Ethiopia and the availability of an ungoverned but raidable territory was not an intolerable situation for Alulā. The continuous razzias were not only a reason for the existence of his army but also probably the main source for its maintenance. Thus, Alulā led another expedition to Bogos in December 1881, and did not evacuate the Egyptian-claimed territory as hastily as the previous year. On 16 January 1882, he camped with his army at Dabra-Sinā and published an *awādj* regarding rates of taxes for the neighbouring tribes. "Most of these unfortunate people," reported the new French vice-consul at Massawa, "bring the tax, while Rashed pasha [the Egyptian commander] who cannot protect them, burns their villages when he hears that they are paying."[39] Around 15 February, Alulā pillaged for two days in the Ad-Tamāryām and Bedjuk countries and returned to Addi Taklay with 7-8,000 sheep and goats, almost as many cattle, and some 15,000 thalers (Maria Theresa dollars).[40]

Before leaving Egyptian territory, following Yohannes's instructions, the *rās* appointed a new abbot to the monastery of Dabra-Sinā and proclaimed that henceforth the neighboring tribes should pay tribute to the monastery.[41] This step aroused the adjacent Muslim Habbāb tribes against the Ethiopians, and the Egyptians were quick to send Bāhtā Hagos to organise them.[42] Bāhtā led his new followers to Dabra-Sinā, looted the monastery, and killed ten people.[43]

On the Massawa coast the Egyptians were equally successful in supporting another dangerous outlaw, Dabbab Ar'āyā, who crossed the undemarcated border line to the Egyptian-held Harkikū, to whose traditional ruler he was connected by marriage.[44] Only a few years younger than Alulā, the ambitious Dabbab was still a frustrated *fitāwrāri*.[45] His appeals for higher rank had been rejected by the emperor, and he wrote in early 1882 to the Egyptian governor of Massawa: "My father is *Rās* Arāyā, my brother is the King Yūḥannā but I was deprived by Yūḥannā my country and have come to you. No one is with the king, they will all join me..."[46]

D. "Rival of Shoa": Menilek Again

In June 1882 the emperor's hegemony was threatened again. Menilek of Shoa defeated *Negus* Takla-Hāymānot (formerly *Rās* Adāl) of Godjām in the battle of Embābo, 6 June 1882, and gained control over all the territories south of the Abbāy. Yohannes, who in the previous year had promoted Takla-Hāymānot to undermine Shoa's hegemony in the south, ostensibly intervened to ensure that Menilek did not become too powerful.[47] The emperor's advisers apparently considered that: "Shoa is a strong kingdom let alone with Godjāmi arms. Even without those we fear them; so let us strike now before the weak as well as the horses have regained their strength." Yohannes left Dabra-Tābor at the beginning of July.[48]

The Tigrean army marched eastwards, but again, as in 1878, a frontal clash with the Shoans was avoided. Menilek immediately wrote to the emperor who had camped at Warra Ilu[49] and in early August arrived there with the King of Godjām.[50] After some discussion, Takla-Hāymānot was permitted to depart, after having been given back some of his arms. The greater part of the weapons of the Godjāmi army were transferred by the emperor to Alulā.[51] Menilek was also deprived of the strategically important province of Wallo (recognized as Menilek's by Yohannes in 1878) which was given to *Rās* Ar'āyā-Sellāssē, with *Rās* Mikā'ēl as deputy. Yohannes also took Agaw Meder from Takla-Hāymānot and gave it to Alulā,[52] who never went there.[53]

As a gesture of reconciliation and to reinforce national unity, Yohannes married his only son, *Rās* Ar'āyā-Sellāssē, to Menilek's daughter, Zawditu. According to oral tradition, Alulā much opposed the marriage, arguing absurdly that the bride was not beautiful enough. "Policy is not decided by the straightness of the nose,"[54] Yohannes is said to have retorted. Nevertheless Alulā accompanied *Rās Bitwaddad* Gabra-Masqal and *Rās* Gabra-Kidānē (the governor of Zabul and Yohannes's brother-in-law) to Menilek's camp to escort the bride.[55] On 24 October 1882 the young couple were married with great ceremony.

* * *

During late 1882 and the whole dry season of 1883, *Rās* Alulā was away from the Marab Mellāsh. He and *Rās* Gabra-Kidānē accompanied Yohannes on an expedition to western Wallo before returning in January 1883 to Dabra-Tābor.[56] In March and April, Alulā camped first outside Adwā and then in Aksum.[57] In June he visited Dabra-Tābor to see the emperor before returning to his province.[58] For the next five years Alulā would seldom cross the Marab southward. His province also became the stage for important historical developments.

NOTES

1 According to oral tradition, after he established his government in the Marab Mellāsh, Alulā used this terminology to refer to himself. Interview, Bairu Tafla, Addis Ababā, Jan. 1972.
2 Kolmodin, No. 268. During Alulā's absence, *Belātta* Gabru replaced him as governor.
3 MAE(F), Mass. 4, Raffray to MAE, 16.3.80.
4 See below Section 8.
5 BM. Add. Mss. 51294, Gordon to Augusta, 12.9.79.
6 FO 407/14, Extract from the "Royal Engineer Journal", 1.5.80.
7 FO 407/11, Gordon to Consul in Jedda, 13.9.79.
8 BM Add. Ms. 51294, Gordon to Augusta, 12.9.79.
9 B. Hill, pp. 403, 404.

10 Ibid.
11 FO 407/11, Lascelles to Salisbury, 4.10.79.
12 B. Hill, pp. 410-416. FO 78/3140, Gordon to Malet, 25.12.79. Consult also H. Marcus, *The Life and Times*, p. 78.
13 FO 407/11, Wylde to Alula, 22.9.79.
14 FO 407/11, Wylde's memo, 16.9.79.
15 FO 407/11, Wylde to Salisbury, 20.10.79.
16 Ibid.
17 FO 78/3005, Malet to Salisbury, 29.12.79; FO 407/14, Wylde to Zuhrab, 16.12.79.
18 FO 407/11, Victoria to King John, 12.12.79.
19 A.S.MAI 1/1-3, quoting *Moniteur Egyptien*, 15.2.80.
20 F.O. 407/11, quoting *Moniteur Egyptien*, 21.3.80, MAE Mass. 4, Raffray's, 16.3.80, 12.4.80.
21 Kolmodin, No. 267.
22 Wylde, *'83*, I, p. 205.
23 Kolmodin, No. 267; FO 407/14, extract from *Moniteur Egyptien*, 21.3.80.
24 E. Bucci, *Paesaggi e tipi africani*, Torino 1893, p. 232.
25 See /ewde Gabre-Sellassie, *Yohannes IV*, pp. 94-100.
26 J.S. Trimingham, *Islam in Ethiopia*, 2nd ed., Oxford 1965, pp. 112, 123; O. De Lacy, *The Ethiopian Church*, London 1936, p. 76.
27 See below: Section 8.
28 R. Pankhurst, *Economic History of Ethiopia*, Addis Ababa 1968, p. 670, citing J.M. Flad, *Zwölf Jahre in Abessinien*, Basel 1922.
29 A. Eshete, "The Swedish Protestant Mission 1866-1889," unpublished article.
30 MAE(F), Mass. 4, Raffray to MAE, 25.10.80; Eshete, "Conflict Egypto-Abyssinien," 179-184.
31 See: MAE(F) Mass. 4, Raffray to MAE, 20.8.81, 22.11.81.
32 O. Baratieri, "Di fronte agli abissini", *NA*, 1888.
33 For the raid, see, among others, MAE(F), Mas. 4, Raffray to MAE, 25.10.80; Pennazzi, *Dal Po ai due Nili*, p. 307; L. Negri, *Massaua e dintorni*, Valenza 1887, pp. 60, 71, 72; E. Littmann, *Publications of the Princeton Expedition to Abyssinia*, vol. IV B; *Lieder der Tigre-Stämme*, Leyden 1915, Song 704, p. 1065.
34 "Spedizione Militare Italiana in Abissinia," *Pensieri di un ufficiale superiore dell'esercito*, Rome 1887, pp. 71, 72.
35 E. Bucci, *op.cit.*, p. 232.
36 Raffray to MAE, 25.10.80.
37 E. Tagliabue, "Egiziani e abissini," *L'Esploratore*, 1881, p. 64.
38 G. Rohlfs, *L'Abissinia*, Milano 1885, p. 110.
39 MAE(F), Mass. 4, Herbin to MAE, 1.4.82.
40 Ibid. Also *Annales de la Congregation*, 1882, pp. 249, 250.
41 C. Conti Rossini, *Principi di diritto consuetudinario dell'Eritrea*, Rome 1916, pp. 419, 420. Asrata Māryām, *Zēnā Dabra-Sinā* (with Italian trans.), Rome 1910.
42 A.S.MAI 3/6-40, Baratieri to MAE, 15.10.91.
43 Conti Rossini, *Principi*, p. 420.
44 Wylde, *'83*, I, p. 51. MAE, Mass. 4, Herbin to MAE, 1.3.82, 1.7.82. Takla-Ṣādeq Makuriya, p. 58.

45 The young Dabbab killed a man and had to live as an outlaw; see Takla-Ṣādeq Makuriyā, pp. 58, 59.
46 AA Soudan 3-6, Rubenson coll. IES. Dabāb to Tawfīq and Dabab to Rashīd Pasha, 1882, n.d.
47 For background consult Marcus, *The Life and Times*, pp. 68-71.
48 Aṣmē, p. 92.
49 MAE(F), Mass. 4, Alula to Raffray, Wara Ilu, 14 Hamle 1874/20.7.82.
50 MAE(F), Mass. 4, Yohannes to Raffray, 17.8.78.
51 Zewde, *Yohannes*, p. 234, quoting Heruy, "History of Ethiopia," p. 60.
52 Takla-Ṣādeq Makuriyā, p. 58.
53 According to one of Alulā's descendants it was subsequently governed by *Wāgshum* Beru. Int. Fit. Bayyana Abrehā.
54 Int. with a Tigrean teacher who wishes to remain anonymous.
55 Guébrè Sellasisé, *op.cit.*, p. 185.
56 FO 407/27, 'Ala' ad-Dın to Eg. Gov., 14.2.83, in Malet to Granville, 15.2.83.
57 G. Branchi, *Missione in Abissinia (1883)*, Rome 1889, p. 20.
58 MAE(F), Mass. 4, Herbin to Soumagne, 8.6.83.

4

1883: Brink of a Second Egyptian-Ethiopian War

A. *Egyptian Initiative*

While the Ethiopians in the Marab Mellāsh continued profitable raids on the Egyptian-occupied territories,[1] the khedive's authorities in Massawa were trying to reorganize their defences. In December 1881, they combined all Egyptian holdings bordering Ethiopia into a new *Hukūmdāriyyat hudūd al-Habasha*, i.e., "the Hukūmdāriyya [Administrative District] of the Ethiopian frontier."[2] and they started a new road from Karan to Kassala. In late 1882 a commission of four Egyptian officers headed by Zakī 'Abd ar-Rahmān was sent to study the border problems. In a long report submitted in early 1883,[3] they suggested a reorganisation of the frontier "in order to prevent Ras Alula and Belata Gabru from pillaging [our] tribes." The officers recommended that a chain of forts should be erected in Kumaliya, Sabarguma, Ira and other places, to be supported by newly-organized administrative centres in Massawa, Karan and Amidib. The strongholds were to house over ten thousand troops; and neighbouring tribes would be organized under new shaykhs known to oppose the Ethiopians. These proposals could not be sustained by Egyptian resources in 1883, and it seems that little was done to implement them. Yet the report reflected the will to regain strategic positions and foreshadowed a new Egyptian initiative.

B. *The Brother of Emlasu*

The Egyptian authorities at Massawa returned to their old system of harbouring and financing Ethiopian outlaws. Dabbab Ar'āyā, the rebellious son of *Rās* Ar'āyā and Alulā's brother-in-law, was even given a monthly salary[4] and started raiding the borderlands. Leading a well armed gang of 400 Assāwurta tribesmen, he robbed his first Ethiopian caravan in October 1882,[5] and intensified these activities throughout the next year. In April 1883 he even robbed a caravan carrying the property of the French Vice-Consul.[6] The loot was openly sold in the markets of Massawa and Harkīkū.

In June 1883 *Rās* Alulā returned to Addi Taklay to find that the commercial links with Massawa were paralysed,[7] not only because of Dabbab's activities, but also because the Egyptians were interfering with trade as part of their new initiative. In January 1883 an Egyptian detachment was sent to the coast near Zulā, from where Alulā long had smuggled in arms, and confiscated a consignment of 840 rifles with 32 boxes of ammunition. In May, while still in Adwā, Alulā unsuccessfully sought to obtain the release of these arms,[8] and once back in his province wrote to Mukhtār Pasha. He vowed that Massawa would be devastated unless the arms were restored and Dabbab turned over to him. Alulā's first demand was instantly met. Immensely pleased, Alulā summoned his European agent from Massawa and ordered another 1,800 rifles, promising to make payment in September.[9]

That month Dabbab carried out his most daring raid. Just two hours away from Massawa he looted a very rich caravan, confiscating goods owned by Alulā's wife and a sum of 3,000 thalers,[10] probably Alulā's down-payment for the rifles and their ammunition. Pleased with himself, Dabbab sent a letter to *Rās* Alulā mockingly asking him to thank his wife—Dabbab's sister—for the presents she had sent him.[11]

These insults came at a bad time. A few weeks later, in October, Emlasu died.[12] Alulā's biographer reported that the sorrowful *rās*:

> wept greatly, saying Amläsu was the covering of my head, the epaulettes of my collar and the shield of my arm. Behold, the wall of my house has fallen, woe is me, woe is me, for my light is darkened and my lamp extinguished, woe is me, woe is me. My praise has become silent, my thought is weakened and my strength trembles. . .'
>
> He [Alulā] wrote a letter about her death to his lord, Yohannes. The King sorrowed and grieved on account of her strong faith and noble deeds, for he loved her greatly, more than all the female relatives of his father and mother.

It was undoubtedly at this time that the *rās* developed a strong personal hatred for Dabbab, whose capture became Alulā's obsession. Meanwhile, he prohibited trade to Massawa and wrote to Mukhtār Bey in an effort to obtain Dabbab's surrender:

> The reason why I have not sent you the merchants and the caravans is that the other day I have sent you a letter that I would send you the merchants if you catch and send me Debbub. Now imprison him and send him to me. He is sitting with the family of the Naib of Herkeeko and his children. You yourself also know it.[13]

This was the situation on the eve of the first direct Ethiopian-Egyptian clash since the battle of Gurā.

C. October 1883: Sahāti, "Dogali of the Egyptians"

The lack of a defined Egyptian-Ethiopian frontier resulted from an earlier failure to negotiate a peace treaty and from the nature of the acrimonious relations between the two powers. While a common commercial interest necessitated some agreement about caravan routes, the Ethiopian "taxing" and raiding system contradicted any concept of a boundary. Thus, a tactical defence based on a fortified line, as suggested in the report of the Egyptian border commission, was actually an offensive plan. By proposing a line passing west of Sabarguma, the four officers clearly sought to rearrange areas which for years had been regarded as under Ethiopian control.

The Ethiopians were also in an aggressive mood. Yohannes was aware of the Egyptian collapse in the Sudan; he suspected a British-Egyptian action against him; and therefore prepared his armies for a quick preventive campaign. Menilek was ordered to move to Wallo, Takla-Hāymānot to Bagemder, *Rās* Mikā'ēl to Tigre, and Alulā's forces on the border were much reinforced.[14] The latter was undoubtedly eager to exploit his military advantage to regain territories lost since 1872, an interest strongly reinforced by his desire for revenge in the case of Dabbab and his supporters.[15]

In early October 1883, either because of Alulā's threats or because they were acting according to their new tactical plan, the Egyptians sent a company of troops to fortify Sahāti (then an almost deserted water-hole) on the Massawa-Hamāsēn road.[16] The *rās* protested to Mukhtār Bey, only to receive the reply that the troops were sent there to protect Ethiopian caravans.[17] In the last days of October 1883,[18] he therefore marched there:

> Ras Alula, having heard the matter of their coming . . . he could not be patient, and he rose up to fight them. He said to the officers and troops who were with him, 'In faith be brave, and do not fear. . .'
> And going they found them [the Egyptians] digging the ground, gathering wood and piling up stones to make a strong wall. . .[19]

Surprised by the Ethiopians, the Egyptian company was annihilated, 45 of the troops being killed and 15 taken prisoner.[20] Probably remembering Dabbab's last letter to him, "Ras Alula", wrote a British visitor, "with his usual pleasantry, sent word to Massawa, thanking the authorities for sending him so many excellent Remington rifles."[21]

★ ★ ★

Alulā's attack at Sahāti, later described as the "Dogali of the Egyptians,"[22] was apparently ordered on his own initiative. It was not the first time he had confronted the Egyptians, and he undoubtedly did not need Yohannes's approval to attack a small unit. He was after all, governor of the Marab Mellāsh. This time, however, things were different: the elimination of the company at Saḥāṭi was no longer a mere border clash. Egypt was already under British control, and the changed international situation would turn the incident into the starting point of a new period in Ethiopian history, enabling Alulā to develop his local independence and to become a leading figure in diplomacy.

NOTES

1 For Ethiopian raids on Egyptian-protected tribes in Bogos and the coast, see: A.S.MAI 36/2-11, Coanoti to MAE, 19.1.83, Branchi to MAE, 10.1.83. FO 403/81, Dowding to Moncrief, 21.2.83. SOAS M.518 R.8, 'Alā'ad-Dīn to Eg. Govt., 15.3.83, 18.4.83.
2 FO 78/3326, Malet to Granville, 12.12.81. SOAS M.518 R.8, Rep. 49.
3 SOAS M.518 R.8, Rep. 49.
4 AA 3/6 No. 41 and 42, Rashīd Kamāla to Eg. Gov., 16.5.83. Memo. on Dabbāb 1883, n.d., *Rub.Col., IES*.
5 Wylde, *'83*, I, pp. 337, 51; FO 406/1, V. Baker, Memo., 9.1.84 in Baring to Granville, 18.1.84.
6 FO 407/27, Stewart to Malet, 18.4.83.
7 For commerce with Massawa, see below Section 8.
8 Rohlfs to Allen in *The Times*, 11.7.83. A.S.MAI 36/2-11, Branchi to MAE, 10.11.83. MAE(F), Mass. 4, Müller-Vogt Co. to Soumagne, 15.4.86.
9 Ibid.
10 Perino, p. 76.
11 Ibid.
12 FO 406/1, Hewett to Admiralty, 7-10. I. 1884.
13 Wylde, *'83*, I, p. 59.
14 Zewde, *Yohannes*, p. 121, citing *Bosphore Egyptien*, 24.12.83.
15 FO 407/60, A. Baker to Granville, 5.1.84. Following Alula's demand for the surrender of Dabbab, the Egyptians in Massawa advised the latter to go to Sawakin for a while.
16 A. Salimbeni, "Diario d'un pioniere africano," *Nuova Antologia*, 1936, p. 131.
17 FO 407/28, Moncrief to Baring, 4.11.83.
18 G. Branchi, *op.cit.*, p. 51.
19 Ms. Mannawē.
20 FO 407/28, Moncrief to Baring, 4.11.83. According to *The Times*, 26.11.83 and Branchi, *op.cit.*, all sixty Egyptians were killed.
21 "A Journey to the Court of King John," *The Daily News*, 7.5.84; and several articles, 7.5.84 to 8.7.84. They were probably written by Mr. Villiers, the artist of *Graphic*, who accompanied the Hewett Mission.
22 For further details, see: Camera dei deputati: *Discorso dell'onorevole Luigi Chiala sul credito di 20 milioni per l'azione militare in Africa 29.6.87*, Rome 1887, p. 24. *The Times*, 22.12.83; FO 407/60, Hewett to Admiralty, 18.12.83.

5

1884: Treaty with Britain

The Sahāṭi clash could well have foreshadowed more intensive hostilities between Ethiopia and Egypt. In fact, Yohannes's next moves clearly indicated his eagerness to march. Following the mobilisation of various provincial armies, the Bogos tribes were again put under Ethiopian pressure, and the Sanhīt-Massawa telegraph line was cut by Alulā's troops.[1]

By the end of 1883, the overall situation of the Egyptian African empire was becoming critical. On 5 November 1883, a few days after the Sahāṭi clash, Hicks Pasha's expedition was annihilated by Mahdist forces. Moreover, the Mahdiyya movement was rapidly spreading among the eastern Sudanese tribes, and the Egyptians there, still organised in their "Ḥukūmdāriyya of the Ethiopian frontier," were apparently slow to understand that they were possibly facing total destruction. Their garrisons in the Ḥukūmdāriyya, those of Al-Qallābāt (Matammā), al-Jīra and Kassala, were actually besieged by superior Mahdist armies and tribes in late 1883 and the first half of 1884.[2] Rumours spread that the Mahdist leader of the eastern Sudanese marches, 'Uthmān Diqna, had written to Yohannes and Alulā suggesting common action.[3] In fact, the Muslim tribes in the areas between Massawa and Kassala were put under Mahdist pressure and influence. Thus, the Egyptian garrison of Amidīb and Sanhīt, though not surrounded by aggressive armies, became isolated from Massawa.

But British officials, now in charge of Egyptian affairs, were fully aware of the new developments. Their traditional policy (since 1868) of minimising relations with Ethiopia finally had to be altered, and the newly adopted line sought Ethiopia's active cooperation to obtain a stable frontier and assistance in relieving the besieged garrisons.[4] London decided, and Cairo agreed—over Gordon's opposition—to contact Yohannes and offer him the Bogos country and free trade in Massawa in return for a peace treaty. Lacking any existing diplomatic channels to the emperor, it was Alulā, the man in charge of the Egyptian frontier, whom the British preferred to contact.

In December 1883, simultaneously with the appointment of Rear-Admiral Sir William Hewett to head a diplomatic mission to Ethiopia, General V. Baker was sent to Massawa to make overtures to the *rās*. En route, the general arrested Dabbab in Sawākīn[5] and reached Massawa in late December. Baker immediately replaced Mukhtār with the American Mason Bey,[6] and charged A.B. Wylde with the pacification of the frontier. Writing to Alulā on 29 December 1883, General Baker promised the arrest of other outlaws and asked the Ethiopians to agree to receive British and Egyptian envoys in the near future in order to establish friendly relations between the Khedivial Government and Emperor Yohannes.[7] A follow-up letter from Wylde reminded Alulā of their previous cordial meeting of 1879. Wylde promised to do his best about Dabbab's followers, and asked the *rās* to normalise the situation by again permitting commerce with Massawa, which elicited Alulā's immediate and positive response.[8] Ethiopia still sought restoration of lost territories and guaranteed access to firearms through Massawa, and Alulā would do his best to obtain them.

A. French Interference

The French Government, embittered by the British occupation of Egypt and already in fairly close contact with Alulā and Yohannes, started to undermine the projected British mission.[9] The new Vice-Consul at Massawa, François Soumagne, wrote to Alulā on 12 January 1884, warning him against London and urging him not to decide anything before consulting a French representative. Soumagne wrote a similar letter to the emperor, offering, moreover, to act as his commercial agent at Massawa for the import of French arms.[10] Yohannes was already aware of the fact that the British were the new masters of Egypt, and so the French admonitions had the desired effect: "*Atsē* Yohannes was suspicious of the British envoys," wrote a contemporary Ethiopian historian. "He thought that they were followed by an army, for white traders on the coast used to warn him."[11] In early April 1884 Yohannes wrote to Soumagne appointing him commercial agent (*Wakīl*) in Egyptian-occupied Massawa.[12] Two weeks later he asked a newly-arrived French official, Lucien Labosse, to come to him before the arrival of the Anglo-Egyptian mission.[13] As for Alulā, it is apparent that he was interested in negotiating with the British. His future activities clearly show that he perfectly understood that, though France could provide arms, Great Britain actually controlled all disputed territories and Massawa.

B. Alulā's Initiative

From the beginning, the British were convinced that *Rās* Alulā was the key to successful negotiations. This conclusion, soon to be justified, was probably a result of the impression that Alulā was actually conducting an independent policy on the border. Regarded as "the mouthpiece of the Emperor,"[14] Alulā was considered as more than a mere channel to Yohannes. In Massawa Hewett was undoubtedly informed by the local Egyptian authorities and by Wylde about the *rās*'s strong position at court and about his interest in the Massawa trade. "Ras Alula," wrote Hewett,[15] "the Abyssinian generalissimo and apparently the moving spirit of that country . . . is well disposed towards Great Britain and anxious to arrive at a peaceful solution of the present lock-up of trade: a properly accredited British Commissioner could alone do this."

Returning to Addi Taklay on 31 January 1884, *Rās* Alulā found a British officer, Lieutenant Walter Graham, awaiting him with a letter from Hewett. The lieutenant told the *rās* about the mission, and obtained permission for the admiral to come inland by way of Addi Taklay. Alulā may have suspected that the emperor might instantly reject the British overtures and wanted to take charge of the preliminary stage of the negotiations. He then gave Graham a letter to Hewett stating that Yohannes was "not very far, at Wofillah Hashenghi," and inviting the ambassador to come "whenever he likes," promising to receive him and to send him on to the emperor.[16]

The hot springs in Lake Ashangē were not close, by any stretch of the imagination. In fact, for a mission as large as Hewett's (of about 150 men), it would have required several weeks to get there. In any case the British wanted a meeting near the coast as London thought that it safer, in case Yohannes became hostile.[17] Thus in early February 1884, Commander Ernest Rolfe visited Alulā, to arrange a more convenient meeting place.

Rolfe was warmly received in Addi Taklay on 10 February 1884, and, in the security of his tent, the anxious Alulā again took a forward action:

> He again answered that he could not order the King [to come to the coast], but that he [*Rās* Alulā] had authority to receive letters, and if necessary conclude treaties, and would come down to Massawa if desired. I [Rolfe] told him I did not think you [Hewett] would deliver the letter otherwise than personally to the king of Abyssinia.[18]

Asked about Ethiopia's demands, Alulā told the Lieutenant "that Abyssinia wanted Bogos and a seaport."[19] Nine days later, the *rās* reported that "'he had sent letters to the king begging him to settle the time and place' for a meeting."

Alulā again wrote to Hewett asking him to come by Addi Taklay and promising to take him to Yohannes.[20] When the letter reached Massawa, the British perceived that the emperor's man was anxious to conclude the much needed treaty. V. Baker's defeat by the Mahdists at Tokar seriously aggravated the situation; "Kassala is only provisioned for one month," telegraphed Hewett, "I think that the mission had better go."[21]

C. Persuading Yohannes

On 18 April 1884 the Hewett mission accompanied by the American, Mason Bey, as the Egyptian envoy, entered Asmara. Alulā's reception "was most cordial and magnificent."[22] The *Daily News* correspondent provided an interesting account:

> Sir W. Hewett dismounted a few paces from the door of the tent, and Ras Aloola walked forward and shook him by the hand. The Admiral, Mason Bey and Captain Speedy entered the marquee, and were seated on the right of the Ras, who squatted on a dais in the centre of the tent... with his toga gracefully thrown about him, he looked as nearly as possible like some of the statues of the great Caesar. But all this majesty soon disappeared. Squatting on his throne, the swaying to and fro of his body, and his long curved sword, worn on the right side and ever sticking behind, broke the illusion.[23]

The *rās* had good reason to be nervous. When Hewett asked about Yohannes, "Alulā again said he did not know as the King is always unpredictable about his movements."[24]

Alulā and his visitors proceeded to Addi Taklay, at the same time having preliminary discussions on the proposed treaty. "I am able to report," Hewett wrote from Addi Taklay on 18th April 1884,[25] "that so far my interviews with Ras Aloula have been satisfactory," but he was not optimistic about a quick meeting with Yohannes. During the slow march inland towards Adwā, no letter came from the emperor to instruct Alulā about the mission. At their camp in Gurā on the night of 23 April 1884, Hewett drafted a detailed letter for Yohannes: "I stated the terms which I was empowered to offer. To the Ras at his own request, I gave a copy of my letter to the king: the former appeared pleased with the object of my mission, and hastened to dispatch my letter to the King."[26]

The next day, when the *rās* was carrying Hewett's letter to the emperor, Alulā encountered a messenger with a letter from Yohannes, instructing him to bring the mission to Maqalē. Alulā nevertheless continued towards the imperial camp situated at the hot baths of Dabbah Hadra, Tambēn. Meanwhile, the annoyed British envoy (probably having in mind Rolfe's report of the *rās'* readiness to act on his own) wrote to Yohannes: "If your Majesty is unable to come to Adowa... [and] if you should be desirous of settling the affairs on which we have come, you will send such of your counsellors as we have confidence in, to discuss and conclude the said affairs."[27]

D. *May-June 1884: Drafting the Treaty*

On 30 April 1884, Alulā wrote to Hewett to inform him that the emperor would meet him in Adwā.[28] Four days later the *rās*, "to whose interest is doubtless due the decision of the king,"[29] arrived at Adwā carrying Yohannes's letter to Hewett: "I have sent you Ras Alula to assist you in counsel, provision and everything... I am coming soon."[30] When the emperor was not quick to come, Alulā and Hewett had the time to work out a draft treaty: "Availing myself of the opportunity of discussing with the Ras the matters which were embodied in the treaty," Hewett reported,[31] "I was enabled to draw up the treaty in rough, in order that as little detention as possible should take place after the King's arrival."

At last, on 26 May 1884, the emperor arrived, and immediately received the mission with only Alulā and the *echagē* present. "Alulā, who a few weeks ago was playing the haughty chieftain with surroundings more regal and a retinue as large as the king's . . . now stood abashed and humble before his monarch with his Shemma down to his waist and lowered head."[32]

During the next few days the emperor and the envoys discussed the future of Massawa and Kassala. According to Hewett, Yohannes was persuaded that "he would not be a gainer by having ports of his own . . . but declared his intention of taking Kassala from the Arabs [the Mahdists] should it fall into their hands."[33] On 3 June 1884, in a ceremony attended by the emperor's son, *Rās* Ar'āyā-*Sellāssē* (later that month to become the crown prince), *Rās* Mikā'ēl and *Rās* Alulā, the peace treaty of Adwā, better known as the "Hewett Treaty," was signed by Yohannes, Hewett and Mason Bey.

By Article III,[34] Yohannes agreed "to facilitate the withdrawal of the troops . . . from Kassala, Amedib, and Sanhit through Ethiopia to Massowah." In return Ethiopia was promised "free transit through Massowah . . . for all goods, including arms and ammunitions, under British protection," and the return of fugitives from justice. Of special importance to Alulā was Article II's retrocession of Bogos:

> On and after the 1st day of September 1884, corresponding to the 8th day of Maskarram, 1877, the country called Bogos shall be restored to His Majesty the Negoosa Negust; and when the troops of His Highness the Khedive shall have left the garrisons of Kassala, Amedib, and Sanhit, the buildings in the Bogos country which now belong to His Highness the Khedive, together with all the stores and munitions of war which shall then remain in the said buildings, shall be delivered to and become the property of His Majesty the Negoosa Negust.

* * *

The "Hewett Treaty" was the only one Emperor Yohannes ever signed with a foreign power, and it was undoubtedly Alulā who gained the credit for what was considered by Ethiopians as a "moral and political victory."[35] Alulā was proud of the diplomatic achievement: the emperor's demand that any treaty with Egypt be guaranteed by Britain, a requirement which had seemed impossible in 1879, "had become an accomplished fact."[36]

The British soon interpreted Article I of the treaty as an abandonment of Ethiopian claims to Massawa, though the emperor considered the stipulation a first step towards making these claims good.[37] In fact, on 25 June he wrote to Queen Victoria asking her "to make me take hold of the port of Massawa."[38] Article II, on the other hand, formally recognized what had actually been the case for several years, that Bogos, except for the fort of Sanhīt, was under Ethiopian sovereignty, in Alulā's hands. The status of Kassala remained ambiguous,[39] however, and Al-Qallābāt (Matammā), though much desired by Yohannes, was not even mentioned. (The British thought it already had fallen into Mahdist hands.) Perhaps Alulā, who was little interested in districts outside his immediate sphere, had neglected pressing Hewett to be specific about places other than in Bogos. On the other hand, Article V about extradition was apparently initiated by Alulā, since Hewett had no instructions about this. The *ras* clearly remembered his problems with Walda-Mikā'ēl, Dabbab, Keflē Iyāsus and Bāhtā Hagos.

It has been rightly said that in the Treaty of Adwā Ethiopia traded one weak enemy (Egypt) for two strong ones.[40] The Ethiopians committed themselves to provoking the Mahdists actively[41] and received no guarantee about the port of Massawa which was soon to be occupied by the Italians. Indeed, on the eve of such a critical period of history, Ethiopia might have been able to obtain a better arrangement or have used her military superiority more advantageously. It may also be argued that the desire, which especially motivated the Ethiopian architect of the treaty, to have a European partner in international affairs rather than an African neighbor, was based on harmful naiveté. Alulā was soon to be disillusioned by the treaty and with the Europeans.

NOTES

1 FO 407/28, Granville to Baring, 26.12.83; FO 407/60, Baker to Baring 27.12.83; SOAS A.518 R.8, "Affairs in eastern Sudan"; *The Times*, 22.12.83.
2 See P.M. Holt, *The Mahdist State of the Sudan* 1881-1898, Oxford 1970 (2nd ed.), pp. 166, 167.
3 A. Eshete, "Conflit Egypto-Abyssinien," pp. 240, 241.
4 FO 407/60, Granville to Baring, 10.3.84.
5 FO 407/60, Baker to Granville, 5.1.84. Dabbab was then transferred to Cairo, FO 407/61, Granville to Egerton, 30.4.84.
6 FO 406/1, V. Baker's Memo, 9.1.84 in Baring to Granville, 18.1.84.
7 Baker's letter was in Arabic. Text: AA Rub.Coll. Soudan 3/6, Baker to Alulā, 27 safar 1301 A.H.
8 Wylde, *'83*, I, pp. 48-49. FO 407/72, Wylde to FO, 13.2.88.
9 Consult H. Marcus, *The Life and Times*, p. 82.
10 Eshete, *Evol.*, pp. 273-278.
11 Aṣmē, p. 94.
12 Eshete, "Conflit Egypto-Abyssinien," p. 244.
13 MAE(F), Mass. 4, Labosse to MAE, 29.6.84.
14 FO 401/6, Hewett to Baring, 6.3.84.
15 FO 406/1, Hewett to Admiralty, 7-10 Jan. 1884.
16 FO 406/1, Alula to Hewett, 31.1.84, in Graham to Hewett, 1.2.84.
17 FO 401/6, Pauncefote to Admiralty, 29.1.84.

18 FO 406/1, Rolfe to Hewett, 12.2.84.
19 FO 401/6, Hewett to Baring, 6.3.84.
20 FO 406/1, Rolfe to Hewett, 12.2.84, 21.2.84.
21 FO 407/60, Baring to Granville, 29.2.84.
22 FO 406/1, Mason to Nubar, 7.5.84.
23 [Villiers?] "A Journey to the Court of King John," *The Daily News*, 16.5.84 (Several articles, 7.5.84 to 8.7.84).
24 Ibid.
25 FO 406/1, Hewett to Admiralty, 18.4.84.
26 FO 1/31, Hewett to Admiralty, 9.6.84.
27 Ibid., Hewett to John 25.4.84.
28 Ibid., Alula to Hewett 30.4.84.
29 FO 407/61, Hewett to Adm. 5.5.84.
30 FO 1/31, John to Hewett 1.5.84.
31 FO 1/31, Hewett to Granville, 9.6.84.
32 "Journey", *DN*, 8.7.84.
33 FO 1/31, Hewett to Granville, 9.6.84.
34 English text in FO 1/31.
35 Zewde, *Yohannes*, p. 315.
36 Wylde, *'83*, II, p. 19.
37 S. Rubenson, "The Adwa peace Treaty of 1884," *Proceedings of the Third International Conference of Ethiopian Studies*, Vol. I, Addis Ababa 1966, p. 225; (also his newly-published *Survival* pp. 335-346).
38 FO 95/743, Yohannes to Victoria 25.6.84.
39 See below p. 52.
40 S. Rubenson, "Some Aspects of the Survival of Ethiopian Independence," *Univ. Coll. Rev.*, Addis Ababa 1961.
41 For the implications of the Hewett Treaty of the Mahdist-Ethiopian relations, see below, p. 127.

6

1884: Disillusionment

A. The Emperor and "his Mouthpiece"

While the Hewett mission was wending its way back to the coast, everything seemed to be going smoothly in the Ethiopian camp. *Rās* Mikā'ēl's 20,000 Galla (Oromo) horsemen were said to be attached to Alulā's army, awaiting the first rains in order to march on Kassala.[1] The *turk bāshā* himself returned to Hamāsēn for further preparations, and the emperor was said to be organising another force to march through Addi Abo, parallel with Alulā's, to the besieged town.[2] Yet, Yohannes may have felt that his beloved *"bālamwāl"* was growing too great. Though standing with his *shammā* down and humbly introducing the foreign envoy, was it not Alulā who actually shaped and imposed the treaty?

Moreover, many of the influential Tigrean dignitaries could hardly stomach the fact that the "wadi qubi" had become such a moving spirit in the country's high policy. Some of these men were said to be open enemies of Alulā.[3] For example, the governor of Adwā (probably *Dadjāzmāch* Hagos or *Rās Bitwaddad* Gabra-Masqal) had done his best to create difficulties for the Hewett Mission.[4] Yohannes was made aware that the treaty, which meant the opening of a arms trade route to Massawa, might overstrengthen Alulā's position. Alula was obviously liked by the British, and he was in control of the district of Akalla-Guzāy through which imports were carried to Tigre. Yohannes thus directed Hewett not to permit arms from Massawa to pass into Ethiopia unless they were certified as ordered personally by the emperor.[5] Moreover, the emperor withdrew Akalla-Guzāy from Alulā's authority, replacing *Bāshā* Gabrē with *Badjerond* Lawtē, the emperor's loyal follower.[6] Indeed, in early August 1884 a consignment of 3000 rifles was released by the Massawa customs, which carefully heeded Yohannes's request that the weapons not be carried inland by Alulā's men.[7]

With Alulā out of the picture, Soumagne, the new *wakīl*, started conveying arms to Yohannes through the Roman Catholic Mission in Akrur.[8] In late September, Alulā wrote to an assistant of Coulbeaux with evident surprise: "Why have you brought the firearms by some other route when Yohannes has ordered that all should pass through here [Hamāsēn]."[9] The missionary was relieved by *Badjerond* Lawtē's assurances: "The man from Hamāsēn, whom you know well and whom I would not even name, you say has written to you demanding to know why you brought arms some other way: do not worry. It was I who required you to do so by order of Yohannes, so do not let this person—however great he may be—bother you."[10]

B. *July: Again into Bogos*

On 24 July 1884 *Rās* Alulā led his army into the Bogos country but did not, as expected, head for Kassala. Though the emperor was anxious to occupy the town, the *rās* was apparently more concerned about the immediate establishment of his government in the Bogos and, as the frontiers of that country were not defined, to extend his authority over the neighboring Muslim tribes. For nine days, Alulā's troops raided the Banū 'Āmir and the Ḥabbāb, who were forced to pay a tribute of 5,000 thalers. *Ledj* Fantā's men cut the Sanhīt-Massawa telegraph line and clashed with an Egyptian-organized company of Banū 'Āmir horsemen.[11]

Alulā's raid on Bogos six weeks before official restoration to Ethiopia was poorly timed. It caused panic among those tribes which could have supported Alulā's future government over Bogos. The Banū 'Āmir, who had already applied to Yohannes for support against the Mahdists,[12] now desperately opposed the Egyptian evacuation of Bogos, and among the Banū 'Āmir's traditional rivals, the Ḥabbāb, pro-Mahdist tendencies emerged. Meanwhile, Alulā appointed *Kantiba* Ḥamīd as the supreme shaykh of the Ḥabbāb[13] and ordered him to pay tribute, further inciting the pro-Mahdist party in that tribe.[14]

The raid also warned the British that sending Alulā to Kassala might not be such a good idea. Speedy wrote:

> The tribes hitherto loyal to the Khedive . . . prefer anything rather than become subjects of a Christian Monarch . . . it is quite possible that Ras Aloola . . . [is] . . . merely looking forward to a grand foray, on a larger scale than usual.[15]

Finally, the razzia probably caused further disappointment to the emperor, who subsequently ordered Alulā to apologise to Mason Bey and Captain Speedy. "I have done nothing to break the peace," Alulā then wrote to Mason, trying to minimise the whole affair, "I am ever your friend."[16]

C. *September: "Restoration" of Bogos*

In the meantime, in early July 1884 the British suddenly discovered that the besieged Egyptian garrison at Al-Qallābāt (Matammā) had not actually fallen. A new policy was subsequently adopted: the projected Ethiopian march on Kassala was cancelled, and the military effort was to be diverted to Al-Qallābāt. In the Massawa-Kassala area, the newly arrived Governor of the Red Sea, Colonel Herbert C. Chermside, hoped to organise an anti-Mahdist Muslim tribal front for which the fort of Sanhīt (Karan) was designated as the main base. It was therefore decided that this fort would not be ceded to Ethiopia, when Bogos was restored.[17] *Rās* Alulā was of course unaware of the new British decision.

In late August 1884, he met Mason Bey and Captain Speedy between Addi Taklay and Sanhīt. "The Ras was anxious to know if he would be put in possession of the fort . . . when Bogos [would] be ceded. Mason Bey explained that the fort and buildings must be retained until the arrival of the Kassala and Amadeb garrisons. *Rās* Alulā after some argument merely dropped the subject saying: 'We ask no more than what is in the Treaty'."[18] The alarmed *rās* reported to Yohannes, who, in turn, wrote to Speedy:

> You are thoroughly acquainted with the whole affair of the Treaty, yet you say Ras Aloolah has made a mistake. He has made no mistake. Is it not written in the Treaty that the soldiers of the Khedive stationed at Bogos should be withdrawn on the 1st September? Now this Treaty has been ratified by all. 'Words may be forgotten, but writing cannot alter'. However, if the soldiers are not ready to leave at once, I will not insist on the literal rendering of the Treaty, but let them remain till the end of Maskarrem (10th October), as I am anxious that the country should be governed by my Chiefs in accordance with the Treaty. Are we not one, bound by friendship?[19]

While the English version of article II could have been interpreted as stipulating the evacuation of Kassala and Amadib as a precondition to the cession of the buildings and equipment in Sanhīt,[20] the Amharic version was significantly different:

> When the troops of the Egyptian khedive leave, having left Kassala Amadib and Sanhīt, the buildings [*bētoch*] of the Khedive in Bogos, the equipment and war materials, everything left in those places [*safāroch*] shall become the [property of the] Emperor.[21]

The Ethiopians clearly considered that Kassala and Amadīb were included in the promised country of Bogos and believed therefore that after evacuation, the buildings in those three *places*, including the fort of Sanhīt, would revert to the emperor's sovereignty. Captain Ernest Rolfe, member of the Hewett mission, revealed his understanding of the talks at Adwā: "The Bogos country, including the fort of Sanhīt and Amadib, were to be given to Abyssinia on the first of September or sooner if the garrisons could be withdrawn. Kassala should be given over to Abyssinia as soon as that country is ready to take it over and garrison withdrawn."[22] In this way, the emperor's objections were dismissed.

On 12 September 1884 "the country called Bogos was publicly restored to the Negusa Negust of Ethiopia." But what was actually handed over to Alulā's officer was a small fort four miles from Sanhīt. It was a disillusioned *rās* who sat down in

Addi Taklay to draft a letter of protest to Captain Speedy. Repeating the demand for Sanhīt itself, Alulā concluded: "what was done was simply to make a public pronouncement and [to] hand . . . over a small subsidiary fort, while the Egyptian garrison still remained in full strength in possession of the main fort."[23] The fort of Sanhīt remained in Egyptian hands for the next seven months.

D. British Refusal to let Alulā March on Kassala

At a meeting with Yohannes in Aksum, September 1884, Alulā planned his next step. The British wanted him to relieve Al-Qallābāt because they were anxious to avoid an Ethiopian march on Kassala and further raids on the Muslim tribes, whose alliance they hoped to obtain. Yohannes, on the other hand, wished to send Alulā to Kassala because, as he understood the treaty, the town had been promised to him. Moreover, as the British now stipulated the relief of Kassala as a precondition to the cession of Sanhīt, the emperor may well have considered it as his right and duty to march there. Thus, in late October 1884, while accepting the British request to facilitate the relief of the Al-Qallābāt garrison,[24] Yohannes ordered Alulā to ready his armies and lead them to Kassala.[25]

The British reaction to the emperor's new initiative was definite and clear. Instructed by Baring "to use firm language to King John,"[26] Speedy requested the emperor "to suspend all preparations relative to your contemplated movements regarding the evacuation of Kassala."[27] For Alulā, however, who had priorities in Bogos, British opposition to Yohannes's march on Kassala was probably a fortunate development.

E. Growing Opposition Among the Ḥabbābs. Dabbab.

In June 1884, just after the safe return of the Hewett mission, the British decided to extradite *Fitāwrāri* Dabbab to Massawa for trial.[28] He arrived there in early October and almost immediately, on the night of 8th October 1884, he managed to escape and rejoin his Assāwurta followers.[29] Yohannes angrily wrote to Speedy and, reminding him of Article V, stated: "How disgraceful to break a treaty."[30]

Alulā's disappointment must have increased when the emperor, aware of Alulā's personal quarrel with his own nephew, ordered *Badjerond* Lawṭē and another of Alulā's enemies, *Rās* Gabra-Kidānē (the emperor's brother-in-law), to capture Dabbab.[31] The two men raided the Assāwurta, hitherto considered to be under Alulā's care, and burned the coastal village of Zulā.[32] Dabbab himself fled to the Habbāb and recruited one of its sub-tribes, with which he soon raided Alulā's Mansa tributaries.[33] Thus, at the end of October 1884, three of Alulā's personal enemies: Dabbab, Bāhtā Hagos and Keflē Iyāsus, were active among the Habbābs.

The various Ḥabbāb sub-tribes were then in a delicate situation. As traditional rivals of the loyal Mansa and as Muslims, they were reluctant to submit to Alulā's rule in Bogos.[34] They were also bitter rivals of the Banū 'Āmir, who were loyal to the Egyptians, and therefore could not cooperate with Massawa. Under the growing pressure of 'Uthmān Diqna's envoys, the pro-Mahdists among the Ḥabbāb, led by *Shaykh* Ḥaddād and *Shaykh* 'Umār of the Ad Tamāryām, began to cooperate with the Sudanese. When they intensified their activities,[35] Mason Bey had no alternative but to ask Alulā to "enter their country and crush them."[36] Similarly, *Kantibā* Ḥamīd, seeing his own position challenged, "went to Abyssinia and prayed Ras Alula to come with his troops."[37]

Alulā made no haste to interfere. During November 1884, he was busy constructing a stronghold in Bogos near the old Egyptian fort at Shabbāb.[38] Only around the middle of December, when he had secured his position near Egyptian-occupied Sanhīt, did he move off towards the Ḥabbābs. His mission proved only partially successful:[39] none of the pursued outlaws were captured, and the Ḥabbāb's resistance was not broken. Alulā returned to Hamāsēn in late December, having apparently realised that there was a Mahdist threat to his domains.

F. Late 1884:
Failure of Anglo-Egyptian "Local Muslim Government" in the Kassala-Massawa Area

Colonel Chermside, who was in charge of the relief of Kassala, strongly believed that Alulā's army would not be able to relieve the besieged town[40] and that the Muslim tribes would not work with the Ethiopians in a common operation.[41] He therefore supported the idea of "a local Muslim government"[42] in the Kassala-Massawa area.

With Baring's agreement,[43] Chermside considered that the Mīrghanī family, headed by *Sayyid* 'Uthmān,[44] was capable of supplying spiritual leadership to the desired front, although political and military matters were left to the skillful *Shaykh* 'Alī Bakhīt of the Banū 'Āmir. The fort of Sanhīt, which had been deliberately denied to Alulā, was to become a *point d'appui* for the Muslim tribesmen.[45] At the request of *Sayyid* 'Uthmān, it was heavily reinforced in order to prevent Alulā, then building his fort near Shabbāb, from interfering with the new "government."[46]

Though Chermside reported that the plan was an immediate success,[47] the plan proved to be a failure. With the exception of the Banū 'Āmir, almost all the other tribes who were expected to join the cause failed to do so. "Reaction in favour of the Mahdi," admitted Chermside, "has swept almost to the gates of Massawa."[48] This situation, though partly caused by Alulā's raids,[49] was mainly the result of an overly soft policy towards those tribes which were threatened by Mahdist envoys.[50] The sudden death of *Shaykh* 'Alī Bakhīt on 18 November 1884, the defeat of the Kassala garrison in January 1885,[51] and the fall of Khartum, 26 January 1885, were final blows to the idea.[52] In January 1885, Chermside was still "unwilling to bring down this Christian power on the Moslem population,"[53] but the situation in Kassala continued to deteriorate,[54] Thus, finally, on 8 February 1885, Chermside wrote to Yohannes urging him to send Alulā to Kassala. He promised to hand over the fort of Sanhīt,[55] whose garrison was now actually besieged by the neighboring pro-Mahdist tribes. Then, he wrote directly to Alulā asking him to decide on a relief expedition.[56] Ironically, three days earlier the Italians had landed in Massawa.

* * *

From the end of 1884 to the beginning of 1885, *Rās* Alulā had been busily constructing Asmara, his new capital in the Marab Mellāsh. This creation was the culmination of Alulā's efforts to try to establish his government on an economic basis, based on trade with the coast. In his continuing dilemma of whether to march against Kassala or to establish his rule over the territories between Hamāsēn and the coast, Alulā's economic interest lay definitely with the second option.

NOTES

1 It was impossible to lead Ethiopian soldiers in the western Eritrean plains without the "Khawrs" being full of rainwater to drink. See FO 78/3806, Alulā to Gov. of Massawah, 11.6.85.
2 FO 1/31, Hewett to Adm., 22.6.84.
3 Unfortunately the documents consulted did not list Alula's opponents. Yet judging from events and information regarding a later period, it may be assumed that those were mainly leading figures in *Ras* Ar'aya's family, *Rās Gabra-Kida*ne, the emperor's brother-in-law, and *Dadjazmach* Hagos (later *ras*).
4 FO 1/31, Hewett to Adm., 9.6.84.
5 FO 407/62, John to Speedy, 13.8.84.
6 MAE(F), Mass. 4, Coulbeaux to Soumagne, 30.6.84. Lawṭē's background is unknown to me. He was probably another *bālamwal*, who became Yohánnes's *badjerond*, or treasurer. In 1878, he served as go-between for Yohannes and Menilek.
7 FO 407/62, Egerton to Granville, 5.8.84; Speedy to Egerton, 27.7.84.
8 MAE(F), Mass. 4, Coulbeaux to Soumagne, 30.6.84.
9 Ibid., Alulā to Abba Yohannes, 23.9.84. For Alulā's interest in the arms trade, see below, p. 82.
10 MAE(F), Mass. 4, Bajerond [Lawṭe] to Abba Yohannes, 27.9.84.
11 MAE(F), Mass. 4, Labosse to MAE, 5.8.84, 9.8.84. FO 407/62, Speedy to Egerton, 30.7.84, 19.8.84. Detailed descriptions also: K. Winqvist. *En liten aterblick*, Stockholm 1908, p. 7; *DN*, 27.12.84.
12 FO 78/3673, Egerton to Granville, 7.5.84.

13 O. Baratieri, "Negli Habab", *NA* 1892, p. 205.
14 FO 407/62, Speedy to Egerton, 30.7.84; Ras Alulah to Mason Bey, 12.8.84.
15 FO 407/62, Speedy to Egerton, 30.7.84.
16 FO 407/62, Ras Alulah to Mason, 12.8.84. Also: John to Speedy, 13.8.84.
17 FO 407/62 Egerton to Granville, 16.7.84. FO 78/3799, Chermside to Nubar, 27.12.84.
18 "Abyssinia out of its Treaty obligations," *The Daily News*, 27.12.84; FO 78/3678, Speedy to Egerton, 31.8.84.
19 FO 407/63, John to Speedy, 10.9.84.
20 See FO 1/31, Hewett to Admiralty, 22.6.84: "There is a possibility, however, that King John, knowing that the date on which he will acquire possession of the garrison of Keren depends on the relief of Kassala and Amedib, intends to precipitate matters by effecting the relief of those two garrisons as soon as possible."
21 See S. Rubenson, "Adwa treaty."
22 FO 1/31, Rolfe's account, 5.7.84.
23 FO 78/3678A, Speedy to Baring, 15.9.85, in Baring to Granville, 30.9.84.
24 The garrisons of Al-Qallabat and of al-Jira were relieved by Ethiopian forces supervised by the brilliant Egyptian officer Major Sa'd Rif'at. Sa'd reached Asmara from Massawa in December 1884 (and not in August as claimed by Sa'd) but failed to persuade Alula to march with him to Al-Qallabat. See Major Sa'd's long report in SOAS M.518, English translation by Professor P.M. Holt, SOAS. See also Holt, *The Mahdist State*, pp. 167-169.
25 FO 78/3679, Alulā to Speedy (received 21.10.84) in Speedy to Baring, 22.10.84.
26 FO 407/63, Baring to Granville, 8.11.84.
27 FO 407/63, Speedy to John, 21.10.84.
28 FO 407/61, Egerton to Granville, 23.6.84.
29 FO 407/63, Molyneux to Hay, 21.10.84, Speedy to Baring, 15.9.84.
30 FO 407/63, John to Speedy, 22.10.84.
31 FO 407/66, Report by a chief from Harkeeko, 11.12.84, and an enclosure by M. Manopole.
32 FO 407/63, Baring to Granville, 18.12.84.
33 K. Roden, *Le Tribu dei Mensa*, Stockholm and Asmara, 1913, p. 124.
34 For the hesitations of a member of that tribe, see Littmann IV.B, Song 633, p. 975.
35 FO 407/63, Speedy to Baring, 20.9.84; Chermside's Report, 18.11.84. FO 406/66, Crowe to Molyneux, 24.12.84. *Daily News*, 16.10.84, 30.10.84.
36 FO 407/63, Speedy to Baring, 20.9.84. Molyneux to Hay, 4.10.84.
37 FO 406/66, Crowe to Molyneux, 24.12.84. See also: FO 407/63, Speedy to Baring, 22.10.84.
38 FO 407/36, Chermside to Baring, 12.11.84; 406/66, Crowe to Molyneux, 24.12.84.
39 Crowe to Molyneux, loc.cit.
40 The most detailed descriptions of the siege of Kassala are in Na'ūm Shuqayr [Shouchair], *Ta'rīkh as-sūdān al-qadīm wal-ḥadīth wajighrafiyatuhā*, Cairo 1903, pp.331-343; Holt, *The Mahdist State*, pp. 166-169; F.R. Wingate, *Mahdism and the Egyptian Sudan*, London 1901, pp. 150-151, 241-242, 247-248.
41 FO 78/3799, Chermside to Nubar, 27.12.84; FO 78/3805, Chermside to Mudir of Taka (Iffat Bey), 29.1.85.
42 Chermside to Iffat, 29.1.85.
43 FO 78/7678, Baring to Speedy, 24.9.84.

44 On the Mīrghanīs' influence on Eritrean tribes, *vide* Trimingham, op.cit., pp. 244-245.
45　FO 78/3799, Chermside to Nubar, 27.12.84.
46　FO 407/63, Chermside to Morghani, 13.11.84. Morghani to Chermside, Sanhit, N.D.
47　FO 407/63, Chermside to Alula, 16.11.84.
48　FO 78/3805, Chermside to Baring, 28.6.85. For Alulā's punitive mission against the Assāwurta in January-February 1885, see: FO 403/83, Chermside to Baring, 18.1.85; FO 78/3801, Chermside to Watson, 21.2.85. For Mahdist influence over the Ḥabbāb and others, see Littman, *Publications*, vol. II; *Tales, Customs*, Leyden 1910, pp. 194, 195.
49　FO 78/3799, Chermside to Nubar, 6.1.85.
50　As predicted by Wylde in early 1884. *The Times*, 18.2.84.
51　On 2.1.85, see "Sa'd Report," also: FO 78/3801, Chermside to Watson, 21.2.84, Baker to Baring, 1.3.85; SOAS M.518, Reel 8, "Report on the Fall of Kassala" by Ibrāhīm Eff. Kharyāllah.
52　FO 78/3805, Chermside to Baring, 28.6.85; FO 78/3809, Chermside to Egerton, 16.9.85.
53　FO 78/3805, Chermside to Iffat Bey, 29.1.85.
54　FO 78/3800, Baring to Granville 3.2.85; Baker to Baring, 4.2.85; FO 78/3802, Baker to Baring, 15.3.85.
55　FO 78/3805, Chermside to Yohannes, 8.2.85; FO 78/3805, Chermside to Baring, 28.6.85.
56　FO 78/3804, Baring to Granville, 31.5.85.

7

1885: "The Year in Which the Dervishes were Cut Down"[1]

A. *February-May: The Italian Landing and the Emergence of Alulā's Dilemma*

For Alulā and Yohannes, the Italian arrival at Massawa was a surprising development.[2] The Italian Giacomo Naretti, then visiting the emperor and the *rās* at Maqalē, testified that Yohannes' first reaction was: "But why did England not warn me?"[3] Alulā immediately returned to Asmara and lost no time in sending troops to the outskirts of Massawa. Seven Egyptian soldiers were killed by Alulā's *fanno*,[4] whose mission was undoubtedly to collect more information about the newcomers.

In fact, it seems as if Alulā was not unduly alarmed by the arrival of the Italians. Though surprising, their appearance was not *ipso facto* contradictory to the Hewett Treaty, and it could make no practical difference to him if the port, as a free one, was to be run by other Europeans. He was also preoccupied by the construction of his new capital and, in any case, was mainly concerned with the fort of Sanhīt still held by the Egyptians, and with the Mahdist danger in Bogos and in the coastal lowlands. For example, on 18 March 1885 the official Italian envoy to Yohannes, Vicenzo Ferrari, was well received by Alulā in Asmara. Together with Cesare Nerazzini, who joined him four days later, he explained to the *rās* the circumstances leading to the Italian landing and assured him of Rome's friendship towards Ethiopia. Alulā then raised the subject of the Hewett Treaty, "and especially regarding the country of Bogos," and was assured by the envoys that "what was concluded between H.M. the King of Abyssinia and the representatives of the British Government will not be changed by our government."[5] According to the Italians, Alulā appeared convinced and sent a calming letter to the worried emperor.[6] Having other priorities, Alulā was undoubtedly relieved to learn from the envoys that Rome would function in Massawa as the long desired European neighbour.

In the meantime the negative implications of the past British "Muslim and diplomatic" policy became more obvious as pro-Mahdist, or rather antigovernmental, tendencies[7] among the peoples in the still Egyptian-held territories were strengthened. The Ad-Tamāryām became turbulent, especially after its Shaykh 'Umar was replaced by Shaykh 'Abd al-Qādir,[8] the more energetic ex-qāḍī of Sawākin and a faithful follower of 'Uthmān Diqna. Shaykh 'Abd al-Qādir organised a substantial force which threatened the Egyptians in Karan and actually cut the road from Asmara to Massawa. He also initiated friendly terms with *Kantibā* Ḥamīd, hitherto considered Alulā's man among the Ḥabbābs. Though 'Abd al-Qādir did not succeed in persuading Ḥamīd openly to join the Mahdist camp, he strengthened the latter's will neither to ally with his traditional rivals, the Banū 'Āmirs, nor to cooperate with his Ethiopian master, *Rās* Alulā, against the Sudanese.

The new British approach envisaging an Ethiopian expedition to Kassala necessitated shifting from the "Muslim policy" towards encouraging co-operation between the tribes and the Ethiopians. The promise to hand over Sanhīt, it was thought, might persuade Alulā to march, but without the aid of the Banū 'Āmirs and other tribes, he might be unsuccessful. Thus, simultaneously with the letters to Alulā in early February, Chermside instructed the *mudīr* in Kassala, 'Iffat Bey, and *Sayyid* 'Uthmān al-Mīrghanī in Daqqa to organise the loyal tribes and prepare them for future common action with Alulā.[9] Chermside also advised the *mudīr* to offer Alulā and Yohannes money, arms and the buildings in Kassala, thus retrospectively recognising the Ethiopian version of Article II of the "Hewett Treaty".

Alulā must have been pleased with the new developments. On 10 April the Egyptian garrison at Sanhīt (Karan) and at Amidīb left for Massawa and *Belāttā* Gabru, Alulā's lieutenant, occupied the long sought fort of Sanhīt.[10] In Asmara, Alulā demonstrated his goodwill by warmly receiving the Egyptian Major Sa'd Rif'at and his newly freed garrison:

> He ordered that we were to have everything necessary for our comfort . . . his music played to welcome our arrival. He gave us hospitality for three days and showed true friendship. . .[11]

In order to facilitate the transfer of the Egyptian evacuees to Massawa, Alulā had to clear the road of pro-Mahdist Ḥabbābs. In a battle near Aylēt in late April, 'Abd al-Qādir was defeated but managed to escape. The Mahdist leader then wrote to 'Uthmān Diqna in Sawākin and was subsequently strongly reinforced.[12] Meanwhile, a new crisis was developing.

Contrary to Alulā's hopes, the Italians had no intention of merely staying in Massawa,[13] and their commanders in the town were not closely supervised by Rome. On 10 April 1885, the same day the fort of Sanhīt was transferred to Alulā, the Italian commander, Colonel Tancredi Saletta, sent his troops to occupy Arafali. Then, on 21 April 1885, while Alulā was still heading back to Asmara, Saletta occupied Harkīkū, and a few days later, announced his intention to take over Sahāti from the Egyptians.[14] Alulā considered the site to be within Ethiopian territory, even though Egyptian irregulars, with Alulā's permission, had been in occupation during the time of the Hewett Mission. The *rās* had agreed that the Egyptians could remain there for a time, to secure the newly-opened commercial route,[15] but Col. Chermside, worried about Ethiopia's possible reaction, had refused to let the Italians take over.[16] From the Anglo-Egyptian point of view, Saletta's decision was poorly timed. With Karan already in Ethiopian hands, even if quite seriously threatened by Mahdist forces, and the very suspicious and dangerous developments in the more important coastal areas, *Rās* Alulā was really losing interest in relieving the besieged Egyptians in far-off Kassala.

The British, the *mudīr* from Kassala and the influential Mīrghanī, promised Alulā arms, money, property and the co-operation of the tribes,[17] but he now had no reason to hurry. Although he wanted the money and arms, he also understood that his bargaining position was strengthened by the passage of time.

B. *May-June: Alulā Hopes for Italian Aid Against the Mahdists*

Alulā's attitude to the Italian presence at Massawa nonetheless remained far from hostile. The Mahdist threat in the Asmara-Massawa-Karan triangle seemed much more acute, and the Italians did their best to persuade the *rās* that they were fighting a common enemy. On 9 May 1885 Saletta sent a company of irregulars to occupy Ambā, but they were defeated the next day by pro-Mahdist forces.[18] Keflē, Alulā's Ḥabbāb-based rival, was said to have been nominated as the future Mahdist governor of Bogos.[19] From Aylēt on 11 May 1885, Alulā wrote to Saletta that he was going to fight the Mahdist sympathizers,[20] and on 12 May 1885, at the head of 5,000 troops, the *rās* encircled 1,000 followers of *Shaykh* 'Abd al-Qādir near Ambā and annihilated a third of them.[21] Happy with his victory, Alulā announced to Saletta that: "Those who call themselves Dervishes were destroyed and annihilated by me, I am very pleased with that and hope that you will share my pleasure."

Alulā also asked the Italian officer to facilitate the passage of a new consignment of arms which he expected to be brought to Massawa by his Greek agents.[22] Saletta was agreeable (the customs were in any case still in Egyptian hands) but repeated his request to occupy Sahāṭi. To this Alulā replied with a diplomatic but quite clear refusal: "I have seen Scialaha Arhaia to Sahaṭi to receive rifles, and the Italian soldiers [who accompanied them] can return from Sahaṭi."[23] During the rest of May and the first three weeks of June, the Italians remained passive and Alulā seemed less suspicious about their intentions. Ferrari and Nerazzini who visited Asmara in June 1885, reported that the *rās* was happy about his good relations with Saletta.[24] He also permitted an Italian detachment to proceed to Aylēt in order to escort the two men back to Massawa.[25] Two Italian journalists, Giacomo Belcredi and Colaci, were permitted to come to Asmara, where they were well received on

17 June 1885. Alulā, however, refused their request to proceed to Karan, but they were allowed to stay in Asmara as long as they liked.[26]

C. June-July: Alulā's Growing Concern over Coastal Affairs while the Kassala Situation Worsens

On 11 June 1885 Alulā replied to Chermside's letter:

> "I received your letter concerning Kassala, . . . I am ready to do what you require. The cause of my delay is my waiting for rains to fall."[27]

Meanwhile, the situation in Kassala continued to deteriorate, and the frustrated Chermside continued his efforts to conciliate Alulā. He arranged for the Massawa customs to release an additional 1,015 rifles which the *ras* had purchased from his Greek merchants.[28] Though Chermside undoubtedly remembered the emperor's demand not to sell arms directly to Alulā, the Englishman instructed Massawa's Egyptian governor to:

> do everything according to Alulā's request . . . ask him [Alulā] whether he wants any ammunition for rifles and supply. In case of your making sure of his advance to Kassala you may supply him also with rifles and ammunition if he asks for the same.[29]

Indeed from early June, until after the battle of Kūfīt in late September, Yohannes's name was not mentioned at all in the correspondence concerning the Kassala issue. During March-November, the emperor remained in Bagemder and the British and the Egyptians approached Alulā. Yohannes repeatedly had promised that upon occupation, Alulā could have Kassala,[30] but it was up to the *ras* to decide on the expedition. Alulā, however, had lost interest in the proposed campaign because of the deteriorating situation in the coastal plain and the areas east and north of Asmara.

Many of the Ad-Tamāryām and the Ḥabbāb warriors were fully cooperating with 'Uthmān Diqna's envoys, headed by *Shaykh* 'Abd al-Qādir, and in early June they were reported as intending to mobilise 12,000 men.[31] They not only had survived their defeats by Alulā in April and May, but also had dared to renew their attacks on Ethiopian caravans to Massawa.[32] The ability of the pro-Mahdists to achieve a real success was entirely dependent on the hitherto wavering Ḥabbābs and on supplies which could be obtained only through Ḥabbāb-land. Alulā, who had every reason to be angry with the Kantibā Ḥamīd, his nominee among these tribesmen, had demanded that Egyptian authorities in Massawa not trade with him.[33] The kantibā, afraid of Alulā, of the Banū 'Āmir[34] and of the Mahdists, contacted the Italians in Massawa, and in early June was allowed to purchase food there.[35] Extremely annoyed, Alulā wrote to Saletta:

The Muslims are encouraged and they all say they are Dervishes. The people of Habab provide the rebels with supplies. Why do you permit them to purchase it there?. . . Hereafter do nothing of the kind and have the greatest hatred for them.[36]

The Italian step, though it might have been justified as a measure taken to prevent Ḥamīd from joining the Mahdists, sustained Alulā's growing suspicion about Rome's intentions, made even more evident by the Italian occupation of Saḥāṭi on 24 June 1885.[37]

In the meantime, Chermside was still doing his best to persuade Alulā to march westward. Following his instructions, *Shaykh* Mūsā al-Fīl, *Shaykh* 'Alī Nūrīn and some other Muslim leaders arrived in June at Alulā's camp in Asmara.[38] They were warmly received by the *rās*, the man whom they had hitherto considered their most implacable enemy.[39] In response, Alulā wrote to Col. Chermside, on 6 July 1885, 8 July 1885 and in mid-July, promising him that he was about to move to Kassala, from where he had just received a new plea for assistance.[40] But it was too late, since on 30 July 1885 Kassala finally fell into Mahdist hands. The expectation of Alulā's arrival was the only thing that had given hope to the starving garrison during the last six months.

By 9 June 1885 the *mudīr* had already written four unanswered letters to Alulā,[41] and, after a fierce battle which took place on 13 June,[42] he was ready to surrender, when, on 23 June 1885 a messenger arrived from the *rās* saying: "Take courage, I am coming to help you soon."[43] The starved and exhausted garrison went on fighting, and *Rās* Alulā was again petitioned.[44] Alulā's biographer saw the whole affair purely as a Christian-Muslim conflict and claims that the people of Kassala wrote to the *rās*:

> If you get us out of this trouble and affliction and great pain, will we not give you much gold and silver without measure? He [Alulā] said to them: 'I do not want your much gold and silver, but I desire your faith. If you worship the word [Christ] and bow down to him. I will get you out of this amazing trouble'.[45]

This requirement could hardly have encouraged the Egyptian garrison. When the *mudīr* surrendered, the town was plundered but, contrary to all expectations, there was no bloodshed. Furthermore, fierce quarrels began among the victorious besiegers which lasted till 'Uthmān Diqna's arrival in late August. Though "the usual severities were practised on the officers to extract booty,"[46] the garrison and inhabitants were allowed to leave in peace,[47] and thus the problem of Kassala was finally resolved. However, more than three weeks passed before the news about Kassala reached Sawākin.

Was it really the rains which prevented *Rās* Alulā from marching on the besiegers of Kassala? To answer that question one must quote the following passage written by A.B. Wylde, who discussed the situation with Alulā eleven years later:

The Ras has repeatedly told me that he informed the Egyptians that the majority of his army is always disbanded in the month of June to enable the men to go to their villages to plant their crops, and it is only on Holy Cross day, in September, that they come back to headquarters, when all planting has been finished.[48]

Wylde was not privy to official British correspondence[49] which reveals that Alulā used the affair as a diplomatic and polite excuse for not undertaking the Kassala expedition. From the eyrie of Asmara, he observed developments in the coastal plains, in the newly-restored Bogos country and the Shoho district, where he faced new Mahdist and Italian threats; no wonder the *rās* was reluctant to lead his soldiers to Kassala in order to save a few hundred of his ex-enemies. On the other hand, it seems that Alulā fully understood that he could not refuse an offer by which he could gain arms and money and reestablish Ethiopian hegemony in eastern Eritrea. He was in a dilemma, but he was not in a hurry.

D. Growing Pressure on Alulā

Colonel Chermside and his superiors understood, by now, that the new circumstances had diverted Alulā's attention to the coast. In late July, he therefore suggested that Ethiopia receive Zulā as the price for Alulā's immediate move to Kassala.[50] The idea, which would have been most attractive to Alulā and a great blow to Italian ambitions, was refused by London, but Chermside continued his machinations. On 24 July 1885, the colonel instructed 'Izzat Bey "to do everything in your power to induce . . . [Alulā] to start as soon as possible [for Kassala]." An Egyptian, Marcopoli Bey, was to be sent to Asmara "to use every persuasion to get him to move quickly." The envoy was authorized to offer arms, ammunition, and supplies, to hand Alulā a sum of 50,000 thalers "payable on condition of his really advancing" and to promise expenses up to 300,000 thalers for the expedition.[51]

Marcopoli Bey reached Asmara on 11 August 1885, and was very well received by Alulā "who showed a great desire to be agreeable to the government by assisting Kassala."[52] Alulā was given the 50,000 thalers and was told that some 800-1,000 Remington rifles would reach his camp from Massawa.[53] The next day, 12 August 1885, Alulā summoned the envoy, and in sharp contrast to his earlier cordiality, he exhorted the Anglo-Egyptian authorities at Massawa:

> Why do you not turn out the Italians from Massawa? What business have they to remain there?. . . Why have you allowed them to camp at Saati, this is a neutral ground. They must abandon the place! . . . No, I will not march to the relief of Kassala before I see what the authorities at Massawa shall do on these matters.[54]

While the *rās* remained unmoved, *Shaykh* 'Uthmān al-Mīrghanī left on 8 August

1885, for the Banū 'Āmir centre in Daqqa to prepare the neighbouring tribes for Alulā's expected expedition.[55] He sought to threaten the pro-Mahdist tribes "with the Abyssinian sword" and, on the other hand, to motivate Alulā by creating a convenient anti-Mahdist atmosphere in the Kassala area. He was most successful in the first part of his mission; his agents infiltrated the al-Jādīn, Sabdrāt, Baraka and Baria tribesmen, spreading tales about powerful Ethiopian forces aided by Banū 'Āmir warriors and supplied with British arms.[56] These reports caused panic among the neighbouring tribesmen[57] and the Mahdists in Kassala. The head of the Hadendowa warriors, who constituted the main element among the garrison, *Shaykh* Mūsā Ṣadīq, hastened to consult the *mudīr* about the situation. Consequently, the chief of the Hadendowa declared he would not follow the Mahdist 'Uthmān Diqna, but he returned the wounded prisoners *Shaykh* Bakrī al-Mīrghanī to the town and sent a conciliatory letter to *Rās* Alulā in Asmara.[58] The Hadendowa's revolt against the Mahdiyya really created a new situation, much more critical than *Shaykh* 'Uthmān al-Mīrghanī, or his British employers, had expected.

E. Mahdist Threat to Invade Ethiopian Territories

On 12 August 1885, 'Uthmān Diqna was informed about Alulā's preparations and the new development in Kassala. By then, the British blockade had reduced Mahdist-followers in the Sawākin area to starvation,[59] so 'Uthmān prepared to fight the non-Mahdist Muslim tribes and the Ethiopians in the Massawa region.[60] There, under Shaykh 'Abd al-Qādir, he had the nucleus of an army to exploit the vacuum created by the Egyptian evacuation. After sending troops to reinforce Shaykh 'Abd al-Qādir, then near Karan,[61] 'Uthmān and a few followers hastened to Kassala, which they entered on 21 August 1885. 'Uthmān granted security to the inhabitants and garrison, urging them to join the Mahdiyya; recruited the frightened tribes of al-Ḥalāniqa and Shukriyya; and put the disobedient Hadendowas into flight northward to Filik.[62]

A few days later 'Uthmān heard that Mīrghanī's men were confiscating cattle only a few miles from the town.[63] Having undoubtedly read Marcopoli Bey's letter to the *mudīr* which promised that Alulā would capture Kassala by 18 September 1885,[64] 'Uthmān Diqna declared war on the Ethiopian *rās*. In late August he collected his warriors and left Kassala for the Baria country, from where his commander-in-chief Muṣṭafā Hadal[65] wrote to Alulā on 29 August 1885:

> From the slave of God and faithful Mustafa Hadal to the King of Infidels, to Ras Alula his devil, and to Mussa Mohammed [al-Fīl] . . . This is to tell you that I know you said you would bring English troops to fight against the servants of the Prophet. But all your sayings are a delusion. They have not come, and now you say you will fight me with an Abyssinian army; but in this you cannot succeed. The emir of emirs, Osman Abu Bakr

Digna, has now decided to conquer every province; he came to Kassala, where all the inhabitants joined him, and now we have come down to the hills in your neighbourhood. Therefore come out and meet us. Do not delay, but if you cannot come and are afraid, then let me know by the bearer of this and I will come to you with my 'ansar', and will fall upon you and utterly exterminate and destroy you and all those who do not believe in God and His Prophet, and all your souls shall go down straightway to hell.[66]

Did 'Uthmān Diqna really intend to assault Ethiopia? This question, whose answer is vital to an understanding of the period, has been neglected. A study of 'Uthmān Diqna's correspondence with the Khalīfa leads, however, to the clear conclusion that he did mean to invade.[67] 'Abdallāh wrote his general:

We heard the news of your advance to Ethiopia . . . but my beloved, things should be arranged according to their importance and we have heard that the problems in Kassala are still unsettled . . . and so is the situation in Sawākin . . . and the desired need is that you will pay attention to what is the more important.[68]

Do not attach great importance to the Ethiopian affair . . . leave the Ethiopians and do not enter their country now . . . return to Sawākin, that is what we want.[69]

'Uthmān Diqna could not follow the *khalīfa*'s advice, since the letters reached him two months after his defeat. It is clear, however, that he wrote to *Khalīa* 'Abdallāh about his intention to divert military efforts from the Sawākin area to Ethiopia, probably to Bogos and the Massawa coast.

'Uthmān Diqna first sought to mobilise the various Baria tribes to join his campaign. However, Shaykh Arāy of the Baria disappeared with his cattle and warriors and so did the tribesmen of Al-Jadīn, Sabdrāt, Ḥamrān and others.[70] Thus, 'Uthmān Diqna was able neither to mobilise the Hadendowas, hitherto the strong backbone of Mahdist power in the Kassala area, nor the warriors of the Baria, Sabdrāt, Ḥamran or Al-Jadīn. His army was therefore made up of the Ja'aliyyīn tribesmen, al-Ḥalānīqa, a very few Hadendowa[71] and some of the "bāshībazūks" of the Kassala garrison, a total of between 6,000 to 12,000 warriors.[72] The fact that the Mahdists stayed more than three weeks in Baria country and could not mobilize a stronger army took Alulā mid-way to victory, though the *rās*, from far off Asmara, could not appreciate 'Uthmān's weakness. The latter, however, must have either underestimated Alulā's power or, more probably, overestimted the strength of his followers in Bogos under Shaykh 'Abd al-Qādir. 'Uthmān left for Kūfīt on 12 September 1885, ordered his troops to entrench there, and wrote to *Rās* Alulā "threatening him [again] with invasion."[73]

F. New British Interest in Alulā's March. The Rās's Decision to Go

By mid-August, concentrated near Karan was a combined force of 2000 Banū 'Āmir warriors and Ethiopians commanded by the governor of Karan and Alulā's lieutenant, *Belā*ttā Gabru. This force had to counter 'Abd al-Qādir's Mahdists, who, camped in the Ad-Tamāryām area, not far from Karan, threatened Bogos.[74] By late August, Alulā began to consider sending Gabru against Kassala. On 26 August 1885, he ordered him (in the presence of Marcopoli Bey and possibly in order to please him) to prepare for a march to the Banū 'Āmir centre of Daqqa.[75] Meanwhile, Gabru sent patrols towards Kassala, one of which was annihilated around mid-September,[76] but his main function remained that of facing the immediate threat and, later, of collecting cattle and transport animals for an expedition which Alulā planned for September.[77]

On 20 August 1885 the British authorities in Sawākin received information that the town of Kassala had already fallen and that the Egyptians had been spared.[78] For *Rās* Alulā, the Kassala expedition had become pointless, but the British had a different view. With 'Uthmān Diqna known to be moving his headquarters there and to be making efforts to revive Mahdist power, possibly through a renewed march towards the Massawa area, the question of mobilising Alulā had become much more important. Neither the *rās* nor his sovereign were informed, therefore, about the fall of the town which they were so energetically urged to save.[79] Chermside and his superiors had to use Ethiopian power to face Mahdism in the eastern Sudan. "I have no wish to stop him," Chermside wrote to Marcopoli Bey, "Alulā's advance may prove of great assistance."[80]

In Asmara on 25 August 1885, Marcopoli Bey transferred 640 Remington rifles to a grateful Alulā who re-emphasized that "what he was doing for Kassala is for the greater glory of God and not for presents and rewards." Alulā claimed, however, that he had "many preparations [to make] and could not leave before his new year's day, 8 September 1885." The *rās* also informed Marcopoli that he was expecting troops to guard the frontier against the Italians.[81] Alulā remarked:

> What are the Italians doing at Massawa? It is not their country. Let them go home and the sooner the better. . . Why did not the Italians stop Debbeb[82]. . . There is no necessity to have a garrison at all at Saati. Tell England and Egypt that Abyssinia is not pleased at the presence of the Italians at Massawa and other places on the coast.[83]

Upon receiving this report, Col. Chermside finally began to realize that, even with the arms and the money, the Ethiopian *rās* would not budge from his position facing the coast. Yet he tried to convince Alulā that the coast held no dangers for Ethiopia; on 4 September he ordered Marcopoli to promise Alulā that he would do his best to catch Dabbab. Indeed, a few Anglo-Egyptian patrols, mostly in pretense, were sent after the outlaw.[84]

But *Rās* Alulā did not base his moves on Chermside's assurances or on the state of the Egyptians in Kassala. Mahdist moves and words now threatened invasion, so the *rās* planned a military expedition, during which Kassala could be taken as a by-product. He hesitated briefly because of the risk to his "eastern front," but, luckily enough, the Anglo-Egyptians saw their own interests in supplying him the means he needed for warfare on west and security on the east.

G. *Alulā's Imperial Army*

A long wait by *Rās* Alulā might cause the wavering tribes to side with 'Uthmān Diqna[85] or permit 'Abd al-Qādir's forces to link up with the latter. In such circumstances even the Banū 'Āmir, encircled by Mahdist forces, would be in a very bad situation, while the Ḥabbāb would inevitably join the enemy's camp. From Alulā's point of view it was not impossible that he might soon find himself facing both the Italians and the "dervishes." His option of marching westward would soon lapse because "in about mid-October the water in *khors* dries up and there is malaria in the plains which punishes the Abyssinian hill men very heavily."[86]

Though convinced he should march away from the "eastern front," Alulā had to neutralize the Italians, and, on the eve of his departure from Asmara, on 13 September 1885, he replied positively to Col. Saletta about the despatch of an Italian mission to sign a treaty of friendship with the emperor.[87] The strong anti-Italian feeling in his camp, no doubt sustained by Alulā himself, was however convincingly described by both an Egyptian[88] and an Ethiopian visitor to Asmara.[89]

The Ethiopian visitor, Haylu, an interpreter employed by the Italians, was in Alulā's camp during the two days before the army moved to Kūfīt. He was deeply impressed by the strength of the Ethiopian army which he placed at 10,000 troops, "all armed with Remingtons."[90] There are other estimates, and they are not necessarily contradictory, because on march the army was constantly augmented by local forces. The reinforcements arrived as scheduled, since the *rās* and his emperor proclaimed heavy penalties for absentees.[91] Alulā, wrote the biographer[92], "sent round a herald, who said: 'Every man who goes here and there at the time of battle, I will kill with a cruel death, and he will have no hope of life in the Kingdom of Heaven'." Thus, Marcopoli Bey, who stayed in Asmara until the beginning of September, estimated the army as numbering 8,000 troops.[93] Italian sources, based probably on Haylu's evidence of 13 September 1885, put the number at 10,000,[94] and Mahdist sources derived from battlefield evidence claim as many as 20,000.[95] This was actually the first time that Alulā led such an imperial force on the northern frontier, and the first time that he and his army were not under the emperor's direct guidance and command. Consequently, not a single prominent Tigrean personality joined that army; only *Belāttā* Gabru, Alulā's lieutenant, is known to have fought under the Alulā in the forthcoming battle.

Praising Alulā's ability as an organiser and his diplomatic success in uniting

Christian and Moslem, a British official concluded: "Everything there promises success, and in all probability we are on the eve of the most remarkable and extraordinary episode in the history of the rebellion in the Sudan."⁹⁶ But for *Rās* Alulā the coming battle was not a chapter in Sudanese history. On 14 September 1885, he received 'Uthmān Diqna's threatening letter,⁹⁷ which was probably the final argument in favour of beating the *Nagārit* and ordering the army to march. He wrote the same day to 'Uthmān, "I will not trouble you to move from your place, make ready all your preparations, and I will come to you."⁹⁸

Alulā's biographer regarded the *rās*'s letter to 'Uthmān Diqna as a Christian reply to the Mahdist challenge:

> How have you dared to come against me, O evil and troublesome man? Do you not fear the Lord God who made heaven and earth and all that is in them?⁹⁹

But according to other sources, Alulā's reply was more pointed:

> I heard that you came to Kūfīt and your aim is to penetrate Ethiopia. Wait for me three days and God willing I shall send you soon to hell.¹⁰⁰

H. *The Battle of Kūfīt*

> May we tell you the accounts of Kūfīt?
> The Dervishes came like clouds.
> Can it be that they had not heard of Abbā Naggā?¹⁰¹

Not a single European participated in or witnessed the fierce battle which took place in Kūfīt on 23 September 1885 between *Rās* Alulā and 'Uthmān Diqna.¹⁰² Mahdist sources neglected the subject for obvious reasons,¹⁰³ and the scattered pieces of evidence provide only an incomplete picture. From Karan, *Rās* Alulā sent ten horsemen to Baria country. They returned with the incorrect information that about 3,000 "dervishes" were entrenched in the *khawr* of Kūfīt.¹⁰⁴ Subsequently, the *rās* divided his army into three columns: *Belātā* Gabru and his horsemen in the front, Alulā with the infantry in the rear, while another column of riders was on the wing. On 22 September 1885 the Ethiopian army arrived at Kūfīt.

Mahdist forces commanded by both 'Uthmān Diqna and Muṣṭafā Hadal¹⁰⁵ were entrenched along the steep banks of the *khawr*, whose broken bed was full of bush,¹⁰⁶ in positions invulnerable to surprise. *Belātā* Gabru nevertheless ignored the nature of the ground and Alulā's order to outflank the enemy,¹⁰⁷ underestimated Mahdist power, and decided to assault the entrenched enemy frontally. Marcopoli Bey had promised him a sum of $1,000 "If he could assist [sic] Kassala before the arrival of Alula . . . [and] he promised to do his best."¹⁰⁸

> The forces of Blata Gabru were in front of the force of Ras Alula and they hastened their advance, hoping to encounter the dervishes in order to take

the glory from Ras Alula. His troops met those of 'Uthmān Diqna and fighting began between them. The dervishes won the victory while Blata Gabru and his troops were defeated. The only persons to escape from that fearful engagement were those who brought the news.[109]

Gabru's attack was a disaster: the bush and the broken ground created a trap for the Ethiopian and Banū 'Āmir horsemen,[110] the latter probably wearing their clumsy armour.[111] Even had conditions been better, Gabru's army would have had only a small chance as the Mahdists were entrenched on higher ground, and 3,000 of them were armed with rifles. In such circumstances, there was no opportunity of a direct assault, and *Belātta* Gabru's brashness cost his life. The remnants of his force "rallied when they found themselves some way in the rear of the Dervish position . . . [with] only camp followers to oppose them, and reformed.[112]

Rās Alulā's first move repeated his lieutenant's mistake:

> When the news reached Ras Alula who was in the rear of the army, it filled the hearts of his troops with fear and they didn't wish to advance and fight. When they reached the battlefield 'Uthmān Diqna met them with firm hearts and sharp swords and high spirit. Fighting took place. The troops of Ras Alula were defeated and dispersed. His horse was killed and threw him. His nephew[113] brought him . . . [another] steed and they fled in disguise and stopped on a high mountain at four hours' distance from the battle-field. He beat his drum to muster the fugitives as it was rumoured in his country that Ras Alula was slain.[114]

Although slightly wounded,[115] the *rās* reorganised his troops and attempted what he should have done originally, to force the Mahdists out of their trenches. He ordered two reformed detachments to outflank the enemy position from both sides. This movement surprised the dervishes, whose positions had been arranged only to counter frontal attack.[116] The Mahdists, either in response to Alulā's manoeuvre or because of their recent success (or, probably, because they were low on ammunition) decided to counter-attack[117] and marched towards Alulā's army. Meanwhile, the *rās* had arranged his main force "in phalanx formation":[118]

> He set his forces in order by means of Mūsā al-Fīl, *Nāzir* of the Banū 'Āmir. The cavalry surrounded the infantry and he ordered that anyone who avoided the battle should be killed by the cavalry. By this means he kept them steady and they advanced until they reached the headquarters of 'Uthmān Diqna on the morning of 23 September 1885. The two armies met and the battle lasting four hours took place on that day. The cavalry were only employed in keeping watch on the infantry. When the Abyssinian troops realised that they had fallen between the two enemies, their hearts were strengthened. They stood firmly in the battlefield and slaughtered the dervishes.[119]

The wounded *Rās* Alulā was reportedly at the head of his men shouting, "We must conquer or die."[120] Soon the clash was no longer a battle but a massacre:

> There was a great killing from sunrise until sunset, and Ras Alula conquered and killed off the wicked and apostate men who brought division on the name of Christ and who make arguments over the Messianic law. There was not one of them left.[121]

In fact about 3,000 "dervishes" were annihilated in the battle,[122] and most fugitives were killed by Alulā's cavalry and the hitherto passive Baria warriors. The latter, headed by Shaykh Arāy, had arrived near Kūfīt on the evening of 22 September 1885, when the battle was to begin. They anticipated the result and destroyed the fleeing Mahdists and their camp followers.[123] At the same time, the opportunistic al-Jadīn warriors intercepted Mahdist reinforcements consisting of al-Ḥalāniqa tribesmen from Kassala.[124]

An Ethiopian officer estimated 5,050 Mahdist dead,[125] whereas others claimed 10,000,[126] with only 150 survivors. The Mahdist leadership in the eastern Sudan suffered heavily as almost all the shaykhs and commanders were identified among the corpses,[127] although 'Uthmān Diqna himself had managed to escape.[128] His defeat, however, "had a cooling effect on the ardour of the local tribes," and he experienced difficulties in maintaining an adequate fighting force, even in the Sawākin area, where he subsequently returned.[129]

Ethiopian casualties were not small either: no less than 1,500 warriors were reported killed and 300-500 wounded. Besides *Belāttā* Gabru, some forty officers did not return from the battle-field.[130] The fact that their names were not known or mentioned by any of the sources is indicative of the fact that prominent leaders from Tigre had not joined Alulā's army but probably preferred to send only their followers.

> From his troops, many faithful died, those called Blatta Gabru, Assallafi[131] Hagwas Warrata . . . For the rest no one knows their names, but their names are written in Heaven, in the book of life . . . for they became martyrs for the faith. . .[132]

I. Alulā's "Retreat" from Kūfīt and its Effect on Western Eritrea

Contemporary British officials cited Alulā's heavy casualties, sickness in the exhausted army and the *rās*'s wound as the reasons why Ethiopian authority was not extended to Kassala after the Mahdist defeat.[133] Others suggested that the rains prevented Alulā from doing so,[134] or that he withdrew because the retreating dervishes could still be easily reinforced by neighbouring tribes.[135] On the other hand, it was considered that "he believed that such a signal victory as he had gained must enable the garrison to retire without further help on his part."[136] Marcopoli Bey, however, offers the most reasonable explanation:

> Ras Alula was exceedingly nervous as to the possible hostile action of the Hababs, supported by or co-operating with the Italians . . . solicitude as to Italian action was one of the principal reasons which decided Ras Alula not to advance after Kufit.[137]

The basic reason must lie in the inevitable conclusion that *Rās* Alulā never intended to go to Kassala: he did not consider the operation a relief expedition but a defensive measure against the Mahdists. Had 'Uthmān Diqna not come to Kassala and advanced to Kūfīt, threatening Ethiopia by words and deeds, Alulā probably would have sent an expedition similar to *Belāttā* Gabru's advance guard to demonstrate his goodwill towards the British. Had the Italians not come to Massawa, *Rās* Alulā would surely have been delighted to establish Ethiopian hegemony over Egyptian-evacuated Western Eritrea and even to annex the town of Kassala. But in the circumstances he could not afford to stay even in the Kūfīt-Karan area, a fact which proved to be important in the long run.

Deciding to return to his "eastern front," *Rās* Alulā tried to exploit his victory to create an anti-Mahdist tribal front in the western marches. On 25 September 1885, Alulā began his march to Karan,[138] where, upon arrival, he issued a proclamation to the various tribes around Kassala instructing them to assist and supply its garrison or else they would be destroyed.[139] He promised the tribesmen that he would soon be back and ordered the Baria and the al-Jadīn to make the appropriate preparations, including the digging of new wells.[140] A new but rather small detachment consisting of the remnants of Alulā's advance guard, with their Banū 'Āmir companions, was told to be ready to move back to the tribal country.[141] Ordering the various local politicians to come to Karan, *Rās* Alulā announced that he had appointed the local Shaykh Mūsā al-Fīl of the Banū 'Āmir as "Shaykh 'Umūmī" (i.e. general chief),[142] making him a sort of unofficial Ethiopian governor to replace the Egyptian *Nāẓir*. Shaykh Arāy of the Baria, who attacked the Mahdists only after their defeat had become obvious, and who had previously disobeyed Alulā's instructions to collect cattle for the expedition, hastened now to appease Alulā—unsuccessfully as it later turned out—by bringing a present of 100 oxen to Karan.[143] The loyal Shaykh 'Alī Nūrīn, whose return to his tribe caused his warriors to assist Alulā by intercepting pro-Mahdist reinforcements, came to Karan with the captured shaykh of al-Ḥalāniqa, Shaykh Muḥammad b. 'Awaḍ. The latter, a former Egyptian-nominated *nāẓir*,[144] who had become one of the important Mahdist *amīrs* in the eastern Sudan,[145] was accompanied by his lieutenant, Shaykh Nāfi' al-Ḥalāniqī, and sixteen of his followers. As ordered by *Rās* Alulā, these pro-Mahdists were executed by hanging;[146] later the bodies of Shaykh Muḥammad and Shaykh Nāfi' were brought to Asmara where, on 17 March 1886, Harrison Smith, a visiting British envoy,[147] saw them displayed "as a warning to the Musulmans . . . not to join the cause of the Mahdi."[148]

But Alulā's idea of creating a buffer zone on the "western front" by forming an anti-Mahdist tribal front proved to be as much a failure as Col. Chermside's earlier "Muslim policy."[149] The various Muslim tribes of northern Eritrea and eastern Sudan proved too weak to maintain an independent role, and Alulā's failure to return there undermined the credibility of his promise and threats. The tribesmen demonstrated their anti-Mahdist line by helping Egyptian refugees from Kassala to cross their country and reach Asmara, and thence to Massawa.[150] Facing, however, an immediate threat from the Mahdists and lacking Alulā's support, the tribes in the Kassala area, who had deserted 'Uthmān Diqna in the first months after the battle, were obliged to resubmit themselves to the Mahdists by the end of the year.[151] Many of the other tribes, fearing revenge and lacking Ethiopian support, hastened to ask for Italian protection.

J. October: Alulā's Return to Asmara

In early October, *Rās* Alulā travelled to his new headquarters in Asmara.[152] Shortly thereafter, 'Uthmān Diqna returned to Kassala and immediately arrested the *mudīr* whom, he was told, had tried to regain control and had reported the weakness of the Mahdist force at Kassala to *Rās* Alulā.[153] The Mahdist leader had very good reasons to be afraid of a possible Ethiopian advance. His anxiety that the Egyptian *mudīr* might persuade Alulā to renew hostilities was described by the secretary of 'Iffāt Bey, Ghabriyyāl Effendi Jārallāh, who fled from Kassala on 23 September 1885. On his way to Massawa he heard that 'Uthmān Diqna's envoys were looking for him "as some of the rebels accused me of carrying letters to *Ras* Alula to call him to destroy them."[154] In order to minimize such dangers 'Uthmān Diqna ordered the execution of the *mudīr* and six of the most important Egyptian functionaries.[155] Thus for the Egyptians in Kassala, Alulā's expedition was a mistake, even a disaster. As a senior Egyptian officer said, referring to the possibility of the expedition's renewal, "If Ras Alula went now to Kassala, it will be an excuse to slaughter the remainder of [our] soldiers and officers there . . . and it is the same with the Arabs[156] and their chiefs who say they write to him about his coming to them with his army to relieve them."[157]

But the *rās* probably did not even consider an advance and especially not in order "to save" a few Egyptians[158] after so many Ethiopians had been killed. Inevitably his thoughts were directed to the "eastern front," where the Italians had taken advantage of the situation. Col. Saletta had strenghtened his relations with chief of the Ḥabbābs, *Kantibā* Ḥamīd, and officially granted him protection.[159] The *rās*, who "was exceedingly nervous as to this possibility," preferred therefore to stay in Karan, the natural portal into Ḥabbāb country, and to rest his army. Alulā himself suffered from chest and stomach pains and wanted to restore his own health.[160] But the "cold war"[161] with the Italians necessitated a show of power.

On 6 October 1885,[162] therefore, "Ras Alula made a triumphal entry into Asmara at the head of his army, and preceded by priests in full canonicals, while his victorious troops carrying the captured arms and banners[163] shouted out songs of victory. Alulā himself was directly preceded by a raised dais, on which lay the banner of Osman Digna.'"[164]

> And the men of the land of Hamasen said: 'Praise to you, O Ras Alula, who protected us ... For you saved us from sudden death and took us out of bitter bondage, that is, bondage to the Dervishes, ... ' The priests and monks praised and sang melodious songs, saying: 'Blessed is Ras Alula, who comes in the name of God'.[165]

Emperor Yohannes did not learn about the battle of Kūfīt and subsequent events before the middle of October. In late September he enthusiastically had written to Queen Victoria that he soon would join Alulā to raise the siege of Kassala,[166] and he had made some preliminary arrangements.[167] It was only on 12 October 1885, when Yohannes, then in Dabra-Tābor, received Alulā's letter of 29 September 1885:[168]

> Behold, our foes and enemies, who heaped boasting and pride upon us .. became before me like wax before the face of the fire and like smoke blown by the wind. All the Muslims, whom they call Dervishes, were destroyed.[169]

As will be seen by his reply, the emperor was undoubtedly satisfied with Alulā's success at Kūfīt and probably had to accept the *rās*'s explanations for his return to the Hamāsēn. Though he wanted him to take Kassala, he either did not want to impose on Alulā or was persuaded by his arguments. The emperor replied to his subordinate:

> Let this reach the honoured Rās Alulā, who is a Turk Bāshā, a faithful man after my heart. Peace to you!. . . your pleasant and clear letter reached me on the 3rd of Ṭeqemt . . . and when we opened it and read it . . then our mouth was filled with joy and our tongue rejoiced . . . And all those who have been killed and have fought against those pagans let God pour his mercy over them and give them the merits of their toil.[170]

As for the British, they now preferred to remain passive: "The Abyssinians should no longer be pressed to advance to Kassala," wrote Egerton to Salisbury, "but left to act as they think best."[171] It became clear now in Sawākin, Cairo and London that a renewed effort to divert Alulā from his "Italian front" would be both futile and destructive to their relations with the *rās*, who had proved to be "a man of considerable judgement and ability and has behaved well."[172] The British were also afraid that Alulā's anger over the Italian advance would lead to reprisals against Egyptian refugees still crossing Ethiopian territory.[173] But the *rās* was friendlier to the Egyptians than ever before.[174]

The garrison of Al-Qallābāt and al-Jīra and the refugees from Kassala were so far the only ones in the entire Sudan to avoid falling into Mahdist hands, and

London realised that "it is owing in no small degree to the ability of Ras Alula that the operation of the Abyssinian forces led to a successful result."[175] *Rās* Alulā, however, was fully aware of the fact that, while supporting Italian ambitions on the Eritrean coast, the British were doing their best to use him as an anti-Mahdist weapon. He was actually pleased with their aims, since it helped him to conduct his own policy, but he completely understood Whitehall's cynicism.

Years later, six months before his death, Alulā encountered A. Wylde:

> The Ras turned all his followers out of the room and said, 'Now I want to have a talk with you. Why do you forget your old friends. What does England mean by destroying Hewett's treaty and allowing the Italians to take my country from me?' Pulling from underneath his pillow a copy of Hewett's treaty of June, 1884, he unfolded it before me and went on: 'What single article of that treaty have you kept? Look at the first article . . . You gave Massowah away to the Italians. Arms and ammunition could not be imported by the king . . . As to the second and third articles,' the Ras went on, 'did I not relieve the Egyptian garrison in the Bogos country? Did I not fight at Cassala when it was too late? Have I not done everything I could? You English used us to do what you wanted, and then you left us. . . . Article IV, about the Aboona, is the only thing that you have carried out'.[176]

★ ★ ★

European historiography has almost totally neglected the battle of Kūfīt. The event generally has been described as an Ethiopian military victory which came too late to achieve the relief of the Kassala garrison.[177] Further research however seems to lead to the conclusion that both the circumstances and the implications of the episode were not so simple. In the longer perspective of Ethiopian history, it was an important event in the struggle to safeguard the country's independence. While in the "Adwā treaty", Ethiopia traded one weak enemy for two strong ones, Alulā's military and diplomatic skill liquidated the threat of an immediate Mahdist invasion and supplied some of the arms needed to face the Italian ambitions.

NOTES

1 Littman, op.cit., II, p. 196; See also H. Erlich, "1885 in Eritrea: 'The Year in which the Dervishes were cut Down'", *Asian and African Studies*, 1975, pp. 282-322.
2 LV.XVII, Ferrari to MAE, 23.3.85.
3 A.S.MAI 2/2-13, Naretti to Lucardi, 17.2.85.
4 FO 78/3801, Chermside to Watson, 21.2.85. On this traditional intelligence-gathering unit see: Marcus, *Life and Times*, pp. 65, 66.

5   LV. XVII, Ferrari to MAE, 23.3.85.
6   LV. XVII, Ferrari to MAE, 25.5.85.
7   It would be a mistake to attribute pro-Mahdist tendencies solely to religious motives and especially so in Eritrea, where even Christian or semi-pagan tribes occasionally sided with the Mahdist cause. Diffidence should rather be attributed to centrifugal and anti-government tendencies.
8   Wingate, *Mahdism*, pp. 247, 254. FO 78/3805, Chermside to Baring, 28.6.85.
9   FO 78/3805, Chermside to Mudir, 8.2.85; FO 78/3805, Chermside to Baring, 28.6.85.
10 For details about the evacuation of Karan (Sanhīt) and Amidīb, *vide*: Shuqayr, *Ta'rīkh*, p. 330; FO 78/3803, Baker to Baring, 10.4.85, 14.4.85.
11 Sa'd Report.
12 Sa'd Report; FO 89/3805, Chermside to Baring 28.6.85; Depretis to Ricotti, 1.8.85; C. Giglio (ed.), *L'Italia in Africa, Serie Storica, Etiopia e Mar Rosso*, Ministero degli Affari Esteri, Rome 1959, Vol. V, No. 17, p. 12.
13 See for example, Extract from *L'Opinione*, 15.2.85, in FO 407/65, Lumley to Granville, 22.5.85.
14 Ministero della Guerra, *Storia Militare della Colonia Eritrea*, Rome 1935, pp. 92, 94. Maissa to Mancini, 14.5.85, *Ethiopia e Mar Rosso*, III, No. 493, p. 181.
15 FO 78/3808, Marcopoli to Chermside, 26.8.85.
16 FO 403/90, Chermside to Portal, 22.8.87.
17 FO 78/3805, Chermside to Yohannes, 8.2.85; FO 78/3813, Baring to Granville, 31.5.85; 78/3813, Baring to Granville, 17.6.85.
18 A.S.MAI, 2/2-13, Maissa to MAE, 14.5.85.
19 M. Savelli, *La Spedizione*, Rome 1886, p. 162.
20 A.S.MAI, 2/2-13, Alulā to Saletta, 11.5.85.
21 Savelli, loc.cit.
22 A.S.MAI 2/2-13, Alulā to Saletta, 13.5.85.
23 A.S.MAI ibid., Saletta to Alula, 5.5.85; Alula to Saletta, 14.5.85.
24 A.S.MAI 36/3-23, Ferrari's report, 14.9.85.
25 Maissa to Mancini, 15.6.85; *Giglio, Etiopia e Mar Rosso*, III, No. 504, p. 191.
26 G. Belcredi in *La Tribuna Illustrata*, 26.6.90. Savelli, p. 163. They were later expelled, following the Italian occupation of Sahāṭi.
27 FO 78/3806, Alulā to Gov. of Massawah 11.6.85.
28 FO 78/3806, Ras Alula to Izzet Bey, 7.6.85, 11.6.85.
29 Ibid., Chermside to Izzet Bey, 12.6.85.
30 Ibid., Egerton to Salisbury 26.7.85; Fasolo, op.cit., p. 266.
31 Ricotti to Depretis, 8.8.85; Giglio, *Etiopia e Mar Rosso*, V, No. 20.
32 Alula to Saletta, Asmara, n.d.; Saletta to Alula, 11.7.85; Giglio, *Etiopia e Mar Rosso*, V, No. 20, pp. 14. 15. 16.
33 FO 78/3811, Egerton to Salisbury, 10.11.85.
34 Ibid.
35 Ricotti to Depretis, 8.8.85, Giglio, *Etiopia e Mar Rosso*, V, No. 20, pp. 13,14.
36 A.S.MAI 4/1-2, Alula to Saletta, n.d.; Saletta to Alula, 11.7.85.
37 See below, p. 89.
38 Ricotti to Depretis, 8.8.85; Giglio, *Etiopia e Mar Rosso*, V, No. 20, p. 14. C. Conti Rossini, "Documenti per lo Studio della lingua tigre," *Giornale della Società Asiatica Italiana*, Firenze 1903, XVI, p. 26.

76 BIOGRAPHY OF RAS ALULĀ

39   FO 78/3808, Marcopoli to Chermside, 26.8.85.
40   FO 78/3806, Baker to Egerton, 20.7.85.
41   Shuqayr, *op.cit.*, p. 398; FO 78/3806, Iffat Bey to Chermside, 9.6.85.
42   "Sa'd Report"; Shuqayr, *Ta'rīkh*, p. 398; FO 78/3806, Baker to Egerton, 20.7.85.
43   Shuqayr, *Ta'rīkh*, p. 398; "Sa'd Report," SOAS M.518, Ibrāhīm Khayrallāh Report.
44   FO 78/3808, Marcopoli to Chermside, 12.8.85.
45   MS. Mannawē.
46   Holt, *the Mahdist State*, p. 169.
47   Details: Shuqayr, *Ta'rīkh*, p. 399; "Sa'd Report," SOAS M.518, Reel 8, Khayrallāh's Report.
48   A.B. Wylde, *Modern Abyssinia*, London 1900, p. 36.
49   See above, p. 32.
50   78/3806, Egerton to Salisbury, 26.7.85.
51   FO 78/3807, Chermside to Izzet Bey, 24.7.85.
52   FO 78/3808, Marcopoli to Chermside, 12.8.85.
53   Ibid.
54   FO 78/3809, "Marcopoli Diary" in Egerton to Salisbury, 2.10.85.
55   FO 78/3807, Cameron to Egerton, 11.8.85.
56   A. Pollera, *I Baria e I Cunama*, Rome 1913, p. 46. As might be concluded from Muṣṭafā al-Hadal's letter see below, pp. 64-65, he probably told them also that British troops would come too.
57   For evidence from local informants of fear among the tribes around Kassala concerning Alulā's future advance, see: FO/78/3807, Egerton to Salisbury, 23.8.85.
58   FO 78/3813, Egerton to Salisbury, 15.8.85, 18.8.85.
59   For his failure in Sawākin, see Holt, pp. 186-187.
60   FO 78/3806, Egerton to Salisbury, 4.8.85.
61   FO 78/3806, Egerton to Salisbury, 4.8.85, Chermside to Watson, 30.7.85; FO 78/3808, Egerton to Salisbury, 23.8.85, Depretis to Ricotti, 1.8.85; Giglio, *Etiopia e Mar Rosso*, V, No. 17, p. 12.
62   "Sa'd Report"; FO 78/3807, Egerton to Salisbury, 20.8.85; Holt, *The Mahdist State*, p. 169. Shuqayr, *Ta'rīkh*, p. 400 (according to Shuqayr, the movement occurred on 26.8.85). (According to Wingate, p. 249. 'Uthmān came to Kassala "about the middle of August.").
63   Shuqayr, *Ta'rīkh*, p. 400.
64   FO 78/3809, "Marcopoli Diary" in Egerton to Salisbury, 2.10.85.
65   The other Mahdist *Amīrs* were: Al-Ḥassan Wād Hāshī, Bilāl al-'Awaḍ and 'Abd al-Karīm Kāfī.
66   Wingate, *Mahdism*, p. 250. Wingate's belief that this letter was sent from Kūfīt is definitely false, as the Mahdists had not reached there by then.
67   See also Littmann, *Publications*, vol. II, pp. 194, 195.
68   Mahdia Y80, 1. MSS Letter Book of 'Uthmān Diqna, SOAS 101491 (Collection of the mahdī's and the khalīfa's letters to 'Uthmān Diqna 1881-1888.) Khalīfa to 'Uthmān Diqna, Muḥarram 1303H./October 1885, p. 48.
69   *Ibid.*, Khalīfa to 'Uthmān Diqna, 21 Muḥarram 1303 H./31.10.85.
70   Pollera, *I Baria*, pp. 46-47.
71   FO 78/3811, Egerton to Salisbury, 17.11.85.
72   FO 78/3810, Egerton to Salisbury, 12.10.85; FO 78/3811, Egerton to Salisbury,

10.11.85; Shuqayr, *Ta'rīkh*, p. 401 and H.C. Jackson, *Osman Diqna*, London 1926, p. 112. estimated the army at 10,000, Wingate, *Mahdism*, p. 205, at 8.000-10,000, "Khayrallāh Report," at 9,000, Shaykh Musā al-Fīl in FO 78/3813, Egerton to Salisbury, 25.10.85, at 6,000-9.000.
73   "Sa'd Report."
74   FO 78/3806, Chermside to Watson, 30.7.85; FO 78/3807, Egerton to Salisbury, 24.8.85; FO 78/3807, Egerton to Salisbury, 20.8.85.
75   FO 78/3809, "Marcopoli Diary" in Egerton to Salisbury, 2.10.85.
76   "Sa'd Report."
77   Ricotti to Depretis, 23.9.85; Giglio, *Etiopia e Mar Rosso*, vol. V, No. 55, p. 64; FO 78/3810, Egerton to Salisbury, 12.10.85.
78   FO 78/3807, Egerton to Salisbury, 20.8.85.
79   According to Marcopoli Bey, *Rās* Alulā said on 29.8.85, that he did not believe Kassala had fallen: "We are only six or seven days distance from Kassala, how could we not have heard of such a capitulation?" FO 78/3809, "Marcopoli Diary," in Egerton to Salisbury, 2.10.85.
80   FO 78/3808, Chermside to Marcopoli Bey, 21.8.85; FO 78/3813, Egerton to Salisbury, 19.8.85.
81   FO 78/3808, Marcopoli Bey to Chermside, 26.8.85. FO 78/3811, Egerton to Salisbury, 10.11.85.
82   Sahāṭi was occupied by Italian irregulars on 24.6.85 (see above, p. 62). For this important issue see below, p. 89. For Dabbab's raid on villages considered as Ethiopian (Ricotti to Depretis, 23.9.85; Giglio, *Etiopia e Mar Rosso*, V, No. 55, p. 63) and Alulā's suspicion that he was encouraged by the Italians, see below, p. 88.
83   FO 78/3803, Marcopoli Bey to Chermside, 26.8.85.
84   FO 78/3808, Chermside, to Marcopoli, 4.2.85. Depretis to Ricotti 20.9.85, Giglio, *Etiopia e Mar Rosso*, V, No. 50, p. 47; Zerboni to Depretis, 22.9.85, p. 55; FO 78/3810, Marcopoli to Chermside, 20.9.85; Egerton to Salisbury, 21.10.85.
85   According to Luca dei Sabelli, 'Uthmān Diqna intended to make the al-Jadīn, Sabdrat and the Baria the advanced guard of the Mahdiyya. Sabelli, *Storia*, vol. III, p. 339.
86   FO 78/3809, Chermside to Egerton, 16.9.85.
87   Zerboni to Depretis, 8.9.85; Depretis to Ricotti, 20.9.; Giglio, *Etiopia e Mar Rosso*, Nos. 39, 50, pp. 32, 33, 46.
88   FO 78/3809, "Marcopoli Diary," in Egerton to Salisbury, 2.10.85.
89   Zerboni to Depretis, 23.9.85, Report of the interpreter Hailu on his visit to Alulā's camp, 11-13.9.85; Giglio, *Etiopia e Mar Rosso*, V, No. 54, pp. 58-62.
90   Zerboni to Depretis 23.9.85. "Thousands of Remington rifles and an abundance of ammunition have been conveyed during the last months from Massawa up to Alulā's headquarters . . . the Abyssinian expeditionary force is now all armed with breech loaders." FO 78/3808, Cameron to Egerton, 9.9.85.
91   FO 78/3808, Cameron to Egerton, 8.9.85.
92   Ms. Mannawē.
93   FO 78/3813, Egerton to Salisbury, 2.10.85. Wingate, *Mahdism*, p. 250, calculated the whole army, including the advance guard, as 10,000 men.
94   Sabelli, *Storia*, III, p. 339.
95   Shuqayr, *Ta'rīkh*, p. 401.
96   FO 78/3808, Cameron to Egerton, 9.9.85.

97 "Sa'd Report."
98 *Ibid.*
99 Ms. Mannawē.
100 Shuqayr, *Ta'rīkh*, p. 401; see also H.C. Jackson, *Osman Diqna*, London 1926, p. 113.
101 A song from a Ms. found in the monastery of Dabra-Bizan by Ato Māmo Wudnah, Asmara. (Abbā Naggā *i.e.* "The father of he who dawned" was Alulā's horse name.)
102 The idea that a British officer would accompany the mission was dropped after it was learned that Kassala had fallen.
103 The only Mahdist description of the battle of Kūfīt is a false exposition based on a report from 'Uthmān Diqna. On 9 Ṣafar 1303 H./18.11.85, the khalīfa wrote to 'Uthmān Diqna: "We want to inform you, my beloved, that your entertaining letter of 20 Muḥarram [30.10.85] reached us . . . in which you told us how you had gone to the Sabdirāt and al-Jadīn and others because they became enemies of God and how they positively responded to you and joined your army, and that you advanced to Kūfīt in order to spread the real faith and thus reached the country of the Ethiopians, the enemies of God, and that you invited them to join the God . . . which they refused. You therefore fought . . . the war of the victorious God, destroyed, ruined and defeated them, till God annihilated no less than six thousand of them . . . so we became happy . . ." MS Letter Book of 'Uthmān Diqna, SOAS, p. 50.
104 FO 78/3810, Egerton to Salisbury, 12.10.85.
105 Some sources claimed that 'Uthmān Diqna was the commander and others, Muṣṭafā Hadal. 'Uthmān was reported as not taking active part in the fighting as he was wounded in 1883. It seems, therefore, that Hadal was in charge of combat actions, and 'Uthmān was present on the battlefield, or somewhere in the neighbourhood, in order to encourage his followers and influence the wavering tribes.
106 Pollera, *I Baria*, p. 47; Wylde, *Modern Abyssinia*, p. 36.
107 Report on Muḥammad al-Fīl in Zerboni to Robilant, 9.10.85, in *Etiopia e Mar Rosso*, V, No. 71, p. 77.
108 FO 78/3809, "Marcopoli Diary" in Egerton to Salisbury, 2.10.85.
109 "Sa'd Report." Written in 1889, Major Sa'd Rif'at's Report was based on participant evidence and is the most detailed account of the battle.
110 Wingate's version that Gabru attacked with infantry seems unlikely, *Mahdism*, p. 251.
111 They reportedly fought in armour against *Ledj* Fantā in August 1884. "Abyssinia out of its treaty obligations," *The Daily News*, 27.12.84.
112 Wylde, *Modern Abyssinia*, p. 36.
113 According to Muḥammad al-Fīl, the person who gave Alulā the new horse and thus saved him was Shaykh Mūsā of the *Nabtab* sub-tribe of the Banū 'Āmir. See Zebroni to Robilant, 9.10.85, in Giglio, *Etiopia e Mar Rosso*, V, p. 76.
114 "Sa'd Report."
115 Pollera, *I Baria*, p. 47.
14 *Ibid.*
117 *Ibid*; Shuqayr, *Ta'rīkh*, p. 401.
118 Wylde, *Modern Abyssinia*, p. 36.
119 "Sa'd Report."
120 Wingate, *Mahdism*.

121 Ms. Mannawē.
122 Wylde, *Modern Abyssinia*, p. 37; Wingate, *Mahdism*; FO 78/3813, Egerton to Salisbury, 7.10.85.
123 Pollera, *I Baria*, p. 47.
124 FO 78/3813, Egerton to Salisbury, 7.10.85; FO 78/3810, Egerton to Salisbury, 14.10.85.
125 FO 78/3811, Cameron to Egerton, 25.10.85.
126 Wylde, *Modern Abyssinia*, p. 38. Wylde explained his estimate, commenting that: "nearly all the wounded that escaped died afterwards from want of food".
127 For a list of their names see Zerboni to Robilant, 9.10.85, in Giglio, *Etiopia e Mar Rosso*, V, No. 71, p. 77.
128 *Ibid*; Depretis to Ricotti, 5.10.85; Giglio, *Etiopia e Mar Rosso*, V, No. 62, p. 69; FO 78/3813, Egerton to Salisbury, 7.10.85.
129 A. Paul, *A History of the Beja Tribes of the Sudan*, Cambridge 1954, p. 114.
130 Wingate, *Mahdism*; Seven according to Zerboni to Robilant, 7.10.85, in Giglio, *Etiopia e Mar Rosso*, V, Nos. 71, 77; FO 78/3811, Memorandum, Chermside, 10.11.85.
131 An officer in charge of setting the troops in order during the battle.
132 Mannawē MS.
133 FO 78/3811, Cameron to Egerton, 25.10.85, and Egerton to Salisbury, 10.11.85. For the Ethiopian soldiers suffering from the heat in the plains see "Our Abyssinian Allies", *The Daily News*, 15.7.84.
134 See Wingate, *Mahdism*, p. 252.
135 Pollera, *I Baria*, p. 47.
136 Wingate, *loc.cit*. FO 78/3811, Egerton to Salisbury, 10.11.85.
137 FO 78/3811, Memorandum by Chermside, 17.11.85.
138 FO 78/3813, Egerton to Salisbury, 7.10.85, 25.10.85; FO 78/3811, Egerton to Salisbury, 10.11.85.
139 FO 78/3811, Memorandum, Chermside, 10.11.85.
140 FO 78/3813, Egerton to Salisbury, 7.10.85, 25.10.85; FO 78/3811, Egerton to Salisbury, 10.11.85.
141 *Ibid*.
142 *Ibid*.
143 Pollera, *I Baria*, p. 47.
144 At the time of the battle, al-Ḥalaniqa Nāẓir was Shaykh 'Abd al-Qādir, who remained loyal and accompanied Alulā's army.
145 For his activities, see: "Sa'd Report," Shuqayr, *Ta'rīkh*, p. 401; MS 'Uthmān Diqna Letter Book, p. 49; SOAS M.518 Reel 8, Ibrāhīm Khayrallāh Report on the Fall of Kassala; Jackson, *Osman Digna*, p. 114.
146 FO 78/3811, Egerton to Salisbury, 10.11.85, 22.11.85; SOAS M.518, Reel 8, Report of 'Abd al-Qādir Aghā.
147 See below p. 98.
148 FO 403/87, Harrison Smith's Diary in Baring to Rosebery, 21.5.86.
149 See above, pp. 54, 55, 58, 59.
150 SOAS M.518 Reel 8, contains much evidence to this effect. See Reports of Faraj Effendi, Ghabriyāl Eff. Jārāllah, 'Issā Ismā'il Agha and others.
151 "Sa'd Report."
152 FO 78/3811, Egerton to Salisbury, 10.11.85.

153 "Sa'd Report." Farāj Effendi: "Report on the Fall of Taka", SOAS M.518; Shuqayr, *Ta'rīkh*, p. 401.
154 Ghabriyyāl Eff. Report, SOAS, M.518, The Egyptian secretary fled subsequently to Walqayt province, where he joined the refugees of al-Jīra garrison with whom he reached Massawa in February 1886. For details on Jīra garrison, see Shuqayr, *Ta'rīkh*, pp. 328-329.
155 "Sa'd Report."
156 i.e., tribesmen in the terminology of that period.
157 "Report on the Fall of Taka", SOAS M.518.
158 Most of the Sudanese and some of the Egyptian troops of the garrison joined the Mahdiyya and fought against Alulā in Kūfīt. 'Abd al-Qādir Bey, SOAS M.518.
159 See below, pp. 90, 91.
160 Winqvist, *op.cit.*, p. 10.
161 R.A. Caulk, "The origins and development of the Foreign Policy of Menelik II, 1865-1896," unpubl. Ph.D. thesis (SOAS, 1966), p. 137.
162 FO 78/3810, Egerton to Salisbury, 18.10.85.
163 "The Abyssinians brought to Asmara somewhat over half the Remingtons supposed to be in the hands of the dervish force", FO 78/3811, Egerton to Salisbury, 10.11.85.
164 Wingate, *Mahdism*, p. 252. (The date in Wingate's text is 22.10.85).
165 Ms. Mannawē.
166 FO 78/3810, Egerton to Salisbury 2.10.85.
167 Zerboni to Robilant 7.10.85; Giglio, *Etiopia e Mar Rosso*, V, No. 71, p. 78.
168 The dates are according to Yohannes's letter of 14.10.85.
169 Ms. Mannawē.
170 Yohannes to Alulā, Ṭeqemt 5th (1878 E.C.); written at Samera (Dabra-Tabor); was kept by the late Fit. Asbehā Abrehā of Aksum, a grandson of Alulā; and was given to an Ethiopian student of Dr. R. Caulk, then at Addis Ababa university.
171 FO 78/3811, Egerton to Salisbury, 10.11.85; and Chermside, Memorandum, 11.10.85.
172 FO 78/3810, Egerton to Salisbury, 10.11.85.
173 FO 78/3811, Chermside, Memorandum, 11.10.85.
174 "Report on the Fall of Taka", SOAS M.518. Also "The Fall of Sennar", SOAS, M.518.
175 FO 1/31, Salisbury to Treasury, 30.12.85.
176 A.B. Wylde, "An Unofficial Mission to Abyssinia", *The Manchester Guardian*, 14.5.97. (17 long articles, *ibid.*, 10.5.97 to 1.7.97.)
177 See among others: R. Hill, *A Biographical Dictionary*; Jackson, *Osman Digna*, p. 112; Longrigg, *Eritrea*, p. 112; Pollera, *I Baria*, p. 46; G.H. Portal, *My Mission to Abyssinia*, London 1892, pp. 6-7; Paul, *Beja*, p. 114; Puglisi, *Chi e?* p. 14.

8

Asmara

The establishment of Asmara, Alulā's capital from late 1884[1] onwards, took place just before the Italian landing at Massawa. According to oral tradition, it was Emperor Yohannes himself who told the *rās* that the old capital of Addi-Taklay "can not serve as a barrier against the enemy" and ordered him to "choose a better place and establish the camp there".[2] The emperor sought Asmara's establishment not merely to counter the Italians, but also to provide Alulā with a province of his own. Yet, in the Marab Mellāsh, *Rās* Alulā also encountered Tigre's traditional agrarian system,[3] in which he had no rights.

According to Pollera,[4] Yohannes authorised Alulā to confiscate one-tenth of the Marab Mellāsh for himself and for his officers, but this effort to create large *gults* (territorial fiefs) was fiercely and successfully opposed by the local inhabitants.[5] In any case it seems that those fiefs which were actually established were too small to cover the expenses of maintaining an army as large as Alulā's.

As can be established from the few available facts, Alulā tried to attack the hereditary land tenure system in the Marab Mellāsh, which was based largely on *rest*, an hereditary family ownership; as Nadel comments:

> The right of *resti* can never be forfeited by absence from the land or failure to work it . . . only in certain special cases can women or their offspring claim a share in the paternal hereditary land. [This hereditary right] invests him [the owner] almost for ever with the status of a member of the hereditary families, almost of a landed aristocracy, which looks down upon 'newcomers' who have come later and had to acquire land by purchase or lease. Indeed the term *restenya*, resti-owner, is hardly ever used without this secondary meaning.[6]

During his government in the Marab Mellāsh, Alulā managed to make a few inroads into the *rest* system, to enable newcomers to join the feudal upper-class. The first was the formulation of the "Forty years' right" according to which a squatter who actually cultivated deserted *rest* land could claim legal ownership.[7] The second was an edict which laid down that every tribute-paying owner of land, by whatever title, would retain his holdings by the right of *rest*. This famous edict, issued in 1888, according to Nadel[8] started with the words: "Man is free; land is tributary." It may however, be assumed that this was Alulā's actual policy even before the last year of his administration there.[9]

Another loophole was to give the right of inheritance to local women,[10] many of whom probably married Tigrean newcomers and other outsiders. Alulā also reportedly exploited Hamāsēn's characteristic collective village ownership of land.[11] He confiscated one-quarter of the land of such villages for the use and ownership of his Tigrean soldiers, forcing the others to compensate those deprived of their property.[12] Notwithstanding these few, limited successes, Alulā knew that he could not really fight or even join the well-established agrarian élite of the Marab Mellāsh. He was quickly forced to rely upon the proceeds of urban commerce, which, ironically enough, derived from other outsiders, Muslim traders and Tigrean soldiers.

Immediately after his arrival in Hamāsēn in 1879, Alulā had renewed commerce with Massawa,[13] hitherto adversely affected by the Egyptian campaign and the struggle with *Rās* Walda-Mikā'ēl.[14] From that moment, Alulā did his best to secure the trade route to the coast in spite of the international problems involved. His main interest was the highly profitable arms trade, for which the *rās* was in constant commercial relations with various Greek traders in Massawa. The arms trade was but a part of the commercial life stimulated by Alulā, who was accordingly anxious to have the port of Massawa protected and managed by the British. This anxiety spurred him to work hard for the Hewett treaty: "Ras Alula the Abyssinian generalissimo . . . is well disposed towards Great Britain and anxious to arrive at a peaceful solution of the present lock-up of trade: a properly accredited British commissioner could alone do this."[15]

On the Massawa-Tigre caravan route, the tiny little village of Asmara, described as numbering 150 inhabitants in 1830,[16] was chosen by Alulā as his commercial headquarters. In 1880 (or even before), Alulā appointed a *naggādrās* there to organise the caravans.[17] At the beginning of 1881, Rohlfs reckoned the population of Asmara as numbering a "few hundred."[18] In early 1884 Wylde estimated "three hundred houses":

> The town of Asmara is not laid out in streets, nor is there any regularity about it; it has been built haphazard on two low hills or mounds above the ordinary plateau level, and now consists of perhaps three hundred houses at most, the only clearing in it being near the church, towards which most of the lanes that represent streets run out.[19]

Wylde colorfully described Asmara's weekly markets then developing, and his companion, the correspondent of *The Daily News*, guessed at a population of two thousand.[20]

The first *naggādrās* of Asmara in Alulā's time was a Muslim from Shoate

Ansabā, named Berhānu Hagos.[21] *Rās* Alulā was undoubtedly a devoted Christian,[22] and his dedication to fighting the Mahdist threat also stemmed from a sincere religiosity. While he shared Yohannes's concern about external Muslim threats, his attitude towards Ethiopian Muslims was quite different.[23] In 1880 Yohannes issued an *awādj* ordering all the Muslims in Ethiopia to be baptised or to leave the country, an edict which Alulā ignored. Being much concerned with commercial interests, he actually encouraged Muslims, among them many refugees from areas south of the Marab, to settle in Asmara and to become active there as traders. For the same reason, he also opened the gates of Gindā to them,[24] and ultimately even persuaded Yohannes to rescind the edict forbidding Muslims to own land and property in the Marab Mellāsh.[25] He publicly demonstrated his respect for Islam[26] and was even considered by some of his co-religionists as an "enemy of the Christians,"[27] although Wylde concluded that Alulā was merely a non-fanatic.[28] Muslims, therefore, supported the *rās*, but his main strength derived from his soldiery and their families.

In the Marab Mellāsh these soldiers found a new way-of-life and lost their interest in returning to Tigre. Alulā had encouraged the settlement of his immigrant soldiers, mostly the one to two thousand devoted veterans whom he had commanded since his days as an unknown *shālaqā*. They lived in the Marab Mellāsh, and no longer wanted to return to Tigre, where they had no property. Their needs were met through land alienation and rapid integration into the Hamāsēn peasantry.

Meanwhile, however, Alulā's need for a professional standing army[29] was met by the establishment of a salaried soldiery. As the maintenance of such a paid force depended on the existence of an economic centre, the removal of Alulā's military headquarters from Addi-Taklay to his commercial base at Asmara was inevitable. There, in the new capital, Alulā had a standing force, the nucleus of his armed forces. The salaried soldiers, probably no more than a thousand, were not well paid: their annual salary was five thalers, plus thirty-two litres of *ṭēf* a month.[30] As this central army needed the support of a central economy, its establishment may be regarded as an innovation,[31] and given the hitherto traditional nature of agricultural Tigre, Asmara was also something new in Tigrean history.

People from all over Hamāsēn were mobilised to construct the government headquarters.[32] On a commanding hill, three *tukul*-shaped stone houses,[33] larger than those seen before in Hamāsēn, were constructed. Surrounded by a wall, they resembled, and actually were, a fortified military camp[34] permanently capable of housing some 2,000 troops,[35] and temporarily even 10,000.[36]

The biggest of the three buildings was the *addārāsh* or banquet-hall, some 18 metres in diameter, where the élite of the new régime used to assemble for consultation and frequent war councils. For their own reasons, Italian writers and observers used to refer to Alulā and his collaborators as the representatives of a foreign, occupying power. And, indeed, following the arrest of *Rās* Walda-

Mikā'ēl and the other important members of the Ṣa'zegā house and the weakening position of other local dignitaries,[37] the leading figures of the Hamāsēn élite had no chance of returning to their previous status. Their removal from political power represented a new phenomenon of foreign domination of the Marab Mellāsh.[38]

In the new centralised régime, Alulā's main functionaries were almost exclusively Tigrean: *Belāttā* Gabru "Abbā chaqun," his deputy, a native of Samrē from Tambēn,[39] who was killed in Kūfīt some six to eight months after the construction of the new *Tukuls* in Asmara; *Ledj* Fantā Wudā'ēl from Sar'ē Adwā; *Shālaqā* Ar'āyā from Zuqli,[40] Alulā's birthplace, who governed the strategically vital region of Gindā; *Dadjāzmāch* Engdā "Abbā Shawul" in charge of the munition stores in Asmara; *Bāshā* Tadlā Fanjā, Alulā's nephew,[41] and *Dadjāzmāch* Hāyla-Sellāssē, his son-in-law.[42] They were all from Tambēn, and, like Alulā, they originated from the lower rungs of the Tigrean social ladder.

Except for *Ledj* Fantā's forebearers, people in Tambēn could not remember the names of the parents of Alulā's lieutenants, nor were such details recorded by contemporary writers. As a matter of fact, the importance of these men derived exclusively from their functions as Alulā's subordinates.[43] Their establishment in Asmara was undoubtedly the culmination of a successful immigration. They probably considered themselves the new local élite of Hamāsēn rather than foreign conquerors. In Tigre itself they had left behind nothing of importance, and, when later, for reasons which will be described below, they had to return there, they actually disappeared from the political scene.

While the functions of the Hamāsēn élite were completely assumed by the Tigreans, local functionaries, the *shum addis* and *shum gultis*,[44] continued their offices. The *shum gultis* were recognised by the imperial government (i.e. Alulā) as the heads of the local families. The *shum addis*, or the *cheqqā shums*, were village administrators, a function traditionally kept for *resti* holders, and were subordinated to the mostly hereditary *meslanēs*, or district officers.[45]

The members of this local administrative élite were strictly and directly controlled by Asmara. They not only had to report there from time to time, but they were also checked and inspected by a network of Alulā's *farasanyas* or "horsemen." They served also as tax collectors, deputy governors and as a rapid means of communication to and from the capital.[46] Their functions were not new in the administrative structure of the area, but Alulā's use of Tigrean outsiders was presumably an innovation.

Asmara's permanency spurred a further centralisation of the economic and commercial life of Alulā's province. According to Perini, in pre-Alulā times Ṣa'zega, Godofelasi and Edāgā Hamus were the main markets in the Marab Mellāsh, and trade was free of tax all over the country. Alulā, however, closed all the markets and opened a big one in Asmara, at which a *shum edāgā*, the chief of the market, "who was, naturally, a Tigrean," was authorised to tax commerce there.⁴⁷ Though Perini doubtlessly exaggerates the situation, as local markets could not be suppressed, the bulk of the long-distance trade was diverted to Asmara.

So was much new revenue; Alulā's tax schedule was quite high. According to the evidence of an old Ethiopian trader,⁴⁸ merchants had to pay the relatively enormous sum of about two thalers per mule load, while a farmer, an owner of two oxen, was charged about ten thalers per annum, plus two-fifths of his production.⁴⁹ The *rās*'s provinces paid a substantial revenue to the Ethiopian treasury: during Alulā's administration (1879-1889), Hamāsēn provided taxes of 125,000 thalers,⁵⁰ while in the early seventies the annual return had been around 5,000 thalers.⁵¹ Under Alulā, Akalla-Guzāy, which lay outside the main trade route, paid 7,900 per annum, compared with 5,000 in previous years,⁵² and during the period up to 1889, the tribes of the Ḥabbāb, Bogos, Maria and Banū 'Āmir paid a total of around 7,750 thalers per annum.⁵³

By centralizing the economy, Alulā was able to double the revenue paid to the imperial treasury and at the same time to maintain local administration and support the armed forces needed for facing the continuous threat to his province and Ethiopia. Though this was by no means revolutionary, Alulā made significant social and economic changes in the future Eritrea.

It was suggested, mostly by Italians, that Alulā's central government was so oppressive and untraditional, that it alienated the local peoples and thereby helped a foreign power gain control over the area.⁵⁴ This charge seems to be only partly true. In fact, it looks as if the common people of Hamāsēn, those who had no share in the government during the previous, semi-independent period, accepted the new régime and its flourishing commerce and better security.⁵⁵ Moreover, Alulā established governors in Hamāsēn, Sarāyē, Akalla-Guzāy and Bogos and concentrated his government efforts here.

Alulā's government in the Marab Mellāsh lasted only four years after the establishment of Asmara. The period is recalled by the Christian population of the Eritrean highlands as a period of justice: "Justice like that of Lālibalā; legislation like that of Alulā,"⁵⁶ two lines which are heard nowadays in Eritrea. It may also be concluded that during 1885-1889, when Alulā had to struggle for the future of Ethiopian government over Eritrea, the majority of the Christians there supported him. The Muslim tribal zones later contained in the future Eritrea, Assāwurta, Ḥabbāb, Banū 'Āmir etc., during Alulā's time, were actually part of the raiding zone. They were not directly governed by Asmara and naturally resisted any central government, especially Alulā's which only taxed and raided them. It was mainly the peripheral Muslim tribes which later supported the Italians during the struggle to take the Marab Mellāsh from Alulā.

NOTES

1 *Annales de la Congregation de la Mission* 1885, p. 250. Paillard's letter of 25.12.84: Kolmodin, No. 271.
2 Kolmodin, No. 271.
3 The Eritrean agrarian structure was analysed in: S.F. Nadel, "Land Tenure on the Eritrean plateau", *Africa*, vol. XVI, 1946, pp. 1-21, 99-109.
4 A. Pollera, *Il Regime della proprieta terriera in Etiopia e nella Colonia Eritrea*, Rome 1913, p. 90.
5 *Ibid.*
6 Nadel, "Land Tenure," pp. 7-9.
7 Nadel, pp. 17, 18.
8 Nadel, p. 11.
9 See also Pollera, *Il Regime della proprieta*, p. 90.
10 Conti Rossini, *Principi*, p. 314.
11 Nadel, "Land Tenure," pp. 11, 12.
12 A. Pollera, *L'Abissinia di ieri*, Asmara 1940, pp. 60, 61.
13 FO 407/11, Gordon to Consul in Jedda, 12.9.79.
14 Wylde, *'83*, I, p. 216; Pankhurst, *Economic History*, p. 573.
15 FO 406/1, Hewett to Admiralty, 7-10. Jan. 1884.
16 Pankhurst, *Economic*, p. 693. Wylde's suggestion (*'83*, I, p. 216) that before the war with Egypt the population of Asmara was "some 5,000 people" seems to be a figment of his imagination. We have no estimates for the period of 1830-1880. In an English map of Ethiopia, probably drawn for or after the 1868 campaign (see WO 33/55 Eritrea Report), Asmara appears as a little village, smaller than Ṣa'zega or Aylēt. In 1873 the town was described as "almost deserted"; see Pankhurst, p. 573.
17 Puglisi, *Chi e?* p. 44.
18 Pankhurst, *Economic*, p. 693.
19 Wylde, *'83*, I, p. 222.
20 "A Journey to the Court of King John", *The Daily News*, 16.5.84.
21 Puglisi, *Chi e?* p. 44. A.B. Wylde, "An Unofficial Mission to Abyssinia", *The Manchester Guardian*, 13.5.97; also *'83*, I, p. 216.
22 See P. De Lauribar, *Douze ans en Abyssinie*, Paris 1898, p. 605.
23 See such a distinction in Puglisi, p. 44.
24 A.S.MAI, 3/2-17, Genè to MAE, 22.1.87.
25 Perini, p. 349.
26 F. Martini, *Nell'Africa Italiana*, Milano 1891, p. 109.
27 E. Littmann, Princeton publications, Vol. II, p. 171.
28 Wylde, *Modern*, p. 149.
29 The soldiers had to go back to their villages in the rainy season. (In the late 1880s many of them were apparently too old to fight).
30 F. Fasolo, *L'Abissinia e le colonie*, pp. 206, 207.
31 Troops who were mobilised in the Marab Mellash were rewarded by exemption from tax payment, see Genè to Robilant, 8.10.86; *Giglio, Etiopia e Mar Rosso*, V, No. 257, p. 359. The standing, salaried army of Yohannes is probably to be identified with what Portal described as the emperor's 5,000 guards. See Portal, *My Mission*, p. 257.

32 Perini, p. 387.
33 "Tucul di Ras Alula", Puglisi, p. 14.
34 Walatta-Berhān; Fosolo, p. 207.
35 Perino, *Vita e gesta*, p. 21.
36 The interpreter Ailu to Zerboni, 17.9.85; Allegato 2 in Zerboni to Depretis, 23.4.85; Giglio, *Etiopia e Mar Rosso*, V, No. 54, p. 60.
37 For examples, see Puglisi, *Chi e*? p. 147; Perini, pp. 72, 245, 391.
38 For background, see among others: G. Bonacci, *Il Mareb Melasc*, Rome 1905; Longrigg, *Eritrea*; "Eritrea", *Enc. Brit.*, 11th Ed.; Kolmodin, *Traditions*.
39 Interview, *Kagnāzmāch* Abrehā Fantā, Asmarā, March 1972.
40 Abrehā Fantā.
41 Interview, Ato Yekunuamlāk Ar'āyā, Maqalē, Feb. 1972.
42 See below, p. 130-132.
43 The following passage from the Mannawē Ms may be interpreted as reflecting not only the personal devotion of these followers to Alulā but also their awareness of the fact that his death would automatically end their own careers: "The powerful chiefs of his army, namely *Blatta* Gabru, *Shalaka* Araya, *Lejj* Fanta, *Basha* Talla Waddi, *Basha* Fanja, *Basha* Basta Abba Ga'i, *Basha* Asro Balla, came to him when they heard that he had risen up for battle. They said to him, 'it is not good that you go to the battle, but we ourselves will go, and we will do battle while you help us [praying?] with your great power.'"
44 See Perini, *Di qua*, p. 69.
45 Nadel, "Land Tenure".
46 Kolmodin, *Traditions*, No. 269; Nadel, "Land Tenure".
47 Perini, *Di qua*, p. 386.
48 Int. Kan. Abrehā Fanta. Asmara, March 1972.
49 *DN*, 4.6.84.
50 Corazzini, in *La Tribuna*, 20.6.90.
51 Pankhurst, *Economic History*, p. 536.
52 F. Martini, *Diario*, III, p. 380.
53 A.S.MAI, Eritrea 109, Report by Al-Husayn Hamīd, 3.1.89.
54 Perini, s.t. pp. 38, 192, 193; V. Mantegazza, *Gl'Italiani in Africa*, Firenze 1896, pp. 242, 245.
55 See description in FO 403/88, "Report by Mr. Bearclerk on the commerce of Massowah," in Lumley to Iddesleigh, 13.10.86. For a general description of commerce in Eritrea, see Wylde in *The Manchester Guardian*, 29.6.97.
56 Māmo Wudnah, *Ya'ertrā tārik*, Asmara 1962, EC, p. 59. See examples in A. Sapelli, *Memorie d'Africa (1883-1906)*, Bologna 1935, p. 53 (unlike Perini, *Di Qua*, p. 373); H. Smith, *Through Abyssinia*, p. 111; Longrigg, *Eritrea*, p. 112.

9

1885-1886: The Italians in Massawa: From a European Neighbour to a Local Rival

'The Faranje and Qunqun are the same.
Qunqun is the smallest of insects but it eats
up a large tree, causes it to dry up and fall down.'[1]

A. *The pre-Kūfīt Period: Increasing Italian Involvement and First Signs of a Rupture with Alulā*

When *Rās* Alulā left Asmara in September 1885 to face the Mahdist threat in Kūfīt, he was already in a situation of a "cold war" with the Italians on the coast. Even such inactive belligerancy was by no means a desirable state of affairs for the newcomers. In fact, the original Italian idea was to create friendly relations with the neighboring *rās*:

> ... Alula is the most serious the most influential and the strongest personality in today's Abyssinia. The word of Alula is heard with enthusiasm and confidence by the king ... one can say that it is very easy to get anything from the Negus of Abyssinia once Ras Alula is interested in it.[2]
>
> Ras Alula is the Ethiopian chief with whom we shall be in contact most frequently and directly as his province is on the border. We must neglect nothing in order to have him as a friend.[3]

But their slow advance out of Massawa, which they began in April 1885, the occupation of places evacuated by the Egyptians, and their friendly relations with "Ethiopian" tribes eliminated the chance "to have Alulā as a friend." Moreover Alulā suspected the Italians of supporting Dabbab who was in close contact with the *nā'ib* of Italian-held Harkīkū.[4] When Dabbab continued raiding Ethiopian caravans, and Alulā retaliated in late July 1885 by plundering Dabbab's Assāwurta supporters, Col. Saletta wrote to the *rās* demanding an explanation and threatening to stop arms deliveries to Asmara.[5] Astonished by such an insolent demand, Alulā did not even reply "As if he wanted to say that it was not our business."[6]

On 24th June 1885, Saletta secretly sent Italian troops to occupy Sahāṭi, but it was only on 12 August 1885, shortly after Sahāṭi's Egyptian garrison had finally departed, that Alulā reacted. He demanded that Marcopoli Bey, then staying in his camp, ask his superiors to order its abandonment.[7] When Saletta wrote to Alulā regarding Sahāṭi and reported his intention to construct a few huts to protect his troops during the coming rainy season, Alulā categorically replied:

> You have told me that you had come to plant your huts in Saati. This can not be. Not only the huts but also the people who are at Saati cannot stay there. The land belongs to the Negus . . . Therefore, evacuate Saati.[8]

Then the Italians learned that Alulā had received Yohannes's instructions "to attack Saati if the Italians would construct there houses, and not to do so if they remain in Zariba."[9] Rome decided to ignore Alulā's demand and the emperor's reported threat, but to calm the *rās* and his master.[10] On 7 September 1885 Saletta therefore wrote to Alulā notifying him of Italian plans of an official mission to the emperor to sign a treaty between Ethiopia and Italy.[11] Threatened by the Mahdists in Kūfīt, Alulā was relieved to receive this sign of at least temporary peace along his eastern front. "Your welcome letter has reached me," he replied to Saletta, "I shall forward it direct to the Negus."[12] And on the next day he started his march to fight 'Uthmān Diqna in Kūfīt.

B. *Victorious Alulā and the Italian Question*

Yohannes originally seems to have had access to knowledge of the developments in the Massawa arena only through Alulā himself. Yet when the relations between his vassal and the Italians began to deteriorate, Yohannes, still desirous for an amicable settlement with Rome,[13] carefully supervised his confident general, to restrain him from careless activities.

In early July 1885 Alulā had initiated an anti-Catholic campaign in Akalla-Guzāy, where, at the head of a small expedition, he maltreated some missionaries,[14] possibly as a preventive measure against possible Italian influence there.[15] If Coulbeaux is to be believed, the emperor sent to Alulā the following angry words:

> Don't you know that the French and the Italians are of the same faith? If you indulge in this sort of activity I shall send someone else to take your place. My throne is established only on prayer and cautious diplomacy, not on the force of my arms.[16]

This admonition, together with Yohannes' instructions not to attack Sahāṭi, "if . . [the Italians] remain in the Zariba," and encouragement of Alulā to march on Kassala, suggests that the emperor was worried about the *rās*'s policy vis-à-vis the

Italians. But this caution seems to have changed after Alulā's return from Kūfīt.

Alulā's victory over the Sudanese on 23 September 1885 was undoubtedly a great relief for Yohannes, who must have been extremely worried about possible Mahdist influence on the rebellious Muslim Oromo (Gāllā) tribes, currently giving his son so much trouble.[17] The emperor had to hurry to Oromo country, and before leaving he appointed the victorious Alulā over the north of his empire. Consul Soumagne reported:

> Alula, is 'premier ministre' of the Emperor and his powers have been extended by the sudden diversion of Yohannes to the south . . . at Yohannes's orders all the other Commanders remaining in Tigre have joined forces with Alula at Asmara under his command. At the time that I arrived [Feb. 86] Dadjazmach Tedla [Ayba], governor of Meqelle, Dadj. Hagos, governor of Adwa, and Balambaras Debab, in charge of Tambien, were in Alula's camp.[18]

Alulā's new position represented Yohannes's recognition of his political judgment, as might be illustrated by the evidence of *Mamher* Walda-Samāyāt, who visited Massawa in May 1886 en route to Jerusalem. The priest told General Genè that Yohannes had told him:

> You want a letter to the Italian general? Some people tell me that the Italians came to invade my country, others say they are my friends. I give you a letter to Ras Alula, as he is there near them he is better than me in this business.[19]

But in spite of his strong position, the *rās* did not have authority to take any military initiative against the Italians.[20] With the imperial army involved in the Oromo campaign, with Alulā's forces still exhausted from the Kūfīt massacre, and with the promised Italian diplomatic mission creating the illusion of an imminent understanding, the possibility of hostilities diminished for a while.

C. *September-October 1885: Italian Involvement in Alulā's Affairs*

Alulā's victory in Kūfīt only partly impeded the Mahdist movement in Eritrea's western marches, but it destroyed 'Uthmān Diqna's aspirations in the coastal zone. Ironically it was mainly the Italians who were to profit from the resulting power vacuum. In late September 1885 *Bālambārās* Keflē Iyāsus, who, before Kūfīt, was known to be siding with 'Uthmān Diqna, contacted Colonel Saletti in Massawa. Well received, he persuaded *Kantibā* Ḥamīd and other chiefs of the Ḥabbāb to strengthen their relations with the Italian authorities.[21] The *kantibā* had not participated in Kūfīt and was consequently ordered by Alulā to report to Asmara; he was therefore prepared to try an Italian ploy. On 7 October 1885, Ḥamīd was ceremoniously received by Saletta in Massawa and, two days later, signed a document putting his tribes under Italian protection.[22] This treaty, which was also signed by Ḥamīd's brother and former pro-Mahdist rival Shaykh Ḥassan Ḥaddād,[23] was clearly against Alulā's interests and claims.

Alulā's reaction was bitter and determined. On the same day, 7 October 1885, when the Ḥabbāb tribesmen entered Massawa, an Italian medical mission composed of six members left the town heading toward Asmara to help wounded Ethiopian soldiers returned from Kūfīt. The mission had been sent "to obtain the Ras' friendship on the eve of the [promised] mission"[24] but obviously was destined to fail. Hearing the news of the Ḥabbāb-Italian treaty, Alulā expelled the medical team from Asmara without even giving its members provisions for the road.[25] The group reached Massawa on 18 October 1885, carrying Alulā's letter demanding the extradition of *Kantibā* Ḥamīd.[26] Saletta's reply of 28 October 1885 claimed that he thought Ḥamīd was Alulā's friend. The Italian added that, upon hearing Alulā's complaints, he had stopped selling food to the Ḥabbāb and concluded, "I believe I proved to you my friendship to Ethiopia which is Christian like Italy."[27]

D. *November-December 1885: Italian Attempt to Appease Alulā and Yohannes*

Notwithstanding Alulā's insulting attitude to the medical mission, the Italians attempted a policy of appeasement.[28] Saletta was instructed by Count Carl Robilant, the new prime minister, to order the Italian troops at Saḥāti to evacuate the place and to replace them with irregulars.[29] Robilant favored a more moderate approach to the Ethiopian question and sought to restrain the energetic Italian commanders in Massawa. Colonel Saletta was subsequently replaced by Major-General Carlo Genè,[30] who immediately opened a friendly correspondence with Alulā. He underlined his good intentions by facilitating the passage of a new consignment of arms.[31] On 2nd December 1885 the Italians finally assumed the administration of the port of Massawa and, probably due to Robilant's policy, the transition turned out to be a non-event from the Ethiopian point of view. The British Captain Harrison Smith reported from Massawa on 19 February 1886, that "The relations between the Italians and the Abyssinians seem to have changed much for the better of late."[32]

E. *December 1885-January 1886: Alulā's Attempt to Outmanoeuvre the Italians through a French Treaty*

It was again the French, as in 1884, who were invited to intervene before a treaty was to be negotiated with another European power. On 25 November 1885 the vice-consul at Massawa, Soumagne, left for Asmara to meet *Rās* Alulā. In his report[33] the Frenchman wrote that the *rās* had actually initiated the meeting. Disillusioned with the British and already suspicious of the Italians, Alulā turned to the only other possible diplomatic option.

Confident in his new position as chief of Ethiopia's northern border, Alulā probably thought that, as in 1884, he could conduct high policy and make the emperor sign the papers. As Soumagne noted:

> He alone could not do so [sign the Treaty] but he assured me that Yohannes would accept our work and the *pourparlers* were begun and concluded rapidly.[34]

Alulā's idea was to let the French have the small port of Zulā from where—as a European neighbour should do—they would supply Ethiopia with firearms and act on the emperor's behalf if the empire's integrity were threatened by the Italians. Alulā was interested in a French presence at Zulā, to help him subdue the Assāwurta and catch Dabbab.[35]

At Alulā's prompting, in order, as he put it, "to settle this treaty in calm,"[36] Soumagne wrote to Yohannes from Asmara suggesting that:

> Till such time as I can come to see you we should seal a treaty as events at Massawa go quickly and the enemy's [the Italian's] encroachment may outdistance us if we wait.[37]

In late December 1885, Yohannes left Oromo country and made his way to Ashangē to meet the Frenchman but was forced by events in the south to return there.[38] He therefore wrote to Alulā instructing him to conclude the matter with Soumagne.[39]

The vice-consul returned to Asmara on 3 February 1886, and on the next day he agreed verbally to a draft treaty which merely confirmed his nomination of 1884 as a *wakīl* in Massawa.[40]

> In the final evidence Alula invited all the chiefs in Asmara . . . to attend so that they might witness his success as a diplomat! . . . He told me: Yes, telegraph to your government that I have done all this by the Emperor's orders and that 'everything is settled definitely'.[41]

In fact, the idea of Soumagne and Alulā to invite the French to Zulā was not that straightforward, as the place was actually (though still not officially) under Italian control. It seems, however, that both men left the question to be decided by future events. Even less realistic was Alulā's attempt to establish diplomatic relations with Russia through the adventurer Nikolai Ashinov who visited during the last three weeks of 1885. The Russian falsely claimed to represent the tsar and promised to purchase arms for the *rās* in Europe. In spite of Alulā's efforts, Yohannes refused to meet the adventurer, and nothing resulted from that episode.[42]

F. December 1885-March 1886: Last Attempt to Reach Understanding Between Italy and Ethiopia

While *Rās* Alulā was vainly trying to make a successful diplomatic move before the arrival of the promised Italian mission, Rome decided not to rely on the *rās* as a channel to the emperor. On 17 November 1885 Robilant wrote to Genè that because of Alulā's behaviour with the medical group no mission would leave for Ethiopia until its acceptance was signalled by Yohannes.[43] But the emperor never replied positively, since he believed that the Italians:

> are not people of good faith they are intriguers. . . . The Italians have not come here because they lack pastures and fat in their own country, but they come from ambition to better themselves, because there are many of them and they are not rich. With the help of God they will depart again, humiliated and disgraced in the eyes of the world.[44]

In late January 1886 the head of the planned mission, General Giorgio Pozzolini, arrived at Massawa carrying detailed instructions from the foreign minister. The mission's aim was "to rival the Hewett Treaty in its entirety, but at the same time give it a new twist for their [the Italians'] benefit."[45] Ethiopian sovereignty over Bogos was to be recognised, with the exception of the tribes to the north of Massawa—Mansa Ḥabbāb and others—where the Italians wanted to retain "complete liberty of action." Concerning Sahāṭi, Pozzolini was permitted to leave it to the Ethiopians, if really desired by them, but Italian protection over the coast from Massawa to Assab was to be recognised. Dabbab was to be denied Italian help but also was not to be extradited to the Ethiopians.[46]

With these objectives, the Italians were right to try to avoid Alulā as a negotiator. Pozzolini, in Massawa from late January 1886, was well aware of the fact that the *rās* never recognised Italian occupation outside Massawa,[47] and Alulā's subsequent activities merely emphasised this fact. In early January 1886 Alulā ordered the *Nā'ib* of Harkīkū, Dabbab's relative, to report to Asmara, and on 15 January he notified Genè of his action.[48] The Italian hurried to exploit the chance to declare indirect Italian protection over the Assāwurta. He wrote to Alulā:

> The subjects are free to go to you because I do not stop people or merchandise to come from or go to the kingdom of Abyssinia, for this is the will of my king because of his friendship with Emperor Giovanni.[49]

Alulā's reaction was to raid the Zulā plain in late January, killing ten Assāwurta, but Dabbab managed to escape.[50]

In mid-December 1885 Alulā wrote to Genè about the Ḥabbāb, again warning him not to let them purchase food in Massawa and demanding the extradition of *Kantibā* Ḥamīd. Genè's reply was evasive,[51] and on 16 February 1886, Alulā raided the Ḥabbāb as "a protest against the Italian activities there." Leading his force in a deep penetrating raid, the *rās* reportedly killed 200-400 people and took a lot of cattle.[52]

Alulā's attitude derived not only from Italian territorial claims, but also from their own attitude to him. Even though he had received friendly letters from Saletta, Genè and Pozzolini, Italian newspapers were derisory when referring to Alulā, to Yohannes or to the Ethiopians. Extracts were translated and sent, probably by French agents or Greek merchants, to Alulā in Asmara.[53] The *Popolo Romano* of 16 March 1886 stated: "The semi-barbarous sovereigns of Central Africa cannot be reckoned upon as though they were civilised European monarchs." Alulā sent such "gems" on to the emperor, who extracted some of them for quotation to Menilek.

Alulā wrote to Yohannes on 9 February 1886, warning that the Italian envoy "seeks only to trick you."[54] On 23 January 1886 General Pozzolini, the head of the mission, had arrived at Massawa, and quickly sent Dr. Nerazzini[55] to Alulā, to prepare the ground for the mission and ensure the emperor's acceptance. Reaching Asmara on a second visit on 2 March 1886, Nerazzini was told by *Rās* Alulā:

"You Italians came to Massawa, according to your declarations, in order to facilitate the commerce with Abyssinia, with amicable intentions towards our country and not in the spirit of conquest . . . You, our friends, have taken not only Massawa but also other places, and now, for the sake of your friendship I demand that you withdraw the troops [from there]."

Though Alulā and his lieutenant, *Shālaqā* Ar'āyā, stressed that the mission was welcome to negotiate,[56] it must have been quite clear to both parties that it was impossible to come to terms without one of them giving up territories and prestige. On 16 February 1886 Antonelli's report quoting Yohannes's letter to Menilek reached the Italian Foreign Ministry.[57] Its contents, together with the fact that the emperor was camping at Boru Mēdā, some fifty days' march from Massawa,[58] brought about the final Italian decision to abandon the mission.[59]

* * *

The cancellation ended a period in which diplomatic methods only helped to delay the inevitable hostilities. Rome's appeasement, which was supposed to culminate in the mission, could never succeed as it was accompanied by expansion over areas and involvement in affairs regarded by the Ethiopians as exclusively theirs. For *Rās* Alulā, the man in charge of the frontier's problems, the issue was not merely a question of national prestige, or even of national security, but of direct political competition.

When, in 1884, the *rās* was working enthusiastically to bring the British to Massawa, he probably viewed all Europeans in the same way as he saw the Greek merchants of Massawa who came and went, traded and profited. Those representatives of a higher technology imported arms and could work wonders with watches and geological apparatus. European governments could run and manage Massawa and continue it as a source of manufactured items. They had of course their own economic interests, but their real focus was elsewhere. They never participated in the local game consisting of Christian-Muslim, tribal-governmental, Tigrean-Eritrean and other rivalries. Even in the Ethiopian-Mahdist or Ethiopian-Egyptian conflicts Europeans were only indirectly involved. The British under Napier, or under Hewett, arrived and left leaving arms and illusions. But when Europeans, such as the missionaries, came to stay, and started to participate in politics, they began to be regarded as part of the local scene and could no longer be seen as privileged Europeans. The slow Italian penetration into Ethiopia was not for Alulā just a question of losing territories. In July 1896, he told the Italian officer Mulazzani, "With you I have made a great problem over a small piece of land, arid, sandy and of no value."[60]

It was a question of outsiders trying to participate in what the Ethiopians regarded as their own game. Alulā had hoped the Italians would limit themselves to Massawa and facilitate trade (as he had thought that the British would do, or planned that the French would do at Zulā); but, once they started interfering in internal politics, they had to be countered. Now they were no longer purely local political enemies, but also religious enemies. A contemporary chronicle of Yohannes refers to the Italians in the following words:

> After this many powerful and conceited pagans came from Jerusalem intending to exterminate the religion of our Lord Jesus Christ, to construct their temples and destroy our churches."[61]

Thus, the Italians were sometimes regarded as Muslims,[62] even Dervishes.[63] A harsh exposure to the merciless rules of the local game.

NOTES

1 Pētros Giyorgis to *Rās* Alulā, Massawa, 18.1.87, as quoted in Garimā Tāffērē, *Yemakarā dawal*, Asmara, 1963, E.C., p. 8.
2 A.S.MAI, 36/3-23, Ferrari's report, 14.9.85.
3 LV, XVII, Maissa to MAE, 20.3.85.
4 FO 78/3808, Marcopoli to Chermside, 26.8.85.
5 A.S.MAI 2/2-13, Saletta to Alula, 28.7.85, 15.8.85.
6 A.S.MAI 2/2-13, Saletta to MAE, 22.8.85.
7 See above, p. 66.
8 *LV*, XVII, Zerboni to MAE, 1.9.85; *Storia Militare*, p. 94.
9 A.S.MAI, 41/1-2, Zerboni to MAE, 3.9.85.
10 *LV*, XVII, MAE to Zerboni, 2.9.85.
11 Zerboni to Depretis, 8.9.85; *Giglio, Etiopia e Mar Rosso*, V, No. 39, pp. 32-33.

12 Alula to Saletta (misdated 4.9.85, must be 13.9.85, see Giglio, V, p. 61) in Zerboni to Depretis, 23.9.85; *ibid.*, No. 54, p. 57.
13 Consult: Marcus, *The Life and Times*, p. 84.
14 *Annales de la Congregation de la Mission*, 1886, p. 261.
15 And probably also in retaliation for the missionaries' role in diverting the arms trade in late 1884. See above, p. 50.
16 MAE(F) M. et. D. 105, Aby. IV, Coulbeaux to Soumagne, 7.8.85.
17 FO 403/87, Smith to Baring, 12.3.86. L'Informatore Ghermai Arcu to Genè, 21.1.86 in Genè to Robilant, 21.1.86. Giglio, *Etiopia e Mar Rosso*, V, No. 165, p. 205. See also H. Marcus, *The Life and Times*, p. 84.
18 MAE, Mas. 5, Soumagne to MAE, 26.2.86.
19 A.S.MAI, 2/2-13, Genè to MAE, 21.5.86.
20 L'Informatore Ghermai Arcu to Genè, 21.1.86, in Genè to Robilant, 21.1.86; Giglio, *Etiopia e Mar Rosso*, V, No. 165, p. 205. Antonelli to MAE, 11.5.86, LV, XV, p. 228.
21 Puglisi, *Chi e?* pp. 161, 174.
22 L. Chiala, *La Spedizione di Massaua*, Torino 1888.
23 Zerboni to Robilant, 9.10.85; Giglio, *Etiopia e Mar Rosso*, V, No. 72, pp. 80, 81.
24 A.S.MAI 2/2-13, Saletta to MAE, 8.10.85.
25 FO 408/125, Tornielli to Salisbury, 30.4.90. A.S.MAI 2/2-13, Zerboni to MAE, 23.10.85.
26 A.S.MAI 4/3-12, Alula to Saletta, 15.10.85.
27 A.S.MAI 4/3-12, Saletta to Alulā, 28.10.85.
28 A.S.MAI 2/2-13, MAE to Saletta, 20.10,85, Robilant to Genè, 6.11.85; Giglio, *Etiopia e Mar Rosso*, No. 100, p. 126.
29 Ricotti to Saletta, 21.11.85, in A. Bizoni, *L'Eritrea nel passato e nel presente*, Milano 1897, p. 138. For unfavourable reaction, see FO 78/3811, Cameron to Egerton, 5.11.85.
30 Giglio, *Etiopia e Mar Rosso*, V, p. 383.
31 A.S.MAI 2/2-13, Alulā to Genè, 21.11.85; 17.12.85, Genè to Alulā, 20.12.85.
32 FO 403/87, Smith to Baring 19.2.86.
33 MAE(F), Mass. 4, Soumagne to MAE, 19.2.85.
34 Ibid.
35 MAE(F), Mass. 5, Soumagne to MAE, 27.1.86.
36 MAE(F), Mass. 4, Soumagne to MAE, 19.12.85.
37 Ibid., Soumagne to Yohannes, 9.12.85.
38 Ibid., Alula to Soumagne, 3.1.86, 15.1.86.
39 Ibid., Soumagne to MAE, 26.2.86.
40 See above, p. 44.
41 MAE(F), Mass. 5, Soumagne to MAE, 26.2.86.
42 Le Vicomte de Constantin, "Une Expédition Religieuse en Abyssinie," *La Nouvelle Revue*, 1 and 15 February 1891, pp. 13-17; P.J. Rollins, "Russia's Ethiopian Adventure 1888-1905," Ph.D. thesis, Syracuse University, 1957, p. 43; FO 403/87, Morier to Salisbury, 27.1.86.
43 Giglio, *Etiopia e Mar Rosso*, V, No. 115, p. 140.
44 Yohannes to Menilek in A.S.MAI, 36/3-28, Antonelli to Robilant, 26.11.85. The letter reached Menilek 18.11.85.
45 Zewde, *Yohannes IV*, p. 193.
46 Robilant to Pozzolini, 8.1.86; Allegato 3, Giglio, *Etiopia e Mar Rosso*, V, No. 158,

pp. 189-200.
47 Pozzolini to Robilant, 21.2.86; Giglio, *Etiopia e Mar Rosso*, V, No. 190, p. 228.
48 Genè to Robilant, 21.1.86; Giglio, *Etiopia e Mar Rosso*, V, No. 165, p. 204.
49 Ibid.
50 MAE(F), Mass. 5, Soumagne to MAE, 27.1.86; FO 403/87, Watson to Baring, 6.2.8.
51 A.S.MAI 2/2-13, Alula to Genè; Genè to Alula, 24.12.85.
52 MAE(F), Mass. 5, Soumagne to MAE, 26.2.86; FO 403/87, Smith to Baring, 27.2.86.
53 FO 403/87, Lumley to Salisbury, 12.1.86, 15.1.86.
54 Alulā to Yohannes, 9.2.86, in MAE, Mass. 5, Soumagne to MAE, 26.2.86.
55 Chiala, pp. 310, 311.
56 Nerazzini to Genè, 2.3.86; Giglio, *Etiopia e Mar Rosso*, V, No. 200, p. 241; Pozzolini to Robilant, 14.2.86, No. 184, p. 225.
57 See Giglio, *Etiopia e Mar Rosso*, V, p. 148 (not for the letter itself).
58 F. Crispi, *La prima Guerra d'Africa*, Milano 1914, p. 14.
59 A.S.MAI 2/2-13, Robilant in Camera dei Deputati; Robilant to Genè, 18.3.86; Giglio, *Etiopia e Mar Rosso*, V, p. 248.
60 A.S.MAI 3/17-136, Mulazzani Report, 26.7.86; Conti Rossini, *Italia ed Etiopia*, p. 465.
61 Ge'ez chronicle of Aksum, written by *Abbā Hayla-Māryām*. Translated by Tesfayohannes Fessehaye.
62 C. Conti Rossini, "Canti Popolari Tigrai," *Zeitschrift für Assyriologie*, 153 (1906).
63 Ms. Mannawē.

10

1886-1887: Dogali

A. War With the Italians

After the cancellation of the Pozzolini mission, the Italians first occupied areas in the peninsula of Buri on the eastern coast of the Bay of Zulā. A dissident local shaykh sped the news and himself to Asmara. Alulā interpreted the move as a threat to Agāmē,[1] and he subsequently led a counterforce to Sanāfē where a new fort was being erected.[2]

Back in Asmara on 18 March 1886, Alulā received the British envoy, Harrison Smith, who had been sent to thank him and Yohannes for their help in relieving the Egyptian garrisons. Alulā nonetheless complained:

> When a man comes for friendship and commerce, he keeps in his own place, and does not take places outside, and get nearer to another man's country. Why have the Italians occupied places in Buri and Raguali, which is on the way to my country?[3]

Alulā was also bitter that Dabbab Ar'āyā was still acting freely in the Assāwurta territories, tolerated at least by Italian authorities. The anarchy caused by Dabbab could be used to justify further occupation under the pretext of security. In a long statement, Alulā complained to Smith that the Italians purposely refrained from stopping Dabbab and other outlaws.[4] With the emperor still in the Oromo area, Alulā was not, however, permitted yet to open hostilities, but started fortifying Asmara and awaited further instructions.[5]

B. Yohannes's Policy: Appeal for British Mediation

Informed by *Rās* Alulā about the situation on the frontier, Yohannes subsequently shared his vassal's views about the new neighbours. According to the Greek physician Dr. Parisis, who spent a long period with the emperor, Yohannes even instructed Alulā not to let Pozzolini's mission enter the country.[6] But, upon hearing of Smith's arrival, Yohannes left Oromo country and met the British envoy near Lake Ashangē. On 17 April 1886, after a long discussion Smith was led to believe that:

> it is the object of the Italians to annex territory claimed by Abyssinia, and eventually Abyssinia itself. He [Yohannes] states that they have already done this by the occupation of Arafale, Sahaati, and places in Buri.[7]

While agreeing with Alulā, the emperor still believed that European mediators could restrain the Italians. In contrast, the *rās* coldly received the British envoy and openly demonstrated his distrust.[8] He even stopped aiding those Egyptian troops who were still escaping from the Eastern Sudan via Asmara and Massawa.[9] Yohannes, on the other hand, influenced by the envoy's arguments and Queen Victoria's letter to him,[10] applied for British diplomatic help and told Smith that "he looks to England to protect his interests at Massowah."[11] As Yohannes wrote the Queen:

> ...We had no quarrel before because you told me to be in friendship with the Italians. Now I do not know how to be in friendship with them. Write to me explaining how to do it.[12]

C. May-July 1886: Alulā is in Disgrace with Yohannes

In late April Yohannes left Ashangē for Maqalē where he summoned Alulā,[13] whom he had not seen since February 1885. This time the two men had what was probably their first open argument. Smith reported, "*Rās* Alulā was far more bigoted againt them [the Italians] than the king and I think the feelings of the latter were considerably influenced by Her Majesty's letter."[14] Smith's visit marked the end of the period in which Yohannes considered Alulā as "better than me in that [Italian] business." Since the British had led the emperor to believe he could coexist with the Italians,[15] he was angry with his general. Yohannes sought a diplomatic solution to the border situation, while Alulā seemed to doubt if conciliation was the right step. Alulā stood for an immediate war, and was also uncompromising about minor questions like the Ḥabbāb. He was still under the influence of his victory at Kūfit and surely more confident than his master about a military threat. Yohannes, psychologically still in debt to the British for his throne, was more willing to rely on their asurances regarding the Italians than Alulā, whose recent experiences with European diplomacy undoubtedly caused him to be sceptical.

Alulā stayed with Yohannes in Maqalē during May and June 1886. Information about the *rās*'s disgrace repeatedly reached Massawa,[16] and, in fact, he was deprived again of the government of Akalla-Guzāy.[17] It was even rumoured that Yohannes was about to release old *Rās* Walda-Mikā'ēl from Ambā Salāmā and place Alulā under his command.[18] The Tigrean chiefs headed by *Rās* Hagos, *Dad-*

jāzmāch Tadlā of Ayba and *Badjerond* Lawṭē who, just six months before, had to praise the victorious "Wadi Qubi," now did their best to describe Alulā as irresponsible and uncompromising. Yohannes, though he still had confidence in Alulā, could hardly ignore them. Indeed, spies reported in Massawa that it was only due to the influence of the old and the now non-ambitious *Rās* Ar'āyā Demṣu that Alulā remained in office as governor of Hamāsēn and Sarāyē.[19]

D. August-October 1886: Yohannes Diverts Alulā to the Mahdist Front

The rainy season was imminent, and it was the Mahdists who took the initiative in raiding the Bogos, Banū 'Āmir and other tribes. The emperor, already worried about Sudanese activities elsewhere,[20] reportedly ordered Alulā to prepare an attack on pro-Mahdist tribesmen who were concentrating at Kūfīt.[21] On 9 August 1886 Alulā led his followers[22] to Ḥabbāb for the most effective raid he had ever launched on that tribe: he confiscated about two-thirds of their cattle and camels.[23] From Ḥabbāb he proceeded to the Bogos country in September and clashed with some unimportant pro-Mahdist groups near Karan and the Hallal plateau.[24] Returning to Asmara later that month, he was again summoned to the emperor who was camping between Adwā and Aksum.[25]

The Italians in Massawa were convinced that Alulā's position in the court was deteriorating constantly. According to their informants in Tigre, *Badjerond* Lawṭē, the finance minister of the emperor and ex-governor of Akalla-Guzāy, was continuously trying to convince Yohannes that Alulā was untrustworthy. He was supported by the newly appointed governor of Akalla-Guzāy. The latter (whose name is not mentioned in the informer's report) complained that Alulā, when he was temporarily given back the government of that province, purposely mobilised too many troops, thus exempting their families from paying taxes.[26]

But Yohannes was apparently not seriously considering the removal of Alulā from the future Eritrea. Mahdist pressure on the Ethiopian western frontier was growing, and since the Italians were inactive,[27] Yohannes probably wanted to take the initiative in western Eritrea and send Alulā to occupy Kassala, which he regarded as Ethiopian territory according to the Hewett Treaty.

E. November-December 1886: The March on Kassala. Alulā Loses his Reputation of Invincibility

On 31 October 1886, after three weeks with Yohannes in Dabra-Dāmo, Alulā must have been optimistic when he entered his capital.[28] Yohannes had ordered him to march on Kassala, and Alulā was undoubtedly pleased with the projected move. Under his command was an imperial force of 10,000 troops headed by *Dadjāz-*

mâch Tadlā of Ayba, *Dadjāzmāch* Walda-Gabre'ēl, and *Bāshā* Gabre'ēt of Addi Abo, who had already left Adwā for Karan and awaited Alulā there.²⁹ The *rās* probably thought he could make a better use of that power by leading them against the Italians. But, on the other hand, he knew that, by a successful march on Kassala, he might regain his master's grace. Alulā badly needed a success, and an impressive one.³⁰

In the meantime, Alulā's envoys were sent to the Baria tribes informing them about the march to Kassala and ordering them to prepare cattle for the coming troops.³¹ Alulā reached Karan on 13 November 1886, where he was awaited by the Ethiopian army and also by Banū 'Āmir warriors led by Shaykh Mūsā al-Fīl and Shaykh 'Alī Nūrīn.³² The Baria's Shaykh Arāy arrived with no supplies, was nonetheless well received by the *rās*, but was ordered to return in order to collect and bring to Kūfīt as many rifles and cattle as he could obtain from his followers.

Reaching Kūfīt on 17 November 1886, Alulā camped with his army at the site of the previous year's battle and sent spies towards Kassala. Since Shaykh Arāy had met him with only fifty oxen and fifteen rifles, he again sent the Baria leader to collect more cattle and arms. On 22 November 1886 the *rās* ordered his army to march some eight miles southwards to the spring of Magalo. There he camped again, became frustrated with his inability even to contemplate an attack on Kassala, and therefore ordered the greatest plunder in the history of the Baria tribes.³³ During the last week in November, two-thirds of the people and cattle of the Baria and Kunama north of the Gash were destroyed. On 1 December 1886 Alulā ordered his army to march back to Tigre, even though, as in the previous year, he had not seen the gates of Kassala. Alulā's biographer excused his hero's failure by stating it was the emperor's order which stopped him:

> After this he went to the land of Käsäla, and the king sent after him 3 times, saying, 'My son, return, and do not go there. If you go, you are not a doer of my will and a fulfiller of my wishes.'
> Hearing this, he [Alulā] returned, and reached a place which they called Mägälo. He stayed there a short time, not very long, and he destroyed all the rebels and apostates of that place, and took much spoil and captured many men and women, young men and virgins; he did not leave any cattle, goats or sheep. In this majesty of appearance he returned and entered his country by another way, and arrived at the reception-room of the king.³⁴

But this argument cannot be accepted. Yohannes anxiously wanted success in Kassala. His son *Rās* Ar'āyā-Sellāssē, together with *Negus* Takla-Hāymānot of Godjām, was facing Mahdist pressure in Gondar,³⁵ and it seems that much depended on Alulā's campaign. Trying to explain Alulā's retreat, Pollera suggested that the *rās* never really intended to go to Kassala but to devastate the Baria country to create a deserted buffer zone between the Mahdists and Ethiopia and simultaneously to feed and supply his troops in preparation for his coming Italian campaign.³⁶ This analysis can hardly be accepted. Alulā, accompanied by many devotées of Yohannes, was in no position to disobey his master. His retreat also can not be fully explained by lack of water on the route to Kassala³⁷ because, according to Shaykh Arāy's evidence, "It was unfortunately raining."³⁸ Alulā's return is better explained by intelligence received from Kassala that the town was fortified and ready for the invaders.

On 6 September 1886 'Uthmān Diqna had been defeated at Tamai, in the Sawākin area, by the Amrār tribesmen. Again, as in 1885, he moved to the neighbourhood of Kassala and, upon hearing about Alulā's advance, 'Uthmān entered the town and strenghthened its defence.³⁹ Though so badly in need of the prestige of a victory, Alulā knew that to besiege a strongly fortified town, which was surrounded by Muslim tribesmen, could only lead to his destruction. Frustrated and "in order not to return empty handed,"⁴⁰ he destroyed the long-suffering and unlucky Baria.

Before ordering his army to return, Alulā was careful enough to consult with his lieutenants, who unanimously approved his decision.⁴¹ Yet Alulā had good reason to be afraid of the emperor's anger, and not only because of his military failure. One of the participants in the Kassala expedition, *Bāshā* Gabre'ēt of Addi Abo, complained to Yohannes about Alulā's maltreatment of the Baria,⁴² and, according to Pollera, Shaykh Arāy himself followed the returning army in order to raise the matter with the emperor.⁴³ Alulā travelled via Addi Abo and Shirē and reached Adwā on 10 December 1886, three days after Yohannes had left for Maqalē.

F. November-December 1886: Further Italian advances; Alulā's Position Improves

Yohannes's movement from Adwā to Maqalē resulted from a deteriorating situation in the Oromo area and on the Mahdist Matammā front.⁴⁴ He was undoubtedly displeased, and Alulā was probably busy looking for excuses to save his shaky position, when he learned of the new developments on the coast. The Italians had exploited Alulā's absence and, on 23 November 1886, occupied Wi'ā,⁴⁵ finally proving to Yohannes that the *rās*'s fears were not exaggerated. As Alulā later explained:

> At that time I was in a mission against the Muslims who threatened Keren and its territory. When I returned I heard about the occupation of Ua'a and Saati. If we could have a dispute about Saati, we should not have it about Ua'a which was undoubtedly in Imperial territory.⁴⁶

In late December, when Alulā arrived at Maqalē, he did not have to explain his failure in Kassala, rather he was put in charge of the future anti-Italian campaign, as described in the following passage from Yohannes's Aksum chronicle.⁴⁷

He [Yohannes] said the following to Ras Alula who was his favourite, as David was the favourite of God. He [Alulā] knew what he [Yohannes] thought and at what he pointed. He was God-loving and firm in his faith and love of Yohannes, the Negusa Şion, the Negusa Nagast. He [Yohannes] said to him: 'Go in your faith and you will defeat your enemies and do not hesitate.' Ras Alulā said to him, 'Alright my Lord, I shall never fear the evil doer, for you are on my side.'

Judging from subsequent events, Alulā was again given command over all the troops then available in northern Ethiopia. His biographer described this nomination:[48]

And he [Yohannes] said to him, 'Rejoice and be glad, my son, who have been faithful over one; I appoint you over many. . .' He [Yohannes] commanded the troops and said to them, 'All that he commands you, do; and that which he says to you, observe.'

G. *January 1887: "May I Tell You the Accounts of Ted'ali"* [49]

Alulā's return to Asmara on 5 January 1887,[50] was interpreted by the Italians as a preliminary step to an Ethiopian attack. On 6 January 1887, General Genè sent substantial reinforcements to Wi'ā. On 10 January 1887, when he received a letter from Alulā demanding evacuation, Genè sent Italian troops equipped with some artillery to replace the irregulars at Sahāṭi.[51] That same day, Alulā jailed some private Italians and threatened their lives.

On 12 January 1887 Alulā led his forces down to Gindā.[52] He was still unaware of the recent Italian occupation of Sahāṭi and told his prisoners that he still hoped that the Italians would peacefully return to Massawa "where he would like them to stay."[53] He again wrote Genè, asking him to stop commercial relations with the Ḥabbābs. He concluded his short letter:

The troops who camp at Ua'a must be cleared out by the 13 of Terr [21.1.87], those who camp at Zula must be cleared out within a month [6.2.87]. If friendship is to continue you must do this. Otherwise you must know that the friendship is at end.[54]

Alulā's insistence on the evacuation of Zulā suggests that he was still hoping for a free port to be run there by the French.[55]

The Italians took this letter as an insulting ultimatum, and Genè replied accordingly on 15 January,[56] rejecting the demand and concluding: "I tell you that in order that you will know that the Italian Government respects others, but wants to be and must be respected in its turn."[57] Alulā received Genè's reply together with the news about the occupation of Sahāṭi. "I told you," he addressed his prisoner

Count Augusto Salimbeni, "to write to the General in order that he would evacuate Ua'a and instead he sent to occupy Saati."[58]

On 16 January 1887 Alulā sent a warning to Genè that he would execute his prisoners, whom he accused of being spies, if the two places were not evacuated.[59] In reply, Genè threatened Alulā:

> Now if you want to break the friendship which exists between us and hurt Christian and Italian brothers, you will be responsible before your king the Negus Neghest and before my king.

The next day Genè wrote directly to Yohannes informing him "that Ras Alula is breaking our friendship," and asking for the release of the *rās*'s prisoners.[60] The Italian general was then confident that the Ethiopians would not attack,[61] but Alulā's subsequent letter of 20 January should have convinced him that the situation was critical:

> You sent to tell me: 'You will be responsible before the Negus Neghest and my king.' You are responsible. In order to avoid war you stayed in the middle of the sea like fishes. Later you came out and like rats you have dug trenches inside which you established yourselves. You who are sad for the bad fate of Salimbeni, what will happen to you and your troops?[62]

The Italians considered that two encumbrances prevented Alulā from attacking them. They believed that Yohannes had ordered Alulā to remain passive. An Ethiopian informant alleged on 21 January 1887 that *Bālambārās* Tasammān had told him that Alulā had received a letter from Yohannes saying:

> You have plundered the Baria . . . Now you want to fight those who say that they are my friends. You do not have to move against them. If they advance write me about it and I shall come with my troops.[63]

The other reason for Alulā's hesitation, as it was regarded in Massawa, was his soldiers' reluctance to fight a modern army. According to another piece of information, the *rās* ordered his troops to march on Sahāṭi on 19 January 1887, but "all chiefs lay around him with stones on their necks . . . asking him not to advance." One of the chiefs, a certain *Bālambārās* Warqu, said "that the Italians did no harm, and that the Ethiopian will find nothing at Sahaṭi but lead [bullets], which will kill them all."[64] The next day, on 20 January, the confident Italians took an undoubtedly hostile step. Keflē Iyāsus, Alulā's old rival, joined Genè's forces and was stationed with some one hundred followers at Otumlo.[65] This move, together with the reception of a letter from Soumagne, the French Consul to Massawa, renewing proposals to establish a French port in the coast,[66] was probably what convinced Alulā to take the initiative.

On 23 January 1887 he wrote to the emperor that he was going to attack Sahāṭi,[67] and, according to one eye-witness recollection, Alulā's address to the troops encouraged them to fight the better-armed Italians.[68] The events of the 25 and 26

January 1887 are detailed fully in Italian accounts. On the first day, Alulā led a direct attack on the fortified camp of Sahāṭi in which hundreds of Ethiopians were massacred by cannon fire, and only four Italians were injured. The next day at Dogali, Alulā ambushed a battalion consisting of five hundred Italian troops which was on its way to reinforce Sahāṭi. The Italians, surrounded by thousands of Ethiopians, fought heroically, but were destroyed, almost to a man. Only eighty wounded troops managed to escape the notice of the Ethiopians and were eventually rescued.

Alulā's biographer recorded the victory with the following lines:

> He rose up and travelled by night, while an angel led him. Fear did not enter his heart, because our Lady had made the matter certain for Ras Alula, from the beginning to the end. He prayed and besought God . . . And further he said, 'why does the powerful Italian boast in his evil, and rebel all the time?' . . . After he had finished his prayer, he went to the place of battle shaking like a calf filled with its mother's milk, and like a bridegroom going to the wedding. . . . When he went, many powerful men followed him, and passed him, and waited in ambush on a difficult path and a narrow pass. They surrounded them from one evening till the next, and in the morning they joined battle. When Ras Alula heard the battles and the sound of battle, he drew near and arrived, while the Holy Spirit, which rested on him encouraged him. And when his powerful men — namely Lejj Fänja Täsämma Shärif, Basha Märsha, Basha Täla Wäddi, Basha Fänja, Basha Tälla Addi Mellale, Basha Dästa Abba Ga'i — when they saw him, they were strengthened and given power in the time of battle, and they did not turn their faces from side to side, for Ras Alula, a man resolute, powerful and warlike, was among them. They made a great slaughter, and many of the troops died.[69]

H. *Dogali – Alulā's Own Initiative*

Alulā's military campaign of 25 and 26 January was not directly ordered by Yohannes. In fact, on 26 January the emperor was still hoping for a peaceful solution, as he then wrote from Maqalē to Genè: "In the first place you took Ua'a; and now you have also come to Saati to erect a fortress . . . Is not this country mine? . . . Evacuate my country . . . ".[70] Yet, three years after Dogali, when *Rās* Alulā discussed the subject with some Italian officials, he spoke convincingly as if he had been following his master's instructions:

> In any case you have to pardon me. Before attacking I asked instructions from the Emperor, and such were the orders. Being a soldier I executed them.[71]

And Yohannes's Ge'ez chronicle, too, gives firm impresion that Alulā was authorised to attack.⁷² Finally, Count Antonelli, who had reason to identify the emperor with what the Italians regarded as a horrible crime, suggested that the *rās* was acting on Yohannes's orders.⁷³

The Mannawē Ge'ez manuscript provides no new evidence: the biographer wrote nothing about Yohannes and Alulā planning an anti-Italian campaign during their meeting of December 1886. He merely hints that, on his way to Asmara, Alulā dreamt about his future victory over "the pagans" and subsequently attacked them at Sahāṭi and Dogali.

Yohannes's letter to Queen Victoria of 9 March 1887, does, however, provide some insights:

> But when at last he [the Italians] came where the Egyptians had been [Sahāṭi] he said: 'We shall occupy this'. Then I said, 'What have you to do with my country?' Therefore, they came by force and made in two places forts, and stopped there. Ras Alula went down to inquire 'What business have you to do with other people's country?' The Italian chief gave an order to prepare to meet him, and fought with him.⁷⁴

The emperor, who was most irritated about the Italian activities, sent his most uncompromising general at the head of a large army "to inquire" or threaten those whom Yohannes regarded as invaders. For two weeks Alulā was making "inquiries" and in his own diplomatic style tried to reach a peaceful solution. Having failed to do so, the *rās* probably thought that he had the option to fight. Actually, he urgently needed a spectacular victory to reestablish his prestige and had reason to believe that his military success would be followed by a political one. His previous campaign in that area, his annihilation of the Egyptian Company at Sahāṭi in late October 1883, resulted in the arrival of the Hewett Mission. Destruction of the Italians at Sahāṭi and their expulsion from Zulā might well lead, Alulā may have thought, to a favourable treaty with the French. The fact that Alulā fought and killed European troops was probably the reason for Yohannes's reluctance officially to back his general. It seems that Yohannes wanted Alulā to expel the Italians from the occupied territories, but he could not foresee that Alulā would do this in such a bloody way.

* * *

The battle of Dogali was undoubtedly one of the most important events in the history of Ethiopia in the late 19th century. The open enmity it created between the emperor and the Italians assisted the rise of Shoa's hegemony. The personality of *Rās* Alulā, whose activities were a main factor in the history of Ethiopia until his death, was associated with Dogali. This identification, as described below, was an important factor from 1887-89 to the battle of Adwā in 1896.

NOTES

1 FO 403/87, Smith to Baring, 20.5.86.
2. A.S.MAI, 2/2-13, Genè to MAE, 19.3.86.
3 FO 403/87, Smith to Baring, 20.5.86.
4 Ibid.
5 A.S.MAI 2/2-13, Genè to MAE, 16.4.86.
6 *La Tribuna*, 25.9.86. Quoted in Chiala, *La spedizione*, p. 312. Yohannes's letter reached Alulā only in early April.
7 FO 403/87, Smith to Baring, 30.5.86.
8 Ibid.
9 A.S.MAI 2/2-13, Sa'd to Genè, in Genè to MAE, 15.4.86.
10 FO 95/747, Victoria to John, 8.12.85. The letter contained a promise that Britain would ensure that Italy would follow the Hewett Treaty, i.e., maintain a free port in Massawa.
11 FO 403/87, Smith to Baring, 30.5.86.
12 FO 95/747, Yohannes to Victoria, 12 Miyāziā 1878 E.C. (19.4.86).
13 Genè to Robilant, 23.4.86; Giglio, *Etiopia*, V, No. 216, p. 253.
14 FO 403/87, Smith to Baring, 30.5.86.
15 FO 403/90, Smith to FO, 22.10.87.
16 A.S.MAI, 2/2-13, Genè to MAE, 29.7.86.
17 A.S.MAI, 2/2-13, Genè to MAE, 22.7.86.
18 Ibid.
19 Ibid.
20 See Holt, *Mahdist State*, p. 170.
21 Genè to Robilant, 8.10.86; Giglio V, *Etiopia*, No. 257, p. 358.
21 A.S.MAI, 2/2-13, Genè to MAE, 12.8.86.
23 Chiala, *La spedizione*, p. 325.
24 A.S.MAI 2/2-13, Genè to MAE, 23.9.86.
25 A.S.MAI, 2/2-13, Genè to MAE, 5.10.86.
26 Genè to Robilant, 8.10.86; Giglio, *Etiopia*, V, No. 257, p. 359.
27 The Italians enjoyed a quiet period as a result of Alulā's disgrace, and in May 1886 Genè sent home some 2,000 troops to save them from the heat of Massawa. *Popolo Romano*, 1.6.87.
28 A.S.MAI 2/2-13, Genè to MAE, 25.11.86; A. Salimbeni, "Diario," *NA*, 1936, p. 431.
29 A.S.MAI 2/2-13, Genè to MAE, 25.11.86.
30 Before leaving for Karan, Alulā found out that *Shālaqā* Ar'āyā had been in touch with Dabbab in order to persuade him to come to Yohannes. See below p. 118. Alulā nominated his brother *Bālambārās* Tasammā to Gindā and Asmara and took Ar'āyā to Karan, where he was put in prison. A.S.MAI 2/2-13, Genè to MAE, 25.11.86.
31 Pollera, *I Baria*, pp. 50-51.
32 The dates given below of Alulā's activities during the Kassala expedition are according to a report by one of the participants, Muḥammad Maḥkūmī of Harkīkū, in A.S.MAI 2/2-13, Genè to MAE, 31.12.86.
33 For a colourful description, see Pollera, *I Baria*, pp. 50-52.

34 MS. Mannawē.
35 MAE(F), Mass. 5, Soumagne to MAE, 30.12.86; Also: Genè to Robilant, 17.12.85; Giglio, *Etiopia*, V, No. 272, p. 373.
36 Pollera, *I Baria*, p. 54.
37 As in Genè to Robilant, 17.12.86; Giglio, *Etiopia*, V, No. 272, p. 373.
38 Pollera, *I Baria*, p. 51.
39 *The Times*, 26.1.87.
40 MAE(F), Mass, 5, Soumagne to MAE, 30.12.86.
41 Ibid.
42 Genè to Robilant, 17.12.86; Giglio, *Etiopia*, V, No. 272, p. 375. According to Pollera, *I Baria*, Bāshā Gabriet himself was very active in plundering the Baria.
43 Pollera, *I Baria*, loc.cit.
44 MAE Mass. 5, Soumagne to MAE, 30.12.86.
45 This Italian encroachment was also facilitated by Alula's removal of *Shālaqā* Ar'āya [see note 30]. According to Alula's biographer, the *ras* regretted the imprisonment of *Shālaqā* Ar'āyā: "Why did I put him in prison and order that his hands and feet be bound. If he had been there, the Italians would not have come to the field of Sahati and would not have made a wall there." The Italian advanced under the pretext of a need to protect the commercial route from Dabbab. A.S.MAI 2/2-17, Genè to MAE, 22.1.87.
46 N. Corazzini, "La pace," *La Tribuna*, 8.6.90.
47 A. Ge'ez book. A chronicle of Yohannes found in Aksum written by Abbā Hāyla-Māryām. Translated by Tesfayohannes Fessehaye.
48 MS Mannawē.
49 From a poem found by Ato Māmo Wudnah in a Ge'ez manuscript of Dabra-Bizan. Ted'ali is the Ethiopian name for Dogali.
50 Salimbeni, *Pionere*, p. 437.
51 A.S.MAI 3/2-17, Genè to MAE, 22.1.87.
52 Salimbeni, *Pioniere*, p. 437.
53 A.S.MAI, Eritrea II, Salimbeni to Genè, 12.1.87.
54 Crispi, *La prima Guerra*, p. 15.
55 In fact on 17 January 1887, Soumagne despatched Alula another draft treaty according to which the French, once given authorisation to establish a port, would promise not to extend their possessions. It seems also that Greek arms traders, such as Nicola Giorgi Kaligi, whom the Italians suspected stiffened Alulā's resistance, supported the idea of a French port at /ulā. MAE(F), Doccuments Diplomatiques Français, 1871-1914, Afrique 138 Aby.V., Soumagne to Alula, 17.1.87. A.S.MAI 2/4-32, Baldissera to M.d.G., 5.7.89.
56 See text in Crispi, *La prima Guerra*, p. 15.
57 In a meeting which took place three and a half years later, Alulā explained that it was his duty "to fix time for the evacuation." Antonelli retorted: "This was exactly your fault. You can not say to Europeans 'Get out from there or I attack you.' This is the way to make a retreat impossible for them. They will all prefer to die than give up [like that]." N. Corrazini, "La pace," *La Tribuna*, 8.6.90.
58 Salimbeni, *Pioniere*, p. 437.
59 Salimbeni, *Pioneer*, p. 437.
60 A.S.MAI, Eritrea II, Genè to Alulā, 18.1.87.
61 L.V. XVII, Genè to MAE, 22.1.87.

62 Alula to Genè, 20.1.87 in Genè to Robilant, 21.1.87; Giglio, *Etiopia*, VI, p. 11.
63 Genè to Robilant, 21.10.87; Giglio, *Etiopia*, VI, No. 6, p. 10.
64 Ibid.
65 Puglisi, *Chi e*? p. 174.
66 See above p. 92.
67 According to Alulā's Italian prisoner Savoiroux as told to the correspondents of *Riforma*. See Antona Traversi, *Saati*, p. 69.
68 Ishaq Yosef, *Hade Eritrawi*, chapter 12.
69 MS. Mannawē.
70 Giovanni to Genè, 26.1.87, Giglio, *Etiopia*, VI, No. 14, Allegato 3, p. 30.
71 N. Corazzini, "La Pace," *La Tribuna*, 8.7.90.
72 See above, p. 103. A chronicle of Yohannes found at Aksum, written by Abbā Hayla-Māryam.
73 Antonelli in Camera dei Deputati, 5.5.91, vide: *Discussione sull' Africa*, p. 5. Antonelli to MAE, 19.9.87; Giglio, *Etiopia*, VI, No. 209, p. 240.
74 FO 95/748, Yohannes to Victoria, Yakatit 30th, 1879 E.C. 9.3.87.

11

1887: The End of Alulā's Government in the Marab Mellāsh (Eritrea)

A. February-March 1887: Alulā Condemned for Dogali but Needed on the Threatened Frontier

After Dogali, Alulā did not proceed towards Massawa, a lapse which the Italians attributed to his great losses at Dogali.[1] In fact, it appears as if the *rās* merely awaited Yohannes's instructions. From Dogali Alulā sent emissaries to the emperor, who was in Maqalē.[2] Other emissaries were sent to Menilek of Shoa carrying letters in which the Italian defeat was colourfully described.[3] On 29 January Alulā passed through Gindā, and he entered Asmara on 31 January 1887.[4]

According to Augusto Salimbeni, Alulā's prisoner, the *rās*'s letter to the emperor contained an urgent petition for reinforcements enough to resume his march to the coast. Upon reading Yohannes's reply, "Alulā's face darkened ... and returning to his hut he did not want to eat."[5] The letter reportedly contained the following passage:

> Who gave you permission to go and make a war there? Those soldiers are not yours but mine; I shall cut off your right hand.[6]

Salimbeni testified that Alulā did not, however, give up his aggressive ideas and that during the next month the *rās* often petitioned for reinforcement and permission to resume hostilities.[7] On the other hand, Alulā resumed the correspondence with Genè, emphasizing an interest and will for peace, but only if the Italians limited themselves to Massawa.[8] Genè's reply of 5 February accepted Alulā's call for peace and demanded the release of the Italian prisoners,[9] Alulā had taken on 10 January.

But the *rās* had his reasons not to hurry about freeing his hostages. He wanted to force the fulfillment of article V of the Hewett Treaty and the extradition of Keflē Iyāsus, Dabbab and some Assāwurta leaders, the last of whom deserted during Dogali.[10] Besides, the hostages might come in handy if there were an Italian counter attack. Finally, Alulā was also doing his best to gain time in order to persuade his master to take the military initiative.

Through February and early March, Alula continued his negotiations with Genè.[11] The general warned Kefle Iyasus about Alula's demand and sent him from Massawa to Ḥalḥal and promised him a monthly stipend of 1,000 Thalers.[12] In early March, however, he sent the eight Assawurta leaders and their rifles to Asmara.[13] F. Piano and Salimbeni were subsequently released on 11 March 1887 but the third prisoner, T. Savoiroux, was kept in Asmara,[14] undoubtedly as agreed by the emperor.

According to Salimbeni, it was around 20 February 1887 that the emperor, though still disapproving of Alula's initaitve in Dogali, consented to send reinforcements, but only as a defensive measure.[15] Expecting an Italian counterattack, Yohannes could not continue to punish the general upon whose military prowess he had to rely. In late March he summoned Alula to Maqale,[16] and it was rumoured that he again appointed him as "a governor of all the Taccazze country as far as the Red Sea, excepting the province of Makkale."[17] In fact, Alula's power was limited by the emperor. He had to return to Asmara together with the loyal and calm *Rās* Hagos, whom Yohannes appointed as "a companion and a watchman" to Alula.[18]

B. Repercussions in Europe to Dogali

Dogali seriously damaged the prestige of the Italian army and caused great sadness and vengeful emotions in the Mother country. The defeat was followed by a governmental crisis and changes in leadership at Massawa. Parliament voted finance for a large-scale punitive expedition, and war in the near future seemed to be inevitable. *Rās* Alula, hitherto regarded by officials and the press as a leader of "forty thieves,"[19] was now described as a monster, whose destruction became almost a national obsession.[20]

Dogali's immediate diplomatic result was the French decision to recall Soumagne and to cancel further negotiations for the treaty with Ethiopia.[21] In Britain, where Yohannes appealed for mediation, a possible Ethiopian-Italian war was regarded as a negative development. According to an editorial in the *Manchester Guardian* of 2 February 1887:

> It is not yet clear whether the KING is responsible for what has happened, or whether RAS ALULA has struck that blow on his own account. We hope the latter. A war between Italy and Abyssinia could lead to nothing.[22]

Mr. Harrison Smith, in a memorandum also written on 2 February 1887, expressed what later became Whitehall's opinion:

> The attack referred to may have been an overprecipitate action on the part of Ras Alula, in which case there is yet time to make honourable terms

with the king, and humble Mr. Ras Alula as well, for the King will do that by shutting him up in an 'Amba', or punishing him with death.²³

C. April-August 1887: Religious Policy in the Threatened Marab Mellāsh

Another immediate consequence of the Dogali affair was the beginning of the collapse of Alula's regime in the Marab Mellāsh. Facing the threat of Italian retaliation, the *rās* began to intimidate the Muslim population of Hamāsēn and Sarāyē, hitherto his commercial collaborators. The Muslims of Hamāsēn and particularly of Asmara suffered heavily from the deterioration of commerce following the Dogali clash, especially after 1 May 1887, when Alula's prohibition of trade with Massawa²⁴ was matched by a complete blockade declared by Saletta, the newly-promoted Italian C.-in-C.²⁵ On 7 April 1887, Alula issued an *awādj* by which the Muslims of Hamāsēn (or rather those who were the Asmara-based traders) were concentrated in two places outside the province where their activities were strictly controlled.²⁶

The stoppage of trade, followed by the temporary removal from Asmara of the Muslim traders, was virtually a mortal blow to the economic basis of Alula's regime in the Marab Mellāsh. The *rās*'s anti-Muslim policy could be effective only in the area directly controlled by his government. As for the peripheral tribes, the Italians gained the upper hand. Greater cooperation with these tribes was suggested by General Genè immediately after Dogali.²⁷ Alula's new anti-Muslim policy and the weakness of the Mahdiyya in that area after Kūfīt enhanced Italian efforts. In early May 1887, immediately after an official state of war was declared by Saletta, Italian-Ḥabbāb relations were renewed.²⁸ "The chiefs of the tribes of the Beni Amer," it was reported by a British observer,²⁹ "seem disposed to make common cause with Italy." The Assāwurta and Dabbab were also said to be considered "allies and friends" of the Massawa authorities.³⁰ Alula's reaction was to obtain hostages,³¹ but he apparently met no success.

Simultaneously with the confrontation with his own Muslim population, Alula seemed to be wary of possible cooperation between the Italians and the French Catholic missionaries, a suspicion which was possibly strengthened following the French diplomatic withdrawal. During the months of May-August 1887, the French Father Paillard mediated between Alula and the Italians for Savoiroux's release. Alula agreed to exchange the prisoner for 15,000 thalers and the release of the head of the Ethiopian convent in Jerusalem, Walda-Samāyāt,³² who had been detained on his way back to Ethiopia. Alula also demanded that Father Coulbeaux guarantee the deal. On 17 August 1887 Savoiroux was liberated, and the money transferred to Alula but not in a currency accepted in Ethiopia; moreover, Walda-Samāyāt was not permitted to enter Ethiopia and had to return to Jerusalem. Father Coulbeaux was subsequently arrested and kept in prison for a period of two months.³³ Alulā was so enraged that his suspicion overwhelmed him and, on 23 August 1887, "with 500 soldiers encircled the mission of Chern, chained 6 native priests, 40 students and 13 members of the sect and forced them to march, chained in couples, to Asmara."³⁴ Father Picard, the head of the mission, reported that "Alulā said that Yohannes had ordered him to bring all of us to Asmara," where he was told to stop prosyletizing.³⁵ Judging from the following passage from the Mannawē MS, the action against the mission of Keren was not a unique episode.

> He [Alula] said to Abba Takla Maryam [an Ethiopian priest mentioned many times in the manuscript as being an adviser of the Rās] 'Remember me, father, in your holy prayer, and give me permission that there be an assembly in this place and settlement; because there are wicked priests who divide the Word [Christ] from his Father and from the Holy Spirit, in honour and in form, in wish and in volition.'
> They had an assembly, and he set up for them a quotation from the books, which says, 'And as the Father has life, so to the Son he gave life, in order that life might be with him.' There was this and more like it. The men of Saraye and Hamasen who were assembled in that assembly lacked anything to say, and were troubled on that day... The faith was corrected and they worshipped the Word.³⁶

D. *November-December 1887: British Mediation: An Effort to Remove Alulā in Order to Prevent a War of Revenge*

After Dogali the Italians evacuated Sahāṭi and Arāfali and concentrated in Massawa. For Yohannes this state of affairs was satisfactory:

> For my part, if the Italian government does not come to take possession of my country and allows the free passage of goods at Massawa, I am disposed to make peace and come to an agreement.³⁷

Alulā, who was most active in preparing his province for a defensive war, and annoyed over Italian activities among the peripheral Muslim tribes, was also reported as prepared to seek peace on such terms. On 17 August 1887, he said "that he was most ready to make peace, to forget the past and ask you [Saletta] to open the roads to commerce and that he would never cause any more troubles to the Italians."³⁸

But the cry for Dogali's revenge was growing in Italy during 1887. On 14 July 1887 a "Corpo speciale d'Africa" was organised by General Tancredi Saletta, eventually to number some 20,000 troops with thirty-eight pieces of artillery. It was clear, however, in London and to some in Italy that no strategical or political benefit could be derived from such an expedition,³⁹ which was purposely aimed at restoring the honour of the Italian army and taking revenge on those responsible for

Dogali. For Britain an Italo-Ethiopian war was undesirable, and London used Yohannes's letter of 9 March as a call for mediation.[40] This démarche was accepted by Crispi for reasons which had nothing to do with Ethiopia.

The British Foreign office, "wishing to do all that is possible for King John without, however, in any way giving umbrage to the Italian government,"[41] decided to send a special envoy, G.L. Portal, to outline Italian conditions for peace. Yohannes had to express his regret "for the unjust attack" and to recognise Sahāti and Wi'ā as "definitely Italian territory," with Gindā as the Ethiopian frontier town. The Assāwurta and Ḥabbāb were to be put under Italian protection and "the region of Sanhit" occupied by the Italians. "A treaty of Peace, Amity and Commerce" was then to be signed between Italy and Abyssinia.[42]

Though not included in the written conditions, *Rās* Alulā's removal from the political scene, as has been suggested by Harrison Smith, was clearly one of Portal's main objectives. Portal enthusiastically adopted this condition after he learned that General Saletta believed that "Italy should be amply satisfied by cession of Sahati and Oua and removal of Ras Alula from this district."[43] This view was fully supported by Baring, who added: "I am of opinion that these conditions could be obtained. The last one may be worked by urging that Ras Alula command an army for Sennar."[44]

As it was impossible to travel to meet the emperor, then in Debra-Tābor, without crossing Alulā's territory, Portal decided, against Italian advice,[45] to meet the *rās* on his way. On 30 October 1887, he sent a letter to Alulā, then camping in Gurā "threatening the Assaurta,"[46] notifying him about his mission.[47] On 4 November 1887 Alulā replied, calling for peace according to the Hewett Treaty:

> We have no conflict between our two governments. What causes enmity between us, traders having been impeded, is on account of this rebel called Dabbab, . . . let it be that you seize him in accordance with our treaty [Hewett Treaty] and our friendship. It is Dabbab who has involved us in conflict with the Italians. I mean that, if the rebels who stand between the two governments were to be eliminated, it is my contention that the friendship between the governments would be strong and traders would be able to trade as usual. But my saying this is not in the nature of a command but is in view of our friendship.[48]

Alulā again expressed his wish for peace and demanded extradition of Dabbab, now in close relations with Saletta,[49] and also in command of 1,900 men[50] who raided into Assāwurta and Gindā regions.[51] Portal was probably led astray by his interpreter,[52] who, for some still unexplained reason, was interested in jeopardising any agreement between Alulā and Portal. The diplomat's understanding of the *rās*'s letter was as follows:

> The Ras said that he would receive me at Asmara and begged me to come on to him at once. So far the letter was civil, but the latter part of it

consisted entirely of violent abuse of the Italians, which was less encouraging.[53]

Thus, when Alulā and Portal met in Asmarā on 11 November 1887, the Englishman was convinced that the *rās*'s policy was "war at any price,"[54] and, as he later analysed in his letter to Baring:[55]

> Ras Alula is determined to do everything in his power to bring about a war with Italy. He alone is responsible for the massacre of Dogali. A peace with Italy would imply censure of his action on that occasion, and would entail his downfall; he has already many enemies among the King's immediate followers, and, indeed, throughout the country, and it is only by achieving some brilliant military success that he can hope to triumph over them all, and to raise himself to the level of the great Chiefs of the Abyssinian Empire.

In their meeting Portal avoided telling Alulā the aim of his mission, "as it was easy to see that the acceptance by King John of the Italian terms . . . would probably lead to . . . [Alulā's] downfall, or at least to his removal to another province."[56]

But the Ethiopian was undoubtedly aware of the significance of Portal's mission and even was informed about Italy's territorial demands, which he most emphatically decried:

> The Ras proceeded to speak with great excitement and said that the Italians should come to Sahati only if he could go as Governor to Rome; that he had beaten them once, and if they advanced he would beat them again.[57]

On 12 November 1887 Alulā sent emissaries to the emperor,[58] who, in the meantime, had left Dabra-Tābor to march to Ashangē. He did not let Portal and his retinue proceed inland before 19 November 1887, when he received Yohannes's affirmative reply. It looks as if Alulā was playing his cards slowly in order to gain time. The Italian expedition was already concentrated on the coast, anxious to march, and any delay could only serve the Ethiopian cause. He also needed time to enable the emperor to reach Ashangē from Dabra-Tābor and to supply him with more evidence of Italian aggression before his own fate might be decided between Yohannes and Portal.

It was only on 7 December 1887, a week after Portal was supposed to finish his mission,[59] that the Englishman was received by Yohannes in Ashangē. He presented his introductory letters from Queen Victoria and Salisbury and a written document that he had drafted which strictly distinguished between the offender and the friend:

> Her Majesty Queen Victoria, whilst deeply regretting the massacre of 450 Italians committed by Ras Alula in January last, is very sorry to see

that her friend, His Majesty King John, is in a state of war with the King of Italy.[60]

The aide-mémoire continued with the Italian peace proposals. The emperor's reply was bitter, and he rejected the conditions with the following words:

> I did not give them Massowah; England gave it to the Italians, but I will not give them an inch of land. If they cannot live there without Sahati, let them go; and as for Senhit, it is mentioned in the Treaty, and England cannot ask me to give it up.[61]

After seeing that the emperor was uncompromising, Portal appealed to Yohannes about the unwritten condition:

> I then remarked that the whole population of . . . the civilized world, had been surprised and made indignant by the news of the massacre at Dogali . . . I even went so far as to hint that I thought—though I added that I was not authorised to say so—that if Ras Alula were appointed to some other province not on the frontier, some of the difficulties in the way of peace might, perhaps, be removed. . . . His Majesty then continued: 'Ras Alula did no wrong; the Italians came into the province under his governorship, and he fought them, just as you would fight the Abyssinians if they came into England'.[62]

Portal's mission was a failure. His presentation of Rome's conditions was too one-sided and only persuaded Yohannes that Alulā might be right about Italian intentions.[63] The territorial demands, and the request to remove his best general, while the Italian expedition concentrated on the coast, amounted to an ultimatum which Ethiopians, no more than Europeans, could accept. Portal's only achievement was to delay the hostilities.[64]

On 23 December 1887 Portal passed through Asmara carrying a letter to Queen Victoria in which the emperor blamed the Italians for the developments leading to Dogali:[65]

> If your wish were to make peace between us, it should be when they are in their country and I in mine. But now on both sides the horses are bridled and the swords are drawn; my soldiers like the sand, are ready with their spears. The Italians desire war, but the strength is in Jesus Christ. Let them do as they will, so long as I live I will not hide myself from them in a hole.[66]

E. December 1887-February 1888: Alulā Persuades Yohannes to Fight the Italians

> Alulā Abbā Naggā go soon to Massawa,
> I do not like people beyond the sea.
> Bad weeds grew in lowland Massawa
> Get rid of it before it is multiplied.[67]

While Portal was still with the emperor at Ashangē, General Alessandro San Marzano assumed command over the Italian expedition concentrated at Massawa. Directed by four generals, its 20,000 troops were occupied in entrenching and securing the positions around Massawa. They soon moved inland and by the beginning of January 1888, the 1st and 2nd Brigades, commanded by the Generals Genè and Cagni, were encamped in the neighbourhood of Dogali.[68]

Alulā reported the Italian activities while the emperor was still with Portal, who believed that the *rās*'s reports were exaggerated and had led to the emperor's refusal to come to terms.[69] In fact, the correspondence between Yohannes and Menilek clearly indicates that the emperor would not comply with Portal's terms.[70]

Alulā's biographer described the message as a prayer to God made at the king's side:

> Rise up, O Lord, from your resting place and from the Ark of your sanctuary. For behold, our foes and enemies have exulted and have heaped pride upon us, and surrounded the land of Hamasen. For they do not know that which the book says, 'Do not be proud and do not shout in houses'.
> The king, hearing this word, was angry. 'How has Satan filled the heart, and how have you dared to come against me'? And the Italian rose up and went to the land of Hamasen.[71]

Threatened by an Italian army and feeling deserted by the British, Yohannes fully responded to Alulā's call for a national war. "The whole country is under arms, very large armies are advancing towards the frontiers."[72] By Portal's own account, *Rās* Alulā had 16,000 men at Asmara, mostly armed with rifles. At Karan, *Rās* Hagos commanded a further 20,000 men, again mostly riflemen. *Rās* Mikā'ēl, also in the north at Agulā, led 25,000 men, largely Oromo cavalry. The emperor directed an imperial guard of some 5,000 men, while his nephew Mangashā's force was about the same size. *Rās* Hāyla-Māryām had over 16,000 men, who were on their way from Wādlā to join Yohannes at his camp, and *Rās* Ar'āyā-Sellāssē's army of 40,000 was concentrating near Adwā.[73]

From a strategic point of view, it was dangerous for the emperor to concentrate such a massive army on the Italian front. Mahdist pressure was growing on the Sudanese frontier,[74] where *Negus* Takla-Hāymānot was ordered to face this threat alone. *Negus* Menilek, "who was now potentially stronger than the emperor, at a time when both Italian and Shoan policies aimed to remove Yohannes,"[75] was suspected by Yohannes of possible treachery.[76] The sovereign now ordered Menilek to Boru Mēdā to guard Wallo and to assure communications in the rear while the army of Wallo Oromo, under *Rās* Mikā'el, marched to the aid of Alulā To supply the huge armies, Alulā ordered the people of the Marab Mellāsh to bring cattle to Asmara,[77] where Muslim inhabitants were being disarmed.[78] In early January 1888 Yohannes was in Adwā and constantly in touch with Alulā.[79] But when everything seemed ready for the anti-Italian campaign, alarming news reached the emperor in the Tigrean capital.

The Mahdist advance into Amhara under Abū 'Anja seemed to be much more serious than expected, and rumours were circulating about Menilek's rebellious intentions.[80] On 16 January, Alulā and Hagos were therefore summoned to Adwā for consultations,[81] where Yohannes again blamed Alulā for placing Ethiopia in peril,[82] but ordered no new troop dispositions.[83] As he had demonstrated in the past, the emperor preferred to fight foreign enemies rather than rebels. Alulā therefore returned to Asmara to face the Italians, who had reoccupied Dogali, and had constructed a light railway to Sahāṭi,[84] which they heavily fortified with artillery.[85]

F. February 1888:
Dabbab's Return to the Ethiopian Camp

The Italians' plan included an effort to coordinate the activities of Eritreans who opposed Alulā's regime. This part of their plan suffered a heavy blow in late February, when Dabbab Ar'āyā, the chronic rebel, who served as adviser and as commander of irregular troops, defected to the Ethiopian camp on 22 February 1888.[86] According to Lamlam, Dabbab's father, *Rās* Ar'āyā Demṣu wrote from Adwā:

> 'The Italians have come to fight us. Do you dare to fight us being one of them? And now if you do not come, I shall curse you. Be cursed.' And Dabbab fearing the curse of his father, sent to the *Jānhoy* saying '. . . I have sinned. Please have mercy on me . . . and send an army to escort me.'[87]

Accompanied by some 300 followers, Dabbab was received by Alulā in Asmara. It must have been a terrible moment for the *ras* to be forced by his master honourably to receive his most bitter personal enemy. Alulā accompanied Dabbab to Adwā, where the latter with a rope around his neck[88] fell before Yohannes and declared:

> 'I deserve to be hanged. I deserve to be executed. Forgive me!' Being pleased with him, the *Jānnoy* rewarded him with everything except the crown.[89]

Earlier in late 1886, when *Rās* Alulā had been diverted from the Italian front, it had been reported that Yohannes was about to pardon Dabbab.[90] The emperor, judging from his subsequent policy, probably considered Dabbab influential enough in Akalla-Guzāy to replace Alulā as governor in the Marab Mellāsh. Now in 1888 Dabbab was not only pardoned by the emperor, but, to Alulā's great sorrow, was also appointed as Yohannes's personal adviser for Italian affairs.[91] It was but little comfort to Alulā that the rehabilitated Dabbab also urged the emperor to take the offensive against the Italians.[92]

G. March 1888: Alulā's Fails to Entice the Italians to Fight in the Open

On 16 March 1888 the most dramatic and worrying news reached the emperor at Adwa.[93] Abu 'Anja's Mahdists had heavily defeated King Takla-Haymānot's army on 21 January 1888. The Sudanese entered Gondar on 23rd January 1888,[94] where, as claimed by Abū 'Anja,[95] forty-five churches were set on fire. The appeal of the clergy of Godjām must have deeply moved Yohannes: "'O Lord! the pagans have invaded thy preserve, thy sacred shrine they have profaned, Gondar have they laid in ruins.'"[96]

Most of the emperor's counsellors advised him to abandon the Italian front and to march to Amhara. But *Rās* Alulā apparently said, "Your return without fighting the Italians not only would be useless, but may well prove to be a cause for the destruction to your throne."[97]

Rās Mikā'ēl supported Alulā:[98]

> 'Give authority to me and to Ras Alula, that we may go to the snake and to the scorpions — who are the Italians. . .' And he [Yohannes] said to them, 'Go in peace . . . May God give you power and strength in time of battle. I will come with you, and I will not leave you to be orphans.'[99]

Alulā's plan, as approved by the emperor, who subsequently moved down to Sabarguma, was anticipated by the Italians.[100] As the new fort of Sahāti was justifiably considered invincible, Alulā thought he would again, as in Gurā, Kūfīt and indirectly in Dogali, entice the enemy from his fort and meet him in the open. The next developments were fully described by a British observer, who concluded that:

> It is difficult for the moment to satisfactorily explain the Negus' motives, and various are the opinions expressed; but I am of the opinion that all along he has only had one object in view, and that of endeavouring to entice the Italian force to leave their entrenchments and fight him in the open, and that he never advanced with the view of attacking Saati, and this, I consider, is borne out by the flank movement of the Abyssinian cavalry, evidently to be held in readiness to attack either in flank or in

rear, as opportunity afforded. . . . Again, his advance at the last moment was evidently with the intention of throwing down the gauntlet in the hopes that it would lead to a fight in the open.[101]

Alulā's failure of 25 March 1888[102] was characterized in the following way by his biographer:

> The two of them [Rās Alulā and Rās Mikā'ēl] went to the place of battle, Rās Alula leading them. And when he came to the edge of that place in which the Italians were, Rās Alulā, taking off his adornments, made a crown of gold and clothes of gold braid and of silver, and he took a shield of gold and silver and girded his sword that was adorned with gold and silver. . . . He said [to the Italians], 'come, come out of this den, and let us see each other face to face'. And he [the Italians] said to him 'I will not come out of this house of mine, unless you have gone away'. The king [Yohannes] and his troops went away, and he [the Italians] went away.[103]

From the Italian side Alulā's effort seemed ridiculous:

> When the army with the emperor approached the Italian camp, the Italian General ordered a balloon to be raised to watch the enemy from above. The effect of the balloon frightened the Ethiopian soldiers who, without listening to their commanders, turned back. Many took the way to their homeland saying: 'We can face an army of human beings, but not the army of God which comes from the sky.' In the night Ras Alula sent near the Italian fortress some twenty Tigrean soldiers who shot a few shots. The Italians illuminated them with the electric lights.[104] The soldiers of Tigre being illuminated like in daytime stood terrified and frightened not knowing what to do. The Italians did not even shoot at them but remained laughing watching the Tigreans' flight.[105]

H. *March-May 1888: The Italian Front Abandoned; the End of Alulā's Government in the Marab Mellāsh*

In Aylet on 26 March 1888, faced with the sack of Gondar and Alulā's failure, Yohannes decided to turn to the Mahdist front. He wrote to San Marzano, calling on him to "abide by the treaty that the English have made me make with the Egyptians" and to join hands together against the Mahdiyya. "Ras Alula," Yohannes added, "did what he did [in Dogali] without writing to me and you also told me nothing. It was the work of the Devil."[106] But Yohannes's appeal to return to the Hewett Treaty was not accepted by Rome. Though the bulk of the expeditionary force had to return home, and no military revenge for Dogali was taken, the Italians still insisted on the "conditions communicated by Mr. Portal to the

Negus."[107] Thus, while the emperor was leading his armies back into Ethiopia, the problem of his Italian frontier was farther than ever from being solved.

Yohannes's decision to abandon the Italian front signified the end of Alulā's government in the now ruined province of Hamāsēn. Yohannes now realised that under the care of his hitherto invincible general the northern frontier had become a source of diplomatic isolation and a military threat. Silhouetted against the background of what then seemed to be Menilek's friendly relations with the Italians, Yohannes had abundant proof that Alulā's policy in the Marab Mellāsh had been based on two contradictory and irreconcilable elements: the encouragement of trade with the coast and a tough policy towards Massawa. The inevitable friction had led to the decline of trade, the alienation of the Muslim inhabitants, the extinction of Alulā's regime and the exacerbation of coastal problems.

According to rumours, Yohannes was seriously considering Alulā's removal from the area,[108] the only Italian-British condition for peace that he could accept without giving up the Hewett Treaty. Spies returning to Massawa constantly reported on Alulā's disgrace but differed about the future governor of Hamāsēn.[109] Alulā's brother, *Dadzāzmāch* Tasammā, described by Portal as his *bāldarabā* (host), and a commander of 3,000 of the emperor's troops,[110] was deprived of his office on 7 April 1888, and his property was confiscated.[111] Even *Rās* Ar'āyā-Sellassē, the emperor's son, for whom Alulā had been a guide and protector, was quoted as complaining to his father: "I told you not to listen to him. He will lead to our destruction in order to serve his own purposes."[112] In Godofellasi on 12 April 1888, the emperor ordered the *rās* to return to Asmara and prepare a list of the firearms distributed among his devotees in Hamāsēn. Since only 1,000 Remingtons[113] were involved, one can safely conclude that Yohannes's aim was to disarm Alulā's old followers, the veterans of his brigade as a *shālaqā* and the backbone of his government in the Marab Mellāsh. Accompanied by some of Yohannes's officers, the humiliated Alulā returned to Asmara on 13 April 1888, and was reported as not emerging from his *tukuls*.[114] The man who was for more than a decade the undisputed master of Eritrea was facing the end of his role there. On 19 April 1888, Alulā's servants packed up his belongings and made for Adwā; the next day, the emperor's officers, with the list of firearms, left; and on 23 April 1888, after issuing a pathetic *awādj*[115] calling on the people of Hamāsēn to be tranquil and return to their work, the *rās* quietly slipped out of Asmara, leaving behind only sixty of his soldiers![116]

Alulā's position was obviously delicate, and during late April and the first half of May, while he waited on the emperor at Adwā and Aksum, his enemies worked diligently to remove him from the political scene. On 9 May it was reported by informants in Massawa that *Rās* Hagos and *Fitāwrāri* Dabbab again accused Alulā of leading Yohannes to disaster.[117] On 19 May 1888 the same informants wrote to Baldissera that Dabbab Ar'āyā not only had demanded Akalla-Guzāy from Yohannes[118] but also had charged Alulā with maladministration. The turncoat even managed to obtain a share in Emlasu's property, which must have deeply humiliated Alulā. Yohannes forced him, in accordance with Ethiopian law, to hand over some of the property and fifty retainers.[119] Judging from the emperor's letter to San Marzano of 10 May 1888, Yohannes may have been ready now to sacrifice Alulā's career in order to appease the Italians:

> You say that Ras Alula offended you. Therefore, let an high-officer of yours come and I shall summon Ras Alula in front of him and in the presence of the Abuna, the Echege and all the officers. If he is found guilty, I shall make him pay and restore all that he had unjustifiably taken.[120]

* * *

As if to confirm his offer, Yohannes left the Marab Mellash without making any serious arranements for its defence, even nominating Dabbab to govern Akalla-Guzāy. Alula's removal from Asmara was soon to prove a great mistake, an action which undoubtedly enabled the Italians subsequently to become such an important factor in Ethiopian history.

Yohannes, however, was not the only leader responsible for losing Eritrea; it was mainly the policy of his devoted general which led to the end of Ethiopian government beyond the Marab. In defending his government in the Marab Mellāsh, *Rās* Alulā had to deal with three major elements: the presence of an ambitious European neighbour, the existence of an undefined border and the establishment of his capital as a commercial centre. Alulā failed to create the necessary balance between these elements which could only have been achieved through compromise. Had he been able to permit Italian participation in governing what he regarded as his territorial sphere of raids, Asmara could well have become a flourishing commercial centre. But Alulā was too proud to compromise; he wanted to raid the peripheral tribes, to limit the Italians to the port of Massawa and he sought an active and peaceful commercial contact with the port there. Though from a legal and national point of view he was right, such an inflexible approach proved disastrous.

NOTES

1   A.S.MAI Eritrea II, Genè to MAE, 4.2.87. But Antona-Traversi suggested that Alulā lost only 730; C. Antona-Traversi, *Sahati e Dogali*, Rome 1887, p. 54.
2   Alula also sent emissaries to Karan to release *Shālaqā* Ar'ayā, whose arrest had proved to be such a mistake. Salimbeni, "Pioniere," Genè to MAE, 14.2.87. LV, See above, pp. 107, 108.

3 Antonelli to MAE, 2.4.87; LV, XV, C. Zaghi, *Le origini della Colonia Eritrea*, Bologna 1934, p. 145. For Menilek's reaction see: H. Marcus, *The Life and Times*, pp. 87, 88.
4 Salimbeni, "Pioniere"; Antona-Traversi, p. 50.
5 Salimbeni, *Pioniere*, op.cit.
6 Ibid. The two other Italian prisoners, Piano and Savoiroux, also testified that Yohannes condemned Alulā's initaitve. See: A.S. MAI, Eritrea II, 1887, Verbal note by Piano, 8.3.87; FO 403/90, Savile to Salisbury, 6.10.87. See also Puglisi, *Chi e?* p. 14. Cutting off one's right hand was a traditional punishment for traitors and thieves.
7 A.S.MAI 3/2-15, Salimbeni to the editor of *Gazzetta Piemontese*, 7.5.88.
8 Alula to Genè, 2.2.87, LV XVII. Also Giglio VI, No. 14, Allegato 4, p. 30.
9 LV XVII, Giglio, *Etiopia*, VI, p. 31.
10 A.S.MAI 3/2-16, Genè to MAE, 27.2.84.
11 Vide A.S.MAI Eritrea II, Alulà to Genè, 14.2.87, 25.2.87; Salimbeni, "Pioniere."
12 A.S.MAI, "Collection Vitale", Saletta to M.d.G., 7.5.87.
13 The tribesmen were immediately released by Alulā, *The Times*, 22.3.87.
14 *La Tribuna*, 16.3.87.
15 Salimbeni to editor of *Gazzetta Piemontese* 7.5.88.
16 A.S.MAI 3/2-15, Genè to MAE, 26.3.87.
17 *La Tribuna*, 22.5.87; *The Times*, 23.5.87.
18 De Simone to Crispi, 4.1.88, quotes Antonelli's letter of 9.12.87, Giglio, *Etiopia*, VI, No. 257, p. 286; FO 403/91, Portal to Baring 1.1.88; Antonelli to MAE, 19.12.87, LV XVII.
19 *La Tribuna*, 24.1.87.
20 For the image of Rās Alulā in Italy, see the play of A. Castelleto, *La Figlia di Ras Alula*, Milano 1888. See English translation in *Ethiopia Observer*, 1972, No. 3, and a short article there by R. Pankhurst.
21 MAE(F), *Documents Diplomatiques Français*, 138, Flourens to D'Aunay, 19.2.87, and Alula to Soumagne, 5.3.87.
22 *The Manchester Guardian*, 2.2.87.
23 FO 493/89, Memorandum by Mr. Harrison Smith, 2.2.87.
24 *The Times*, 23.5.87; A.S.MAI "Vitale Collection," "Nota del segretario per gli afari indigeni," 18.4.87.
25 *Tribuna*, 3.5.87.
26 A.S.MAI, "Vitale Collection", "Nota del segretario per gli affari indigeni, 18.4.87.
27 Genè to Robilant, 29.1.87, LX XVII, Giglio, *Etiopia*, VI, No. 11, p. 23.
28 *La Tribuna*, 9.5.87.
29 FO 403/89, Kennedy to Salisbury, 19.6.87.
30 Saletta to Bertolè-viale, 17.8.87; Giglio, *Etiopia* VI, No. 174, p. 208.
31 *Storia Militare*, p. 193.
32 See above, p. 90.
33 Mercinier to d'Aunay, 23.4.87, as quoted in Aleme Eshete, *La Mission catholique Lazariste en Ethiopie*, Institut d'Histoire. Université d'Aix-en-Provence, Etudes et Documents No. 2 (1970-1971), p. 84.
34 Da Nembro, *La Missione*, p. 18.
35 MAE(F) Mass. 5, MAE to Mercinier, 9.9.87.

36   MS Mannawē.
37   Yohannes to Menelik, 21.11.87 in A.S.MAI 36/4-42.
38   Savoiroux to Saletta, 22.8.87; Giglio, *Etiopia* VI, No. 173, p. 207.
39   See FO 403/90, Savile to Salisbury, 2.11.87.
40   See FO 403/90, Salisbury to Kennedy, 2.8.87. In fact Yohannes's letter requested further explanations about the British attitude to the Italian presence in Massawa.
41   *The Times*, 20.4.87.
42   FO 403/90, Salisbury to Baring, 31.10.87.
43   Portal to Baring in FO 403/90; Baring to Salisbury, 1.11.87.
44   FO 403/90, Baring to Salisbury, 1.11.87.
45   FO 403/90, Salisbury to Savile, 21.11.87.
46   *Popolo Romano*, 1.11.87.
47   FO 403/90, Crispi to Catalani, 12.11.87.
48   E. Ullendorff, "Some early Amharic Letters," *BSOAS*, vol. XXXV, part 2, 1972, pp. 250, 251.
49   See above, p. 112.
50   B. Melli, *L'Eritrea*, Milano, 1902, p. 19.
51   *The Times*, 13.12.87, 19.12.87.
52   See FO 403/91, Portal to Baring, 6.1.88.
53   Portal, *My Mission*, p. 66.
54   Ibid., p. 85.
55   FO 403/91, Portal to Baring, 1.1.88.
56   FO 403/91, Portal to Baring, 1.1.88.
57   Portal, *My Mission*, p. 81.
58   FO 403/90, Salisbury to Savile, 21.11.87.
59   FO 407/90, Salisbury to Baring, 31.10.87. Portal was supposed to finish his mission in late November in order to let the Italians, if he failed, start their campaign on schedule.
60   Portal, *My Mission*, p. 167.
61   Portal, *My Mission*, p. 158.
62   Ibid., pp. 159, 160.
63   While Portal was on his way to Yohannes Alulā wrote to the emperor that the Italians were actually advancing. FO 403/90, Portal to Baring, 25.12.87. Portal, pp. 161, 162.
64   See M. Perham, *The Government of Ethiopia*, 2nd Ed., London 1969, p. 54.
65   Portal, *My Mission*, p. 217.
66   Yohannes to Victoria, 12.12.87 in FO 95/748; also Portal, *My Mission*, pp. 172-174.
67   A song from an Amharic calendar book, *Qedus Abrehā*, Addis Ababa 1963 E.C.
68   For a good and detailed account, see WO/33/55 A322, "Eritrea Report."
69   FO 403/90, Portal to Baring, 25.12.87. Portal, *Mission*, pp. 161, 162.
70   Yohannes to Menilek, 21.11.87, A.S.MAI 36/4-42, as quoted by Caulk, "The Origins", p. 232. Also in LV, XV.
71   MS Mannawē.
72   FO 403/90, Portal to Baring, 25.12.87.
73   PP.C. 5431, Enclosure 4 in No. 65; Portal, *Mission*, pp. 256-261.
74   See below, pp. 127-129.
75   For Italian-Shoan cooperation and Menilek's policy see: H. Marcus, *The Life and Times*, pp. 96, 97.
76   A.S.MAI, "Diarii Informazioni" 1888, 24.1.88. The "Diarii Informazioni" are two

ETHIOPIAN LOSS OF ERITREA   125

files kept in A.S.MAI which contain the information received from indigenous spies returning from Ethiopian territory throughout 1888 and 1889. The file "Diarii Informazioni" 1888 is kept in "Collezione Vitale" and contains mainly the summarised reports. The "Diarii Informazioni" 1889 is kept in "Archivio Eritrea" No. 109 and contains many original reports. [D.I.]

77   A.S.MAI D.I., 8.1.88, 9.1.88. San Marzano to M.d.G., 20.12.87, LV. XVII.
78   A.S.MAI D.I., 23.1.88.
79   A.S.MAI D.I., 9.1.88.
80   A.S.MAI D.I., 24.1.88, Informant: Adam; 25.1.88, 30.1.88, 8.2.88.
81   A.S.MAI D.I., 16.1.88, 24.1.88. Also FO 403/91, Kennedy to Salisbury, 26.1.88.
82   A.S.MAI D.I., 2.2.88. Evidence collected among Alulā's troops in Gindā'.
83   A.S.MAI D.I., 3.2.88, 8.2.88.
84   See the long report by Lt. Col. Slade in FO 403/91, Savile to Salisbury, 12.1.88.
85   For a detailed account of this operation to re-occupy Sahāṭi, see: *Relazione A.S.E. Il Ministero Della Guerra sulla Operazione Militare eseguita Nell' Inverno Del 1887-88 per la Rioccupazione di Saati*. This report is based on an Extract from the *Rivista Militare Italiana*, 1888. See also: "Eritrea Report."
86   FO 403/91, Kennedy to Salisbury, 4.3.88. Zewde, *Yohannes IV*, p. 520.
87   Lamlam, *Ya'atsē Yohannes tārik*, p. 34. According to other pieces of information, Dabbab was annoyed because the Italians dealt with other Ethiopian deserters, some of them superior to him. One of them was, according to British sources, *Dadjāzmāch* Mangashā, a nephew of the emperor. See: FO 403/91, Slade to Kennedy, 24.2.88; Slade to Savile, 19.3.88; WO 33/155, Eritrea Report, p. 22; IO, L/p & s/9/7, Debeb to Hogg, 23.12.88. This individual was apparently the future *Rās* Mangashā who, as described below, played a most significant role in Ethiopian history from 1889 to 1897.
88   See also Antonelli to MAE, 10.5.88, LV, XVII.
89   Lamlam, *Ya'atsē Yohannes tārik*, p. 35.
90   Genè to Robilant, 16.11.86; Giglio, *Etiopia*, V, No. 262, p. 362.
91   Int. *Dadjāzmāch* Zawdē. Addis Ababa, March 1972.
92   Antonelli to MAE, 10.5.88, LV, XVII.
93   A.S.MAI, D.I., 20.3.88.
94   Holt, *Mahdist*, p. 172; Shuqayr, *Ta'rīkh*, pp. 475-477.
95   Shuqayr, *Ta'rīkh*, p. 477.
96   Heruy's MS, *History of Ethiopia*, pp. 86-87, as quoted by Zewde, p. 526. See a similar text quoted from "An Ethiopian informant" in D. Levine, *Wax and Gold*, Chicago, 1965, p. 28.
97   A.S.MAI, D.I., 20.3.88.
98   Rās Mikā'ēl and Alulā then apparently enjoyed very good relations, and Alulā was reported as having Rās Mikā'ēl's son in his camp. D.I., 8.2.88, 29.2.88.
99   Mannawē MS.
100 FO 403/91, Savile to Salisbury, 12.1.88. Slade to Kennedy, 24.2.88, reports on his conversation with Colonel Dal Verme.
101 FO 403/91, Slade to Savile, 4.4.88.
102 FO 403/91, Slade to Savile, 4.4.88; San Marzano to M.d.G., 3.4.88, LV. XVII.
103 Mannawē MS.
104 For the effect on the Ethiopians, see Kolmodin, *Traditions*, No. 276.
105 LV.XV, Information received from Ambaciera, 17.5.88, in Antonelli to MAE,

10.6.88.
106 Yohannes to General Marzano, Ailet, 26 March 1888; Giglio, *Etiopia*, VI, No. 307, p. 331.
107 FO 403/91, Kennedy to Salisbury, 30.3.88.
108 According to informants returning from Adwā in early May 1888. A.S.MAI, D.I., 19.5.88.
109 Among those mentioned were *Rās* Hagos and *Wāgshum* Gabru. See: San Marzano to M.d.G., 4.4.87, LV. XVII.; A.S.MAI, D.I., various documents, 8.4.88, 18.4.88, 9.5.88, 12.5.88.
110 Portal, *Mission*, p. 152.
111 D.I., 9.4.88.
112 D.I., 9.4.88.
113 D.I., 12, 13, 15.4.88.
114 D.I., 15.4.88, 18.4.88.
115 D.I., 21.4.88.
116 D.I., 20.4.88, 23.4.88.
117 D.I., 9.5.88.
118 Which he visited on his way to Adwā, D.I., 11.4.88.
119 D.I., 6.6.88.
120 *Storia Militare della Colonia Eritrea*, I, p. 170.

12

1888-1889:
The End of the Tigrean Emperor

A. May 1888: The Mahdist Threat — Personal Relief for Alulā

As analysed by P.M. Holt,[1] "warfare against the Abyssinians aroused some repugnance among Sudanese Muslims because a tradition ascribed to the Prophet excepted them from the *jihād*, on account of the asylum granted by the Negus to the Prophet's Companions." But this repugnance disappeared following what the *khalīfa* regarded as Ethiopian aggression against his state:

> So we did not allow the army of the Muslims to raid your land until from your side serious aggressions repeatedly took place against the weak Muslims who are near your country . . . while the apostates from their Faith as Muslims took refuge with you.[2]

It can be quite clearly established that the Mahdist decision to launch a *jihād* derived largely from Yohannes's attempts to fulfil his part of the Hewett Treaty. Judging from the following passage in a manuscript by the Mahdist historian Ismā'īl b. 'Abd al-Qādir, it appears that Alulā's role in these developments was not underestimated in 'Umm Durman:

> When Yūḥanā ascended the throne of Abyssinia . . . he became proud, exorbitant and insolent . . . and looked to the land of Islam. And he sent his troops to the Red Sea coast where he took from the Turks [the Egyptians] several cities and put on the frontier the best of his men who are famous for cunning, bravery and steadiness such as Rās Alulā and others. Rās Alulā was one of the famous and brave men in war, very experienced in the tactics of battles. He was a bone in the throats of the British, Italian and Turkish [Egyptian] Empires.[3]

The Mahdist invasion of Amhara, which culminated in the defeat of Negus Takla-Hāymānot (referred to in the Mahdist correspondence as *Rās* 'Adār), and the destruction of the old capital of Gondar was the first anti-Ethiopian battle initiated under the slogan of the *jihād*. 'Uthmān Diqna's plan of 1885 to invade the Egyptian-evacuated areas of the future Eritrea was an attempt to exploit a certain strategical situation. He aimed at the conquest of mainly Muslim-populated areas, an idea then rejected by the *khalīfa*. Abū 'Anja's expedition of 1887 and the razing of churches was, however, a totally different matter, as was clearly explained in one of the *khalīfa*'s letters to Yohannes:

> And later we have written you the same as the Mahdi had written to you and told you that if you do not act according to our command [i.e. adopt Islam] there will be no alternative to the entrance of the armies of the Islam into your territories, their fighting you and their killing of your men.[4]

Deeply moved by this new Muslim threat, Yohannes undoubtedly consulted his vassals in Adwā about his future action. Alulā, more than ever before, needed a military campaign to save his lost prestige and status. He could not suggest a renewal of the anti-Italian campaign, but he reminded the emperor his previous successes against the Mahdists. The Mannawē manuscript describes an imperial council held in Aksum:[5]

> [And the king] of kings revealed their impure religion [the Mahdists'] and hateful works. Their religion says as follows—'Say "No" to God, and "Yes" to the demon which is Mohammed.'
> Ras Alula . . . opened his mouth and said, 'What really are these pagans, who do not know God? Let us go and do battle with them, on behalf of the name of our Lord Jesus Christ'.
> The king said to him, 'you have spoken well, O elect Ras Alula, a man faithful after my heart'. And the matter ended with this good counsel.[6]

In late May 1888 *Rās* Alulā returned to Asmara to recruit in the Marab Mellāsh for the forthcoming campaign.[7] The emperor left Adwā for Maqalē to spend the coming rainy season there. The *ras* stayed in his *Tukuls* up to 14 June 1888.[8]

B. June 1888: Menilek and Takla-Hāymānot Revolt Against Yohannes

In February 1888, when Yohannes was camping in Adwā, he ordered Menilek to march northward from Wallo. Yohannes was said to have written the Shoan:

> The Muslims want to massacre the Christians and burn the churches of Gondar. . . I am occupied with my battle; order your soldiers and come to Gondar. If they come against you, fight them.[9]

The king welcomed the invitation to march to Amhara, far away from the front. He had already been in touch with the Italians about a secret treaty, and it was thought that he was actually awaiting Yohannes's defeat. As Antonelli wrote in late May,[10] "I am sure he wanted an absolute Italian victory over the emperor so that he could present himself to the people as the saviour of Ethiopia." Menilek slowly led his army to Dabra-Tābor on 8 March 1888, and camped near the ruined Gondar on 18 April 1888. Yohannes was aware of his vassal's relations with the Italians and was angered by Menilek's relative inaction.[11] The Shoan army was camping in Bagemder, actually ruining the country, and in May, Yohannes brusquely ordered Menilek to return to Shoa. The Shoan king crossed the Abbāy River and, on 2 June 1885,[12] met Negus Takla-Hāymānot. "He received him with joy," Lamlam wrote, "they took an oath never to submit to Atsē Yohannes for the second time."[13]

Antonelli's description was, however, closer to the truth:

> Menilek, vexed by Yohannes' treatment of him . . . found Tekle Haimanot who treated him as if he were the empror. The King of Gojjam was even more annoyed than Menilek with the emperor because he believed that the defeat inflicted by the Dervishes had been provoked by the emperor to weaken him.
> They [Menilek and Takla-Hāymānot] have made a pact of mutual aid. Each has fixed to stay in his own kingdom, to obey no orders from the emperor and in case he should invade and occupy their territories, they would unite to fight him.[14]

C. June-July 1888: The Death of Yohannes's Son. Alulā's Departure from Asmara

On 13 June 1888, while *Rās* Alulā was still in Asmara trying to mobilise an army before the rainy season, he received a letter from the emperor informing him that Menilek had entered Wallo without authorization.[15] The next day, on 14 June 1888, with a force of no more than a thousand men, Alulā left Asmara for Maqalē. While camping at Addi Rāsi, Alulā learned that crown prince *Rās* Ar'āyā-Sellāssē (then leading a 40,000-men army towards Bagemder to face a newly rumoured Mahdist invasion)[16] had died of smallpox on 10 June 1888.[17] An interviewer of Alulā later reported:

> It was a great blow for him, as he was accustomed to see the son of Emperor Giovani as the future emperor. . . He was for many years the second father of Ras Area Sellassia[18]. . .
> . . . Hearing the sad news Ras Alula ordered the drums beat and ordered all the people to pray for the soul of the dead prince.[19]

The death of *Rās* Ar'āyā-Sellāssē, the husband of Menilek's daughter Zawditu, was perhaps the end of any hope of saving the emperor's relations with Shoa. The event apparently also had an enormous psychological effect on Yohannes, who henceforth suspected almost everyone, even God, as a potential enemy. With the Italians, the Shoans, the Godjamis and the Mahdists as his enemies, Yohannes again turned to his Turk Bāshā. *Rās* and emperor spent a period of two weeks together in late June and early July in Maqalē, during which they undoubtedly discussed strategy. They received further details of the Menilek-Takla Hāymānot agreement and about the new invasion of Ḥamdān Abū 'Anja, who started on his way to Gondar from Matammā (al-Qallabāt) on 17 June 1888.[20]

On 6 July Alulā returned to Asmara with his 1,000 men. He was again accompanied by his officers and two of his relations—his brother *Dadjāzmāch* Tasammā and nephew *Bāshā* Tadlā—previously the emperor's prisoners and now freed to accompany the rehabilitated *rās*.[21] The emperor left Maqalē on 7 July 1888[12] heading, under heavy rains, for Dabra-Tābor and Godjām, there to fight the weakest of his rivals. Meanwhile Alulā mobilized all available troops, including the garrison of Karan commanded by his son-in-law *Dadjāzmāch* Hāyla-Sellāssē.[23] On 13 July he left Hāyla-Sellāssē and one hundred troops in Asmara and hastened to Ashangē to join up with Yohannes.[24] Alulā was not appointed commander-in-chief of the imperial army. The *rās* might have some credibility in the Marab Mellāsh, but in Tigre, where he had no hereditary rights, his nomination would have caused bitterness and even resistance among the great chiefs. Thus, *Rās* Hāylā-Māryām Gugsā, Yohannes's nephew, was nominated as commander-in-chief and possibly as a crown prince.[25]

D. *August-September 1888:*
The Imperial Army in Godjām. Alulā
Establishes his Position at Court

On 6 August 1888 the emperor crossed the Abbāy River to Godjām, where King Takla-Hāymānot took refuge on the fortified ambā of Gibellā.[26] Alulā was ordered to stay at Dabra-Tābor and march to Dambiyā to face Abū 'Anja,[27] but the latter had already left the area on 30 July 1888.[28] The *rās* was thereupon instructed to stay near Gondar, where he spent the next month.

In early September Alulā was reported to be crossing the Abbāy and joining the imperial forces.[29] In Godjām, meanwhile, Negus Takla-Hāymānot was successfully withstanding the siege of Gibellā. With Alulā's arrival, an intensive action started, to be finished after three weeks with no success. The province of Godjām, particularly the district of Damot, was systematically devastated by the angry Tigreans led by the frustrated emperor. Yohannes's paranoia reflected anxieties that might have been stimulated and exploited by Alulā. The emperor again began to suspect his vassals as traitors. Even faithful *Rās* Hagos was accused of being Menilek's friend and was deprived of his new post over Bagemder which was subsequently given to Alulā, who once had been insulted by the *rās*. Moreover, there was a natural rivalry between these two natives of Tambēn, Alulā the son of a peasant, and Hagos the son of Mirtcha, a former governor of Tambēn and a relative of Yohannes.[30] Another of Alula's enemies, *Badjerond* Lawṭe, recently promoted to *fitāwrāri*, who had led the advance guard to Godjām, was accused of secretly contacting Takla-Hāymānot and was subsequently placed in chains.[31] Informants reaching Massawa reported that *Rās* Alulā, *Rās* Hāyla-Māryām and *Dadjāzmāch* Mangashā were among the few prominent leaders trusted by Yohannes.[32]

E. October-December 1888: Asmara is Threatened While Alulā is With Yohannes

The retreat of the imperial forces in early April 1888 was not immediately exploited by the Italians, and they retained Sahāṭi as their advance post. Meanwhile, General Baldissera's policy of encouraging local opposition to Alulā's government in the Marab Mellāsh became effective. On 15 July 1888, a few days after Alulā's son-in-law, *Dadjāzmāch* Hāyla-Sellāsē, had left Karan, the pro-Italian *Dadjāzmāch* Keflē Iyāsus wrote Baldissera seeking permission to take the town. Keflē was promised supplies and money but was instructed to remain in Ḥabbāb and Banū 'Āmir,[33] where he commenced raiding. In one of these skirmishes, which took place in late October, *Bāshā* Gabra-Māyrām, Alulā's deputy commander in Asmara, was reported killed.[34]

At his headquarters at Saganieti, as the new governor of Akalla-Guzāy, Dabbab Ar'āyā did nothing but protect himself against the Italians.[35] Soon his attention became fixated on the almost deserted capital of Hamāsēn, and he began fighting with *Dadjāzmāch* Hāyla-Sellāsē, the governor, in early October. On 18 October the latter received a written ultimatum from Dabbab: "Evacuate Asmara because I am going to assume its government. If you disagree prepare yourself for battle." Hāyla-Sellāsē refused to move, "before I receive a written order from my master Alulā. If you want to use force, I am ready."[36] Dabbab was apparently looking beyond the government of Hamāsēn and did not want, for the time being, to risk provoking a direct clash with Alulā's nominee. Instead, he marched in early December 1888 to Adwā and established his headquarters in the Tigrean capital itself. While the emperor and Alulā occupied Godjām and Bagemder, he vainly tried to persuade Alulā's Greek arms traders to supply him with new rifles.[37] Dabbab revealed his ambitions in a letter, which he sent on 23 December 1888 to the British Resident at Aden:

> I am no way in accord with the Negus ... I am of Royal birth. If, with the help of Jesus Christ, I secure your goodwill, I shall have no more troubles. I have given my heart to you. Love me. I love you. It is you who have put King John upon the Throne; consequently after Jesus Christ, I look to you for support.[38]

Meanwhile, encouraged by the threats to Alulā's government in December 1888, old *Rās* Walda-Mikā'ēl, at Ambā Salāmā, had drafted a letter to the Italians in Massawa and to his son-in-law Keflē 'Iyāsus camping near Karan, calling on them to take the road inland. His letter was intercepted by *Dadjāzmāch* Hāyla-Sellāssē and despatched to Alulā in Bagemder.[39]

Another potential threat to Alulā's government in the Marab Mellāsh, and indeed to the whole Tigrean government of the emperor, was *Dadjāzmāch* Seyum Gabra-Kidān, "Abbā Gubaz." Yohannes's nephew, he had been imprisoned for many years on an *ambā* in Godjām. After Takla-Hāymānot's agreement with Menilek, Seyum was released and with the advance of the imperial army to Godjām, he was sent to Shoa. Following the Tigrean siege of Takla-Hāymānot and the devastation of Godjām, Menilek was reported intensifying Shoa's preparations for possible invasion. The king did not keep to defensive measures only but did his best to outmanoeuvre Yohannes by enticing an Italian advance from the coast to Asmara.[40] For his part, Menilek undertook to instigate a revolt in Tigre to be headed by *Dadjāzmāch* Seyum.[41] In the middle of December 1888, Seyum was reported en route to Endartā and not far from Maqalē.[42]

With Tigre and Asmara thus threatened, Alulā was with his master in Bagemder and Godjām. He was constantly informed by *Dadjāzmāch* Hāyla-Sellāssē on the developments in the Marab Mellāsh, but was apparently unable to do very much about them. Around mid-August 1888, upon hearing in Dabra-Tābor about the activities of Keflē Iyāsus, he sent 120 troops with *Ledj* Fantā and *Shālaqā* Ar'āyā to Asmara,[43] the only small force he could detach. Threatened and surrounded as it was, Asmara had been retained by *Dadjāzmāch* Hāyla-Sellāssē only because it was constantly rumoured that Alulā was about to return. During the months of November and December 1888 the *ras* sent many letters to his nominee instructing him to announce his imminent arrival.[44] Cattle were frequently gathered at Asmara, as if supplies for a returning army.[45] But Alulā, though he undoubtedly wanted to go to Asmara, was ordered by Yohannes to remain in camp.[46] Apparently the emperor trusted Dabbab Ar'āyā and wanted Alulā close-by for counsel and advice about an anti-Shoan or anti-Mahdist campaign.

F. January 1889: Yohannes Decides to Fight the Mahdists

During late December and up to 17 January 1889, the emperor tried to solve his problems with Menilek through diplomacy. Menilek, threatened by possible invasion, fortified his frontier and simultaneously, cautious as ever, worked hard to appease Yohannes, placing all blame for the current situation on the helpless *Negus* Takla-Hāymānot.[47] The latter, in late December 1888, after a long siege, realized that he had been abandoned by Menilek, submitted to Yohannes, and was pardoned.[48]

Once the Godjami problem was solved, Alulā argued against crossing the Abbāy, for tactical reasons,[49] although it looks as if Yohannes, towards the end of December 1888, was ready to march into Shoa. In a long letter of 25 December 1888 to Abu 'Anja at al-Qallabāt, the emperor offered cooperation against the Europeans (*Afrānj*) and asked for peace, presumably in order to secure his rear: "I have no wish to cross my frontier into your country nor should you desire to cross your frontier into my country."[50] Abū 'Anja received the letter on 11 January 1889, and replied on the same day,[51] insulting Yohannes and calling on him to adopt Islam:

> If you have power and courage as you claim, attack us. You would not have hesitated up to the present, had it not been for your cowardice. And if you do not come, stay in your place and you will have no choice, but to be destroyed by the followers of God. . .[52]

Yohannes received Abū 'Anja's riposte probably simultaneously with Menilek's conciliatory letter of 17 January 1889.[53] As suggested by a Mahdist historian, Yohannes could not stand by and watch Hamdān Abū 'Anja invade his country.[54] At court Yohannes was presssed by the clergy and the senior officers to abandon the projected Shoan campaign. According to Heruy, they believed that it would not:

> be convenient to march to Shoa leaving the Dervishes behind. Let us first destroy the Dervishes, and then, when we return back we shall go to Shoa.[55]

According to Lamlam, Yohannes was persuaded: "if I come back I can fight Shoa later on when I return. And if I die at Matammā in the hands of the heathens I shall gain heaven."[56] He therefore wrote an appeasing letter to Menilek and marched to the Sudanese border.[57]

G. *February 1889: Dabbab Takes Asmara*

By late January the imperial army was concentrating in Dambiyā to march on Qallabāt (Matammā). In Yohannes's camp the following leaders, beside Alulā, were reported assembling: *Negus* Takla-Hāymānot, *Rās* Mikā'ēl, *Rās* Hāyla-Māryām and *Rās* Mangashā.[58] *Rās* Alulā was reported to be the commander of a well equipped force of 15,000 riflemen.[59]

From Asmara worrying news reached Alulā that the town was threatened by both Dabbab and Keflē Iyāsus. Thus, while the emperor was planning his campaign in the western frontier, Alulā sought for leave to return and settle affairs in his own provincial capital.[60] But Yohannes was reported to have full confidence in Dabbab Ar'āyā to whom he sent, in the middle of December 1888, a present of a horse and a sword. "With the horse travel into the country you like," the attached letter was rumoured to have advised,[61] "and with the sword cut whomever you like." Alulā could only obtain permission to send his nephew, *Bāshā* Dastā, with a few armed followers to reinforce *Dadjāzmāch* Hāyla-Sellāssē in Asmara.[62] But Dabbab was too ambitious merely to be a provincial governor.

Simultaneously with his letter to the British Resident in Aden, he directed a communication to Baldissera seeking forgiveness and renewed Italian support.[63] In late January 1889 he led his 2,000 followers to Saganeiti where, on 2 February 1889, he met the Major Piano and General Baldissera. Immediately afterwards he marched on Asmara and in a short and decisive battle which took place on 9 February 1889, he killed *Dadjāzmāch* Hāyla-Sellāssē and some 150 of his followers at Addi Baro and entered Alulā's capital on the same day.[64]

Dabbab made his headquarters in the *tukuls* of his great rival.[65] As can be concluded from Dabbab's letter of 10 February 1889 to Baldissera, Yohannes still hoped to have him govern the Marab Mellāsh:

> I have just received a letter from the king saying: 'Dear brother, return to me and leave the Italians... I am your brother. I shall give you the title of your father [*Rās*]. Answer me.'

But Dabbab had other ideas concerning his future career:

> The king only gave me a title [*Dadjāzmāch*] but I was not convinced he was my friend. I want to be a ruler... I have now half of Ethiopia in my hands. You and I should help each other to our victory... I ask you no arms and no money but your friendship.[66]

Meanwhile the Italians were already in action. Three days prior to Dabbab's occupation of Asmara, an Italian expeditionary force accompanied by Keflē Iyāsus entered Karan, where the latter was to remain under the Italian flag.[67] Karan, then Asmara and the whole of Eritrea, would see this flag during the next five decades.

H. March 1889: The Death of Yohannes in Matammā. His Heir, Mangashā, Put Under the Care of Alulā

Rās Alula was not the commander of the Ethiopian army in the battle of Matammā (Al-Qallabat), 8-11 March 1889. Hearsay even suggests that he did not want to participate in the battle or that he opposed the emperor's tactics.[68] According to the report by *Echagē* Tēwoflos given six and a half years later,[69] Yohannes's new young favourites, Mangashā[70] and Hāyla-Māryām, commanded the two wings of the imperial forces. The two princes were Yohannes's nephews,[71] and Hāyla-Māryām was reportedly the superior and was regarded by the emperor as his heir.[72] Alulā was described as fighting in the right wing together with *Rās* Mangashā,[73] and probably was really in charge.

The Mahdist army, led by Az-Zākī Ṭamal, recently nominated following the death of Ḥamdān Abū 'Anja in January 1889, was entrenched in a zariba.[74]

According to the description given by *Echagē* Tēwoflos,[75] the armies confronted each other on Saturday, 9 March 1889, and the Ethiopian right wing under Mangashā managed to penetrate the Mahdist strong point. In that early stage of the battle, Alulā suffered four minor wounds which apparently did not affect his activities.[76] On the left wing, however, the death of *Rās* Hāyla-Māryām led to confusion and disaster, in strong contrast to the right wing, where success pushed Mangashā to advance, in turn causing the emperor, hitherto inspecting the battle from the rear, to move forward and encourage the army.[77] "Rās Mangashā sent [to Yohannes] saying: 'There is an entrance which we have broken, come'."[78] According to Tēwoflos, Yohannes moved forward enthusiastically, firing his rifle:

> A bullet hit his right hand. But he wrapped it in his *shamma* as if it were nothing. Still he advanced wanting to fire. Another bullet pierced his left hand, struck his chest and lodged there. The *Negus* was carried to his tent.[79]

While the emperor was being taken to the rear, the demoralized Ethiopians broke and ran, suffering many loses. Nightfall was a relief for them, but not for the wounded emperor:

> That night the king passed the time in great pain. When it was morning [Sunday, 10 March 1889] Ras Alula came to him to know his condition, and he [Yohannes] told him secret mysteries concerning the house of the kingdom and concerning the house of his son Ras Mangasha...[80]

Mangashā hitherto had been considered to be Yohannes's nephew. Now, the dying Yohannes declared that Mangashā was his son, not his brother's, and recognised him as his successor.[81]

When Yohannes finished this surprising statement he ordered *Rās* Alulā:

> 'O my beloved and faithful one, behold your son, this Ras Mangasha. Protect your trust which I have handed over to you.' And to his son he said, 'My son, behold your father, Ras Alula, do not depart from his counsel, nor transgress his commands.'
> Having spoken like this, he [Yohannes] made a promise, and rested from the toil of this transitory world...[82]

Yohannes's hopes were dashed not only by immediate opposition to Mangashā but also by the break-up of the Ethiopian army.[83]

Deserted by most of their troops and their officers,[84] *Rās*es Mangashā and Alulā began a hasty retreat to Tigre.[85] The emperor's body was captured, and old *Rās* Ar'āyā Demṣu was killed by the pursuing Mahdists.[86] According to a Mahdist chronicler who was not an eye-witness, on 12 March 1889, near the Atbara River, a second clash developed into a real battle:

> Most of the Abyssinian chiefs who escaped from the first battle were

killed in this. Rās Alūlā, although he was the fire of the Abyssinians's fire [this time] he ran away.[87]

That day Az-Zakī Ṭamal proudly wrote to the khalīfa boasting that he had forwarded the heads of Yohannes and *Rās* Alūlā to 'Umm Durmān. *Rās* Alūlā's head was never received; he remained its possessor although he lost almost everything else.

* * *

Yohannes's death robbed Alūlā of his main source of power. Though frequently upset with the *rās*, Yohannes justifiably regarded Alūlā as his most loyal and trusted vassal. While others proved to be rivals and contenders, the *turk bāshā* could only be blamed for being inflexible with Europeans. Even Alūlā's interest in creating an independent base for himself in the Marab Mellāsh was aimed at securing wealth and social status, and he never sought to create a politically independent unit. Had Yohannes survived the battle of Matammā, he again would have given Alūlā important new military and civil responsibilities.

Now, however, Asmara and Hamāsēn gone, *Rās* Alūlā lost the chance to surmount his patron's death through deriving power from a provincial domain. He lost his source of finance and manpower, his safe base and his home. All he could do now was to return to Tigre where he was actually the "Wadi Qubi," deprived of wealth and hereditary rights.

NOTES

1 Holt, p. 150. Also see Khalīfa to Yohannes, Jan.-Feb. 1887, quoted by Holt.
2 Holt, quotes Shuqayr, *Ta'rīkh*, pp. 467-469.
3 Isma'īl b. 'Abd al-Qādir, *Aṭ-ṭirāz al-manqūsh bibushrā qatl Yūḥanā malik al-ḥubūsh*, Ms., Library of the School of Oriental Studies, Durham, pp. 33, 34.
4 Shuqayr, *Ta'rīkh*, p. 474. This letter written after Abū 'Anja's expedition reached the emperor in April or May 1888.
5 Yohannes and his court were in Aksum on 10.5.88. See above p. 122.
6 Mannawe MS.
7 D.I., 6.6.88.
8 D.I., 16.6.88.
9 Anonymous Amharic biography of *Ras* Gobana, Institute of Ethiopian Studies, Addis Ababa University.
10 Antonelli to MAE, 22.5.88, LV, XV.
11 Antonelli to MAE, 10.6.88, LV, XV.
12 Zewde, *Yohannes IV*, p. 243.
13 Lamlam, *Ya'atse Yohannes tarik*, p. 36. For background, consult Marcus, *The Life*

and Times, pp. 102-104.
14 Antonelli to MAE, 11.6.88, LV, XV.
15 A.S.MAI F.I., 16.6.88.
16 A.S.MAI D.I., 13.6.88.
17 Zewde, *Yohannes IV*, p. 244.
18 N. Corazzini, "La pace," *La Tribuna*, 30.6.90.
19 D.I., 18.6.88.
20 Holt, *Mahdist State*, p. 173.
21 D.I., 8.7.88, 10.7.88. Informant Muhammad Ibrahim.
22 A Ms. from Dabra-Berhān Sellāssē, Gondar, Institute of Ethiopian Studies.
23 The son of *Fitāwrāri* Walda-Taklay, a local chief, *Dadjāzmāch* Hāyla-Sellāssē was the governor of Karan and married Alulā's daughter Ṣahāywarada. Interview w. Yashashwarq, Abbi Addi, December 1971.
24 D.I., 16.7.88. Informant Keflu Drar.
25 Interview, *Dadjāzmāch* Zawdē, Addis Ababa 1972. Sahle Woldegaber, "The Background to the battle of Metemma", BA Thesis, H.S.I.U., 1968, p. 17. Hāylā-Māryām Gugsa was the son of one of Yohannes's elder brothers and was appointed governor of Wādlā in 1878; see Zewde, *Yohannes IV*, Appendix, biographical data.
26 A MS. From Dabra-Berhān Sellāsse, Gondar, IES.
27 Antonelli to MAE, 12.10.88, LV, XV, D.I. 30.8.88.
28 Holt, *Mahdist State*, p. 173.
29 D.I., 7.9.88.
30 See Martini, *Diario*, II, p. 411 and Wylde, *Modern*, p. 174.
31 Antonelli to MAE, 10.12.88, LV, XV. He was later condemned to death by Yohannes, but was saved by Alulā's appeal. A.S.MAI, D.I., 16.1.89, informant Gabra Masqal.
32 D.I., 3.11.88.
33 A.S.MAI, "Vitale," Kafel to Baldissera, 15.7.88; Baldissera to Kafel, 9.12.88.
34 D.I., 28.10.88.
35 WO 33/55, A322, Eritrea Report, p. 25.
36 D.I., 20.10.88.
37 D.I., 15.12.88.
38 IO, L/P&S/9/7, Dadjasmuk [*Dadjāzmach*] Debeb to Brig. Gen. Hogg, 23.12.88. Dabbab's self-reference as a dadjāzmāch could be a false pretention, but Yohannes may have accorded him that rank following his defection in the spring.
39 D.I., 12.12.88.
40 Antonelli to Crispi, 23.9.88. LV, XV. According to a report sent in September 1888 (Dhū al-Ḥijja 1305 H) to the Khalīfa (SOAS, M.518, Reel 9), Abū 'Anja was corresponding with Menilek. He added that "Minilīk spread the rumours that after destroying Yuḥannā he would adopt Islam and would rule the Abyssinians under the auspices of the Mahdiyya." While this was obviously untrue, Menilek probably did attempt to obtain Mahdist intervention.
41 Antonelli to MAE, 12.10.88, 30.10.88, 10.12.88, LV, XV.
42 D.I., 24.12.88.
43 D.I., 25.8.88.
44 D.I., 9.11.88, 13.12.88.
45 D.I., 20.12.88, 21.12.88.
46 D.I., 15.12.88.

47 See Zewde, *Yohannes IV*, pp. 542-544, as quoted from Heruy Walda-Sellāssē MS, *History of Ethiopia*, pp. 81-85.
48 A.S.MAI, D.I., 4.1.89, Suliman /akariya, 16.1.89, informant Ali Kabssay; Lamlam, *Ya'atse Yohannes tarik*, f. 38.
49 Antonelli to MAE, 26.12.88, LV, XV.
50 Shuqayr, *Ta'rıkh*, p. 479.
51 SOAS, M.518, reel 9, Abu 'Anja to Khalıfa, 11.1.89.
52 Shuqayr, *Ta'rıkh*, pp. 480, 481.
53 Zewde, *Yohannes IV*, pp. 268-269, as quoted from Heruy's MS, *History of Ethiopia*.
54 Isma'il, *Aṭ-Ṭirāz*, p. 108.
55 Heruy Walda-Sellasse, *Ityopyānā Matammā*, Addis Ababa 1901, EC, p. 11.
56 Lamlam, *Ya'atsē Yohannes tārik*, f. 38.
57 A.S.MAI, D.I., 26.1.89, informant Abd al-Karim.
58 Mangasha had been recently made *rās* and given the provinces of the late crown prince, including Bagemder. A.S.MAI, D.I., 21.2.89, informant Kefle Maryam, who left Godjam on 30.1.89. This contradicts *Echage* Tewoflos's 1895 statement that in the battle of Matamma, Mangasha was still a *dadjāzmāch*. See Conti Rossini, *Italia ed Etiopia*, p. 461.
59 A.S.MAI D.I., 21.2.89, the informant Kefle Māryām who left Godjam 30.1.89.
60 A.S.MAI, D.I., 22.1.89, 23.1.89, informant: Berhano.
61 A.S.MAI D.I., 3.1.89, informant: Haylu.
62 D.I., 22.1.89, 23.1.89, informant: Berhano.
63 A.S. MAI D.I., 12.1.89, Dabbab to Baldissera, 24.12.88.
64 *Storia Militare*, p. 192; D.I., 13.2.89, 10.2.89, informant: Muhammad al-Fīl, FO 403/12, Slade to Dufferin, 15.2.89.
65 A.S. MAI D.I., 13.2.89, informant: Sulimān.
66 A.S.MAI, D.I., Dabbab to Baldissera (Arabic), 10.2.89.
67 WO 33/55, "Eritrea Report".
68 Tesfai Seyoum, BA Thesis, 1970, p. 34, quoting an informant, Bashai Tzegai Ghebremikael. Also int. with Bairu Tafla of *IES*, Jan. 1972.
69 Conti Rossini, *Italia*, pp. 461, 462.
70 Mangasha was born in 1868, see C. Zaghi (ed.), *Crispi e Menelich; Nel diario inedito del Conte A. Salimbeni*, Torino 1956, p. 24.
71 For Mangasha being the son of Gugsa, Yohannes's brother, see Takla-Ṣadeq Makuriya, *Yaitopyā tārik*, p. 63.
72 Wylde, "Unofficial," *MG*, 10.5.97.
73 Wylde, "Modern", p. 41. In Heruy, *Ityopyānā Matammā*, p. 12, Mangasha is not mentioned among the *rases*, but on p. 13 Yohannes refered to him as *rās*.
74 Holt, *Mahdist State*, pp. 173, 174. Abū 'Anja fell ill and died on 29 January 1889.
75 Conti Rossini, *Italia*, pp. 461, 462.
76 Mannawe MS, A.S.MAI, D.I., 2.4.89, informant: Uthmān 'Umān.
77 Wylde, "Unofficial," *MG*, 10.5.97.
78 Lamlam, *Ya'atsē Yohannes tārik*, f. 39.
79 Conti Rossini, *Italia*, pp. 461, 462.
80 Mannawē MS.
81 See Tēwoflos's description in Conti Rossini, *Italia*, pp. 461, 462. See also Takla-Ṣadeq Makuriyā, *Ya'ityopyā tārik*, p. 63.
82 Mannawē Ms.

83 In July 1896 Alula told A.B. Wylde: "It was not till the next day [Sunday 10 March 1889] when quarrels arose as to the succession to the throne, that the Abyssinian army retreated." Wylde "Unofficial," *MG*, 17.5.97. [Consult also Mem. et Doc. 138, p. 161, Report by Labosse, 17.2.90.] On the same occasion, Alulā rejected Slatin's account of the battle (see Slatin, pp. 439-442) as inaccurate. After Wylde read it to Alulā, he reacted: "How can Slatin describe a battle which he never saw?"

84 Immediately following Yohannes's death, *Rās* Mikā'ēl left for Wallo with his men. See A.S.MAI, D.I., 6.4.89, informant: Gabra Masqal Kāfil.

85 LV, XV, Antonelli to MAE, 27.3.89.

86 Heruy, *Ityopyānā Matammā*, p. 14; Conti Rossini, *Italia*, p. 26, note 2.

87 Ismā'īl, *At-Tirāz*, ff. 125-130. Ismā'īl provides the only evidence about such a clash.

88 Shuqayr, p. 485. A.S.MAI, D.I., 28.5.89. A letter of Aḥmad al-Jīr to Muḥammad al-Fīl, 21.4.89. He was in Khartum and claims to have seen the heads of Alulā and Yohannes. For similar stories, see FO 407/88, Baring to Salisbury, 8.5.89, and Smith to Grenfell, 11.4.89. Also J. Ohrwalder, *Ten Years' Captivity in the Mahdi's Camp*, London 1892, p. 268.

13

1889-1890: Alulā's Failure to Preserve Tigrean Hegemony

A. *Tigrean Hegemony–Alulā's Only Hope for Political Survival*

Having no traditional rights in Tigre, no feudal domain, and consequently no military or economic power, Alulā had to return again to the status of a king's man. He again must become the future Mangashā's prestigious *turk bāshā*, the same position he had enjoyed in the late seventies and early eighties at Yohannes's court. Alulā's destiny was now totally dependent on the preservation of Tigrean hegemony, and his relations with *Rās* Mangashā stemmed from the need to survive politically. Limited to Tigre, Alulā thus had no chance of imperial office and would have to find his place within the province's political framework. Here the best for which he could hope was to be given a small *gult*, or, as Alulā himself said later, to enter a convent[1] and finish his life with prayers. (Indeed it was most probably in 1889 that Mangashā granted him the profits from the custom of Adwā,[2] but given the unstable political situation the revenues were small).

The task of reestablishing the Tigrean imperial court was beset with difficulties. *Negus* Takla-Hāymānot, *Rās* Mikā'ēl and other important leaders, whose loyalty to the Tigrean throne was hitherto pragmatic and conditional, sided with Shoa's now powerful Negus Menilek. In fact almost immediately after Yohannes's death, Menilek was in position to proclaim his accession and receive the submission of Lāstā, Godjām, Wallo and Bagemder.[3]

The Tigrean hegemony was threatened also by the traditional local rivalries hitherto partly restrained by Yohannes. Those tendencies had become stronger during the eight months of Yohannes's absence.

As described by Conti Rossini,[4] there were three great, historic lineages in Tigre which competed for its government: Mangashā's family had originated in Tambēn and was known for great figures like *Rās* Mikā'ēl Sehul, who governed Tigre for about forty years before he died in 1780. The second family was that of *Rās* Ar'āyā Demṣu from Endartā, headed now by Dabbab Ar'āyā, whose forefathers included *Rās* Walda-Sellāssē who controlled Tigre after *Rās* Mikā'ēl Sehul until 1816.

Third were the descendants of Sabāgādis, a *dadjāzmāch* from Agāmē, who governed the province from 1818 to 1831. The family was headed by *Dadjāzmāch* Sebhat Aragāwi, the hereditary prince and governor of Agāmē.

To these chronic rivalries, one can add contenders whose power derived from a non-Tigrean source, such as *Dadjāzmāch* Seyum, "Abba Gubaz," of Yohannes's family, soon to be nominated by Menilek as governor of Tigre.

The internal political situation was complicated by disastrous economic conditions, the result of one of the worst periods of famine and epidemic in Ethiopian history.[5] Feeding a small army even for a very short time was soon to become impossible in the shattered Tigre. Notwithstanding such adversity, *Rās* Alulā apparently tried to persuade *Rās* Mangashā to crown himself Emperor of Ethiopia.[6] Probably for that purpose he guided the young *ras* to Aksum, the traditional site of Ethiopian coronations. According to the Mannawē Ms., they marched from Matammā to Semēn,[7] thence to Tambēn where they arrived in early April:

> Passing on from there, they arrived at the country of Aksum [on 20 April 1889[9]] and the people of Zion received them, weeping and making lamentation for themselves and for Yohannes their king... They assembled and went to Ras Alula, and they said to him, 'Praise to God in heaven ... for he has shown us your face, and has spared you for us, the seed of Yohannes. If he had not spared you for us from death, we would have been like Sodom, and we would have resembled Gomorra.'[10]

B. *April-May 1889: Sebhat and Dabbab Refuse to Unite Under Mangashā*

Rās Mangashā had practical reasons for refusing Alulā's demand to proclaim himself monarch. While he may have been weak-willed,[11] the establishment of his supremacy in Tigre itself, a most necessary precondition for a claim to the throne, was far from being achieved. Threatened by both Shoa and Italy, soon to become officially allied under the Treaty of Uccialli (2nd May 1889), Mangashā and Alulā had not yet achieved that aim.

The ruler of Agāmē, *Dadjāzmāch* Sebhat Aragāwi, at first seemed a possible ally. He had participated in the battle of Matammā, in the subsequent clash at the Atbara between the Mahdists and the retreating Tigreans, and in the later battle in Semēn. He had accompanied Alulā and Mangashā on their way through Tambēn to Aksum and Adwā. There, in the Tigrean capital, in wake of an argument over an old problem with *Dadjāzmāch* Tadlā of Ayba, a follower of Mangashā,[12] he secretly left camp and returned to Agāmē, to await developments.[13] In the later part of 1889, he started cooperating with the Italians, hoping that they would help him to achieve political prominence.

Another Tigrean was already on his way to political prominence. Dabbab

Ar'āyā lived in "Alulā's Tukuls" in Asmara for about a month (from 9 February 1889), exchanging written threats with Yohannes's devotées in Adwā and Aksum *Dadjāzmāch* Tadlā Ayba and the *Nebura-'ed* (governor of Aksum) Walda-Giyorgis.[14] Then in early March he decided to move to his natural base in Saganeiti, probably in order to mobilise more troops for a possible return to Adwā.[15] Consequently Tadlā Ayba marched to the deserted capital of Hamāsēn and entered it in mid-March, proclaiming that he was acting in Yohannes's name.[16] At Saganeiti Dabbab was reluctant to move to Adwā as rumours about the return of Yohannes and Alulā were heard everywhere. In late March Dabbab and Tadlā Ayba clashed between Saganeiti and Asmara, each of them suffering some 10-20 casualties.[17] Tadlā Ayba marched to Adwā,[18] while Dabbab, who had meanwhile learned of Mangashā's and Alulā's arrival at Tambēn, returned to Saganeiti.

Following the death of *Rās* Ar'āyā Demṣu at Matammā, Alulā was shrewd enough to detain two of his sons[19] in an attempt to control the behaviour of their rebellious brother, Dabbab. From Adwā in early May, Alulā sent an agent, to arrange a settlement. In reply, Dabbab demanded his brothers' release and refused to negotiate with one whom he called a usurper of others' rights. He simultaneously wrote to Mangashā assuring him of his desire to compromise but asked for the delivery of Alulā into his hands as a sign of sincere friendship. Mangashā retorted that Alulā was his father, and that a son should never betray his father.[20] The incident, however, demonstrated that Mangashā's identification with *Rās* Alulā could cause difficulties in reuniting Tigre under his dominance.

C. *April-May 1889: Failure to Unite with the Local Élite of Hamāsēn*

Together with the diplomatic effort to unite Tigre, Alulā conducted another diplomatic campaign to regain the Marab Mellāsh. Reaching Tambēn in early April, he camped with Mangashā near Ambā Salāmā, where the leaders of the old aristocratic families of Hamāsēn were still imprisoned. Alulā understood that he had no chance of forcibly restoring Ethiopian government beyond the Marab: after Matammā, many of his followers had either returned to Tigre or had disappeared from the political scene. He therefore had no other choice but to free the old leaders in return for their support.

Rās Walda-Mika'ēl, however, refused to leave the *Ambā* on which he had spent the last ten years,[21] even though he was now a free man. His son Masfen, on the other hand, seemed willing to cooperate; he accompanied Alulā to Aksum and Adwā,[22] and rumours were spread that he would marry the *rās*'s daughter, the widow of Hāyla-Sellāssē.[23] But Masfen could not forget recent history, and from Adwā he secretly offered to help undermine his family's old enemy. He added that his father and younger brother, Hāyla-Malakot, were still on the *ambā*.[24]

Alulā's plan was to influence *Dadjāzmāch* Keflē Iyāsus, Masfen's brother-in-law, to betray the Italians and help him regain Asmara.[25] Kefle, who had some 2,000 followers and 600 rifles,[26] had already raided Asmara around mid-March 1889[27] and actually had captured it for a short time in early April.[28] The *dadjāzmāch* now seemed to be willing to cooperate with Masfen and Alulā and was subsequently reinforced by 'Alāmayahu Gabru, the son of *Belāttā* Gabru and Alulā's devotee in Bogos.[29]

Kefle was encouraged to side with Alulā, probably because he anticipated a move by 'Uthmān Diqna on the Banū 'Āmir and Ḥabbāb[30] and did not believe the Italians would intervene. Indeed, General Baldissera had suggested "that no action should be taken by the [Italian] colonial force until the strength of the conflicting parties [in northern Ethiopia] was entirely exhausted."[31]

But Alulā and Mangashā were doing their best to unite the conflicting parties. In late May it was reported that Alulā was making final preparations to cross the Marab. The Italians, however, aware of their opponent's moves, decided to intervene. From the deserted Asmara, Dabbab and an Italian major led a strong force to Karan and occupied it on 2 June 1889. Kefle was arrested and was sent to die in a prison at Assab.[32]

D. *May 1889: Isolation and Military Weakness*

At Adwā, the following leaders were with Mangashā: *Rās* Alulā, *Rās* Hagos, *Dadjāzmāch* Tadlā Ayba, *Dadjāzmāch* Tasammā, and *Shālaqā* Ar'āyā.[33] The failure to attract additional support not only emphasized the political isolation of those at Adwā, but also indicated that they would not be able to achieve Mangashā's goals. Meanwhile, their army of 8,000[34] was steadily deteriorating because of lack of forage and food.[35] The projected march on Hamāsēn had to be cancelled, and on 10 May 1889 Alulā distributed among his men what was probably his last resource, the sorely depleted royal stores of Aksum, which contained a pitiful few hundred rifles and forty boxes of ammunition.[36] In the third week of May, Alulā sent a detachment of his best troops to raid and feed themselves beyond the Marab,[37] but the others seemed to be losing their patience.

On 24 May 1889 Dabbab wrote to Baldissera that *Shālaqā* Ar'āyā had left Alulā and joined his camp with forty riflemen;[38] a day later, Alulā's brother Tasammā reportedly also deserted.[39] Meanwhile, Alulā had arrested *Nebura-'ed* Walda-Giyorgis because his two sons had left the camp with 150 men,[40] and the *rās* could muster only two hundred troops, as Mangashā's men were in Adwā. In early June came more news about deserters to Dabbab,[41] and Alulā was reported trying frantically to hold on to his men.[42] Tigre, the centre of Yohannes's empire, was virtually isolated and disunited.

E. June 1889: Menilek's Appointee Fails to Enter Tigre

On 2 May 1889 Menilek, aiming "to neutralize Mangashā's pretensions as well as regularize his own status,"[43] signed the treaty of Uccialli with Italy. In order to get official Italian recognition of his accession to the throne and the important right to import military supplies duty-free through Massawa, Menilek agreed in the treaty that a joint commission should fix a frontier line from Arāfali on the Red Sea along the highlands, leaving Asmara and the Bogos with Karan to Italy [Article III]. During the preliminary negotiations on 26 March 1889, Menilek wrote to King Umberto, calling on him to order his troops at Massawa to guard the frontier towards Asmara, and to pay no heed to the appeals of outlaws (*sheftoch*) or rebels against his authority in Tigre, or to allow arms to pass through to them.[44] Since *ras* Mikā'ēl and *Negus* Takla-Hāymānot had come over to Menilek in June,[45] the new emperor was able to send *Dadjāzmāch* Seyum northwards as his nominee over Tigre, his position vastly different than that of Mangashā and Alulā. They had been deserted by most of their troops; they had no possible ally; and they were threatened by Italy and Dabbab from the north and Menilek and Seyum from the south.

In late May it was rumoured that Menilek would personally lead his forces to Tigre,[46] but meanwhile, Seyum advanced to Lāstā from where the local governor *Wāgshum* Beru, a rival of Seyum, fled to Saganeiti and joined up with Dabbab on 6 June 1889.[47] Seyum passed Lake Ashangē and in early June entered the Tigrean province of Endartā where, according to Italian-employed informants, he was well received by the population.[48] This region, and especially Maqalē, its capital, had been the headquarters of the late *Ras* Ar'āyā-Sellāssē and his young wife, Zawditu, to whom Yohannes had given large areas as *gult*. Following the death of Ar'āyā-Sellāsse, the princess had returned to Shoa, but she had many devotees in Endarta who favoured Tigrean recognition of Menilek as emperor.[49]

Meanwhile,[50] Alulā and Mangashā's camp at Adwā continued to suffer increasing desertions. The two *rās*es had to move if they wanted their followers to remain with them. They left Adwā[51] on 4 June 1889, and marched to fight Seyum near Maqalē. The latter, however, avoided the challenge and retreated to Ashangē, while Mangashā and his mentor returned to Tambēn[52] to be in a position to defend both Adwā and Maqalē:

> After this, two rulers [Seyum and Dabbab] rose up in rebellion, and Ras Alula said to Ras Mangasha 'Arise, let us go to fight Dajjach Seyum, because he has come from the eastern land, in order to destroy us and to remove the kingdom of Yohannes.' The heart of Ras Mangasha rejoiced at this counsel, and they went together towards the east [Maqalē is south east of Adwā] to search for him; and they did not find a trace of his path.[53]

Yet Menilek's appointee as a governor of Tigre was not defeated; his retreat to Ashangē was only a tactical step.

F. June-July 1889: Dabbab Takes Adwā and is Imprisoned by Alulā

Before leaving Adwā for Maqalē *Rās* Mangashā appointed *Dadjāzmāch* Embāyē governor. He was Dabbab's nephew, and therefore a potential traitor, but Mangashā and Alulā apparently had no choice. Since they had few followers, they had to make hazardous and quick appointments before leaving the district. On 17 June 1889 it was said in Massawa that Dabbab had left Saganeiti for Adwā,[54] and it was well established by various informants[55] that *Dadjāzmāch* Embāyē had invited him to take the Tigrean capital. In late June Dabbab was reported in Agāmē and on 1 July 1889 that he had met *Dadjāzmāch* Embāyē in Enticho.[56] Dabbab's followers took charge of Adwā, and on 3 July it was learned that a certain *Bāsha* Gabraesgi, an envoy sent by Alulā to collect the revenue of Adwā, had been shot dead in the town.[57]

In early July Mangashā camped with a reported 1,000 men at Abbi Addi in Tambēn, and Alulā was with 500 men in his native village of Zuqli.[58] Reportedly they had a bitter argument, since Mangashā, willing to compromise, was corresponding with Dabbab. Yet an informant returning from Tambēn to Massawa said that "many people believe that the dispute between Mangasha and Alula is but a trap for Debbeb."[59] On 12 July 1889 it was reported that the latter had left for Tambēn,[60] and two days later that he had fought *Ras* Hagos, then returning from Shirē to Mangashā's camp, and killed some one hundred of his followers.[61] Mangashā and Alulā, possibly to avoid battle, left for Maqalē,[62] while Dabbab entered Abbi Addi and devastated Zuqli.[63] During the week between 17 June 1889 and 24 July 1889, many informants reported in Massawa that Mangashā and Dabbab were exchanging many letters.

One of Dabbab's followers later colourfully described how his master was preparing to march on Maqalē, when Mangashā's envoy came and offered Dabbab a share of Yohannes's kingdom. Dabbab responded that he was already in control of Tambēn and that he desired the whole kingdom. "So they brought him the clothes and the horse of Yohannes. Debeb said: 'If I can have it without fighting, it is better' and he made peace."[64]

It was probably between 17 July 1889 and 19 July 1889, that Dabbab entered Maqalē.[65] "Three days they were making a feast. Debeb was dressed in the clothes of the Negus and as Mangascia had promised him he himself declared Debeb as the king of Ethiopia. After 3 days Mangascia invited him to his palace in Makalē where Alulā was waiting to arrest him."[66] Dabbab reportedly entered the palace, was immediately detained by Alulā's soldiers, put in chains and sent to Ambā Salāmā.[67]

Alulā's biographer did his best to characterize the arrest of Dabbab as one of the *rās*'s heroic deeds:⁶⁸

> Secondly, Dajjazmach Dabab followed after them until he reached the land of Enderta, and Ras Mangasha and Ras Alula returned towards him. He [Dabbab] feared and trembled. . . . Dajjazmach Dabab said, 'Have mercy on me, my lords; and especially my lord Ras Alula, forgive me.' And he made reconciliation and peace, and there was great joy at that time.
> On the third day, he [Dabab] wished to return to his former work, and his evil counsel and the deceit of his heart were known to Ras Mangasha and Ras Alula, the good lords. Ras Alula seized with his right hand that man [Dabbab], and with his left hand his brother, and they did not move at all. Is not this man strong of arm like Samson, and resolute like Joab?
> They bound him with a strong chain, and returning, he [Alulā] took him to the high hill which is called the burial place of Abba Salama.

Like the treacherous arrest of *Rās* Walda-Mikā'ēl ten years earlier, still notorious in Eritrea, the arrest of Dabbab, though inevitable and necessary, increased the distrust between Alulā and the Tigrean nobility. Justifiably enough, the removal of Dabbab from the political scene was atributed exclusively to Alulā, and Mangashā was hardly mentioned. Alulā's step also increased the rivalry between Endartā, where many leaders of the royal family lived, and the poor Tambēn, Alulā's native province.⁶⁹ W. Dinqnash, Yohannes's sister, the mother of Seyum and the cousin of Dabbab, was quoted as singing,

> People of Tambēn who are liars killed [Dabbab], and made the son of Qubi a king.⁷⁰

G. August 1889: The Italians Take Asmara. Alulā's New Policy–Appeasement of the Italians

Six days after Dabbab's arrest, *Rās* Alulā left Mangashā and headeu ior Adwā.⁷¹ He had agreed that Mangashā should face Seyum, and had decided himself to regain control over northern Tigre. Alulā passed Adwā and Dabra-Dāmo and in early August crossed the Bellesa river and camped in Co'atit.⁷² He apparently intended to proceed to Saganeiti and take possession of Dabbab's property there,⁷³ since he corresponded with the Shaykhs of the Assāwurta and tried to reach agreement with them.⁷⁴ It was probably then that Alulā heard the news of the Italian occupation of Asmara.

On 25 July 1889 the Italian war minister withdrew his opposition to Crispi's proposal to take the town. Baldissera was instructed to march,⁷⁵ and on the night of 2-3 August the capital of Hamāsēn was entered without opposition. The supreme commander, Baldissera, arrived there a few days later and established his headquarters in Alulā's tukuls.⁷⁶

> Negghe Alula!
> Your master [he was] O Hamasen, and Asmara. In the camp of yours [O Alula] Muslim chiefs [an insulting reference to the Italians] are camping.⁷⁷

"Alula was humiliated and surprised," claimed one of *Belātta* Gabru's sons, *Ledj* Abrehā (who, on 10 August, left the *rās*'s camp and defected to Asmara). As he had only 1,000 men armed with 700 rifles,⁷⁸ Alulā was in no position to react according to his sentiments. With Tigre threatened by Menilek and Seyum and his own personal position quite in doubt, he could not afford to march against the Italians. Alulā was, moreover, perfectly aware that he needed a strong ally to put Mangashā on the throne or even to maintain Tigrean independence.

Henceforth for the next three years, *Rās* Alulā, hitherto the bitter enemy of the Italians, would do his utmost to appease his neighbours and persuade them to cooperate with an independent Tigre. Though fighting the Mahdiyya was probably Alulā's last concern in that period, he raised that matter to establish a possible common interest with Asmara. He wrote to Major Piano on 15 August 1889:

> Some time ago my master Mangascia and I myself have sent you friendly letters . . . Now, our early enmity should end and friendship must be established between us in order that we join hands and destroy the Dervishes. I send you Kantiba Sahle to establish peace with you. I come to Sarae to treat for peace. Send me an answer.⁷⁹

Alulā's courier also asked, in his master's name, for Italian permission to raid Akalla-Guzāy and Sarāyē.⁸⁰ Meanwhile, Alulā had advanced to Godofelasi and was reported heading towards Gurā,⁸¹ probably aiming to reach Saganeiti and contact the Assāwurta.

But the Italians had no intention of cooperating with the person responsible for the Dogali incident; Piano was therefore instructed to pursue and capture Alulā, who, informed of the Italian intention, retreated hastily, marching the whole day of 16 August and the subsequent night. He crossed the Bellesa River and camped in Maraguz.⁸²

On 17 August 1889 Baldissera wrote to Alulā, clarifying Italy's feelings about him:

> You always write me words of friendship but from other people one can conclude just the opposite, therefore it is very difficult for us to understand each other. We came to Massaua (as the whole world knows) in order to help the English fight the Dervishes. It was only after Dogali that we had to vindicate our poor slaughtered soldiers instead of destroying the Dervishes. We desire very much peace with Abyssinia but we do not have to ask for it because it was you who broke it.⁸³

Rome, meanwhile, was agreeable to a détente with Mangashā and Alulā, but only if they recognised Menilek as emperor.[84] From Maraguz on 21 August 1889, Alulā wrote to Baldissera, explaining that he was not to be blamed for Dogali; he added that he had sent on the general's letter to Mangashā and concluded, "I do not like enmity, I like friendship."[85]

H. September-November 1889: Alulā Saves the Hesitant Mangashā from Seyum

Following his initial failure to appease the Italians, *Rās* Alulā did not rejoin Mangashā. The latter was presumably impressed by the negative image of Alulā among his own relatives in Endartā. His next step, therefore, was to pardon *Dadjāzmāch* Embāyē and *Wāgshum* Beru, Dabbab's former allies.[86] As suggested by General Baldiessera, *Rās* Alulā was suspicious that Mangashā might betray him[87] and according to Aṣmē:

> Rās Mangasha was sending messages to Seyum saying 'Let me also submit to Atse Menilek'. But Seyum was refusing saying 'The whole of it [Tigre] is for me.' He was also intercepting all Mangashā's letters [to Menilek?].[88]

In early September Mangashā left Maqalē for Adwā after calling on Alulā to join him there. But Alulā was annoyed with Mangashā's duplicity and ignored his orders.[89]

Alulā spent the months of September and October 1889 camping in Kohayn trying to keep his small army together and fed. At the end of August his force had been estimated at 2,000, of whom 500 were armed with rifles.[90] He managed to maintain that number by raiding various regions in Sarāyē and Akalla-Guzāy. In late August he confiscated the food stores of Maraguz.[91] In the middle of September, however, he was deserted by his nephew *Bāsha* Tadlā Fanjā,[92] and it may therefore be concluded that Alulā had no glorious successes in the southern part of Marab Mellāsh.

Meanwhile, Mangashā came under a serious threat. In late October *Dadjāzmāch* Seyum entered Maqalē and immediately led his 1,500 well equipped troops towards Adwā.[93] Mangashā was reported to be camping there with only 300 troops, many of them ill. When he heard about Seyum's advance, Mangashā called Tadlā Ayba and *Wāgshum* Berru who were foraging in various parts of Tigre.[94]

> After this in the fourth month [after the arrest of Dabbab] Däjjazmach Seyum came towards him [Mangashā] secretly, and not in public; and when he knew the news of his coming, Ras Mangasha sent to the rulers, saying 'Come to me'. But no one came. There were those who stayed away from fear, and those who stayed away from deceit.[95]

While Tadlā Ayba and Berru "stayed away from fear," *Dadjāzmāch* Sebhat "stayed away from deceit." In early September, on his way to Adwā, Mangashā camped for a few days at Hawzen to receive *Dadjāzmāch* Sebhat's submission.[96] The latter was distressed at Italian support for his rival and neighbour *Dadjāzmāch* Bāhta Hagos, who went from strength to strength in Akalla-Guzāy.[97] On the last day of September, he nonetheless secretly betrayed his new master and wrote to Baldissera, declaring himself Menilek's obedient servant.[98]

From Saturday morning to Sunday evening, 2 and 3 November 1889, Seyum and Mangashā fought on the outskirts of Adwā:[99] "They made peace on Sunday. It was said: 'The crown to Degiat Siyum!' and Ras Mangascia submitted. . ."[100] Seyum reported to Baldissera that, on the request of the priests of Aksum, he had forgiven Mangashā, who nonetheless fled that same night, between Sunday and Monday.[101] Seyum immediately went after Mangashā, who apparently was making his way to Alulā's camp in Kohayn. When messengers reached Alulā, he immediately[102] and rapidly marched to Adwā. According to Mannawē, Seyum tried to influence Alulā to abandon Mangashā and submit to Emperor Menilek II:

> He arose [from Kohayn] with a burning heart and came with enthusiasm. He arrived at the place which they call Daero Takli [NE of Adwā]. While he was there, Däjjazmach Seyum sent to him, saying, 'Come to me, my lord, and I will give you up to the half of my kingdom'. But Ras Alula hearing this, was very angry, and became like fire, and said, 'What have I to do with you. For me, I have no king except Ras Mangasha, son of Yohannes the king. But wait for me in the place you have chosen.'[103]

On 6 November 1889, three days after Menilek was officially crowned emperor of Ethiopia, his representative in Tigre was defeated by *Rās* Alulā. The battle of Enda Abuna-Pantaleun, near Aksum,[104] cost Alulā 150 dead and 300 wounded while Seyum had more losses.[105] Menilek's man hastily crossed the Marab and marched to Asmara to be comforted on 14 November 1889 by his Italian allies.[106]

> Ras Alula sent to Ras Mangasha, saying, 'Come, enter your house, for I your father have conquered Däjjazmach Seyum, our enemy'. Ras Mangasha came with joy and gladness, and gave him [Alula] the throne of his father Yohannes, with the result that the officers and troops were amazed, and said, 'How good is all the work of this Ras Alula!' There were those who said 'But I would not have given honour to a non-relative. . .'[107]

I. December 1889: The Battle of Zabān Cha'ā: Alulā and Mangashā Face Seyum and Sebhat

While Mangashā and Alulā were fighting Seyum, *Dadjāzmāch* Tadlā Ayba, the wavering ex-follower of Mangashā, united with Sebhat Aragāwi, the ruler of Agāmē. They both wrote to Baldissera on 8 November 1889, assuring him of their loyalty to Italy and Menilek.[108] Mangashā and Alulā stayed in Adwā until the end of the third week of November awaiting the possible return of Seyum.[109] Their recent success undoubtedly rebuilt their confidence, prestige, and army, which Baldissera estimated as currently numbering 5,000 men.[110] Then they were reported marching towards Agāmē aiming to attack Sebhat and Tadlā Ayba or, as Asmara speculated, to try to influence Sebhat to join them and take Akalla-Guzāy from the Italian-supported *Dadjāzmāch* Bāhtā Hagos.[111] Seyum was therefore immediately rearmed by the Italians and was instructed to unite with Sebhat,[112] who, again, in a letter dated 28 November 1889 to Baldissera, emphasized his devotion and loyalty to Menilek.[113] The next day, 29 November 1889, both Seyum and Sebhat in separate letters informed Baldissera that they had joined up and faced the two *rās*es in Hawzēn.[114] In order to help his allies, Baldissera sent Bāhtā Hagos to Dabra-Dāmo and an Italian-commanded force beyond the Marab towards Enticho.[115] On 2 December 1889, the three pro-Italian *dadjāzmāch*es met the three *rās*es, Alulā, Mangashā and Hagos, at Zaban Cha'ā east of Ambā Ṣiyon in Haramat. The battle lasted for three days, during which Alulā and Hagos were wounded:[116]

> Däjjazmach Sebhat and Däjjazmach Seyum were united in one counsel and one wish. Ras Mangasha and Ras Alula, hearing this, went towards them, and found them in a place which they call Zeban Cha'a. They had a battle and fought until all the officers were scattered separately. Some fled to Tämben and some to Endärta. . . .Ras Alula alone remained with him, and did not leave Ras Mangasha alone. He did battle for three days and three nights . . . But many chiefs of his troops died.[117]

In spite of his losses at Zaban Cha'ā, Alulā found the energy to try and prevent Seyum from re-establishing himself in Maqalē. Alulā followed Seyum down to near Ambā Alājē in Endā Makonni. This area was undoubtedly governed by Seyum's relatives, and, as the Mannawē MS testifies, Alulā's mostly Tambēn and Adwā army suffered another cruel battle:

> That Däjjazmach Seyum escaped as before and preceded them on the path as far as the boundary of Enda Mäkwäni. He arrived there, and they followed after him. They found him at the foot of Alajē, and did battle with him for many days. . . . In this battle Ras Alula was wounded,[118] and fear and trembling entered the heart of the officers. For against them were assembled the men of Enda Mäkwäni and the men of Azäbo, the men of Wajerat and the men of Endärte. Ras Alula led them out of the place of battle as Moses led Israel out of Egypt. And he returned to Tänben [on 19th December 1889[119]], the country of his birth, which is Mänäwe, and Ras Mangasha followed after him.

But though they suffered heavy losses, Alulā and Mangashā were not defeated.

Seyum managed to return to Maqalē and Sebhat to Addigrāt[120] but their combined force proved insufficient to eliminate the *rās*es of Tigre. Back at Tambēn, Alulā and Mangashā awaited an expected direct attack by the Italians and the Shoans.

J. January 1890: Italian Efforts to Catch Alulā

On 3 November 1889, Menilek was crowned emperor of Ethiopia and on 1 January 1890, the Italians, who had already advanced to the Marab River, issued a decree forming their possessions into an autonomous colony called Eritrea. Thus, Shoan-Italian cooperation proved to be mutually beneficial, and the Italian leaders of the so-called "political Scioana" anticipated more gains from their southern ally. The main question was the new colony's southern frontier, since the one stipulated in the treaty of Uccialli was not satisfactory from the Italian point of view.[121] With their forces already camping on the right bank of the Marab, regarded by the Italians as Eritrea's natural border, Rome hoped to persuade Menilek to make favourable modifications. Eritrean authorities also waited the new emperor to march into Tigre and crush opposition chiefs, especially the ex-governor of the Marab Mellāsh, *Rās* Alulā.

In late 1889 Menilek seemed to be cooperating with the Italians. On 17 December, upon hearing of Seyum's failure, he left Addis Ababa and marched toward Tigre, entering Maqalē on 23 February 1890.[122] At Asmara Menilek's advance was interpreted by General Baldassare Orero, the new military and civil governor, as the beginning of the expected action against Mangashā and Alulā. Orero was eager to strengthen cooperation with Menilek in order to obtain a modified frontier and was most desirous "to send Ras Alulā to Italy."[123] Without obtaining permission from the emperor, he therefore crossed the frontier to Tigre and led his soldiers to Adwā, which he entered on 26 January 1890 (and where he commemorated the third anniversary of Dogali). From Adwā he planned to march to Tambēn in order to crush Mangashā and imprison Alulā.[124]

Though the people of Adwā and Aksum welcomed the Italians (or rather the food the Italians supplied), they totally rejected the idea of being ruled by the Shoans. They emphatically expressed their wish to be ruled by *Rās* Mangashā whom they regarded as the only legal heir of the late Tigrean emperor.[125]

Meanwhile, Menilek was pressed by the strong Tigrean party in his court and expressed his disapproval of Orero's unauthorised invasion of Tigre.[126] *Dadjāzmāch* Sebhat of Agāmē, upon whose cooperation Orero hoped to rely, was deliberately slow in his march to Adwā. He was probably aware of Menilek's attitude and was justifiably reluctant to join hands against Mangashā and Alulā.[127] Consequently the Italian general was directed by Rome to withdraw his forces.

K. February 1890: Mangashā Submits to Menilek Against Alulā's Advice

In Tambēn Mangashā and Alulā were facing imminent disaster. Tigre was shattered, hungry and invaded; Agāmē was hostile; Adwā was in Italian hands; and Endartā was occupied and being pillaged by the Shoan army. In Mangashā's court, only *Rās* Alulā rejected submission to Menilek, even though he apparently could offer no reasonable alternative. In the Mannawē manuscript's last page, it was recorded:

> When they [Mangashā and Alulā] were in their country [Tambēn], the king Menelik came, and entered at Makalle, the residence of the king, and entered into the reception-room of the king [Yohannes].
>
> When Ras Alula heard that he had gone into the reception-room of the king, spiritual zeal seized him, and he sorrowed greatly. His viscera blazed like a reed stem before the face of the fire, and he said, 'Where is the land of Yohannes, and where is his resting place? Where will be found the traces of his path?' He further said, 'I will not pay homage to him [Menilek], and I will not bow down to the glory of his kingship, because he is [indistinct word] house of the king.' Ras Alula did not change his word at all, because he did not fear anyone, neither king or anything that is. Was he not a powerful and warlike! And he counselled against him [Menilek] that he [Menilek] should seize him [Mangashā] on the path and take his possessions. But the rulers and princes were not in agreement with this counsel, and they said to Ras Mangasha, 'Go in to him, and bow down to him.' And he [Mangashā] went in against his [Alulā's] will, because the counsel of the rulers overruled him.[128]

Thus, while Alulā and the army remained in Tambēn, Mangashā, in late February 1890, presented himself for submission to Emperor Menilek at Aguddi near Maqalē.[129]

L. March 1890: Mangashā is Recognised by Menilek to be Guided by Another Adviser

Contrary to Alulā's warnings, Menilek did not deprive Mangashā of Tigre: the new emperor already had been criticised for yielding to Italian territorial claims, and his sensitivity had been strengthened by Orero's occupation of Adwā. Moreover, he was now emperor, and his top priority was Ethiopian unity; he probably realised that he never would be able to appease the Tigreans once he deprived them of Yohannes's son and heir. Like Orero in Adwā, Menilek in Endartā could have no illusions about the possibility of installing a Shoan or any other Tigrean but the son of Yohannes over the province.[130] In order, however, to minimise the danger of legitimizing Mangashā's position, in early March Menilek nominated *Dadjāzmāch* Seyum over the eastern parts of Tigre and his old devotée *Dadjāzmāch* Mashashā Warqē[131] as governor of the regions of Adwā and Aksum up to the Eritrean border.[132]

Dadjāzmāch Sebhat of Agāmē, who had also come to Maqalē as the Italian candidate for the Tigrean government, was rejected by Menilek who nominated Seyum over him. Sebhat, however, was quick to leave Maqalē and head back to Agāmē to defend it from Seyum. The latter was left with no choice but to accompany Menilek back to Shoa, when he left Maqalē on 19 March 1890.

In Hawzēn in the middle of March the moving spirit of the Italian "Politica Scioana," Count Antonelli had to confront the partial failure of his policy.[133] Not only had Menilek rejected Sebhat but he also denied the Marab line and agreed only to a minor modification of the frontier.

Menilek must have been very disappointed not to have gained *Rās* Alulā's submission, and it was believed that the emperor did not proceed to Aksum to be crowned because of Alulā's intransigence.[134] Menilek considered the *rās* as the moving spirit of Tigrean resistance to the new Shoan hegemony, and he instructed *Rās* Mangashā to exclude Alula from any military command or provincial government, only permitting him his private property.[135] Menilek gave assurances to the Italians that *Rās* Alulā, "the most offensive culprit in the Italians' eyes, would be excluded from any command in Tigre."[136]

M. May 1890: Alulā Pretends to Recognise Menilek to Appease the Italians

To the surprise of the "pro-Shoan" Italians, it was Menilek who, by recognising *Rās* Mangashā as a governor in Tigre, undermined their own policy. His definite rejection of a modified frontier also contributed to the strengthening of the exponents of a "Politica Tigrina." The latter suggested that the colony's unrecognised southern border would be safer if Tigre served as a buffer between Eritrea and Ethiopia. A semi-independent *Rās* Mangashā could well serve that purpose, particularly since Tigre depended on Italian economic support to overcome famine, and the young governor could also easily be manipulated by threatening Italian support for local rivals like *Dadjāzmāch* Sebhat of Agāmē.[137] For the supporters of the Tigre policy, the main obstacle was the fact that Mangashā still appeared to be under Alulā's influence. The latter was also considered as perhaps the only remaining exponent of the restoration of the Tigrean government in Asmara and, as such, a sworn enemy of the colony.

This interpretation seemed to be based on facts: in early April 1890 *Gerāzmāch* Sadur, Mangashā's uncle, contacted the Italians and informed them that his nephew had written them a friendly letter which Alulā had intercepted. Sadur assured the Europeans that Mangashā would not only recignise the Marab frontier but might also deliver Alulā to them as a sign of friendship.[138] Ironically, as mentioned above, Alulā was, ipso facto, a dedicated supporter of any policy which would permit Tigre some autonomy. Judging from his subsequent actions, Alulā sought to receive Italian aid, or, at least, to secure their neutrality, in order to fight Menilek.[139] As these goals could not immediately be achieved, Alulā's first objective was to appease the Italians and hope for better circumstances. In Adwā on 10 May 1890 Mashashā Warqē, who was cooperating with the Italians, assured Salimbeni:

> That Ras Alula is the one who more vivaciously recommends an accord with the Italians, as a last chance of salvation for the country. Ras Alula said that he was tired of running from Amba to Amba.

He wanted peace and expressed his wish to retire from political life.[140] Alulā was working hard to create a new image as a tired and old man who accepted the established new facts.

An Italian journalist who interviewed him on several occasions in May 1890 described Alulā as:

> One of those medieval knights loyal to one flag, to one man, to one principle . . . One of those faithful men who do not live but for the principle [Tigrean hegemony and Yohannes's will] or for the man whom they support [Mangashā]. . . . Menelik has no son, . . . Mangascia is young, he can wait. The peace with Menelik being accomplished, and the crown of Tigre assured to his protégé. . . . The old hero believes that his mission on earth is finished. In fact he has already manifested his will to go to Jerusalem and shut himself up in a convent there.[141]

On 16 May 1890 *Rās* Mangashā, Mashashā Warqē, Antonelli and Count Salimbeni, who more than three years before had been Alulā's prisoner,[142] assembled in Adwā, where "universal peace and goodwill were agreed upon and sworn to."[143] Mangashā accepted the installation of Mashashā in Adwā and both parties emphasized their intention carefully to execute article XIII of Wichale, which laid down the reciprocal surrender of rebels who might cross the frontier.

Rās Alulā attended the meeting of 17 May 1890; he seemed to be very old,[144] but listened attentively to Mangashā's speech:

> 'And now that we are in peace, it is my wish that that blessed peace would include also Ras Alula. We are in an unfortunate state, a state of blood, but those who died were from both parties. Let us forget the past, Ras Alula wants to justify himself. Listen to him.' Alula now started speaking in a voice which was a little trembling at the beginning and became stronger and clearer later. . .[145]

He explained the reasons for Dogali, blaming the Italians for provocations and adding that he had acted according to Yohannes's instructions.[146]

The proud Tigrean who, less than three months before, had refused to submit to Menilek, continued:

> 'Today I am a servant of Menelik, a servant of Ras Mangascia, whatever they want I want and whatever they love I love. I ask you to make and maintain the peace as I swear to maintain it.' And he waved his right palm in front of himself in a ceremonial act. . . Animated by that speech . . . his face lost any element of vulgarity. . . Ras Mangascia now asked us if we wanted to seal the amnesty with hand-shakes . . . and the first to shake the hand of Alula was Count Salimbeni.[147]

On 20th May 1890, when asked about the frontier question, "Ras Alula shrugged his shoulders. 'We shall respect every decision of the Emperor,' he said. And Ras Mangasha added; 'He is the master, we are his servants.'"[148] Moreover, after a lot of persuasion and argument, Alulā agreed that his picture should be taken.

An Italian wrote that people did not believe that the picture represented the man who had shed so much Italian blood:

> No, this is the portrait of another kind of Alula, an Alula who had to accept the peace, who had seen his army exhausted and diminished not because of battles, but of famine and defections. . . I remember the other Alula, who was completely different from today's one,[149] I remember his riding proudly all dressed in red . . . famous as a just and invincible man . . . Ras Alula honourably accepted the peace, in the same way as he courageously had faced his wars. Would he keep his word? Would he remain obedient under Ras Mangascia?"[150]

Salimbeni must have been sceptical about that question when he wrote in his diary: "Sometimes it looked to me as though he [Alulā] revealed his superiority over Mangascia. Today, for example [during the meeting of 17 May 1890] when he [Mangashā] spoke, he [Alulā] interrupted him saying 'hold your tongue' . . .[151]

★ ★ ★

Alulā's failure to develop Tigre into a united anti-Shoan force was the result of two facts: Mangashā's appreciation that the exhausted province no longer could maintain military superiority; and the Tigrean aristocracy's continued determination to consider Alulā an outsider. His origin and lack of hereditary rights hardly placed him in a position to lead that province. As always, Alulā could only be a follower, and he could not convince his leader, let alone the Tigreans, that it was still possible at least to maintain their independence.

NOTES

1 See below, p. 154. Also: /aghi, *Crispi*, p. 74.
2 A.S.MAI, 3/6-42, Baratieri to MAE, 12.3.93.
3 Consult Marcus, *The Life and Times*, pp. 111-113.
4 Conti Rossini, *Italia ed Etiopia*, p. 26.
5 See Conti Rossini, *Italia*, p. 17, n. 2; R. Pankhurst, "The Great Ethiopian Famine of 1889-1892," *University College Review*, Addis Ababa, Spring 1969, pp. 90-103. See also a detailed description in L. Mercatelli, "Nel paese di Ras Alula," *Corriere di Napoli*, 13-14 May 1891.
6 Interview *Dadjāzmāch* Zawdē Gabra-Sellāssē, Addis Ababa, March 1972.
7 According to oral tradition, /agade, then governor of Semēn, attacked Mangashā and Alulā but was defeated. See Tesfai Seyum, BA Thesis, p. 34. According to D.I., 3.4.89, informant Ghermai Arko, the name of the attacker was Alle, and Alulā lost 150 men.
8 A.S.MAI, D.I., 10.4.89, informant "Wakīl Mulḥaq Harkīkū," 6.4.89, informant Gabra Maskel Kafil.
9 A.S.MAI, D.I., 24.4.89, informant Maḥmūd 'Abd al-Ḥāfiẓ, 22.4.89, informant Berhano.
10 Mannawē MS.
11 This is agreed by many sources. See, among others, Wylde, *Modern*, p. 12; Conti Rossini, *Italia ed Etiopia*, p. 465; FO 403/239, Gleichen, "Memorandum on Ras Mangascia," 13.2.96.
12 On *Dadjāzmāch* Tadlā, see Conti Rossini, *Italia ed Etiopia*, p. 98, note 1. Also *La Tribuna*, 22.1.95.
13 See manuscript in possession of Dr. R. Caulk, "The Life of Ras Sibhat Aregawi," written by one of Sebhat's descendants, a graduate of Addis Ababa University.
14 A.S.MAI, D.I., 11.3.89, informant: Bakhit Scialeb.
15 A.S.MAI, D.I., 4.3.89, informant: Muḥammad Ibrāhīm.
16 A.S.MAI, D.I., 19.3.89, informant: Ali Sciagherai.
17 D.I., 3.4.89, informant: Ghermai Arko; 4.4.89, Di Maio to Baldissera.
18 D.I., 31.3.89, informant: 'Alī Shukrī; D.I., 6.4.89, informant: Muhammad Idrīs.
19 A.S.MAI, 10.4.89, informant: Wakīl of Harkīkū.
20 A.S.MAI, D.I., 11.5.89, informant: 'Alī Adam and Idrīs Zakāriya; 13.5.89, Kuflu Derau; 22.5.89, Muḥammad Idrīs.
21 A.S.MAI, D.I., 22.4.89, 26.4.89.
22 D.I., 30.4.89, 'Uthmān 'Umān.
23 D.I., 18.5.1889.
24 A.S.MAI, D.I., Mesfin to Baldissera, 11.5.89.
25 D.I., 8.6.89, Muḥammad 'Abd al-Hāfiz.
26 LV, XVI, Baldissera to M.d.G., 5.6.89.
27 A.S.MAI, D.I., 16.3.89, informant: 'Abd al-Ḥafīz, 19.3.89; informant: Musa Domfa; Puglisi, p. 174.
28 A.S.MAI, D.I., 2.4.89, informant: 'Uthmān 'Umān, 9.5.89.
29 D.I., 31.5.89.
30 A.S.MAI, D.I., 13.5.89.
31 WO 33/5, Eritrea Report, p. 29. See Baldissera's "Relazione" in LV XVI, 1.9.1889. For more on Italian policy, see Marcus, *The Life and Times*, p. 113.

32 WO 33/55, Eritrea Report, p. 29. Masfen went to the Italians on 11.8.89. LV, XVI Baldissera, "Relazione Sulla Occupazione dell'Asmara," 1.9.89, and "Estratto della relazione... sull'occupazione di Keren...," 16.6.89.
33 A.S.MAI, D.I., 18.5.89, 'Uthmān 'Umān, 20.5.89, informant: Gabru.
34 A.S.MAI, D.I., 2.5.89, XV, XVI, Baldissera to M.d.G., 5.6.89.
35 D.I., 1315.89, informant: Kuflu Derau.
36 A.S.MAI, D.I., 20.5.89, informant: Mensa, 18.5.89, 'Uthmān 'Umān.
37 A.S.MAI, D.I., 20.5.89, informant: Mensa.
138 D.I., Dabbab to Baldissera, 24.5.89; D.I., 27.5.89, 28.5.89, Idris to Zakāriyā, They had been in touch before Dogali, see above, p. 107.
39 D.I., 28.5.89, Muhammad 'Abd al-Hāfiz.
40 A.S.MAI, D.I., 28.5.89, Idrīs Zakāriyā.
41 D.I., 2.6.89, informant: Mensa.
42 D.I., 6.6.89, informant: 'Umār Adam.
43 Marcus, *Life and Times*, p. 31.
44 S. Rubenson, *Wichale* XVII, Addis Ababa 1961, p. 56.
45 D.I., 2.5.89, 24.5.89, 29.6.89. Also LV, XV, Consul-General in Aden to MAE, 12.6.89.
46 Conti Rossini, *Italia*, p. 17; D.I., 28.5.89, Idrīs Zakāriyā.
47 D.I., 8.8.89, Muhammad 'Abd al-Hāfiz.
48 D.I., 22.6.89, "Many informants who left Adwa on 16.6.89."
49 A.S.MAI 3/5-37, Gandolfi to MAE, 6.4.91, *Corriere di Napoli*, 13-14 May 1891; A.S.MAI 3/6-46, Salsa to MAE, 30.7.97.
50 A.S.MAI, D.I., 12.6.89, 'Uthmān 'Umān.
51 D.I., 8.6.89, Muhammad 'Abd al-Hāfiz.
52 D.I., 21.6.89, 5.7.89, Muhammad 'Abd al-Hāfiz.
53 Mannawē MS.
54 D.I., 17.6.89.
55 D.I., 29.6.89, 'Ithmān 'Umān, 27.6.89, Idrīs Zakāriyā.
56 D.I., 1.7.89.
57 D.I., 3.7.89, informant: Mūsā Fākir.
58 D.I., 5.7.89, informant: 'Alī Kassai.
59 D.I., 10.7.89, Report by Albertone.
60 D.I., 12.7.89, Muhammad 'Abd al-Hāfiz.
61 D.I., 14.7.89, informant: Bakit Scialeb.
62 D.I., 17.7.89, Muhammad Idrīs.
63 D.I., 25.7.89, Bāhtā Hagos to Baldissera.
64 A.S.MAI, D.I., 28.7.89.
65 A.S.MAI, D.I., Bāhtā Hagos to Baldissera, 25.7.89, already contained the story of Dabbab's arrest.
66 D.I., 3.8.89.
67 Ibid. Baldissera's "Relazione" in LV, XVI, 1.9.89.
68 Mannawē MS.
69 See Mercatelli's article in *La Tribuna*, 4.6.95.
70 Interview w. Yashashwarq. The song was probably sung two years later when Dabbab was killed in a battle with Alula; see below, pp. 168, 169.
71 D.I., 3.8.89.

72 D.I., 4.8.89, informant: Naib of Arkiku.
73 D.I., 5.8.89.
74 D.I., 4.8.89, informant: Naib of Arkiku; also 11.8.89, 13.8.89.
75 For Baldissera's policy, see his "Relazione sulla occupazione dell'Asmara" in LV, XVI, 1.9.89. Also FO 403/123, Slade to Dufferin, 10.5.89.
76 WO 33/55, Eritrea Report; *Storia Militare*, p. 197.
77 C. Conti Rossini, "Canti Popolari Tigrai," No. 153.
78 D.I., 15.8.89, informant: Abraha.
79 D.I., 15.8.89, Alula to Piano.
80 Conti Rossini, *Italia*, p. 18; A.S.MAI 3/5/33, Baldissera to M.d.G., 19.8.89.
81 D.I., 17.8.89, Piano to Baldissera.
82 Baldissera, "Relazione," LV, XVI, 1.9.89; D.I., 18.8.89, Di Maio quotes Bāhatā Hagos' letter to him of the same day.
83 D.I., 17.8.89, Baldissera to Alula.
84 A.S.MAI 3/5-33, Crispi to M.d.G.
85 D.I., Alula to Baldissera, 21.8.89.
86 They were reported to be with him in Adwā. D.I., "Estratto settimanale," 19-26 Sept. 1889.
87 A.S.MAI 3/5-33, Baldissera to M.d.G., 14.10.89.
88 Aṣme, *Ya'atsē Yohannes*, p. 10.
89 D.I., 27.8.89, Muḥammad Idrīs, 7.10.89, Wakīl of Harkīkū.
90 D.I., Tenente Zuiraghi, 30.8.89.
91 D.I., 27.8.89, Muḥammad Idrīs.
92 D.I., "Estratto settimanale," 19-26 Sept. 1889. Also 14.10.89, Wakīl of Harkīkū.
93 D.I., 9.11.89, 29.10.89, Wakīl of Harkīkū. Unlike Conti Rossini, *Italia*, p. 19.
94 D.I., 27.10.89; also 29.10.89, Wakīl of Harkīkū.
95 Mannawē MS.
96 A.S.MAI 3/5-33, Baldissera to Bertole Viale, 5.9.89. D.I., 10.9.89, Na'ib 'Abd al-Karīm.
97 A.S.MAI 3/5-33, Baldissera to Bertole Viale, 4.9.89. Also: Orero to MAE, 10.3.90.
98 D.I., 30.9.89, Sebhat to Baldissera.
99 A.S.MAI 3/5-33, Baldissera to M.d.G., 15.11.89.
100 "About Dejiat Siyum." L. De Vito, *Esercizi di lettura in Lingua Tigrinya*, Rome 1893, p. 19. This is a passage in Tigrigna written by the Ethiopian Abraham of Adwā, and translated into Italian by De Vito. Also D.I., 10.11.89, informant: 'Alī Ḥamad Nūr and Samra Idrīs.
101 D.I., Seyum to Baldissera, 8.11.89. According to Conti Rossini, *Italia*, p. 19, Mangashā fled assisted by Embāye.
102 D.I., 10.11.89, 'Alī Ḥamad and Samra Idrīs.
103 Mannawē MS.
104 Conti Rossini, *Italia*, p. 19. A.S.MAI 3/5-33, Baldissera to M.d.G., 15.11.89.
105 D.I., 12.11.89, informant: Berhano.
106 A.S.MAI 3/5-33, Baldissera to M.d.G., 15.11.89.
107 Mannawē MS. A descendant of Alulā's relative strongly suggested that Mangashā, being desperate, did offer the throne to Alulā, but the latter refused, saying: "The throne belongs to its owner". [Interview with Fit. Embassā Abbāy, son of *Dadj* Abbāy, Abbi addi, Feb. 1972.] A famous popular song known all over Ethiopia may be also interpreted as

hinting this:

> A brave man is born Alulā Abbā Naggā
> who heard on Monday, marched on Tuesday
> and fought on Wednesday.
> Who smahsed them like pumpkin. . .
> and restored the throne to the owner of the throne.

[Interview with Bayyana Abrehā. Other versions in Abba Gasparini, *Yaityopya tārik*, Asmara 1955, p. 187. I. Guidi, "Storie e brevi testi amarici," a paper prresented to a seminar in Berlin 1907, now in Tel Aviv University Library. C. Conti Rossini, *Proverbi Tradizioni e Canzoni Tigrine*, Rome 1942, p. 297.]

108   D.I., 10.11.89, 'Alī Ḥamad and Samra Idrīs; 8.11.89, Sebhat and Tadlā to Baldissera.
109   D.I., 18.11.89, Wakīl of Harkīkū, 21.10.89, 26.11.89, Muḥammad 'Uthmān.
110   A.S.MAI 3/5-33. Baldissera to M.d.G., 24.11.89, Baldissera's first thought was to instruct Seyum to work for a reconciliation between Alulā and Seyum, but this was rejected by Rome. See 3/5-33, MAE to M.d.G., 20.11.89.
111   D.I., 28.11.89, Albertone to Baldissera, A.S.MAI, 3/5-33, Orero to MAE, 10.3.90.
112   For details about the creation of the alliance, see A.S.MAI, 3/5-33, Orero to M.A.E., 10.3.90.
113   D.I. Sebhat to Baldissera, 28.11.89.
114   D.I., Seyum and Sebhat to Baldissera, 20 Hedar 1882 E.C.
115   Conti Rossini, *Italia*, pp. 19, 20; A.S.MAI, 3/5-33, Orero to MAE, 10.3.90.
116   D.I. Albertone, 9.12.89, 16.12.89; Samuel Giyorgis, 16.12.89; A.S.MAI 3/5-33, Orero to MAE, 11.12.83.
117   Mannawē MS.
118   See A.S.MAI 3/5-33, Orero's "Relazione sul occupazione di Adua," 10.3.90, Allegato: Di Maio's report of 13.2.90.
119   D.I., 23.12.89, informant: Berhano. A.S.MAI 3/5-33, Orero to MAE, 10.3.90
120   D.I., 24.12.89.
121   LV, XXIII bis, No. 12, Perini to MAE, Memoria, 1895.
122   WO 33/55, Eritrea Report, p. 36; Conti Rossini, *Italia ed Etiopia*, p. 27.
123   Orero to Dal Verne, 22.2.90, is quoted in R. Truffi, *Precursori dell'Impero Africano, Lettere inedite*, Milano 1936, p. 179.
124   Berkeley, *Menelik*, 26-27. A.S.MAI, "Vitale" Orero to Sebhat, 17.1.90. See also: B. Orero, "Ricordi d'Africa," *Nuovo Antologia*, 1901, see pp. 200, 201, 202, 203, 500, 501, 511, 679, 683; *Storia Militare*, pp. 214-221; WO 33/35, "Eritrea Report," p. 35. Luca dei Sabelli, vol. III, pp. 367-69; FO 403/125, Dufferin to Salisbury, 27.1.90; A.S.MAI, 3/5-33. Various despatches of Orero, January 1890 and his "Relazione sul occupazione di Adua," 10.3.90.
125   LV, XXIII bis, Perini to MAE, No. 12, Memoria, 1895.
126   See also: Marcus, *The Life and Times*, pp. 118-119.
127   *Storia Militare*, pp. 219-221; A.S.MAI 3/5-33, Antonelli to MAE, 29.1.90; Cossate to M.d.G., 30.1.90.
128   Mannawē MS.
129   Conti Rossini, *Italia*, p. 27.
130   See Berkeley, *Menelik*, p. 27.

131 Mashashā Warqē, a son of *Badjerond* Warqē from Gondar, also had been trusted by Yohannes, and had acted as imperial delegate in Menilek's court after 1886; Zaghi, *Crispi e Menelich*, p. 87.
132 See Berkely, p. 28, note 1.
133 Ibid, p. 28. Conti Rossini, *Italia ed Etiopia*, pp. 28-29. See more in Marcus, *The Life and Times*, pp. 120-21.
134 Un ex-funzionario Eritreo, *La nostra politica africana*, Imola 1895, p. 26.
135 Antonelli to Crispi, Massawa, 13/14-4.90. MAE, Seria Riservatissima, Etiopia I, p. 190. As Alulā's houses in Adwā and Aksum were included in Mashashā Warqē's new province, this probably referred to the poor village of Mannawē.
136 Caulk, *The Origins*, p. 316.
137 See Conti Rossini, *Italia ed Etiopia*, pp. 20, 21. E. Cagnassi, *I Nostri Errori*, Torino 1898, p. 73.
138 Orero to Crispi, 10.4.90. MAE, Riservatissima Etiopia I, no. 209. Also Conti Rossini, *Italia ed Etiopia*, p. 34.
139 See above p. 147, below p. 163.
140 Zaghi, *Crispi e Menelich*, p. 74.
141 N. Corazzini, "La pace — Ras Alula — Un banchetto ad Axum," *La Tribuna*, 3.6.90.
142 He was now on his way to Menilek's court for a new diplomatic mission.
143 WO 33/55, "Eritrea Report," p. 36.
144 Zaghi, *Crispi*, p. 80.
145 Corazzini, "La pace." *La Tribuna*, 8.6.90.
146 See above, p. 105.
147 N. Corazzini, "La pace," *La Tribuna*, 8.6.90.
148 N. Corazzini, "Colloquio con Ras Alula e Mangascia," *La Tribuna*, 20.6.90.
149 Belcredi visited Asmara and interviewed Alulā on 17.6.85. See above, p. 60.
150 G. Belcredi, "Ras Alula," *La Tribuna Illustrata*, 26.6.90.
151 Zaghi, *Crispi e Menelich*, p. 81.

14

1890-1892: Alulā's Failure to Create a Tigrean-Eritrean Front Against Menilek

A. *September 1890-February 1891:*
   War Against Agāmē Prevents Mangashā
   From Travelling to Addis Ababa

After Dabbab Ar'āyā's imprisonment, *Dadjāzmāch* Sebhat of Agāmē remained the only challenger to Mangashā's supremacy over the Tigreans. Described as a clever and intelligent man in his early forties, an excellent administrator but not a distinguished warrior,[1] Sebhat had a new and practical reason to disobey Mangashā. As Menilek's nominee, and especially as an aspirant to the title of *negus*, the latter had to execute imperial policy regarding Agāmē, which, in the partition of Tigre of March 1890, had been assigned to *Dadjāzmāch* Seyum.[2] Since Mangashā would not accept Seyum, Menilek demanded that a certain *Dadjāzmāch* Waldē[3] share the government of Agāmē together with Sebhat.[4] On 20 May 1890, Mangashā demanded that the latter come to Maqalē and submit officially to him. "I fight him," Mangashā told the Italian Corazzini, "only because he refused to submit to the Emperor."[5]

Around mid-June, Sebhat partially agreed to Mangashā's demands by sending his son Dastā to Adwā as an hostage.[6] But, when a few weeks later, Mangashā demanded a share in the revenue of Agāmē, Sebhat refused, but reportedly sent a symbolic sum when threatened with invasion.[7]

With Agāmē at least partially recognising Mangashā's supremacy, Tigre seemed to be reunited under Yohannes's son but also Menilek's nominee. Alulā's influence over *Rās* Mangashā was reported to be rapidly diminishing, while Menilek's man, *Dadjāzmāch* Mashashā Warqē, was considered to be Mangashā's main adviser.[8] As arranged by Mashashā Warqē in August, the Italian supplied 18,000 litres of grain to the Tigreans, for which Menilek paid.[9] The grateful Mangashā, influenced by Mashashā Warqē and tempted by the rumour that the emperor would make him *negus*, reportedly intended to leave for Shoa after the coming *Masqal* (September 1890).[10] The projected visit to Addis Ababa, which was supposed to confirm the Shoan hegemony, became the most important issue in the history of Tigre during the next four years.

Although *Rās* Alulā opposed Mangashā's projected trip to Shoa,[11] he nonetheless supported his young master in other matters. In late August 1890 the son of *Dadjāzmāch* Sebhat fled from Adwā, where he had been kept as a hostage, and returned to his father. Sebhat refused to send him back and war seemed inevitable.[12] In early September Mangashā and Alulā were reported assembling their troops and calling *Rās* Hagos from Shirē.[13] General Antonio Gandolfi,[14] the new Governor of Eritrea, was asked by Mangashā and Mashashā to close the border of Agāmē with Akalla-Guzāy in order not to let Sebhat supply himself by raiding in that direction.[15] From early September 1890 to early February 1891, Alulā and Mangashā's forces camped near the border of Agāmē, reportedly not daring to invade.[16] Militarily they faced a real problem, since Sebhat was fortified on Amba Sardibo and refused to fight in the open. The two armies had great difficulty merely to maintain themselves, and Alulā had to move his camp periodically within the triangle of Hawzēn, Faras Māy, Adwā, while Mangashā did the same in Garaltā.[17]

Though no direct evidence can be adduced, it seems that *Rās* Alulā was this time engaged in a war which he did not want to win.[18] For it was probably in late 1890 that Alulā understood the irony that a Tigre united under *Rās* Mangashā might well be the end of his career and of the hope of regaining Tigrean hegemony. Alulā might have this idea because Mangashā proved over-anxious to become *negus* of Tigre under the rule of Menilek, and it was only the internal troubles, this time the war with Agāmē, which prevented him from taking the road to Shoa.[19]

B. March 1891: Alulā's First Rebellion, to Prevent Mangashā From Going South

In early February 1891, *Rās* Mangashā decided that it was time to leave his province and go to Addis Ababa, where Menilek was discussing Italo-Ethiopian relations with Antonelli and Salimbeni. Mangashā therefore offered Sebhat favourable conditions for peace as well as new territories to govern, especially in Haramat. In return, the *Dadjāzmāch* had to promise his loyalty to Mangashā and Menilek and guarantee his commitment by sending hostages. Relieved at Sebhat's agreement, Mangashā left his camp at Asbi near Agāmē and returned southward to Maqalē,[20] probably heading for Shoa. With Sebhat pacified and Dabbab in prison, it seemed that nothing could stop *Rās* Mangashā, as ruler of a united Tigre, from becoming an honourable vassal of Menilek.

In early January 1891, however, Alulā confiscated a consignment of 400 rifles King Umberto had sent via Massawa and Adwā to Menilek. At first Alulā justified himself by writing to Mashashā Warqē that he had only borrowed the arms for fighting Menilek's enemy, i.e. Sebhat, and would immediately return them after the latter's submission.[21] When Mangashā reconciled with Sebhat, Alulā quickly decamped with 200 of the confiscated rifles, disobeying orders to return them.[22] The *rās* sent raiders towards Shirē but waited near Adwā to ambush *Dadjāzmāch* Mashashā Warqē who, then in Eritrea, was known to have received Menilek's orders to return to Shoa with Mangashā. On 21 February 1891 Mashashā approached Adwā but was astonished to see that, contrary to Ethiopian custom, no one came out to receive him. Entering the town he found that one of his chiefs, a certain *Ledj* Hāylu, had just defected to Alulā with 150 men. Two days later, instead of proceeding to Maqalē, he panicked and recrossed the Marab, notifying the Italians that Alulā was in a state of rebellion against Menilek.[23]

In Maqalē, again among those favouring the Shoan hegemony and therefore Alulā's enemies,[24] *Rās* Mangashā faced further pressure to proceed south. But in Adwā and Tambēn, Alulā's prestige as the only real opposition to apparent humiliation was quickly being rebuilt.[25] After forcing Mashashā from the local political scene, Alulā collected a substantial force (for which figures were not given) and in March 1891 dared to enter Maqalē and face Mangashā.

In Asmara it was thought that the two *rās*es were about "to fortify the independence of Tigre from the Shoan court. They hoped that Italy and Menilek would soon spoil their relations, and then they may rely on us."[26] But it was quickly learned that Mangashā refused to accept such a policy and insisted on his marching to Addis Ababa.[27] In late March Alulā left Maqalē, heading for Tambēn, a step which was justifiably regarded as an obvious act of rebellion.[28]

C. Alulā's Policy: Recognition of Eritrea and War with Menilek

Back at Mannawē, "the most bitter enemy of Shoan hegemony over Ethiopia," as Alulā was then described by Gandolfi,[29] was visited by an Italian correspondent, L. Mercatelli.[30] "Speaking of dignity," Mercatelli quoted Alulā, "Ras Mangascia comes before me, but I am above him in bravery and wisdom."[31] He reported that Alulā's opposition to Mangashā's desire to submit to Shoa had enormously raised his prestige in Tigre, or rather in Tambēn and Adwā:

> In fact Alula is the master. It is sufficient to stay for few days in Tigre to be convinced . . . 'Rassi-imut' [let the *Rās* die] is an oath which comes immediately after 'Johannes-imut'—in Tigre they still swear on the name of the Negus—and before 'Mangascia-imut' . . . If Alula dies, Tigre would fall into such a state of anarchy and exhaustion . . . As a matter of fact even now Tigre is but a corpse that only the strong character of Alula makes walk.[32]

In the tiny village of Mannawē Mercatelli spent a few days with Alulā, whom he described as a lonely and a melancholic leader:

> In the house of Ras Alula not a single woman can be seen except his widow daugher who lives with him[33] . . . His confessor[34] told me that since the death of his legal wife Alula pays no attention to the weaker sex.[35]

Yet, the rebellious Alulā urgently needed a practical alternative to Mangashā's policy, and he thought in terms of Italian support for an autonomous Tigre. *Rās* Alulā was prepared to give the Italians more than Menilek had given them in Uccialli: the whole of the Marab Mellāsh, his previous one and only domain. He told Mercatelli:

> We have been enemies, this is true, but I was serving my king. We have made peace and all I have to say is just one word. Negus Menelick sent an instigator between us, Degiacc Mesciascia, who wants to cause me harm. Why can not we negotiate our own affairs directly? This country is ours, and if we submitted to Menelick this is because we became very few after Metemmah, and caught between two fires. But everyone is the master of his own house only up to his door. He can sell it, let it for money or give it as a gift to a friend. But if he [Menilek] gives as a present what is out of his door [the Marab Mellāsh] the present is of no value. You want the country to the Mareb to cultivate your gardens, to build your houses, to construct your churches. . . ? We can give it to you. [And not Menilek.] Let the Italian soldiers come to Adwa, I shall come to meet them like a friend.[36]

Concerning his motives for establishing an independent Tigre as an ally of Eritrea, Alulā explained:

> But Menelick launched war on Giovanni [Yohannes] when the latter was fighting the infidels, and everyone knows that Giovanni died for a sacred cause. I have my master who is the son of King Giovanni, why should I look for another in Scioa?
> And you why do you look for distant friends? We are neighbours and can serve each other. You want the road open and I want the road open. You should guard it to the Marab, and I shall guard it to Gondar and even beyond Gondar. We must be able to go to the coast where we can trade in order that our country would flourish, with the help of God. Menelick is too far to be of any use to you. Let us make friendship between us.

Alulā probably felt that this economic temptation was not a great attraction for the Italians. He therefore tried to persuade his visitor that it would be strategically beneficial for them to adopt his offered plan: "Tigre can not be a servant of Scioa, because our people are soldiers, while the Shoans fight only against people armed with spears."

When Mercatelli reminded him of Menilek's 50,000 rifles, he answered with a look of contempt: 'It is sufficient that the Italians would be my friends'—And you could hear in that all the bitterness of a year of forced submission.³⁷

But Alulā's plan was not merely based on emotions. Though he only enjoyed a limited knowledge of Shoan-Italian relationships, he understood that the idea of an independent Tigre had supporters (like Mercatelli himself) in the Italian camp.³⁸

D. *April-May 1891: Italian-Shoan Rupture and Dabbab's Mutiny Bring Mangashā and Alulā Closer Again*

After Mashashā Warqē had fled into Eritrea, *Rās* Mangashā successfully persuaded him to return to Ethiopia following a route which avoided Alulā.³⁹ In early April Mashashā arrived at Maqalē, only to find Mangashā extremely reluctant to take the projected trip to the Shoan court.⁴⁰ The activities of Antonelli and Salimbeni in Addis Ababa during January and February 1891 had undermined Shoan-Italian relations.⁴¹ The first obvious signs of the rupture over the Uccialli treaty probably convinced Mangashā that Alulā's advice to approach the Italians independently might well prove a successful policy.⁴²

The second and probably the immediate reason for Mangashā's reluctance stemmed from a mutiny in the fortress on Ambā Salāmā, whose commander, *Ledj* Hāyla-Malakot, the younger son of *Rās* Walda-Mikā'ēl, fled to Asmara. Dabbab Ar'āyā was the ultimate beneficiary of the ambā's large magazines of arms and food, and he prepared for a long siege.⁴³ *Dadjāzmāch* Sebhat of Agāmē, it was reported, was showing signs of wanting to ally with Dabbab, who could help him take Akalla-Guzāy from the Italian-supported Bāhta Hagos. Sebhat therefore allowed many of Dabbab's followers from Akalla-Guzāy to cross his territory, hasten to Ambā Salāmā and join up with their leader.⁴⁴ Simultaneous rebellions against Mangashā's authority in Wādjrat by *Dadjāzmāch* Tadla Wāhid⁴⁵ and by *Dadjāzmāch* Embāyē⁴⁶ made it absolutely impossible for Mangashā to go to Menilek.⁴⁷

Facing such internal threats, Mangashā called Alulā from Mannawē and the two *rās*es met in Chini to lay siege to the *ambā*.⁴⁸ Meanwhile, with Mangashā's permission, Mashashā Warqē left Maqalē for Shoa in late April, although Alulā wanted him arrested.⁴⁹ Nevertheless, Alulā was again Mangashā's first counsellor.

> The accord between Alula and Mangascia, looks at last to be reestablished and in the market of Adua [and probably all over Tigre] Mangascia issued a proclamation saying that a most complete accord exists between him and Alula.⁵⁰

E. May 1891: Dabbab Offers a United Tigrean Action Against Eritrea

On Ambā Salāmā, Dabbab reportedly had some old artillery pieces, which made a successful siege impossible for Alulā's hungry and badly supplied army.[51] Mangashā was back in Maqalē, while Alulā was busy fighting the rebels:

> Mangascia enjoys the comfort of Macalle, but Ras Alula, the loyal and shrewd counsellor, watches restlessly and only with his own troops prevents a general revolt and anarchy, subduing the rebels and brings them to Ras Mangascia.[52]

Confident as he was, and with his followers awaiting him between Faras Māy and Hawzēn, Dabbab demanded complete liberty and recognition of his rights over Sarāyē, Akalla-Guzāy and the Assāwurta from Mangashā.[53]

The latter—it was reported in Eritrea—was inclined to agree to Dabbab's demands,[54] not only to reunite Tigre but also possibly to please Menilek. Asmara learned that the three leaders, the representatives of the houses of *Dadjāzmāch* Sabāgādis, or *Rās* Ar'āyā Demṣu and of Emperor Yohannes, were corresponding and planning an accord.[55] But *Rās* Alulā, now having in his camp *Rās* Hagos and old *Rās* Walda-Mikā'ēl,[56] was reported strongly opposed to such an alliance.[57] Dabbab apparently insisted upon Alulā's extradition to him,[58] so the *ras* could have no illusion about his own future once Mangashā and Dabbab came to an agreement.

Ironically, the Italians now regarded *Rās* Alulā as the only Ethiopian who could save them difficulties on their southern frontier and guarantee "the tranquillity of our colony."[59]

> Ras Alula, the bitter enemy of the Europeans in general and of the Italians in particular, is regarded today in Eritrea as a valuable means to achieve its goals . . . He understood that alone he can hardly match the internal enemies [Dabbab and the pro-Shoans] and that he would die if they manage to unite with external enemies [the Shoans]. This is why he does his best to make the past be forgotten and to calm the Italians.[60]

F. May-June 1891: Alulā Works For An Alliance With Eritrea

Around mid-May 1891, while his three lieutenants were laying siege to Dabbab, Alulā was near Abbā Garima pursuing a certain *Dadjāzmāch* Tagagnā, one of many dissident Tigrean chiefs.[61] Mercatelli wrote: Anywhere that a chief raises his head, Alulā is there to fight him and subdue him. Today he is in Gheralta, tomorrow in Kedia, the day after tomorrow in Nadier.[62]

But the Italian writer was not there just to admire Alulā's energy. He had returned to the *rās*'s camp on a most important political mission. As unofficial envoy of an Italian Commission of Inquiry then visiting Eritrea, he was to check the possibility of a meeting between the commission and the Tigrean *rās*es. In such an encounter it was hoped that the Marab would be recognised as the southern frontier of the colony, and that the Tigreans would guarantee the security of this border.[63]

On 19 May 1891 Mercatelli returned to Adwā with Alulā in order to discuss the matter with De Martino,[64] the Italian resident. According to Mercatelli,[65] the *rās* did not respond immediately to the proposed meeting, but since Mangashā and Dabbab were then considering an anti-Italian action, Alulā decided to frustrate their alliance by responding positively to the Italian offer:

> Finally, one morning, Ras Alula called me and in the presence of degiet Vold-Enkiel[66] and the Bishop of Adua told me: 'From the first day I was convinced that your words were good. But we are dealing with a very serious matter and I wanted my chiefs also to know how the situation lies. I can tell you that if the great generals of the Commission agree to speak to us about our affairs I am willing to meet them. But this meeting cannot take place for eleven days as I want Vold-Enkiel to go to Makalle to seek the advice and assent of Ras Mangascia.

Alulā, however, rejected the idea that the meeting should take place on the northern bank of the Marab. He agreed with De Martino and Mercatelli that he would meet the Italian commission on 2 June 1891 at Daro Takla, between the Marab and Adwā.[67]

Alulā's step forced the hesitant Mangashā on 28 May 1891 (21 Genbot 1883 EC) to write to De Martino in Adwā. He apologised for not being able to come to the meeting but added that he had directed Alulā to receive the Italians and affirm Tigre's friendship with the colony. His instruction to Alulā, however, included no authority to conclude anything with the Italians: "When the Italian dignitaries come, listen to what they say and send it to me in a letter, and then when I see their words, I shall give them my reply in a letter."[68]

Although Mangashā was unenthusiastic about Alulā's policy, it seems that the latter's step was well enough timed to jeopardise the anti-Italian plan offered by Dabbab.

The Italian officials did not cross the Marab on 2 June 1891 to negotiate with Alulā. Governor Gandolfi believed that the commission undermined his authority, and blamed its members for ignoring the fact that Mangashā was the *rās* of Tigre, not Alulā. The idea, attributed to some of the commission members, of paying Alulā a monthly salary of M.T. $1,000 for his promise to keep the peace along the Marab, was published in Italy and was regarded as a national disgrace.[69]

On the same 2 June 1891 Alulā wrote to Borgnini, the president of the commission re-emphasizing his will to meet and "make friendship and that this friendship will be confirmed."[70] Borgnini's reply was polite but evasive. He expressed sorrow that he and his friends were ill and had to leave for Italy, but asked Alulā to send their regards to *Rās* Mangashā.[71]

G. *June-July 1891: Mangashā Sides with Dabbab*

In late May 1891 Dabbab escaped from Ambā Salāmā[72] and came to Wādjrat, to join 500 of his own men and some 3,000 followers of his new ally, *Dadjāzmāch* Tadlā Wāhid.[73] Yet this time Mangasha did not urge Alulā to hurry from Adwā and to subdue the rebels. Mangashā was now apparently convinced that through an alliance with Dabbab and Sebhat, the representatives of the three great Tigrean families, he might finally unite the province. In Maqalē, Mangashā was under the influence of his pro-Shoan counsellors, "all rivals of Alula",[74] who most probably tried to persuade him to submit to Menilek and become the *Negus* of Tigre. Both Sebhat and Dabbab, with whom he started negotiating, were also insisting on Alulā's removal from the political scene.[75] Thus, instead of again calling Alulā, in around mid-June, Mangashā recognized Dabbab Ar'āyā as a *Dadjāzmāch*:[76] "The conditions of peace between me and . . . Mangascia," Dabbab wrote to Gandolfi, "were that Ras Alula must remain our servant, as we are sons of kings."[77]

Alulā had again to oppose such a reunification of Tigre. Though he was "the great fighter for Tigrean independence," he was left with no other choice. First, he could not compromise his own political existence. Second, he had every reason to believe that if he was out of the scene, Mangashā would sooner or later submit to Menilek. Furthermore, as already mentioned, while Dabbab suggested a united Tigrean action against Eritrea, Alulā sought an alliance with the Italians against Menilek.

In the second week of July Alulā moved, trying to surprise Mangashā and Dabbab. According to Dabbab's letter (the only piece of evidence available):

> [Alula] desiring to take our throne came to fight Mangascia. Ras Mangascia fled to a fort which he refused to leave. All the noblemen of the country came to me to ask me to destroy Ras Alula . . . I answered that it was good. Ras Mangascia left the fort. Alula, knowing my accord with Mangascia, immediately asked for peace.[78]

At Zabbā Māryām in Sahartē around mid-July, Mangashā, Alulā and Dabbab made a strange peace,[79] probably arranged by the priests, which had no chance of enduring.

H. September 1891: Mangashā Follows Alulā's Pro-Italian Policy. The End of Dabbab

In late July 1891 Mangashā, accompanied by the two enemies, Alulā and Dabbab, proceeded to Adwā.[80] There, in the proud centre of Tigre, Mangashā was probably struck, as Orero had been in January 1890, by the people's hatred of Menilek and their admiration for Yohannes. Mangashā was undoubtedly aware that the rupture between Menilek and the Italians over the Treaty of Uccialli changed the situation. With Addis Ababa in distant Shoa and the neighbouring Italians eager to cooperate he decided to follow Alulā's policy of trying to obtain Italian aid against the emperor.

Informants who reached Asmara after mid-August 1891, repeatedly announced that Mangashā was now completely under Alulā's influence, and that both men openly expressed their anti-Shoan feelings.[81] On the other hand, Gandolfi reported, "They [Mangashā and Alulā] lose no chance to demonstrate their good will towards us."[82] Indeed, on 6 August 1891, Mangashā wrote to the King of Italy that he sought friendship . . . that . . . will ever grow and become eternal."[83]

Mangashā ordered the still anti-Italian Dabbab to refrain from raiding beyond the Marab.[84] When the latter was insubordinate, Mangashā and Alulā opened hostilities, with Sebhat remaining neutral.[85] Asmara gave direct military aid to Mangashā and Alulā, but an Italian observer was present on 29 September 1891, when they clashed with Dabbab at Abba Garima.[86] Their 1,800 troops faced 1,000 men entrenched on the mountain of Atghebat north of Addi Nafās. On the morning of 29 Septermber 1891,[87] Mangashā's army, with Alulā in the lead, marched towards the mountain but quickly found that during the night Dabbab had moved to the mountain of Alesca, southwest of Addi Nafās. At 7.50 a.m., shouting loudly "and according to the Ethiopian custom arranged in a line they marched forward to storm the enemy." When this attack failed, Alulā reorganised his forces and flanked Dabbab's position. At 8.30 a.m., the fighting was all over, and Dabbab, with some of his followers, was encircled on the summit of the mountain. Even though Mangashā had promised 200 thalers to the soldier who would bring him Dabbab alive,[88] he was killed in combat.[90] The body was carried to Adwā, and ceremonially buried in Trinity Church.[90] Tigre blamed Alulā for his death, and according to the *rās*'s great-granddaughter, he killed Dabbab in retaliation for the death of his son-in-law, *Dadjāzmāch* Hāyla-Sellāssē.[91] Dabbab's demise was fortuitous for Alulā, since it fit into his wider plans to stop Mangashā's wavering: "The battle consolidated Mangascia's authority in Tigre, and many chiefs who regarded themselves as independent since the battle of Matemma are coming to submit to the son of Emperor Giovanni."[92]

I. December 1891: The Meeting on the Marab— Alulā's Greatest Step Towards an Independent Tigre

Mangashā's victory over Dabbab and his repeated failure to comply with Menilek's invitations to come to Shoa made him, towards the end of 1891, the undisputed leader of Tigre. Mercatelli wrote from Adwā that:

> The authority of Mangascia, is absolute and undisputed, they all recognise him as the son and heir of Emperor Giovanni who is worshipped like a saint after he fell fighting the Dervishes. . . . On the other hand Menelik's authority is denied here. Nobody recognises him, and Alula speaks of him always in great contempt.[93]

Mangashā was now confident enough to follow Alulā's advice about an alliance with Eritrea. Governor Gandolfi and his superiors in Rome were quite ready now, for their own reasons, to come to some understanding with the independent Tigreans.[94] On 20 October 1891, Dr. Nerazzini, accompanied by De Martino, arrived at Adwā, at Mangashā's request, to take up the position of Italian resident.[95] Nerazzini also brought King Umberto's reply, dated 15 September 1891, to Mangashā's letter of 6 August 1891. The king wished Mangashā to have a friendly interview with the governor of the colony, but he was careful to refer to Mangashā only as the *Rās* of Tigre and to mention Menilek as the emperor.[96]

During the first half of November, Nerazzini, De Martino, Alulā and Mangashā prepared for an official meeting with Gandolfi. In his report of 2 November 1891, Nerazzini described Alulā as working for Italian friendship in order to fight Menilek.[97] As Gandolfi reported:[98]

> He [Alulā] was tirelessly working for a long time to eliminate any causes of discord with that part of the Mareb, in order to be able, once aid and any kind of help is assured, to divert his attention against Menelik who . .
> is the object of Alula's great contempt, in order to liberate Tigre from the hated Shoan.

The Italians nonetheless conducted their policy according to the spirit of King Umberto's letter. Friendship was to be established with the Tigreans, but they also took care not to alienate the Shoan emperor. Consequently it was agreed that the Tigreans would consider the Marab as their border with Eritrea, but Sarāyē and Akalla-Guzāy were declared parts of Ethiopia, as had been agreed between Menilek and Antonelli on 6 February 1890. No direct military support was promised to Mangashā except for a small quantity of arms and ammunition to be supplied only if Tigre were attacked by the Mahdists. Commercial caravans were guaranteed a safe route from Adwā to Massawa, and the Italians undertook to reconstruct Trinity Church in Adwā, where they would also build a new palace for Mangashā.⁹⁹

The understanding with Eritrea was undoubtedly Alulā's greatest achievement in his long struggle to persuade Mangashā to lead an independent Tigre, his policy for the past two years. Yet Alulā's Dogali image, as Italy's great enemy, led many observers to believe that he opposed the entente and was forced to attend the ceremonial meeting with the Italians on the Marab.¹⁰⁰ It must, however, be remembered that once Alulā gave up the idea of restoring his government in the Marab Mellāsh, he no longer considered the Italians as interfering in his affairs. Alulā was now only interested in restoring Tigrean hegemony or at least in safeguarding the independence of Tigre from Shoa, and he quickly regarded the Italians in Eritrea as European neighbours whose friendship and help had to be obtained.

The meeting between the Tigrean *rās*es and Gandolfi was fixed for 28 November 1891, but it had to be delayed as Alulā had to counter a raid launched by Sebhat,¹⁰¹ the only major chief who did not join Mangashā's camp. On 6 December 1891, on the Italian bank of the Marab River, the official meeting finally took place between the Governor of Eritrea and the leaders of Tigre: Mangashā, Hagos, Alulā and the old *Rās* Walda-Mikā'ēl. According to the correspondent of *Popolo Romano*,¹⁰² Mangashā was the first to cross the Marab and was warmly received by Gandolfi. The governor was then asked by Mangashā to swear that the Dogali affair was entirely forgotten and, after the Italian General assented, Alulā crossed the river:¹⁰³

> On Ras Alula's arrival General Gandolfi addressed him in patriotic language, stating that time had healed a cruel wound, which it was better not to recall. Old difficulties and causes of misunderstanding had ceased to exist, and in common interest it was desirable to work together, and further the interests of the Tigré and the Italian Colony, by a policy of peace and order, and a loyal and honest interchange of intercourse between the two parties. General Gandolfi alluded to Ras Alula as a gallant soldier, willing to sacrifice his life in the interests of his country. Ras Alula, deeply impressed, desired to be allowed to embrace General Gandolfi, to which he acceded.

Negotiations the next day confirmed the previously agreed conditions. Mangashā ceremonially nominated Gandolfi as a *rās*, a fact later humorously treated in Rome.¹⁰⁴ In fact it was quite a significant act, since Mangashā, himself only a *rās*, was not authorised to make such a nomination, and by doing so he was clearly challenging the emperor.¹⁰⁵ The Italians, as mentioned above, were careful to try and minimise the damage to Menilek's prestige, and the meeting resulted in no official paper being signed by the parties. Gandolfi and his officers, in the name of their government, and Mangashā, Alulā, Hagos and the other Ethiopian chiefs swore an oath to be faithful to the engagements entered into. After a cordial leave-taking at which, as a sign of respect, *Rās* Alula kissed General Gandolfi's arm, the two camps broke up, and the negotiations and ceremonies became a matter of history.[106]

J. December 1891-March 1892: Mangashā Regards Himself as Sovereign; Tigre is United

When the Tigrean *ras*es and the Italian officials swore "to be a friend of your friend and an enemy of your enemies,"[107] Alulā's policy of relying on Eritrea against Menilek seemed to be most successful. The coming months saw the strengthening of that policy and of his personal position. During the months of January and February 1892, *Rās* Mangashā and *Rās* Hagos marched southwards to camp in Endartā near Ashangē and to face Menilek's expected advance on Tigre.[108] This time, however, having internal problems of his own and afraid of Tigrean influence in Amhara, where in late 1891 Mangashā and Alulā managed to strengthen pro-Tigrean elements,[109] Menilek's advance halted, and on 17 February 1892, he turned back to his capital.[110]

Meanwhile, *Rās* Alulā was working to remove the last political obstacle to Tigrean unity. He marched to the border of Agāmē, where he met *Dadjāzmāch* Sebhat Aragāwi, to whom he offered Mangashā's pardon and participation in what he hoped would be an anti-Shoan campaign.[111] As a sign of friendship and good faith, the *rās* gave Sebhat the hand of W. Shoanesh,[112] the daughter of his dead brother, *Bāshā* Gabra-Māryām; and Sebhat's brother, *Dadjāzmāch* Abbāy, married W. Damaqach,[113] Alulā's daughter.

In Hawzēn on 8 March 1892, before the *rās*es of Tigre and *Echagē* Tēwoflos, *Dadjāzmāch* Sebhat, carrying a stone on his neck, was ceremonially pardoned by Mangashā. The latter appeared dressed as a *negus* and stood under a royal, red umbrella. Two days later, by appointing Sebhat *rās*,[114] he left no doubt about his claimed status. The combined Tigrean forces of Sebhat, Mangashā, Hagos and Alulā were estimated at 10,000 troops, "by far better trained than the Shoans." Those assembled at Hawzēn addressed Mangashā as *jānhoy*, the appellation of the Emperor of Ethiopia, and demanded that he lead them to Shoa.[115]

K. March-June 1892: Alulā's Policy Jeopardised by New Italian Policy

The economically ruined Tigre could not, however, sustain the type of military expedition to Shoa demanded by Alulā and the Tigrean soldiery. Gandolfi seemed to be willing to assist, and, in early 1892, he sent 35,000 cartridges to Mangashā.[116] The prince of Tigre, aware of the fact that this was only a symbolic quantity, applied for more cartridges and grain.[117] His letters, as befitted those of a sovereign, were now sealed on top.[118]

Gandolfi's straightforward Tigrean policy was however disapproved in Rome, and on 28 February 1891 he was replaced by Gen. Oreste Baratieri, a change which marked the Italian return to a pro-Shoan policy. Immediately after his arrival, Baratieri contacted *Rās* Makonnen, Menilek's major adviser, and started doing his best to appease the emperor.[119] Regarding Tigre, Baratieri attempted to calm Mangashā and to assure him of Rome's friendly intentions but to ignore any request for material support which might encourage an independent line. "I have not sent them even one cartridge," Baratieri reported on 18 August 1891,[120] "and of the 20,000 sacks of grain which they asked for two and a half months ago I have not sent them even a single one."

Baratieri regarded *Rās* Alulā as the most uncompromising Tigrean leader,[121] and, as such, the main obstacle to his policy of calming Mangashā and ensuring Menilek's control over Tigre. *Rās* Alulā, Baratieri thought, was "a turbulent chief, an enemy of the Shoans and of the Italians and indeed of the Tigreans themselves whom he does not let have even one quiet hour."[122] Baratieri's attitude derived from his pro-Shoan policy, a political formulation based on logical analysis, but also on the wrong assumption that the Alulā of 1892 was the enemy of 1887. Baratieri was wrong in thinking that Alulā's ultimate aim was to reoccupy Asmara, and the Italian's subsequent moves even seem to indicate also a politically harmful desire to avenge for Dogali.

The Tigrean *rās*es, still hoping to succeed in their independent policy, were naturally slow to understand the change in Italian policy. Baratieri was pleased to report that Mangashā and Alulā were doing their best to move the colony to their side.[123] An *awādj* of 21 April 1892[124] called the people to assemble in Alulā's camp and forbade any anti-Italian raids. Baratieri was asked to send engineers to build the promised palace at Adwā and to reconstruct the Trinity church. An Ethiopian rebel, *Ledj* Bayyana, who had caused the Italians trouble in Sarāyē and had escaped to Tigre, was hunted by Alulā.[125] Around mid-May all the Tigrean chiefs assembled again in Mangashā's palace in Maqalē, where they jointly reaffirmed their request to Baratieri for cartridges and grain. As there was no positive response, Alulā suggested he would raid the Baria tribes with the dual aim of obtaining the needed food supplies and of putting pressure on the Italians.[126] Yet Alulā was still doing his best to appease Baratieri before spoiling relations with Eritrea by raiding those tribes. Back at Tambēn[127] on 28 May 1892, Alulā wrote to Baratieri trying to arrange a meeting in order "to make our friendship more solid."[128] Baratieri replied on 22 June 1892, praising Alulā and stating that "the pact of friendship sworn by Gandolfi is sacred for me."[129] On the same day, Baratieri answered Mangashā's letter of 20 May 1892 asking again for food supplies.[130] Neither Alulā's request for a meeting nor Mangashā's request for grain were mentioned in Baratieri's polite replies.

Alulā, who fully understood that, without Italian help, no anti-Shoan campaign could take place, still worked to gain Baratieri's confidence. On 3 July 1892, after being strongly advised by De Martino not to raid the Baria, Alulā discussed the matter with *Rās* Hagos and *Echagē* Tēwoflos in Adwā, and subsequently notified the Italian resident that he would refrain from doing so.[131] Simultaneously Alulā invited to Adwā the anti-Italian rebel *Ledj* Bayyana and treacherously imprisoned him.[132] Hearing that Baratieri was visiting Sarāyē around mid-July, he pressed De Martino the Italian resident in Adwā to arrange a meeting with the governor but was again rejected.[133]

* * *

Alulā's failure to unite with Eritrea against Menilek was not his own fault. His political plan seemed realistic and successful, and at Hawzēn in March, Tigre seemed to be about to become an independent buffer province. What rendered the scheme a failure was the change in Italian policy, an unpredictable possibility for someone with Alulā's limited knowledge of Shoan-Italian relationships. The Italian shift, vital and important to the history of the period, can be partly also attributed to Rome's and Asmara's continued identification of *Rās* Alulā with the Dogali massacre of January 1887.

NOTES

1 See an article on Sebhat by Mercatelli in *La Tribuna*, 20.2.96.
2 See above, p. 153.
3 On *Dadjāzmāch* Waldē see Conti Rossini, *Italia ed Etiopia*, p. 465.
4 Corazzini, "Colloquio," *La Tribuna*, 20.6.90.
5 Ibid.
6 Ibid., A.S.MAI 3/3-35, Orero to MAE, 26.5.90.
7 A.S.MAI 3/5-35, Gandolfi, Rapporto 1 July — 15 August 1890.
8 A.S.MAI 3/5-35, Gandolfi to MAE, 21.8.90, "Rapporto politico-militare," 1 July — 15 August 1890.
9 Ibid. L. Mercatelli, "Cronaca di una fuga," *Corriere di Napoli*, 1-2 June 1891.
10 Gandolfi, "Rapporto politico-militare," 1 July-15 August 1890. A.S.MAI 3/5-35, Gandolfi to MAE, 4.9.90, "Rapporto" 15 August-1 Sept. 1890.
11 Marcatelli, "Cronaca."
12 A.S.MAI 3/5-35, Gandolfi to MAE, 22.9.90, "Rapporto," 1-15 Sept. 1890.
13 Ibid.
14 He replaced Orero on 4.6.90 with Baratieri as a deputy.
15 A.S.MAI 3/5-35, Gandolfi to MAE, 22.9.90, "Rapporto," 1-15 Sept. 1890.
16 A.S.MAI 3/5-35, Gandolfi's reports to MAE of 4.11.90, 18.11.90, 4.12.90, 25.12.90, 20.1.90, 6.2.91, 22.2.91.
17 Ibid.

18 See also Belcredi's article "Ras Sebath," *La Tribuna*, 20.2.96.
19 As analysed by Gandolfi in his report of 6.2.91.
20 A.S.MAI 3/5-35, Gandolfi to MAE, 22.2.91, "Rapporto," 1-15 Feb. 1891.
21 A.S.MAI 3/5-35, Gandolfi to MAE, 20.1.91, "Rapporto," 1-15 Jan. 1891.
22 Ibid.
23 A.S.MAI 3/5-35, Gandolfi to MAE, 7.3.91, "Rapporto," 16-28 Feb. 1891. L. Mercatelli, "Cronaca di una fuga," *Corriere di Napoli*, 1-2 June 1891.
24 See above, p. 144.
25 Mercatelli, "Nel paese di Ras Alula," *Corriere di Napoli*, 13-14 May 1891.
26 A.S.MAI 3/5-35, Gandolfi to MAE, 21.3.91, "Rapporto," 1-15 March 1891.
27 A.S.MAI 3/5-35, Gandolfi to MAE, 13.4.91.
28 A.S.MAI 3/5-37, Gandolfi to MAE, 21.4.91, "Rapporto," 1-15 April 1891.
29 A.S.MAI 3/5-37, Gandolfi to MAE, 6.4.91.
30 Mercatelli was a correspondent of *Corriere di Napoli* in the early nineties and of *La Tribuna* in the period prior to the battle of Adwā; probably as a result of his experience in 1891, he became interested in Alulā's subsequent career, as reflected in the many articles cited in my text.
31 Mercatelli, "Nel paese di Ras Alula", *Corriere di Napoli*, 13-14 May 1891.
32 Ibid.
33 Ṣahāywarada, the widow of *Dadjāzmāch* Hāyla-Sellāssē.
34 Alulā's confessor was probably the Bishop of Adwā, mentioned by Ferdinando Martini as Melaka Berakanat, "The Confessor of the Ras and his Adviser," F. Martini, *Cose Africane*, Milano 1897, p. 111.
35 Mercatelli, "Nel paese", *Corriere di Napoli*, 13-14 May 1891. In fact in late 1891 Alulā married W. Kāssā of Haramat, who gave him a child in 1892. See A.S.MAI 3/6-46, Salsa to MAE, 6.11.97; A. Wylde "An Unofficial Visit to Abyssinia," *Manchester Guardian*, 14.5.97; Interview Fit. Bayyana of Aksum, Feb. 1972.
36 Mercatelli, "Nel paese."
37 Ibid.
38 Alula's future policy (see below, pp. 166, 167, 169-171) proves that Mercatelli did not exaggerate the extent to which the *ras* was seeking rapprochement with the Italians.
39 A.S.MAI 3/5-37, Gandolfi to MAE, 13.4.91, 6.4.91, "Rapporto," 16-31 March 1891.
40 A.S.MAI 3/5-37, Gandolfi to MAE, 8.5.91.
41 See Zaghi, *Crispi e Menelich*, Chapter XII, pp. 289-307. H. Marcus, *The Life and Times*, pp. 124-134.
42 As analysed by Gandolfi in his A.S.MAI, 3/5-37, "Rapporto" of 8.5.91 covering 16-30 April 1891.
43 A.S.MAI 3/5-37, Gandolfi to MAE, 30.4.91, 25.5.91, *Corriere di Napoli*, 13-14 May 1891.
44 A.S.MAI 3/5-37, Gandolfi to MAE, 25.5.91, "Rapporto," 1-16 May 1891.
45 A.S.MAI 3/5-37, Gandolfi to MAE, 30.4.91, on Dadjāzmāch Tadlā Wāhid. See Conti Rossini, *Italia ed Etiopia*, p. 463.
46 A.S.MAI 3/5-37, Gandolfi to MAE, 11.6.91.
47 A.S.MAI 3/5-37, Gandolfi to MAE, 30.4.91, 8.5.91, *Corriere di Napoli*, 13.14 May 1891.
48 A.S.MAI 3/5-37, Gandolfi to MAE, 30.4.91. Mercatelli, "Nel paese di Ras Alula,"

Corriere di Napoli, 15-16 June 1891.
49 A.S.MAI 3/5-37, Gandolfi to MAE, 8.5.91; L. Mercatelli, "Cronaca di una Fuga," *Corriere di Napoli*, 1-2 June 1891. Back in Addis Ababa, Mashashā was accused (in early 1893) of advising Mangashā not to go to Menilek. See Marcus, *The Life and Times*, p. 144.
50 A.S.MAI 3/5-37, Gandolfi to MAE, 8.5.91, "Rapporto", 16-30 April 1891.
51 Mercatelli, "Cronaca". For a very good description of Ambā Salāmā, its history and the siege, see Mercatelli's "Nel paese di Ras Alula," *Corriere di Napoli*, 15-16 June 1891. The article was written near the ambā, 20.5.91.
52 A.S.MAI 3/5-37, Gandolfi to MAE, 11.6.91, "Rapporto", 16-31 May 1891.
53 A.S.MAI 3/5-37, Gandolfi to MAE, 30.4.91, 21.5.91.
54 Ibid; Mercatelli, "Cronaca."
55 A.S.MAI 3/5-37, Gandolfi to MAE, 24.6.91, 8.7.91.
56 Conti Rossini, *Italia ed Etiopia*, p. 56.
57 A.S.MAI 3/5-37, Gandolfi to MAE, 8.5.91.
58 See below, p. 168.
59 A.S.MAI 3/5-37, Gandolfi to MAE, 8.5.91.
60 A.S.MAI 3/5-37, Gandolfi to MAE, 11.6.91.
61 L. Mercatelli, "Il Convegno di Ras Alula," *Corriere di Napoli*, 30 June, 1 July 1891.
62 Mercatelli, "Nel paese", *Corriere di Napoli*, 15-16 June 1891.
63 A.S.MAI 11/2-16, De Martino (to Gandolfi?), 20.5.91.
64 A.S.MAI 11/2-16, De Martino (to Gandolfi?) 20.5.91.
65 Mercatelli, "Il Convegno."
66 This was old *Rās* Walda-Mikā'ēl.
67 L. Mercatelli, "Il Convegno di Ras Alula," *Corriere di Napoli*, 30 June-1 July 1891. A.S.MAI 11/2-16, Mercatelli to Piano, 22.5.91; Piano to Baratieri, 23.5.91; De Martino (to Gandolfi?), 20.5.91.
68 A.S.MAI 11/2-16, Mangashā to De Martino, 21 Genbot (1883 E.C.). The letter carried a significant seal: "A seal of Rās Mangashā, Yohannes King of Kings of Zion King of Kings of Ethiopia". Thus, he referred to himself as *ras* on the one hand, while he also emphasised that he was the son of the emperor.
69 A.S.MAI 11/2-16, Borgnini to MAE, 2.6.91, Gandolfi to MAE, 29.6.91; *Corriere di Napoli*, 30-31 May 1891, 14-15 June 1891. The commission was sent by the new Italian Prime Minister, di Rudini, who rejected Crispi's colonial policy. Rudini sought to minimize Italian involvement in Ethiopian affairs, but the commission suggested contacting the Tigrean *Rās*es in order to secure the Marab border. See C. Zaghi, "Il Convegno del Mareb," *Rivista delle Colonie*, Anno XI, [1932], No. 2, pp. 175-184.
70 A.S.MAI 11/2-16, Alula to Borgnini, 26 Genbot (1883 EC). Alula's letter carried a challenging script: "A seal of Ras Alula who is a Turk Basha. Yohannes king of kings of Ethiopia." This seal was not an old one left from the period of the late emperor, as thè seal which Alula had used in his letter to Piano of 15 August 1889 (see above, p. 147) carried the same script but was different in shape.
71 A.S.MAI 11/2-16, Borgnini to Alula, N.D.
72 A.S.MAI 11/2-16, Mangasha to De Martino, 21 Genbot (1883 EC).
73 A.S.MAI, Gandolfi to MAE 24.6.91; "Rapporto," 1-15 June 1891; *Corriere di Napoli*, 30 June-1 July 1891.
74 A.S.MAI 3/5-37, Gandolfi to MAE, 8.7.91, 16-30 June 1891.
75 A.S.MAI 3/5-37, Gandolfi to MAE, 24.6.91, "Rapporto", 1-18 June 1891.

76   Conti Rossini, *Italia ed Etiopia*, p. 56.
77   A.S.MAI, Archivio Eritrea 55/A, Debeb to Gandolfi, 6.9.91.
78   A.S.MAI, 3/5-37, Gandolfi to MAE, 6.8.91, "Rapporto," 1-31 July 1891.
79   Ibid.
80   A.S.MAI 3/5-37, Gandolfi to MAE, 25.8.91.
81   A.S.MAI 3/5-37, Gandolfi to MAE, N.D., "Rapporto," 27 Aug.-18 Sept. 1891, 25.8.91, "Rapporto," 1-25 Aug. 1891.
82   Gandolfi to MAE, 25.8.91.
83   Conti Rossini, *Italia ed Etiopia*, p. 57; Bizzoni, *L'Eritrea*, p. 255.
84   A.S.MAI 3/5-37, Gandolfi to MAE, 25.8.91.
85   Gandolfi, "Rapporto," 27 Aug.-18 Sept. 1891.
86   A.S.MAI 3/5-37, Baratieri to MAE, 6.10.91, contains detailed descriptions by Mulazzani who, on 13.9.91, was sent to Alulā and Mangashā's camp.
87   In *Storia Militare*, p. 233, the battle was misdated 6.10.91 (the date of Baratieri's report).
88   Mulazzani's report in Baratieri to MAE, 6.10.91.
89   According to Conti Rossini, *Italia*, p. 59, Dabbab was killed by one of Alulā's officers.
90   Mulazzani's report in Baratieri to MAE, 6.10.91.
91   Int. W. Yashāshwarq, Feb. 1972.
92   Mulazzani's report in Baratieri to MAE, 6.10.91.
93   L. Mercatelli, "Le trattative Italo-Tigrine," *Corriere di Napoli*, 29-30 Dec. 1891.
94   Consult Marcus, *The Life and Times*, pp. 141-143.
95   C. Zaghi, "Il convegno del Mareb"; also *Storia Militare*, p. 233, Mangasha to Baratieri, 20.8.91.
96   Umberto to Mangashā, 15.9.91, quoted in Bizzoni, p. 255; see also Zaghi, "Il convegno."
97   Conti Rossini, *Italia*, p. 465.
98   A.S.MAI 3/6-40, Gandolfi to MAE, 17.1.92.
99   Gandolfi to MAE, 15.11.91, *La Tribuna*, 17.1.92.
100   For such a passage see Berkeley, pp. 36, 37. Gandolfi explained the source for such misinformation by stating that the pro-Shoan Dr. Nerazzini "had a natural hatred for the greatest rival of that policy and he considered Alula as opposing friendship with us, while in fact he is the most enthusiastic supporter of such friendship", A.S.MAI 3/6-40, Gandolfi to MAE, 11.12.91.
101   *La Tribuna*, 17.1.92; *Corriere di Napoli*, 29-30 Dec. 1891. In November Mangashā nominated *Dadjāzmāch* Waldē and Sebhat's brother *Dadjāzmāch* Abbāy over Agāmē. See Conti Rossini, *Italia*, p. 466. Sebhat's raids were probably an act of retaliation.
102   As quoted in FO 403/177, Slade to Dufferin, 6.1.92. For a similar description see: A.S.MAI 3/6-40, Gandolfi to MAE, 11.12.91.
103   Ibid.
104   *La Tribuna* headline for the article describing the meeting was "Ras Gandolfi", *La Tribuna*, 11.12.91.
105   See below, pp. 171-172.
106   FO 403/177, Slade to Dufferin, 6.1.92.
107   Alulā was reported as changing the agreed text and saying: "I am a devoted servant of Mangascia and therefore swear to be a friend of his friends". See *I Nostri Errori*, p. 131.

108 A.S.MAI 3/6-40, Gandolfi to MAE, 13.2.92.
109 See Conti Rossini, *Italia ed Etiopia*, pp. 72, 73.
110 A.S.MAI 36/16-147, Gandolfi to MAE, 10.3.92.
111 A.S.MAI 3/6-40, Gandolfi to MAE, 13.2.92.
112 W. Yashāshwarq; Mercatelli in *La Tribuna*, 20.2.96; Conti Rossini, *Italia*, p. 77; A.S.MAI 3/17-136, Mulazzani Report, 26.7.96.
113 W. Yashāshwarq.
114 See: Afawarq Gabra-Iyasus, *Dāgmāwi atsē menilek*, Rome 1901 EC, p. 82.
115 Conti Rossini, *Italia*, pp. 74, 75. A.S.MAI 3/6-40, Gandolfi to MAE, 16.3.92, 3/6-42, Baratieri to MAE, 15.4.92. L. Mercatelli, "Ras Sebath," *La Tribuna*, 20.2.96.
116 Conti Rossini, p. 75. According to A.S.MAI 3/6-42, Baratieri to MAE, 15.4.92, only 25,000 cartridges were involved.
117 A.S.MAI 36/16-148, Baratieri to MAE, 18.8.92.
118 Mercatelli, "Ras Sebath"; Conti Rossini, *Italia*, p. 75.
119 A.S.MAI 3/6-148, Baratieri to MAE, 18.8.92.
120 Ibid.
121 Ibid.
122 A.S.MAI 3/6-42, Baratieri to MAE, 13.1.93.
123 A.S.MAI 3/6-42, Baratieri to MAE, 30.5.92.
124 According to Conti Rossini, *Italia*, p. 76, it was proclaimed on 24.4.92.
125 A.S.MAI 3/6-42, Baratieri to MAE, 10.5.92.
126 A.S.MAI 3/6-42, Baratieri to MAE, 30.5.92, 6.6.92.
127 A.S.MAI 3/6-42, Baratieri to MAE, 30.5.92.
128 A.S.MAI 3/6-42, Alulā to Baratieri, 28.5.92.
129 A.S.MAI 3/6-42, Baratieri to Alula, 22.6.92.
130 A.S.MAI 3/6-42, Mangascia to Baratieri 20.5.92.
131 A.S.MAI 3/6-42, Baratieri to MAE, 17.7.92.
132 Ibid.
133 Ibid.

15

1892-1894:
"Wadi Qubi" Challenging the Son of Yohannes

A. *July-September 1892: Mangashā Decides to Go to Menilek. Alulā Fails to Organise an Opposition*

While Alulā's pro-Italian and anti-Shoan policy was collapsing, renewed pressure was put on Mangashā to submit to Emperor Menilek. The emperor asked the Tigrean clergy to persuade their leader to visit Shoa.[1] Mangashā's personal envoy, *Belāttā* Tasfāyē Ḥantālo, Seyum's former supporter, was travelling between Maqalē and Addis Ababa serving as a mediator between Menilek and the *rās*.[2] Moreover, Baratieri, through De Martino, pressed Mangashā to write an appeasing letter to Menilek.[3]

In Aksum in late August and early September 1892, *Rās* Alulā met with *Rās* Sebhat of Agāmē. Both men could not reconcile themselves to the fact that Mangashā was about to submit to Menilek. According to De Martino's reports, Alulā suggested *Rās* Mangashā's overthrow if he went to Shoa, and offered the crown of Tigre to Sebhat.[4] Judging from Alulā's activities immediately following the meeting, it may be assumed that De Martino's sources were fairly reliable.

The two *rāses* had an estimated 7,000 troops, but, according to the Italian resident, *Rās* Hagos's loyalty to Mangashā rendered a march on Maqalē hazardous.[5] So, instead of fighting Mangashā, both Alulā and Sebhat, acting upon Mangashā's *Masqal* invitation, arrived in Maqalē and expressed their loyalty to their master.[6] On the same occasion, Mangashā notified the chiefs present that he was about to leave for Shoa. *Rās* Hagos and *Echagē* Tēwoflos reportedly praised the decision, and Sebhat immediately left Maqalē and returned to Agāmē. Alulā, De Martino reported,[7] reacted furiously and performed the traditional war dances, inciting everyone to shout anti-Shoan slogans. Mangashā ignored Alulā's antics, but the latter preferred to remain in Maqalē to try to prevent the projected journey.

On 22 September 1892 De Martino was instructed by Baratieri to hasten to Maqalē to ensure that Alulā would not cause Mangashā to deviate from his resolve to submit to the emperor. He ordered the resident to promise economic support to Tigre once a peaceful agreement with Menilek was reached.[8] De Martino arrived at Maqalē after the pro-Shoan decision had been announced by Mangashā, and described Alulā's feelings:

> Ras Alula sees in the new Italian policy towards Tigre the downfall of his aspirations and predicts the fall of Mangascia . . . He is afraid . . . and from day to day he is being deserted by his followers. He is aware of his growing isolation . . . but he still has not lost hope and is patiently awaiting the chance to persuade Mangascia not to make peace with Menelik. . . . Mangascia is determined to go to Shoa and only because of the memory of his father and respect for the age, the influence and the rank of Ras Alula . . . he tries to disarm him gently. . .[9]

B. *December 1892: Alulā Openly Rebels Against the Hereditary Prince of Tigre*

On 23 October 1892 Tasfāyē Hanṭalo, Mangashā's envoy, entered Addis Ababa. Two weeks later, before *Abunas* Pēṭros and Mātēwos, Menilek publicly swore not to deceive Mangashā nor cause him any harm. Then, on 9 Nov. 1892, Tasfāyē left for Tigre,[10] carrying the emperor's request that the prince of Tigre and *rās* Alulā should come to Boru Mēdā.[11]

Meanwhile, Mangashā, Alulā and Hagos had marched from Maqalē to Adwā, hoping to make contact with Baratieri, who, unwilling to annoy Menilek, avoided the encounter.[12] To appease the governor, Mangashā ordered Alulā to hand *Ledj* Bayyana over to the Italians. Aware of Baratieri's policy, the *rās* refused. In response, on 18 November 1892, Mangashā sent *Ras* Hagos with an armed escort to Alulā's camp, where they took custody of the rebel and delivered him to the Italians. After this public humiliation,[13] Mangashā left Alulā in Adwā and hastened to Maqalē to meet the envoy returning from Menilek.

Alulā's thereupon informed *Ras* Sebhat of the situation and told him that he intended an open rebellion against Mangashā.[14] On 12 December 1892, Alulā arrested three of Mangashā's devotées, including *Dadjāzmāch* Embāyē; moreover, upon receiving an invitation from Mangashā to come to Maqalē, Alulā responded by beating the *nagārit* to assemble an army.[15]

Ras Sebhat was, however, afraid of fighting Mangashā and exposing his province to a possible Italian punitive expedition. Neither he nor *Echagē* Tēwoflos would come to Alulā's aid.[16] As a matter of fact, the latter left Adwā on 14 December 1892, heading for Mangashā's camp in Maqalē.[17] The abandonment was a great blow to Alulā, since the *echagē* was avowedly anti-Shoan and a dedicated supporter of Tigrean hegemony.[18] He and the Aksum clergy were also known to be Alulā's supporters.[19] For them, the *rās* not only symbolised the Tigrean cause but was also a close personal friend because, when governor of the

Marab Mellāsh, Alulā had endowed Church Dabra-Zion of Aksum[20] with the revenue of Sarāyē. "He," wrote Alulā's biographer, referring to the period during which he was the governor of Hamāsēn, "gave all his property to the poor and wretched, and to all the churches. Most of all, for our mother of Zion [Aksum]."[21] Yet the *echagē* now refrained from supporting the rebellious Alulā against the son of Yohannes. Alulā now retired to Mannawē, where he constructed a *zariba*.[22]

tain a position of power because of his prestige and authority as a *rās*. While he had some financial resources, he had no hereditary feudal domain to serve as a base of power (like Agāmē was for Sebhat). Alulā therefore could promise very little to the people of Tambēn and Geraltā, but he tried to obtain their allegiance.[23]

A declaration of open rebellion against Mangashā had little chance of success in Tigre, even if it issued from a prestigious leader like Alulā. The tired and hungry people of Tambēn saw no value in fighting Mangashā, the Shoans and the Italians. During the year which had passed since the meeting on the Marab, the Tigreans had had enough time to realise that they could not take a military initiative against Menilek. Baratieri's new policy caused disillusion with the slogan of Tigrean independence which had hitherto been Alulā's source of power.

Alulā fortified himself in Mannawē with a few hundred followers and refused to free De Martino and five other Italian hostages he had taken from Adwā. On 27 December 1892, with 2,000 troops commanded by *Rās* Hagos, Mangashā approached Mannawē, took up a position on the surrounding hills, and started ruining the fields and orchards. Around midnight, accompanied by only fifty followers, including *Dadjāzmāch* Abbāy and *Dadjāzmāch* Tadlā Fanjā, "the lame," Alulā left his camp "like a thief running for his life." He led his small group of followers to an *amba* in Avergalle.[24] On the way he was deserted by *Dadjāzmāch* Abbāy, who brought the Italian hostages to Mangashā's headquarters near Mannawē.[25] De Martino reported:[26]

> In Menne, we were received by more than 2,000 soldiers . . . they all shouted: 'Alula kufu, kufu [bad, bad]'.
> Alulā is morally finished even in Tigre. All his chiefs have deserted him, even Degiac Tacle Aimanot and Degiac Abai. He is left only with Tedla 'the lame', Fitaurari Desta and forty followers on an *amba* in Avergalle [Ambā Sarago] from where he sends asking for mercy.[27]

C. *January 1893: Mangashā Rejects Italian Demand to Eliminate Alulā*

Hearing about Alulā's rebellion, Baratieri wrote directly to Mangashā, explaining to him "the danger of setting free such a boastful and perjured enemy."[28] Baratieri wrote that he "spared no effort to persuade Mangascia to finish with that treacherous rebel because he was the greatest obstacle to the pacification of Abyssinia under the hegemony of the emperor."²⁹

By that time, however, Mangashā had learned that Italian-Shoan relations were approaching the rupture which started when Menilek officially denounced the Treaty of Uccialli in Feburary 1893.³⁰ Mangashā, of course, realized that Alulā, hitherto a supporter of an alliance with Eritrea, was now disillusioned enough to return to an anti-Italian policy. He concluded that if he pardoned Alulā, the latter would finally accept his pro-Shoan line or disappear from the political scene. Indeed at the beginning of the third week of 1893, after brief negotiations and the mediation of *Echagē* Tēwoflos, Alulā submitted to his young master. In a ceremony held at the Trinity Church of Adwā, Alulā approached Mangashā with a rope on his neck and a stone on his shoulders.³¹ To the bitter surprise of the Italians, Alulā was pardoned and was given permission to keep 200 riflemen. Mangashā allowed him part of the proceeds of the Adwā customs station, which he now had to share with *Dadjāzmāch* Embāyē. On his side, Alulā promised no longer to interfere in political affairs and was appointed governor over a small area between Avergalle and Tambēn.³²

D. February-May 1893: Alulā Revolts Again

Rās Alulā, however, could not accept his political emasculation, nor could he bear his humiliation, so he wasted no time in breaking his promise of obedience and rebelled again against Mangashā in order to prevent his march to Shoa. On 21 February 1893 *Rās* Alulā attacked a column of Mangashā's troops passing through Tambēn.³³ Mangashā was then in Maqalē, and the Italian Resident in Adwā was convinced that Alulā would arrive there to kidnap him. The English archaeologist T.J. Bent, then researching in Aksum, described the scene:

> Everything was excitement and terror . . . some said Ras Alula was only a few hours off, that he was cutting off the right hands and left feet of all his opponents who fell into his power. 'He is sure to cut mine off' said the terrified Italian 'for I am an old enemy of his. . . .'³⁴
>
> Ras Alulā was spoken of as the devil who came up like smoke from hell, and the Dajatch [Embāyē, the governor of Adwā³⁵] remarked that it would be necessary to put up a cross on either door to keep him out.³⁶

Alulā, however, was not strong enough to enter the Tigrean capital or to risk Italian retaliation. Leading his handful of fifty followers, including *Dadjāzmāch* Tadla Fanjā, he returned to Mannawē, which he fortified. In late February *Rās* Mangashā sent a small force to capture Alulā. It's commander was *Dadjāzmāch* Abbāy, Alulā's relative and ex-follower, who could not bring himself to attack his old master; in fact, the *ras* convinced him to return to his service.³⁸ By early March 1893, Alulā had assembled 200 warriors and climbed up to Ambā Dibuk in Avergalle.³⁸

From early March to early May 1893, Mangashā's forces, commanded by *Rās*

Hagos, beseiged Alulā and his hungry followers. Upon Baratieri's repeated advice, Mangashā agreed to eliminate Alulā.³⁹ Baratieri, however, had instructions to refrain from direct military interference in Tigre⁴⁰ and could not satisfy Mangashā's demands for weapons and ammunition.⁴¹

E. May 1893: Menilek Saves Alulā

Again, for the second time in 1893, Alulā was militarily defeated by Mangashā's men. Putting a stone on his shoulders and a rope around his neck, he prostrated himself before the young *Rās* of Tigre.⁴² Alulā sought pardon and restoration of his former status, but Mangashā refused. *Echagē* Tēwoflos hurried from Aksum in order to prevent Mangashā from doing any harm to Alulā.⁴³

It was undoubtedly at this stage that Emperor Menilek interfered to save the old *rās*, hitherto his greatest Tigrean enemy. With the Ethio-Italian crisis over the Uccialli treaty and the rapid deterioration of his relations with Rome, Menilek shrewdly recognised that the prestigious general, the warrior whose name was identified with a humiliating Italian defeat, could be a useful agent in the future. *Rās* Mangashā, who in early April had assured Baratieri that Menilek was anxious to get rid of Alulā,⁴⁴ was strongly advised by two envoys from Emperor Menilek to pardon the *rās*.⁴⁵

"Ras Mangascia," Baratieri complained,⁴⁶ "who from the end of March was swearing to liberate Ethiopia forever from the rebel Alula pardoned him on conditions which he himself knows cannot be maintained." Alulā was permitted to have an army of 500 men and was probably given adequate financial resources.⁴⁷ On 16 May 1893, near Ambā Dibuk, Mangashā publicly swore allegiance to Menilek. The next day, with Alulā in his camp, the Tigrean leader started for Maqalē.⁴⁸ It was undoubtedly from that time that the grateful Alulā started reconsidering his opinion of Menilek.⁴⁹ Twice humiliated in public by Mangashā, he no longer had strong motives to fulfil Yohannes's will. Alulā's prestige in Tigre, even in Tambēn where he was so miserably defeated, was lost and so was his image as a fighter for Tigrean independence.

Thus, during late 1893 and the first half of 1894, a period during which he was politically inactive, Alulā gave up his dreams about restoring Tigrean hegemony. Having no chance to re-establish his position in Tigre, he could now hope for only two alternatives: a return to his government in the *Tukuls* of Asmara or a return to the status of a "king's man." With Italy and Ethiopia on the eve of war, Alulā had no doubt that his chances lay in Addis Ababa, where his name, as in Rome and Asmara, was still identified with Dogali.

NOTES

1 A.S.MAI 36/13-148, Baratieri to MAE, 9.8.92.
2 See Conti Rossini, *Italia ed Etiopia*, pp. 77, 78.
3 A.S.MAI 36/16-149, Baratieri to MAE, 2.10.92.
4 A.S.MAI 3/6-42, Baratieri to MAE, 13.9.92; A.S.MAI 36/16-149, Baratieri to MAE, 2.10.92.
5 A.S.MAI 3/6-42, De Martino to Baratieri, 5.10.92.
6 A.S.MAI 36/16-149, Baratieri to MAE, 2.10.92.
7 Ibid.
8 A.S.MAI 36/16-149, Baratieri to MAE, 2.10.92; A.S.MAI 3/6-42, De Martino to Baratieri, 5.10.92.
9 A.S.MAI 3/6-42, De Martino to Baratieri, 5.10.92.
10 A.S.MAI 36/16-157, Salimbeni to MAE, 26.1.93, contains Capucci's report of 10.11.92.
11 A.S.MAI 3/6-42, De Martino to Baratieri, 14.12.92.
12 A.S.MAI 3/6-42, Mangascia to Baratieri, 5.10.92; Baratieri to MAE, 17.12.92.
13 A.S.MAI 3/6-42, Baratieri to MAE, 17.2.92. Bayyana was extradited on 18 November 1892. F. Martini, *Il Diario Eritreo*, vol. II, p. 410.
14 A.S.MAI 3/6-42, Baratieri to MAE, 17.12.92.
15 A.S.MAI 3/6-42, Baratieri to MAE, 17.12.92.
16 Ibid.
17 A.S.MAI 3/6-42, De Martino to Baratieri, 14.12.92.
18 See Mercatelli's short article on Tewoflos in *La Tribuna*, 5.7.95. Also A.S.MAI 3/6-42, De Martino to Baratieri, 14.12.92.
19 For his support in Alula's nomination as a *Turk Ba*sha, see above p. 19.
20 Mannawē MS.
21 Mannawē MS.
22 During 1891 and 1892, Alulā had frequently visited his birth-place and constructed a church there. The bell of the church was brought by Alulā from Eritrea. It carries the inscription: "Anno 1891, P. Bastanzetti Arezzo Udine".
23 A.S.MAI 3/6-42, De Martino to Mulazzani, 30.12.92.
24 38⁰ 50', 13⁰ 18'.
25 A.S.MAI 3/6-42, De Martino to Mulazzani, 30.12.92. Interview with *Fitāwrāri* Anbasā Abbāy, the son of *Dadjāzmāch* Abbāy, Abbi Addi, 18.2.72.
26 Ibid.
27 Conti Rossini, *Italia*, p. 462; Martini, *Il Diario Eritreo*, vol. II, p. 411.
28 A.S.MAI 3/6-42, Baratieri to MAE, 12.3.93.
29 A.S.MAI 36/16-150, Baratieri to MAE, 9.4.93.
30 For details consult Marcus, *Life and Times*, pp. 145-149.
31 A.S.MAI 3/6-42, Baratieri to MAE, 12.3.92; *La Tribuna*, 20.1.93.
32 A.S.MAI 3/6-42, Baratieri to MAE, 12.3.93.
33 A.S.MAI 3/6-42, Baratieri to MAE, 27.2.93, *La Tribuna*, 1.3.93.
34 Bent, *op.cit.*, p. 149.
35 Conti Rossini, *Italia ed Etiopia*, p. 82.
36 Bent, *op.cit.*, p. 117.

37 Interview with Fitāwrāri Anbasā Abbāy, A.S.MAI 3/6-42, Baratieri to MAE, 12.3.93.
38 A.S.MAI 3/6-42, Baratieri to MAE, 7.4.93.
39 Ibid.
40 A.S.MAI 36/13-150, Baratieri to MAE, 9.4.93.
41 See also H. Marcus, *The Life and Times*, p. 150.
42 A.S.MAI 3/6-42, Baratieri to MAE, 23.5.93, 30.6.93, quotes Mangashā to Baratieri, 19.5.93.
43 Ibid., 23.5.93.
44 A.S.MAI 36/16-150, Baratieri to MAE, 9.4.93.
45 A.S.MAI 3/6-42, Baratieri to MAE, 23.5.93.
46 Ibid.
47 Alulā's treatment was in sharp contrast with that meted out to Sebhat. Sebhat submitted to Mangashā in late May 1893 and was placed in chains and put on Ambā Salāmā [A.S.MAI 36/16-152, Baratieri to MAE, 18.6.93, 21.6.93.]
48 Ibid.
49 Luca dei Sabelli, *Storia*, III, p. 386.

16

1894-1897: A King's Man Again. Acceptance of Shoan Hegemony

A. *June 1894: Submission to Menilek*

In early April 1894, after being pressed again and again by Menilek and frustrated by Italian passivity, *Rās* Mangashā decided to submit to the emperor. Alulā, whose position in Mangashā's court was described by Baratieri as humiliating,[1] probably had little to say in the discussions held at Adwā which led to that decision.

On 2 June 1894, Mangashā and his *rās*es entered Addis Ababa, where 12,000 well-armed troops, equipped also with twenty-five cannons, were concentrating to impress the visitors.[2]

> The Ras [Mangashā], preceded by the clergy of the holy church of Aksum who carried the shrine of Mary, [and] followed by his Rases, Alula, Hagos and Voldenchiel, modestly advanced towards the Royal residence, where, seated on the throne, with the Royal crown on his head, surrounded by Ras Darghè, Ras Micaèl, Ras Oliè, by his major chiefs and by Europeans, the king of kings awaited him. . . .

At the door, the four *rās*es of Tigre, like rebels who come to submit, loaded a big stone on their naked shoulders: they arrived in front of the king and bowed down to the ground asking pardon. With one word Menilek declared that he granted it. Mangashā was seated; the others were firstly taken away, but after a few moments were called back and were also seated.

> For a quarter of an hour a dead silence prevailed, everyone gazing in absolute immobility, as if immersed in his thoughts. . . For the Tigreans the sacrifice was completed. Only Alula, his shoulders turned to the king, with one hand on his mouth, still seemed to represent the old Tigrean pride.[3]

During the next three days the Tigrean *rās*es and the Ethiopian emperor met for conversation and banquets, during which Mangashā was coolly treated by

Menilek, who did, however, accept the *rās*'s gift of 100 rifles and 6,000 thalers.[4] Then, on 6 June 1894, the four *rāses* were again invited to court where the emperor, in front of a few intimates, demanded the following as a sign of loyalty: a) that Ṣalamti, hitherto governed by *Rās* Hagos, be transferred to Empress Ṭaytu; b) that the *neburā-'ed*, the chief of the holy city of Aksum, be nominated by the emperor; c) that the revenue of Tigre be paid to the imperial treasury; d) and that /awditu's *gult* rights over Endertā be renewed. The *rāses* were given two days to discuss the matter before submitting to those conditions.[5]

According to information received by the Italian intelligence service in Asmara, Mangashā had not permitted Alulā to attend the consultations which he then held with Hagos and the other Tigreans.[6] Undoubtedly, Mangashā suspected Alulā of being already "Menilek's man." If Baratieri could predict on 8 June 1894,[7] that the old *rās* would stay in the Shoan court, then surely Mangashā was also aware of Alulā's shift. Baratieri summarised the situation:

> The opposition of Ras Alula to the Shoan hegemony was overcome by his hatred of the Italians, and by his desire to gain support for the fulfilment of his aspirations to a government on the right bank of the Mareb. To this one can add his disgust at staying any longer with Mangascia in a position by far inferior to his past and to his pretensions.[8]

Alulā was also undoubtedly deeply moved by Menilek's well organised political and military power, by far greater than that which the shattered Tigre could have mobilised, even if united. The British traveller and merchant A. Wylde, who thought that "King Johannes as a monarch certainly ranks before any of his modern predecessors,"[9] was also impressed in his first visit to Addis Ababa in late 1896:

> King Menelek seems to be a very eloquent speaker and a very intelligent man, well informed on all things local and foreign, and certainly the cleverest Abyssinian that I have ever come across. King John was a child compared to him. Ras Mangascha, the would-be pretender to the throne, who says the world is flat, can never hope to make any headway against such a powerful opponent. As long as King Menelek, his nephew Ras Merconnen and his brother-in-law Ras Woly are alive there can be no chance of any rebellion.[10]

Was Alulā also so impressed?

When on 11th June 1894, the Tigrean *rases* came to the court to swear allegiance to Menilek and to ask permission to return to Tigre, Alulā reportedly refused to go North. Instead, "He asked the Emperor's permission to stay with him and not follow Mangascia to Tigre." Menelik quickly agreed;[11] "As my master's son submits," Alulā was quoted as saying when he left the room,[12] "I will go to the real master." Two years later, Alulā explained his *volte-face* to Wylde:

He much regretted the death of King John, and said it was "God's work', but now, he added, Menelek was a good man, and had forgiven him for the attacks the Ras has made on him in the old days by King John's orders. He said: 'I have been to see Menelek, and he was very kind to me.' . . . He then added: 'I then turned to King Menelek as the only man who could restore order, and since that time I have thrown all my influence on his side, in order to unite Abyssinia once more.'[13]

When Mangashā and his retinue left the Ethiopian capital on 13 June 1894, six hundred of the Tigrean troops preferred to remain there with Alulā[14] and camped near his new headquarters in Addis Ababa.[15] When Ras Mangashā reached Maqalē, he reportedly declared Alulā a rebel.[16]

B. November 1894: Full Acceptance of Shoan Hegemony

However much Alulā professed to be an Ethiopian statesman, his goal remained regaining the Marab Mellāsh. In the Shoan court, according to our sources,[17] he became an enthusiastic and strong supporter of war in the immediate future with Eritrea. For the Italians, the fact that Alulā was welcomed by the emperor served as a clear indication of the latter's hostility. Baratieri, for example, understood Rās Alulā to be "the major enemy to the Italian name and the claimant to the domain of the Mareb Melasc."[18] While *Rās* Makonnen was reported as cordially congratulating the Italians for their victory of 14 July 1894, over the Mahdists and the capture of Kassala,[19] Alulā reacted differently. Upon hearing the news from the Italian Capucci, "He made a wry face, twice swallowed his saliva, and told me word by word: 'It is better that the Christians won', a very cold and even villainous phrase."[20] Alulā was probably remembering the days of Kūfīt when "he could have carved out a principality for himself in Kassala" had not the Italians entered the arena.

The emperor treated the *rās* with great honour,[21] but Menilek was playing his cards slowly. Alulā, on the other hand, "keen on active life, tired of the easy life in Addis Ababa" and wanted to return to Tigre.[22] In fact, Alulā was pressing his new master to give him a command and to permit him to march against the Italians, but Menilek wanted him nearby, to act "as a great bogey" for the Italians.[23]

To keep Alulā active, but for the time being out of the Italian-Tigrean arena, the emperor wanted the *rās* to join his projected conquest of Wallāmo.[24] Alulā was promised a command over 700 men, the sum of 2,500 thalers and a monthly payment of 30 thalers, plus salt and pepper, to maintain the troops.[25] Alulā was reticent,[26] since participation in a campaign in the south, while Tigre was threatened by the Italians, was a cause of deep frustration. From Alulā's point of view, if not from an historically objective perspective, Menilek's policy had always been to let Emperor Yohannes face the external threats in the northern arena while he could expand the southern frontier of the Shoan kingdom.[27] Yet when in mid-November, Menilek's Wallāmo expedition left Addis Ababa, it included the proud *Rās* Alulā leading only 200 troops.[28] It was the clearest possible sign of his acceptance of Shoan hegemony in Ethiopia.

C. March 1895: Alulā Nominated to Command an Imperial Army

While Alulā was accomplishing little in the south, *Rās* Mangashā was fighting the Italians in Tigre. As later proved by captured documents,[29] Mangashā was planning to cooperate with the Mahdists against Eritrea.[30] He also was attempting to turn the Italian-nominated governor of Akalla-Guzāy, *Dadjāzmāch* Bāhtā Hagos, against his masters.[31] To prevent Mangashā from joining with the Mahdists in a campaign against Italian-occupied Kassala, Baratieri entered Adwā on 28 December 1894 and, after a powerful demonstration there, returned on 1 January 1895 to Akalla-Guzāy.[32] Mangashā had to respond: leading some 10,000 troops, he crossed the Marab on 9 January 1895, and engaged in a fierce battle at Ko'ātit on 13 and 14 January 1895. Driven back by Baratieri, Mangashā hastily retreated to Sanāfē, where on the following night he was surprised by a brilliant Italian move and suffered a disastrous defeat. Mangashā himself managed to escape, but *Dadjāzmāch* Tadlā Ayba was killed, and *Rās* Hagos defected to the Italians.[33]

In late January and early February 1895, the news of Mangashā's activities, of Baratieri's temporary occupation of Adwā and of the outcome of Bāhtā Hagos's revolt reached Addis Ababa. Alulā was reportedly furious "for not being there to fight for his country."[34] His frustration was undoubtedly embittered by the fact that Bāhtā Hagos, his old rival, was now gaining fame struggling against the Italians, while he was sitting idle in the distant capital. Fortunately for Alulā, Menilek, then making every effort to break the diplomatic blockade fostered by Italy,[35] was in a belligerent mood and started using the *rās* as "the bogey of the Italians." The emperor frequently consulted Alulā and Empress Ṭāytu, both of whom pressed for an early war.[36] By late February, Menilek had decided to send northward a combined force of Tigreans under Alulā, Shoans led by *Rās* Walē, Oromos (Gallas) commanded by *Rās* Mikā'ēl and Godjamis led by *Negus* Takla-Hāymānot.

This plan was opposed by various elements in the Shoan court who were in favour of sending only the Tigreans before undertaking a total war against Italy.[37] Menilek, who considered Alulā's separation from Mangashā as vital to Shoan interests, was reluctant, however, to send the old *rās* alone.[38] Meanwhile, Alulā had difficulties in mobilizing the 3,000 Tigreans said to be in Shoa. The Tigrean warriors, who enjoyed the easy and rewarding campaigns in Southern Ethiopia, did not want to return to an impoverished land to fight the powerful Italians.[39] Even the rumour that Alulā would soon be nominated governor of the Marab Mellāsh[40] did not seem to have the desired effect on the minor Tigrean chiefs in the Shoan capital. These, namely *Dadjāzmāch* Andārgāchawu of Endartā, *Wāgshum* Gobazē of Lāstā, *Dadjāzmāch* Hāyla-Māryām of Ayba, *Kagnāzmāch* Hāyla-Māryām, *Fitāwrāri* Negus and *Azmāch* Abarrā of Hamāsēn,[41] were probably also influenced by the anti-war party in Addis Ababa to remain there. Some of them reportedly told Menilek that they did not recognise Alulā as their leader.[42] Tasfāyē Hanṭalo, Alulā's rival and governor of Agāmē, who had stayed in Addis Ababa since the Tigrean's submission of June 1894, was also reported as trying to convince Menilek that *Rās* Alulā was no longer admired or even wanted in the northern province.[43] In Eritrea in late March, it was wishfully believed that Alulā's nomination as the commander of the Tigreans in Shoa had been cancelled.[44]

In fact, in late March, though he still had not managed to mobilize the Tigreans, *Rās* Alulā was reported to have been appointed to what may be regarded as his highest position since the period prior to Dogali. Menilek, it was said, had nominated him as the commander of a 12,000-man expedition, with *Rās* Mikā'ēl and *Wāgshum* Beru as deputies. Alulā was to lead this column to Adwā, where Mangashā awaited him. The emperor provided a large quantity of ammunition and a sum of 50,000 thalers to help mobilise additional Tigrean troops and to spur the defection of those employed by the Italians. Twelve thousand thalers were immediately sent to Mangashā, but the rest of the money was to be given to Alulā once he started for Tigre. The provinces of Ashangē and Zabul were granted to him to serve as a depot for assembling the soldiers.[45]

D. April-December 1895: Preparations for War

Meanwhile Menilek was still hoping that diplomacy, mainly an alliance with France, might peacefully frustrate Italian ambitions. It was not before September 1895 that he finally realised that war was his only option.[46] The emperor still cautious, *Rās* Alulā who throughout April 1895 was staying in Addis Ababa making preparations for the war, was reportedly having difficulties in assembling the Tigreans.[47] Meanwhile, Baratieri had made the first move: to prevent the Ethiopians from using Tigre as a base against his colony, he marched southwards and, on 25 March 1895, entered Addigrāt, later taking Adwā and Maqalē.[48] With northern Tigre in Italian hands, plans for the Ethiopian offensive had to be changed. Menilek reportedly decided that Alulā would lead his column through the Danāqīl desert, flank northern Tigre, and penetrate Akalla-Guzāy and Hamāsēn. Another column, led by *Rās* Walē, was to march through Walqāyt and unite with Mangashā.[49]

On 2 May 1895, Alulā left Enṭoṭo at the head of 3,000 men, including almost all the Tigreans then in Shoa, namely *Dadjāzmāch* Andārgāchawu of Endartā, *Wāgshum* Gobazē of Lāstā, *Dadjāzmāch* Hāyla-Māryām, *Fitāwrāri* Negus and

Azmāch Abarrā of Hamāsēn and *Dadjāzmāch* Tadlā Wā*h*id, the last recently paroled from prison. Alulā arrived at Warra Illu on 14 May 1895, and proceeded to Boru Medā (17 May 1895), where *Rās* Walē was to transfer Zabul to him.[50] The latter was Ṭaytu's brother and one of the most influential personalities in Ethiopia; he opposed the hazardous military plan, and he hoped to mediate between Baratieri and Menilek.[51]

Rās Walē therefore refused to give up Zabul, and the two *rās*es had to refer to Menilek who, in the meantime, had advanced to Warra Illu. Unwilling to alienate Walē, Menilek ordered Alulā to proceed instead to Saqotā[52] because he was probably persuaded that the coming rains would delay the projected operation. He directed Tasfāyē Hanṭalo instead to reinforce Mangashā,[53] who was reported camping near Hanṭalo with only 300 followers.[54] Alulā, after spending June in Lāstā, pressed Menilek to let him advance immediately and retake Agāmē. "Call me a woman," Alulā told his soldiers,[55] "if we do not spend the rainy season in Hausen or on Amba Augher [in Agāmē]." But the emperor had different ideas, and though Alulā and Mangashā were enemies now, he could not risk letting them unite nor permit the two to gain a prestigious victory in Agāmē. Besides, Mangashā probably did not want Alulā's cooperation, since the latter sought the government of most of the Tigrean territories now held by the Italians.[56]

With the offensive delayed until after the rainy season, *Rās* Alulā was no longer needed to incite the Italians. Since Menilek did not want Alulā in Mangashā's camp, he detached 1,500 Tigreans and sent them to Mangashā. The soldiers lamented Alulā's absence, "the only man, according to themselves, who may stop the adhesion of the Tigrean chiefs to the Italians."[57] Having no real command, Alulā left Lāstā and returned to a domain at Mendjār, where he spent the rainy season of 1895.[58]

E. *Alulā's Political Role in the Preliminaries to the Battle of Adwā*

The fact that Menilek had permitted Alulā to reside in Addis Ababa was not without significance. By persistently suggesting total war on the Italians and demanding Eritrea's reconquest, Alulā had become Menilek's war-drum. The reconquest of the Marab Mellāsh was his only chance to regain the government of an important province and to avoid returning to a lowly position in feudal Tigre. Alulā's role as an adviser in the battles of Ambā Alājē of 7 December 1895, and in the siege on Maqalē of January 1896, where the Italian advance posts and armies were beaten by a column led by *Rās* Makonnen, is well described by the military historian of the period, Berkeley.[59] Menilek, however, was careful enough not to damage any chance of peaceful settlement by giving a significant command to the warlike *rās*. Around mid-January 1896, rumours about Alulā's nomination as the future governor of Hamāsēn and Sarāyē[60] were soon denied, and *La Tribuna* of 15

February 1896 quoted Ethiopian informants bringing the news that "Menelich has driven Alula, who is extremely hostile to us, from the front line, as he is afraid that any reckless move by Alula might damage the negotiations for peace."[61] But, when it became clear that only war would solve the Italian problem, Alulā was given a small force to lead.

F. March 1896: Alulā's Contribution to the Victory of Adwā

While an Ethiopian army numbering some 120,000 troops[62] was camping in Tigre in late February 1896 facing the Italians, most of the province's leaders had little influence on the course of events. *Rās* Sebhat[63] had cooperated with Asmara until the eve of the battle of Adwā, when he secretly joined the Ethiopian camp, but he led no troops. *Rās* Hagos, who stayed in Tambēn in late 1895 as an ally of the Italians[64] was clever enough to change sides in time but was given no command; and poor *Rās* Mangashā had a relatively small force.[65]

As for *Rās* Alulā, his force numbered no more than 3,000 troops,[66] but since he was justifiably regarded by Menilek as well acquainted with the area and the enemy, he served as a kind of chief-of-staff.[67] His image as the great anti-Italian hero doubtless contributed to the morale of the Ethiopians: "I am not afraid of the whip like a maid servant for Abbā Naggā comes spitting fire."[68] As such, *Rās* Alulā had a major role in one of the most important battles in Ethiopian history.

A. Wylde was the only European reporter who managed to penetrate to Tigre just after the battle of Adwā. His account of the hostilities was published in the *Manchester Guardian* of 20 May 1897, and may be regarded as based on research. Wylde claimed to have discussed the battle with Alulā, Mangashā and Menilek, "as well as with most of the other leaders who had taken part in the fight."[69] In Addis Ababa, he had many conversations with the captive General Albertone and enjoyed for six months contact with "the former native secretary of the Italian Intelligence Department." Wylde claimed therefore "to have had exceptional opportunities of getting at the facts, and I hope I shall be credited with the desire to state them as impartially as I can."

After analysing the military and political development prior to Saturday, 29 February 1896, and in which *Rās* Alulā had no share at all, Wylde continued:

> The greater part of the Abyssinian army was collected in and about the town of Adowa, the left wing, under Ras Alula, being posted, however, somewhat further north from Adi Aboona to Gescherworka to guard the northern road. As negotiations for peace were actively going on, and communications on the subject had taken place as late as on the Saturday evening [29.2.96], there was no reason for the Abyssinians to expect an attack, and as the next day was both a Sunday and a feast-day of the Abyssinian Church, many of the soldiers had gone overnight to the sacred

city of Axum, some fifteen miles distant from Adowa as the crow flies, to pray at the churches there. Many, especially of Ras Alula's and Ras Mangescha's men, were absent in this way, thus leaving the left wing of the army, to which they belonged, a good deal weaker than the right and centre. The command of the Abyssinian army was of course with the King and Ras Alula, who may be described as the head of the Abyssinian staff. It is to his skillful dispositions and sleepless vigilance that the sweeping victory of the Abyssinians was largely due. Not trusting for safety to the temporary cessation of hostilities, he had taken care to be informed by means of his spies in the Italian camp of every movement of the enemy's forces.[70]

By eleven o'clock on the night of Saturday, February 29, the whole of the Italian army was on the march, advancing towards Adowa. By four o'clock on Sunday morning Ras Alula's spies had reached his camp, some fifteen miles distant, and at once sent word to the different Generals, and himself made haste to King Menelek to warn him of the enemy's advance.[71]

Alulā's role in the battle itself is not known. He had only a small force, and probably played a limited part in the actual fighting.

G. Governor of Northern Tigre under Menilek

After the decisive defeat of the Italians at Adwā, Alulā pressed Menilek to cross the Marab and drive the Italians out of Eritrea,[72] but the emperor was reluctant to do so. Though his first move was towards Dabra-Dāmo, probably with the dual aim of laying siege to the Italians in Addigrāt and of penetrating into Akalla-Guzāy, he soon decided to leave the area and return to Shoa.[73] Menilek realised that he could not afford pressing the Italians too hard and risk meeting them in Eritrea where they were entrenched in heavily fortified positions. He probably also felt that a reoccupation of Tigrean-inhabited territories would strengthen Tigrean political aspirations. He therefore promised the Italian Major Tommaso Salsa that the Tigreans would not threaten Hamāsēn[74] and created the impression that he was going to do nothing about reincorporating the Marab Mellāsh into Ethiopia. "It appears"—a British observer could report as early as 13 April 1896—"that Menelik is willing to accept the line of the River Mareb as the Italian frontier."[75]

Before leaving Tigre, Menilek reorganised the government of that province. *Rās* Mangashā married *Wayzarit* Kafāi, Empress Ṭāytu's niece, the daughter of *Rās* Walē; was granted the sum of 32,000 thalers by Menilek; and was apparently promised a negusship. "For the time being," wrote an Italian envoy,[76] "the Ras [Mangashā] decided to go on with a policy of complete submission and obedience to Menelich whose power in the eyes of all the Tigreans is really great." As had been agreed in Addis Ababa in June 1894, *Rās* Mangashā had to accept a new *nebura-'ed* in Aksum, *Mamher* Walda-Giyorgis from Amhara, who was known as a strong Shoan sympathiser.[77] *Dadjāzmāch* Tadlā Abbāguben, Dabbab's brother and Mangashā's rival, was made governor over Endartā, with headquarters in Maqalē, so as to be able to report on the attitudes in *Rās* Mangashā's castle there. The provinces of Tambēn and Shirē were given to *Rās* Hagos (together with a certain *Dadjāzmāch* Hadgu), while Tasfāyē Hantalo, whose devotion to the Shoan court was proven, was given Wādjrat and Ashangē. *Rās* Sebhat's government over Agāmē was confirmed, but he had to share it with *Rās* Hagos Tafari,[78] a relative who had cooperated with the Italians and who had governed Agāmē in their name since April 1895.[79]

For the first time in his career, *Rās* Alulā was nominated over a substantial area in the Tigre province, all the territories between Māy Wari and the Marab, with Adwā as his capital. The Tigrean Emperor Yohannes could not or had not wanted to impose an outsider on the Tigrean élite. With Mangashā, or against him, Alulā had to wander from place to place in Tigre in a ceaseless effort to maintain himself and his few men. Menilek, however, in his shrewd strategy of installing outsiders over the various provinces, in which he differed from Yohannes, gave Alulā the most important part of northern Ethiopia, at least from the historical point of view. Thus, paradoxically, but quite significantly for the feudal structure of Tigre, it was the Shoan emperor who installed one of the province's great warriors, though not a member of the provincial élite, as a local governor there. Alulā was, of course, now Menilek's grateful supporter. On 21 June 1896 in his new house at Aksum, he told Wylde how he had turned to Menilek "as the only man who could restore order. . . . I have thrown all my influence on his side in order to unite Abyssinia once more."[80]

Alulā's appointment over the very heart of the historical Tigre did not make him a strong and influential leader. Tigre as a whole and the district of Adwā in particular had paid dearly for the lack of a government since the death of Yohannes; there had been constant internal and external warfare and famine. Wylde pointed out that when he had visited Adwā in 1884:

> it was a flourishing town of about 15,000 inhabitants, the commercial centre of the district. Now it is a ruin and a charnel-house. War and pestilence have done their work, leaving their mark in ruined houses and blackened walls. I do not think there were a thousand people left in Adowa.[81]

Alulā was therefore only able to maintain a small army.

The Italian officer Mulazzani, who visited Alulā's camp at Atzina, 5 km. east of Aksum during 18-22 July 1896, described the *ras* as being worried by the fact that because of lack of food he could hardly support 300 riflemen. Mulazzani wrote that Alulā managed "to maintain his few men by some taxes or gifts given to him by rich people and also by confiscating property from innocent people."[82] The *rās* told Wylde that:

My army now is only a small one, I have but 8,000 troops of my own. When I had the Hamasen I could raise 40,000 men. My property [the government of Asmara] is gone, and I have only my estates near Abbi Adi [Mannawē].[83]

Alulā therefore had to accept Menilek's settlement with the Italians and the loss of Eritrea. In June 1896, according to his visitor A.B. Wylde, Alulā was still restless about Menilek's policy and prayed for the renewal of the war against the Italians;[84] by September, however, he demonstrated his acceptance of the new situation by lifting the ban on commerce with Eritrea,[85] and in the third week of October he wrote to the Italian Resident at Addi Qayh "assuring him of his pacific intentions."[86] Thus, when on 26 October 1896 Menilek signed a new treaty with Italy stating also that "The rivers Mareb, Belesa, and Moona are the lines which by both parties shall not be violated,"[87] it was practically a non-event for the ex-governor of Hamāsēn.

H. Alulā's Share in the Future Fall of Mangashā

The new appointments made by Menilek in Tigre undermined Mangashā's authority in the province, and the *rās* now adopted Alulā's old idea of an alliance with Eritrea against imperial authority. In the present situation, after the Italian defeat and while the emperor was willing to compromise with the existence of Eritrea, this was a most unrealistic policy. Yet on 22 April 1896 Mangashā wrote to Queen Victoria referring to himself as the heir to Yohannes and applied for her mediation between him and Italy.[88]

Rās Alulā, now clearly Menilek's man,[89] was one of the channels through which the emperor was informed of Mangashā's intentions. On 2 October 1896 Wylde was in Maqalē, where *Rās* Alulā was celebrating the *Masqal* with Mangashā. Wylde reported:

> I asked if he had seen what Ras Mangescha had written to England and he said that he had read it. He added that it only confirmed his knowledge that Ras Mangascha had long been intriguing, and that he himself was writing to King Menelek about it all.[90]

We have no direct evidence, but a few clues to support the assumption that in early 1897 *Rās* Alulā planned to take over the government of Tigre,[91] as Menilek's representative. A well informed Italian observer suggested that the emperor planned, as early as the beginning of that year, to remove *Rās* Mangashā and to divide the northern province between Alulā and Sebhat.[92] Alulā was apparently in constant touch with the emperor, as can be concluded from the fact that in late 1896, he was well informed about the Italo-Ethiopian peace negotiations in Addis Ababa, while Mangashā knew nothing about them.[93] The following document also powerfully suggests that Alulā was involved in a plan to remove the hereditary prince of Tigre:

> In the first days of the new year Mangascia said that Menelich had called him to Shoa in order to crown him as a Negus of Tigre. But yesterday Alula secretly told two monks, informants of ours, that Ras Mangascia would never return to Tigre because he was [to be] prosecuted by the Negus. Ras Maconnen would come to govern Tigre. It seems that in the meantime Alula wants to take the government of old Ras Hagos [i.e. Tambēn and Shirē].[94]

1. January 1897: The End of Alulā

While *Rās* Mangashā was making his way to Shoa in January 1897, Alulā assembled a force of 700 men to march on *Rās* Hagos. The fact that he could not organise a stronger force may indicate that the campaign was his own initiative and not coordinated with the emperor. Alulā probably hoped that, once he established himself also in Tambēn and Shirē, he would be recognised by Menilek as the governor of these regions.

For Alulā, conflict with *Rās* Hagos was also a matter of personal revenge. As a devotée of Yohannes and of Mangashā, *Rās* Hagos, the moderate and loyal follower, had been Alulā's rival. The two men had fought in 1892[95] and 1893, when Alulā revolted against Mangashā. In late 1895, when *Rās* Alulā returned to Tigre, *Rās* Hagos started cooperating with the Italians, mainly out of fear of Alulā. On 19 January 1897, at Addi Chumāy in Shirē, the small army of *Rās* Alulā clashed with *Rās* Hagos's forces. Alulā was among the first participants to be wounded—in the leg. His young nephew, *Bāshā* Gabra-Egziabhēr[96] was captured and was immediately shot by Hagos's troops.[97] Nevertheless, Alulā's troops proved to be stronger, and the day resulted in their victory although they suffered fifty dead, compared with one hundred enemy casualties.[98] Hagos himself was captured and brought before Alulā, who ordered him executed immediately. The wounded Alulā was carried to Aksum from where he dictated a letter to the Italian Resident at Addi Qayh narrating the affair.[99] He died of complications on 15 February, and Rome was informed that "Ras Alula died. Tigre is in total anarchy."[100]

★ ★ ★

> 'Were you, Abba-Nagga, met by a killer?' lamented a Tigrean follower. 'You darted like a poisonous snake, camped on the slopes like locusts, with your arms you could break like a lion. The husband of Kassala and lover of the sea.'[101]

NOTES

1 A.S.MAI 36/17-162, Baratieri to MAE, 5.4.94.
2 A.S.MAI 3/6-46, Salsa to MAE, 30.7.94, "Diario Informazioni del mese di guglio, 1894."
3 Conti Rossini, *Italia*, p. 99. Based also on Guèbré Sellasié, p. 354.
4 A.S.MAI 3/6-46, Salsa to MAE, 30.7.94, "Estrato del Diario Informazioni del mese di guglio, 1894."
5 Ibid.
6 Ibid.
7 A.S.MAI 3/6-46, Baratieri to MAE, 8.6.94.
8 A.S.MAI 3/6-46, Baratieri to MAE, 5.7.94.
9 Wylde, *Modern Abyssinia*, p. 45.
10 A.B.Wylde, "An Unofficial Mission to Abyssinia," *The Manchester Guardian*, 28.5.97.
11 A.S.MAI 3/6-46, Salsa to MAE, 30.7.94 ("Diario").
12 Mondon to *Le Temps*, N.D., published in *Le Temps*, 18.10.98.
13 A.B.Wylde, "An Unofficial Mission to Abyssinia", *The Manchester Guardian*, 14.5.97.
14 A.S.MAI 3/6-46, Salsa to MAE, 30.7.94 ("Diario").
15 Alaqā Kenfu's Diary, p. 1, in the possession of Dr. Alame Eshete, IES.
16 A.S.MAI 3/6-46, Salsa to MAE, 30.7.94 ("Diario").
17 It seems that one can rely on the Italian sources, even if they tend to exaggerate Alulā's antagonism. As shown below, Alulā had no other option but to serve as the emperor's war-drum.
18 A.S.MAI 36/17-168, Baratieri to MAE, 10.8.94.
19 *La Tribuna*, 3.10.94.
20 A.S.MAI 36/17-168, Capucci to Baratieri, 29.8.94.
21 Heruy Walda-Sellāssē, *Yahewat tārik*, p. 47.
22 A.S.MAI 36/17-164, Traversi to MAE, 4.9.94.
23 A.S.MAI 36/17-168, Capucci to Traversi, 17.10.94.
24 A.S.MAI 36/17-164, Traversi to MAE, 4.9.94, 36/17-168, Capucci to Baratieri, 18.9.94.
25 A.S.MAI 36/17-168, Capucci to Traversi, 3.10.94; 3/6-46, Salsa to MAE, 6.11.96.
26 A.S.MAI 36/17-168, Capucci to Traversi, 3.10.94; 3/6-46, Salsa to MAE, 6.11.96.
27 For a short summary of Menilek's southern expansion, see H. Marcus, "Imperialism and Expansionism in Ethiopia from 1865 to 1900," in *Colonialism in Africa*, L. Gann and P. Duignan, eds. vol. 1, Cambridge 1969, pp. 420-461, Idem, "Motives, Methods and Some Results of the Unification of Ethiopia," *Proceedings of the Third International Conference of Ethiopian Studies*, Addis Ababa 1966, pp. 269-280.
28 A.S.MAI 36/17-168, Capucci to Traversi, 16.11.94; 3/7-47, Agenzia Stefani from Aden, 3.1.95.
29 See FO 403/221, Ford to Salisbury, 19.10.95 "précis of Italian Green Book" which summarises LV, XXIII. The letters from Menilek to Mangashā were found in the latter's tent after his defeat at Senāfe.
30 Though simultaneously he wrote to the British as the son of Emperor Yohannes asking for friendship and hinted that he was eager to help them against the Mahdiyya. See FO

403/206, Ras Mangasha to Her Majesty the Queen, 21.9.94 and Ras Mangasha to General Kitchener, 22.9.94.
31   Bāhtā Hagos was killed by Baratieri's troops on 18 December 1894. The archival material for the famous revolt of Bāhtā Hagos is mainly in A.S.MAI 3/7. For background consult Marcus, *The Life and Times*, pp. 154-155.
32   FO 403/221, Ford to Kimberley, 5.1.95; Mercatelli in *La Tribuna*, 5.1.95.
33   WO 33/56, Eritrea Report, p. 19. A short article on *Dadjāzmāch* Tadlā Ayba, *La Tribuna*, 2.1.95. For background consult Marcus, *The Life and Times*, pp. 155-156.
34   Capucci to MAE, 6.2.95; Zaghi, *Vigilia*. Hagos started cooperating with the Italians in the second half of 1895. See LV XXIII, Baratieri to MAE, 25.11.95.
35   For background consult H. Marcus, *The Life and Times*, pp. 158-160.
36   A.S.MAI 3/7-49, Capucci to MAE, 3.3.95.
37   Ibid.
38   Ibid. Also FO 403/221, Slade to Ford, 29.3.95.
39   Di Gennaro, "Menelich e Ras Alula," *La Tribuna*, 25.5.95.
40   A.S.MAI 3/7-49, Capucci to MAE, 3.3.95.
41   L. Mercatelli in *La Tribuna*, 5.7.95.
42   Ibid.
43   LV, XXIII bis. Baratieri to MAE, 27.3.95.
44   Ibid.
45   Capucci to MAE, late March 1895; Zaghi, *Vigilia*, p. 545. FO 403/221, Blanc to Ford, 17.5.95, "Intelligence from Massowah," 27.4.95; A.S.MAI 3/7-49, Capucci to MAE, 28.4.95.
46   See Marcus, *The Life and Times*, pp. 158-160.
47   A.S.MAI 3/7-49, Capucci to MAE, Memo., 15.4.97.
48   FO 403/221, Slade to Ford, 29.3.95. LV, XXIII bis, Baratieri to MAE, 30.5.95.
49   A.S.MAI 3/7-49, Capucci to MAE, 20.4.95, 23.4.95. A.S.MAI 36/17-168, Bienenfeld to MAE, 4.6.95. Di Gennaro, "Menelich e Ras Alula," *La Tribuna*, 25.5.95.
50   L. Mercatelli in *La Tribuna*, 5.7.95; LV, XXIII bis, Baratieri to MAE, 2.6.95.
51   LV, XXIII bis, Baratieri to MAE, 25.5.95.
52   Mercatelli, *La Tribuna*, 5.7.95.
53   Ibid.
54   LV, XXIII bis, Baratieri to MAE, 25.5.95.
55   L. Mercatelli in *La Tribuna*, 18.7.95 (From Adwā, 27.6.95).
56   L. Mercatelli in *La Tribuna*, 16.7.95 and 21.7.95.
57   L. Mercatelli, *La Tribuna*, 14.8.95.
58   E. Di Gennaro in *La Tribuna*, 15.12.95.
59   See, *inter alia*, Berkeley, *op.cit.*, especially pp. 114, 134, 137, 146, 147, 163, 205. Also various documents in "Documenti sul combatimento d'Amba Alagi e sulla difesa di Macallè," *Woghera*, Rome, 1896. In LV, XXIII and L. Guido, *L'Assedio di Macalle*, Rome 1901.
60   *La Tribuna*, 21.1.96.
61   *La Tribuna*, 15.2.96. In late January Baratieri reported that Alulā had no troops at all. LV, XXIII bis, Baratieri to MAE, 27.1.96.
62   For various estimates, see Conti Rossini, *Italia*, pp. 340-342.
63   He had been imprisoned by Mangashā in 1893, and was released by the Italians in December 1895.

64 *La Tribuna*, 7.1.96, 23.1.96.
65 For their number, estimated variously between 4,000 and 12,000, see Conti Rossini, *Italia*, pp. 340-342.
66 Conti Rossini, *Italia*, p. 342, note 1.
67 See below, p. 192.
68 Abba Ayla Takla Haymanot, "Il Wata: Una tipica figura folcloristica dell'Etiopia e la sua professione interdetta," *Proceedings of the Third International Conference of Ethiopian Studies*, Vol. II, Addis Ababa 1970.
69 *The Manchester Guardian*, 20.5.97.
70 Unlike R. Greenfield, *Ethiopia, A New Political History*, London 1965, p. 123, who suggested that the victory was a result of Alulā's "master plan."
71 According to oral tradition, Alulā was informed about the Italian advance by a certain Ethiopian named Aw'alom. Int. Fit. Bayyana Abrehā, Aksum, Feb. 1972. A Ge'ez Tarik in *IES* by Kāssā Mashashā Tēwodros. According to one of *Rās* Sebhat's descendents, the latter sent the message to Alulā, "The Life of Ras Sebhat Aragāwi", a manuscript kept by Dr. R. Caulk. For Alulā's role in Adwā, see also Berkeley, pp. 279, 280.
72 See A. Wylde's article in *MG* 14.5.97.
73 For his reasons see Marcus, *Life and Times*, p. 176.
74 Bibliothèque Nationale No. 269, Mondon-Vidailet Collection, No. 82, Gabre Sellasie to Mondon N.D. For a detailed descriptiopn of the military situation after the battle of Adwā, see WO 33/56, J.R. Slade, "Eritrea and Abyssinia," Sept. 1896. Also Berkeley, pp. 362-365.
75 FO 407/137, Slade to Ford, 13.4.96.
76 A.S.MAI 3/17-136, Mulazzani Report, 26.7.96, Lambertinti to M.d.G., 22.9.96.
77 On Walda Giyorgis, not to be identified with the previous *Nebura-'ed* of the same name, see Wylde's article in the *Manchester Guardian*, 21.5.97.
78 See a short article on Hagos Tafari in *La Tribuna*, 20.2.96.
79 For the partition of Tigre by Menilek, see: A.S.MAI 3/17-136, Mulazzani Report, 26.7.96. Also, Mercatelli, *La Tribuna*, 30.5.96.
80 A. Wylde, "An unofficial mission to Abyssinia," the *Manchester Guardian*, 14.5.97.
81 A. Wylde, "An unofficial mission to Abyssinia", the *Manchester Guardian* 17.5.97. For Adwa in 1884, see a detailed description in FO 1/31, Hewett to Admiralty, 9.6.84. "Adowa, as a representative Abyssinian Town". Hewett also estimated the number of the inhabitants as 15,000. "The population of Adowa is estimated at 15,000," Hewett wrote, "it was formerly much greater, but famine following the wake of war swept away over two-thirds of the population only eight or nine years ago."
82 A.S.MAI 3/17-136, Mulazzani Report, 26.7.96.
83 A. Wylde, "An Unofficial Mission", *MG*, 14.5.97.
84 Ibid.
85 A.S.MAI 3/17-136, Lambertini to M.d.G. 22.9.96.
86 A.S.MAI 3/17-136, Baldissera to M.d.G., 23.10.96.
87 See Amharic text sent by Wylde to the *Manchester Guardian*, 16.3.97.
88 FO 403/239, Ras Mangasha to Queen Victoria, Miazia 14th, 1888 E.C., 22.4.96.
89 Together with Ras Sebhat and the Nebura-'ed of Aksum. A.S.MAI 3/17-136, Lambertini to M.d.G., 5.9.96.
90 A. Wylde, "Unofficial mission to Abyssinia," the *Manchester Guardian* 21.5.97.
91 See Mercatelli in *La Tribuna*, 26.1.97.

92 Martini, *Diario* II, p. 411.
93 A.S.MAI 3/17-1549, Baldissera to M.d.G., 22.12.96.
94 A.S.MAI 3/17-27, Baldissera to M.d.G., 9.1.97.
95 For Rās Hagos, see Conti Rossini, p. 462 and Martini, *Diario*, II, p. 411.
96 Conti Rossini, *Italia ed Etiopia*, p. 463.
97 Martini, *Diario* II, p. 412.
98 *La Tribuna*, 27.1.97. For a colourful description of the battle, see Martini, *Diario*, II, p. 412; *La Tribuna*, 25.1.97, 26.1.97, 9.2.97.
99 *La Tribuna*, 25.1.97. I failed to find that letter. According to oral tradition (Fit. Anbasā Abbay) and to an Italian writer (A. Sapelli, *Memorie d'Africa (1883-1906)*, Bologna 1935, p. 48), Alulā refused to take medicines which were sent to him by the Italians. This, explained as a gesture of contempt to Europeans, can hardly be believed as both Vinquist (see above, p. 72 note 160) and Parisis (N. *L'Abissinia*, Milano 1888, p. 130) testified that they had given Alulā medical treatment.
100 A.S.MAI 3/17-229, V. Governatore to M.d.G., 25.2.97. For anarchy in Tigre, see below, pp. 201, 202.
101 Heruy, *Yaheywat tārik*, p. 47. Compare to Tewodros's appellation: "Husband of Ethiopia and lover of Jerusalem." Rubenson, p. 60.

Conclusion

As remembered by the Ethiopians and reflected in their literature, "the famous and brave Ras Alula"[1] was a great warrior whose valour and military skill contributed greatly to various important victories over Ethiopia's enemies. "Since he was feared and well known for his bravery," Heruy summarised,[2] "he always defeated and drove away the external enemies who came from the side of Hamāsēn."

> In Hamasen [where you defeated Ras Walda-Mikā'ēl] you established a market — you brought rifles without paying for them [as booty]. In Cassala you established a market... In Saati you established a market... Stay in peace, my master, Abba Neegà! After you, we shall not find a [resting] bed.[3]

Both Italians and Ethiopians regarded Alulā as the most persistent opponent of Italian involvement in Ethiopian affairs. His policy and activities were sometimes described by foreigners as motivated by xenophobia: "He possessed," a modern historian was impressed,[4] "a fanatical hatred of Europeans approximating that of the Mahdi." Ethiopians, on the other hand, tended to remember his role in Dogali and Adwā but not his pro-Italian policy in the period between these two battles:

> Those Italians how happy they are
> In Rome they have shot the cannons
> Near the sea they have shot the cannons
> In Asmara they have shot the cannons
> In the place of which, in Dogali their testicles were plucked by handfuls
> In the place of which, in Adua their testicles were plucked in handfuls.
> But Negga is dead they can again sleep peacefully.[5]

Yet it seems clear now that Alulā was not motivated by hatred. He wanted Europeans as good neighbours and as partners in economic or political activities and opposed them only when they started interfering in Ethiopian affairs. During the period of 1890-1892, having compromised with the loss of the Marab Mellāsh, Alulā was clearly working for an alliance with the Italians in Eritrea.

Alulā's pride and uncompromising approach to the Italians, especially during the years of 1885-1887, was, and still is, a source of pride for the Ethiopians.[6] From a historical point of view, however, this policy must be criticised. It seems that a more moderate approach and a more constructive diplomacy could have limited the Italians to the Massawa coast and could have prevented further imperialist encroachment on Northern Ethiopia.

★ ★ ★

Alulā's role in the internal history of Ethiopia during that period was no less significant than his role in facing external enemies. In the process of the decline of Tigre and the rise of Shoa, Alulā was a most important figure, and surely the only prominent Tigrean who survived throughout the whole period as an active leader. He started as one of the main builders of Tigrean power and was actually the last one to fight for its continuation. Retrospectively speaking, the Tigreans had little chance of maintaining their hegemony over Ethiopia. The northern part of the empire was constantly threatened by foreign powers: Egyptians, Mahdists and Italians. Costly battles were fought, mainly by the Tigreans, throughout the two decades following the Egyptian invasion of 1875. Northern commercial connections with the Sudan and with the Massawa coast were disrupted, and the famine contributed to the growing military weakness. Finally, the sudden death of Emperor Yohannes left the various proud Tigrean hereditary chiefs without a unifying figure. The combination of the hesitant young *Rās* Mangashā and the proud Alulā, an outsider for the Tigrean nobility, failed to provide undisputed leadership for the shattered and disunited province threatened by Shoans, Mahdists and Italians.

In such unfortunate circumstances, and as victims of their own internal conflicts, the Tigreans could not cope with the rising power of Shoa. There, in the south, through profitable warfare and expansion, the shrewd and clever internal and external policy of Menilek and more favourable political circumstances led to the creation of a more central-minded and strong government.

Fighting for the fulfilment of Yohannes's will and for his own political existence, Alulā had to overcome all these difficulties. His policy was not unrealistic, and Tigre might have been able to survive as an independent entity had the Italians in Eritrea sought a buffer against Menilek. Paradoxically it was Alulā's image as the architect of Dogali, which in part caused the Italians to abandon such a policy.

During late 1893 and early 1894 Alulā finally realised that he was no longer the champion of the Tigrean cause. He could not serve as a unifying element for the Tigrean nobility and could never become an ally of the Italians. This failure and his subsequent recognition of Shoan hegemony may be regarded as a fatal, if not final, blow to Tigrean independence.

★ ★ ★

In early January 1897, *Rās* Mangashā was in Addis Ababa but failed to be nominated *negus*.[7] Insulted, the prince of Tigre returned to his province to learn of the death of Hagos and Alulā. The *rās*'s position was now challenged by the young *Dadjāzmāch* Gabra-Sellāssē Bāriyā-Gaber, a son of one of Yohannes's followers who died in Mattammā.[8] Gabra-Sellāssē returned in October 1896 from Eritrea and entered Alulā's service just before the battle of Addi Chumai. Before dying, Alulā made him a *dadjāzmāch* and left him his arms and followers. Gabra-Sellāssē disobeyed Mangashā who, for his part, openly revolted against Menilek and was supported by *Rās* Sebhat and Tasfāyē Hantalo. In September 1898 Menilek sent *Rās* Makonnen to Tigre with *Rās* Mikā'ēl and *Wāgshum* Beru, and in December Mangashā was surrounded in Adāgā Hamus. Three months later, on 18 February 1899, *Rās* Mangashā and *Rās* Sebhat submitted ceremonially to the emperor, and *Rās* Makonnen was appointed over Tigre. Mangashā and Sebhat were imprisoned in Addis Ababa, from where Mangashā was later transferred to Ankobar, to die there in November 1906.

In Tigre itself the new generation of local hereditary princes went on with their internal rivalries: *Dadjāzmāch* Seyum Mangashā, the son of *Rās* Mangashā; *Dadjāzmāch* Gugsa Ar'āyā-Sellāssē, the son of *Rās* Ar'āyā-Sellāssē Yohannes, the late crown prince; *Dadjāzmāch* Abrehā Hagos, the son of the late *Rās* Hagos; *Dadjāzmāch* Abrehā Ar'āyā, the son of *Rās* Ar'āyā Demsu and the brother of the late Dabbab, *Shum-Agame* Dastā Sebhat, the son of *Rās* Sebhat Aragāwi; and *Dadjāzmāch* Gabra-Sellāssē leading the ex-followers of the late *Rās* Alulā.

In 1909 Abrehā Ar'āyā was imprisoned in Shoa, and on 28 February 1914 *Rās* Sebhat, who had been released from his prison in Shoa after the death of his son Dastā, fought *Dadjāzmāch* Gabra-Sellāssē and met his death on the battlefield. Gabra-Sellāssē, defeated six days later by Seyum Mangashā, took refuge in Eritrea. Seyum, the son of *Rās* Mangashā, was made a *Rās* in the same year by the new ruler of Ethiopia *Ledj* Iyāsu and was appointed as the governor general of Tigre, now quite a remote province of the Ethiopian Empire.

★ ★ ★

Berkeley's statement that Alulā was "the greatest leader that Abyssinia has produced since the death of Emperor Theodore" must be taken with a grain of salt. Alulā did not stand out "in bold relief against the background of intrigues"[9]; neither was he "a turbulent chief"[10]; nor a "treacherous rebel."[11] It seems that Alulā was a brave and fortunate soldier, a great tactician whose tenacity, energy and shrewdness helped him on the battlefields and in the internal political struggles. It was his character, not hereditary rights or economic resources, which enabled him to maintain his prominence throughout his long career. In addition to his tactical skill, Alulā had some vision. He sensed better than Yohannes that Italian ambition rather than Mahdist fanaticism was the real threat to Ethiopia. Yet, as only a provincial governor and later as a leader of hungry people in isolated areas, Alulā had but limited knowledge of the diplomatic and political developments in which he was involved. Thus he was quite slow to realise the nature of Italian-Shoan relations in the early 1890s.

Alulā was not "one of those faithful men who do not live but for the principle" as he was characterized by a sentimental observer.[12] He was quite loyal to his masters in his own way, but mostly served his own purposes without sacrificing his own interests. He was, indeed, too proud to sacrifice anything. First and foremost, Alulā was an Ethiopian whose pride, so generously shared by his fellow-countrymen, was a source of strength and weakness, victory and defeat in an important period of their history.

NOTES

1 Takla-Ṣādeq Makuriyā, *Ya'ityopyā tārik*, p. 48.
2 Heruy, *Yaheywat tārik*, p. 47.
3 Conti Rossini, *Canti popolari tigrai*, song 165, p. 338.
4 D.A. Limoli, *F. Crispi: A Study in Italian Foreign Policy*, unpubl. Princeton Univ. Ph.D. 1961, p. 235.
5 Conti Rossini, *Canti*, No. 164, p. 338.
6 See Garima Taffere, *Yamakara Dawal*, Mamo Wudnah, *Yaertra tārik*.
7 For events in Northern Ethiopia after the battle of Adwa, see Martini, *Diario*. Check index for Annual Reports in FO 371.
8 See Zewde Gabre-Sellassie, p. 547. For Gabra-Sellāsse's career, see Sahay Hayle: "A Short Biography of Dajjazmatch Gabrassallasse Bariya Gabir (1873-1930)," B.A. thesis, H.S.I.U. 1972.
9 Berkeley, *Menelik*, p. 13.
10 A.S.MAI 3/6-42, Baratieri to MAE, 13.1.93.
11 A.S.MAI 36/14-150, Baratieri to MAE, 9.4.93.
12 N. Corazzini, "La pace", *La Tribuna*, 3.6.90.

Glossary

Abun (Abuna if followed by the name):	Title of the head of the Ethiopian church.
Afa-Negus	An official who speaks in the name of the king, a spokesman.
Agāfari	The organiser of meals in the court.
Ambā	Flat-topped mountain.
Ashkar	Servant, follower.
'Atsē	Sovereign, title of the emperors of Ethiopia.
Awādj	Proclamation.
Badjerond	Treasurer
Belāttā	Counsellor. Title of senior official.
Bālāgaı	Inhabitant, peasant.
Bālāmbārās	Military title of intermediary seniority.
Bālamwāl	Favourite.
Bāshā	Chief of riflemen.
Cheqqa Shum	Village chief.
Dadjāzmāch	'Commander at the gate', senior court official, general. Title of high dignitaries, chiefs, etc.
Echagē	Premier monk of the realm.
Elfegn Kalkāy	Chamberlain, door keeper.
Farasagna	An horseman, a military delegate of the governor to the various regions.
Fitāwrāri	'Commander of the spearhead', 'Front invader', title of intermediate seniority.
Gerāzmāch	'Commander of the Left', title of intermediate seniority.
Gult	Territorial fief, land held free of tribute.
Janhoy	Title of emperor of Ethiopia, originally probably a judicial invocation.
Kagnāzmāch	'Commander of the Right', title of intermediate seniority.
Kantibā	Mayor, governor.
Ledj	Title of young nobleman.
Ligabā	Official introducer and master of ceremonies at court; sometimes in charge of the king's personal domains.

Mamher	'Master', title of abbots.
Marab Mellāsh	'Beyond the Marab river', i.e. Eritrea.
Meslanē	District officer, deputy.
Mudīr (Arabic)	District governor in Egypt and its empire.
Masqal	Feast of the Holy Cross, 27 September.
Negus	King.
Negusa-Nagast	King of kings, Emperor.
Nagārit	Drum (preceding royal proclamations).
Nā'ib (Arabic)	'Deputy', indigenous chief of Harkikū and Massawa, originally appointed by Ottoman Government.
Naggādrās	Chief trader.
Nebura-'ed	Chief of Aksum.
Qāḍī (Arabic)	Muslim judge.
Rās	The most senior title, just below negus, comparable to 'duke'.
Rest	Hereditary ownership of land.
Shālaqā	Chief of a thousand.
Shammā	Toga-like garment.
Tukul	Ethiopian domicile.
Tadj	Ethiopian honey-mead.
Wāgshum	Chief of the country of Wāq.
Wayzaro	Lady.
Zabagna	Guard, watchman.
Zarība	A temporary camp fortified by thorn fences.

Bibliography

I Unpublished Documentary Sources

A. *Ethiopian material*

An anonymous Ge'ez Ms of 95 pages narrating the history of *Rās* Alulā kept in the church of
    Mannawē, Tambēn (hence, Mannawē MS) was lent by the priests there to H. Erlich.
    A few additional pages were found later in Abbi Addi. The MS was translated by
    Roger Cowley.
Alaqā Lamlam, *Ya'atsē Takla-Giyorgisnā Ya'atsē Yohannēs tārik*, MS Ethiopiens No. 259
    (Collection Mondon Vidailet No. 72), Bibliothèque Nationale, Paris.
Aṣmē Giyorgis, *Yagāllā tārik*, Institute of Ethiopian Studies (IES), MS 138.
A Ge'ez MS, a *Tārik* of Yohannes in the church of Dabra-Berhān Sellāssē, Adwā.
A Ge'ez MS of Yohannes's history. Found in Aksum, and written by Abbā Hāyla-Māryām.
    Translated by Tesfayohannes Fessehaye. Caulk Collection.
An Amharic biography of *Rās* Gubanā. Caulk Collection.
A Ge'ez MS from Dabra-Berhān Sellāsse, Gondar, kept in IES.
"Alaqā Kenfu's diary," MS in possession of Dr. Alame Eshate, IES.

B. *Egyptian material*

Documents from the 'Abidīn Archives, Cairo (AA), "Rubenson Collection," IES.
Correspondence of Egyptian officers and officials from Massawa to Cairo and reports by
    Egyptian soldiers who escaped from the Sudan through Ethiopia, School of Oriental
    and African Studies, London University, M.518.
Sa'd Rif'at, "Report on the insurrection and evacuation of the Red Sea Stations (1889)"
    (Arabic). English translation kept by Prof. P.M. Holt, SOAS; Arabic version in
    SOAS M.518.

C. *Sudanese material*

Documents from the Central Record Office in Khartoum, SOAS M.518.
SOAS Library, Mahdia Y.80, 1, *MSS Letter Book of 'Uthmān Diqna*, SOAS 101491.
Ismā'īl b. 'Abd al-Qādir, *Aṭ-ṭirāz al-manqūsh bibushrā qatl Yuḥannā malik al-ḥubūsh*,
    School of Oriental Studies, Durham.

D. *British material*

British Museum (BM), Add. MSS 51294 and 51304, Gordon's letters to his sister.
India Office (IO), R/20 AA, L/PS/9-4, etc.
PRO, Foreign Office Papers (FO) 1/30, 1/31, etc.

E. *French material*

Ministère des Affaires Etrangères [MAE(F)], Correspondence Politique des Consuls, Egypte 4: Massauah 1875-1885; Egypte 5: Massauah 1886-1888.
MAE(F), Mémoires et Documents, Afrique [M. et D.]

F. *Italian material*

Archivio Storico del soppresso Ministero dell'Africa Italiana, Rome [A.S.MAI]. In the Ministero degli Affari Esteri [MAE] 36/3-23, 36/2-11, etc.
"Archivio Eritrea" in A.S.MAI
"Collezione Vitale" in A.S.MAI

II Published Documentary Sources

Camera dei deputati, Rome, occasional publications.
Italian *Libri Verdi* (Atti parlamentari) [LV].
L'Italia in Africa, Serie Storica, *Etiopia —Mar Rosso*, ed. Carlo Giglio, Ministero degli Affari Esteri, Comitato per la Documentazione Dell'Opera Dell'Italia in Africa, Rome 1959- , Vols. II, III, V, VI [Giglio].
MAE(F), Documents Diplomatiques français (1871-1914) (Paris, 1929).

III Unpublished Theses

Alame Eshete, *Evolution et Resolution du conflict Egypto-Abyssinien. . .1877-1885*, Doctoral thesis, Aix en Provence, 1965.
———, "The Swedish Protestant mission 1866-1889", unpublished article, IES.
Caulk, R.A., *The origins and the development of the Foreign Policy of Menelik II, 1865-1896*, Ph.D., SOAS, London Univ., 1966.
Ghabr Michael, *Bogos (1849-1890)*, B.A. thesis, H.S.I.U. 1971.
Limoli, D.A., *F. Crispi: A Study in Italian Foreign policy*, Princeton Univ. Ph.D., 1961.
Rollins, P.J., *Russia's Ethiopian Adventure 1888-1905*, Ph.D. thesis, Syracuse Univ., 1967.
Sahay Hayle, *A Short Biography of Dajjazmatch Gabrasallasse Bariya Gabir (1873-1930)*, B.A. thesis, H.S.I.U., 1972.
Sahle Woldegabr, *The Background to the battle of Metemma*, B.A. thesis, H.S.I.U., 1968.
Tesfai Seyoum, *Ras Alula Abba Nega: A Biography*, B.A. thesis, H.S.I.U., 1970.
Zewde Gabre-Sellasie, *The process of Reunification of the Ethiopian Empire 1869-1889*, D. Phil. thesis, Oxford, 1971.

IV Newspapers and periodicals

Annales de la Congregation de la Mission, Paris.
Corriere di Napoli, Naples.
Cosmos, Rome.
The Daily News, London [DN].
L'Esploratore, Rome.
The Manchester Guardian, Manchester [MG].

Popolo Romano, Rome.
Rivista Militare Italiana, Rome [RMI].
The Times, London.
La Tribuna, Rome.
La Tribuna Illustrata, Rome.
Yazāreyitu 'Ityopiā, Addis Ababa.

V Published Works

Abba Ayla Takla Haymanot, "Il Wata: Una tipica figura folcloristica dell' Etiopia", *Proceedings of the Third International Conference of Ethiopian Studies*, vol. II, Addis Ababa, 1970.
Abba Gasparini, *Yaityopā tarik*, Asmara, 1955.
Affawarq Gabra-Iyāsus, *Dāgmāwi atsē Menilek*, Rome, 1901, EC.
Anonimo: *Spedizione Militare Italiana in Abyssinia —pensieri di un ufficiale superiore dell'esercito*, Rome, 1887.
Antona-Traversi, C., *Sahati e Dogali*, Rome, 1887.
Asrātā Māryām, *Zenā Dabra Sinā* (with Italian Trans.), Rome 1910.
Bairu Tafla, "Three distinguished Ethiopian military leaders", A paper presented at the Social Science Conference, Nairobi, 1969.
Baratieri, O., "Negli Habab", *Nuova Antologia*, 1892.
———, "Di fronte agli abissini", *Nuova Antologia*, 1888.
———, *Memorie d'Africa (1892-1896)*, Torino, 1897.
Bent, T., *The Sacred City of the Ethiopians*, London, 1896.
Berkeley, George, F., *The Campaign of Adowa and the Rise of Menelik*, London, 1902; New Edition, London, 1935.
Bianchi, G., *Alla terra di Galla*, Milano, 1884.
Bizzoni, A., *L'Eritrea nel passàto e nel presente*, Milano, 1897.
Bonacci, G., *Il Mareb Melasc*, Rome, 1905.
Bonacucina, Alfredo, *Due Anni in Masawa*, Fabriano, 1887.
Branchi, G., *Missione in Abissinia* (1883), Rome, 1889.
Bucci, E., *Paesaggi e tipi africani*, Torino, 1893.
Castellate, A., *La Figlia di Ras Alula*, Milano, 1888. See English translation in *Ethiopia Observer*, 1972, No. 3.
Caulk, R.A. "Yohannes IV, The Mahdists and the Colonial Partition of North-East Africa," *Transafrican Journal of History*, I, 2 (1972).
Chiala, L., *La Spedizione di Massaua*, Torino, 1888.
[Cagnazzi, E.] *I Nostri Errori*, Torino, 1898.
Constantin, Le Vicomte de, "Une Expedition Religieuse en Abyssinie," *La Nouvelle Revue*, Paris, February, 1891.
Conti-Rossini, Carlo, *Italia ed Etiopia*, Rome, 1935.
———, *Principi di dirirto consuetudinario dell'Eritrea*, Rome, 1916.
———, "Documenti per lo studio della lingua tigre," *GSAI*, XVI.
———, "Canti Popolari Tigrai," *Zeitschrift für Assyriologie*, Strassburg, 1906.
Crispi, F., *La prima Guerra d'Africa*, Milano, 1914.
Da Nembro, Metodio, *La Missione dei Minori Cappuccini in Eritrea (1894-1952)*, Rome, 1953.

De Lacy, O., *The Ethiopian Church*, London, 1936.
De Lauribar, P., *Douze ans en Abyssinie*, Paris, 1898.
De Vito, L., *Esercizi di lettura in Lingua Tigrigna*, Rome, 1893.
Douin, George, *Histoire du Règne du Khédive Ismaīl*, Cairo, 1933-1941.
Dye, W.M., *Moslem Egypt and Christian Abyssinia*, New York, 1880.
"Epistolario Africano," *Italiani in Africa*, Rome, 1887.
Erlich, H., "Alula, 'The Son of Qubi': A 'king's Man in Ethiopia, 1875-1897," Journal of African History, 1974, pp. 261-274.
―――, "A Contemporary biography of Ras Alula: a Ge'ez manuscript from Mänäwe, Tämben, *Bulletin of the School of Oriental and African Studies*, 1976, pp. 1-46; 287-327.
―――, "1885 in Eritrea, 'The Year in which the Dervishes were Cut Down'", *Asian and African Studies*, 1975, pp. 282-322.
Eshete, Alame, *La Mission Catholique Lazariste en Ethiopie*, Institut d'Histoire des pays d'Outre-Mer, Université d'Aix-en-Provence, Etudes et Documents No. 2 (1970-1971).

Fasolo, F., *L'Abissinia e le Colonie Italiane*, Caserta, 1887.
Gabre-Sellasie, /ewde, *Yohannes IV of Ethiopia*, Oxford, 1975.
Garima, Taffere, *Yamakarā Dawal*, Asmarā, 1963 E.C.
Gentile, L., *L'Apostolo dei Galla*, Torino, 1916.
Greenfield, R., *Ethiopia, A New Political History*, London, 1965.
Guèbrè Sellasié, *Chronique du règne de Ménélik II*, 2 vols., Paris, 1930-32.
Guidi, I., "Storie e brevi testi amarici," a paper presented to a seminar in Berlin, 1907, Faitlovich Library, Tel-Aviv University.
Guido, L., *L'Assedio di Macalle*, Rome, 1901.
Heruy Walda-Sellasse, *Yaheywat Tarik*, Addis Ababa, 1914 EC.
―――, *Ityopyana Matamma*, Addis Ababa, 1901 EC.
Hesseltine and Wolf, *The Blue and the Gray on the Nile*, Chicago, 1961.
Hill, G.B., *Colonel Gordon in Central Africa 1874-1879*, London, 1881.
Hill, R., *A Biographical Dictionary of the Anglo-Egyptian Sudan*, Oxford, 1951 (Sec.Ed., London, 1967).
Holt., P.M., *The Mahdist State of the Sudan 1881-1898*, 2nd ed., Oxford, 1970.
Ilyās al-Ayūbī, *Ta'rikh Miṣr fī 'ahd al-Khidīw Ismā'īl bāshā*, Cairo, 1923.
Ishaq Yosef, *Hade eritrawi*, Asmara, 1961 EC.
Jackson, H.C., *Osman Digna*, London, 1926.
Kolmodin, J.A., *Traditions de Tsazzega et Hazzega*, Rome, 1912-1916.
Levine, A., *Wax and Gold*, Chicago, 1965.
Littmann, E., *Publications of the Princeton Expedition to Abyssinia*, vol. II, Leyden 1910; vol. IV, Leyden, 1915.
Longrigg, S.H., *A Short History of Eritrea*, Oxford, 1945.
Māmo Wudnah, *Yaertrā tārik*, Asmarā, 1962 EC.
Mantegazza, V., *Gl'Italiani in Africa*, Firenze, 1896.
Marcus, H., "Menelik II," in N. Bennett, *Leadership in Eastern Africa, Six Political Biographies*, Boston, 1968.
―――, *The Life and Times of Menelik II, Ethiopia 1844-1913*, Oxford 1975.
―――, "Imperialism and Expansionism in Ethiopia from 1865 to 1900," in *Colonialism in Africa*, L. Gann and P. Duignan, eds. Vol. L, Cambridge 1969.
―――, "Motives, Methods and some Results of the Unification of Ethiopia," *Proceed-*

ings of the Third International Conference of Ethiopian Studies, Addis Ababa 1966, pp. 269-280.
Martini, F., Il Diario Eritreo, Rome, N.D.
———, Nell'Africa Italiana, Milano, 1891.
———, Cose Africane, Milano, 1897.
Matteucci, P., In Abissinia, Milano, 1880.
Melli, B., L'Eritrea, Milano, 1902.
Ministero della Guerra, Storia Militare della Colonia Eritrea, Rome, 1935.
Mitchell, L.H., Report on the Seizure by the Abyssinians of the Geological and Mineralogical Reconnaissance expedition, Cairo, 1878.
Nadel, S.F., "Land Tenure on the Eritrean plateau", Africa, vol. XVI, 1946, pp. 1-21, 99-109.
Negri, L., Massaua e dintorni, Valenza, 1887.
Ohrwalder, J., Ten Years' Captivity in the Mahdi's Camp, London, 1892.
Orero, B., "Ricordi d'Africa," Nuova Antologia, 1901.
Pankhurst, Richard, Economic History of Ethiopia, Addis Ababa, 1968.
———, "Ras Alula in Italy," Ethiopia Observer, 1972, No. 3.
———, "The Great Ethiopian Famine of 1889-1892," University College Review, Addis Ababa, Spring, 1969.
Paul, A., A History of the Beja Tribes of the Sudan, Cambridge, 1954.
Pennazzi, L., Dal Po ai due Nili, Milano, 1882.
Perham, M., The Government of Ethiopia, 2nd ed., London, 1969.
Perini, R., Di Qua dal Mareb, Firenze, 1905.
Perino, E., Vita e gesta di Ras Alula, Rome, 1897.
Polera, Alberto, I Baria e I Cunama, Rome, 1913.
———, Il Regime della proprietà terriera in Etiopia e nella Colonia Eritrea, Rome, 1913.
———, L'Abissinia di Ieri, Asmara, 1940.
Portal, G.H., My Mission to Abyssinia, London, 1892.
Puglisi, G., Chi e? dell-Eritrea, Asmara, 1952.
Rif'at, Muḥammad, Jabr al-kasr fī al-khilās min al-Asr, Cairo, 1314 H.
Roden, K., Le Tribu dei Mensa, Stockholm and Asmara, 1913.
Rohlfs, G., L'Abbissinia, Milano, 1885.
Rubenson, S., ———, The Survival of Ethiopian Independence, London, 1976.
"The Adwa peace treaty of 1884," Third International Conference of Ethiopian Studies, Addis Ababa, 1966.
———, "Some Aspects of the Survival of Ethiopian Independence," University College Review, Addis Ababa, 1961.
———, Wichale XVII, Addis Ababa, 1964.
Sabelli, Luca dei, Storia d'Abissinia, Rome, 1936.
Salimbeni, A., "Diario d'un pioniere africano," Nuova Antologia, 1936.
Sapelli, A., Memorie d'Africa (1883-1906), Bologna, 1935.
Savelli, M., La Spedizione, Rome, 1886.
Shuqayr, Na'ūm, Ta'rīkh as-Sūdān al-qādim wal-ḥadīth wajigrafiyatuhā, Cairo, 1903.
Simon, G., L'Ethiopie, Paris, 1885.
Smith, H., Through Abyssinia, London, 1890.
Takla-Ṣadeq Makuriyā, Ya'itopyā tārik, Addis Ababa, 1960 EC.
Trimingham, J.S., Islam in Ethiopia, 2nd ed., Oxford, 1965.

Truffi, R., *Precursori dell'Impero Africano*, Milano, 1936.
Un ex funzionario Eritreo, *La nostra politica africana*, Imola, 1895.
Vanderheym, J.G., *Une expédition avec le négous Ménélik*, Paris, 1896.
Wingate, F.R., *Mahdism and the Egyptian Sudan*, London, 1901.
Winqvist, K., *En liten aterblick*, Stockholm, 1908.
Winstanley, W., *A visit to Abyssinia*, London, 1881.
Wylde, A.B., *'83-'87 in the Soudan*, London, 1888.
———, *Modern Abyssinia*, London, 1900.
Zaghi, Carlo, *Le origini della Colonia Eritrea*, Bologna, 1934.
———, *Crispi e Menelich; Nel diario inedito del Conte A. Salimbeni*, Torino, 1956.
———, "Il Convegno del Mareb," *Rivista delle Colonie*, Anno XI, No. 2, pp. 175-184.
———, "L'Italia e l'Etiopia alla vigilia di Adua," *Gli Annali del'Africa Italiana*, 1941.

VI Informants quoted in the Book

A collective interview with the people of Mannawē, February 1972.
Dr. Abbā Gabra-Iyāsus Hāylu, Addis Ababa, January 1972.
Kagnāzmāch Arbehā Fantā, Asmara, March 1972.
Fitāwrāri Ālamē Tafari, Maqalē, February 1972.
Fitāwrāri Bayyana Abrehā, a descendent of Alulā, Aksum, February 1972.
Ato Bairu Tafla of IES who had collected oral sources in Tigre, January, March 1972.
W. Worqu Imām, Asmarā, March 1972.
W. Walatta-Berhān, Asmarā, March 1972. A tape of an interview with her about Alulā is available in IES.
W. Yashāshwarq Bayyana, a descendant of Alulā, Abbi Addi, February 1972.
Ato Yekunuamlāk Ar'āyā, Maqalē, February 1972.
Dr. Dadjāzmāch Zewde Gabre Sellassie, an historian, Addis Ababa, March 1972.
A Tigrean teacher who wishes to remain anonymous, February 1972.

Indexed Maps

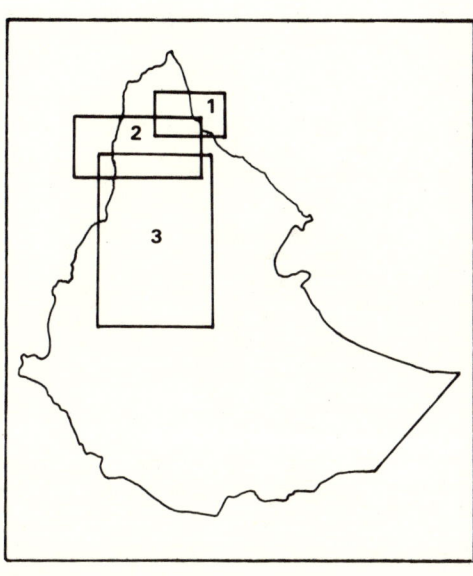

Abba Garima 2
Abbi Addi 2
Ad Tamaryam 1
Addigrat 2
Addi Qayh 2
Addi Rasi 1
Addi Taklay 1
Addis Ababa 3
Ad Taklis 1
Adwa 2
Agame 2
Agaw Meder 3
Akalla-Guzay 2
Aksum 2
Alitiena 2
Amba 1
Amba Alaje 3
Amba Dibuk 3
Amba Salama 2
Amba Sion 3
'Amıdıb 2
R. Ansaba 1
Arafali 2
Ashange 3
Asmara 1
Assawurta 1
Avergalle 3
Ayba 2
Aylet 1
Azebo Galla 3
Bagemder 3
Banu 'Amir 2
Baria 2
Barka 2
Bet Jok 1
Bogos 2
Boru Meda 3
Buri 2

Dabra-Bizan 1
Dabra-Damo 2
Dabra-Sina 1
Dabra-Tabor 3
Dambalas 2
Dambiya 3
Damot 3
Daqqa 2
Daro Takla 2
Dogali 1
Edaga-Hamus 2
Enda-Makonni 3
Endarta 2
Enticho 2
Faras May
Filiq 2
Garalta 3
R. Gash 2
Ginda 1
Godjam 3
Godofelasi 2

Gondar 3
Gundat 2
Gura 2
Hadendowa 2
Halaniqa 2
Halhal 2
Hamasen 1
Hantalo 3
Haramat 2
Hawzen 2
Hazaga 1
Ira 1
Jira 3
Karan 2
Kassala 2
Ko'atit 2
Kohayn 2
Kufit 2
Kumaliyya 2
Kunama 2
Lasta 3

Magalo 2
Magdala 3
Mannawe 2
Mansa 1
Maqale 2
R. Marab 2
Massawa 1
Matamma 3
Otumlo 1
Sabarguma 2
Sabdrat 2
Saganieti 2
Sahati 1
Saharte 2
Salamti 3
Sanafe 2
Sanhit (karan) 1
Saqota 3
Saraye 2
Sa'zaga 1
Seloa 3
Semen 3
Shabbab 1
Shire 2
Shoa 3
Shoho 1
Takkaze 2
Tamben 3
Wadela
Wadjrat 3
Wag 3
Wallo 3
Warra Ilu 3
Wi'a 2
Yedju 3
Zabul 3
Zuguli 2

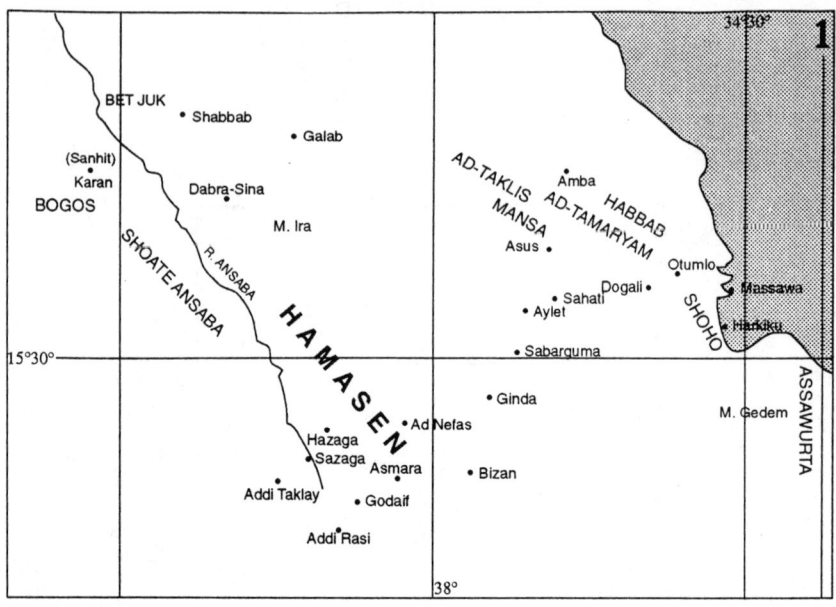

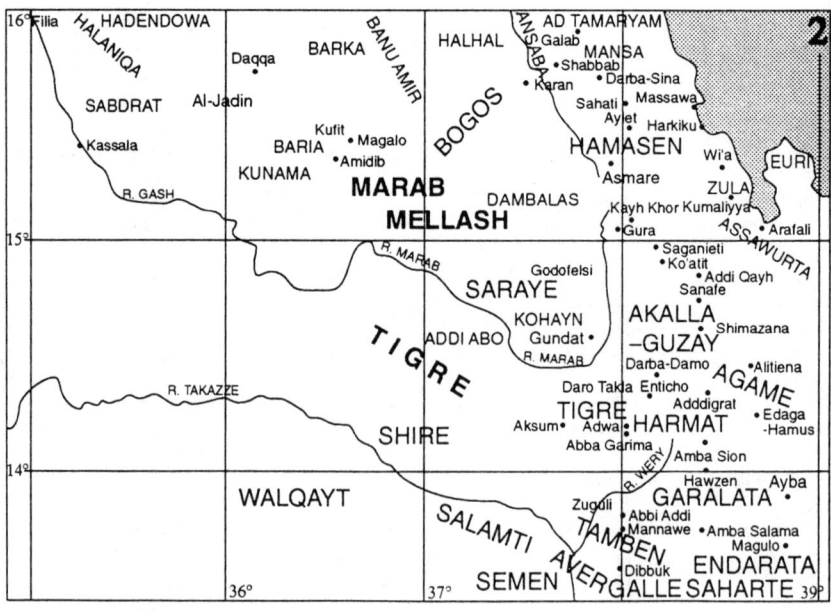

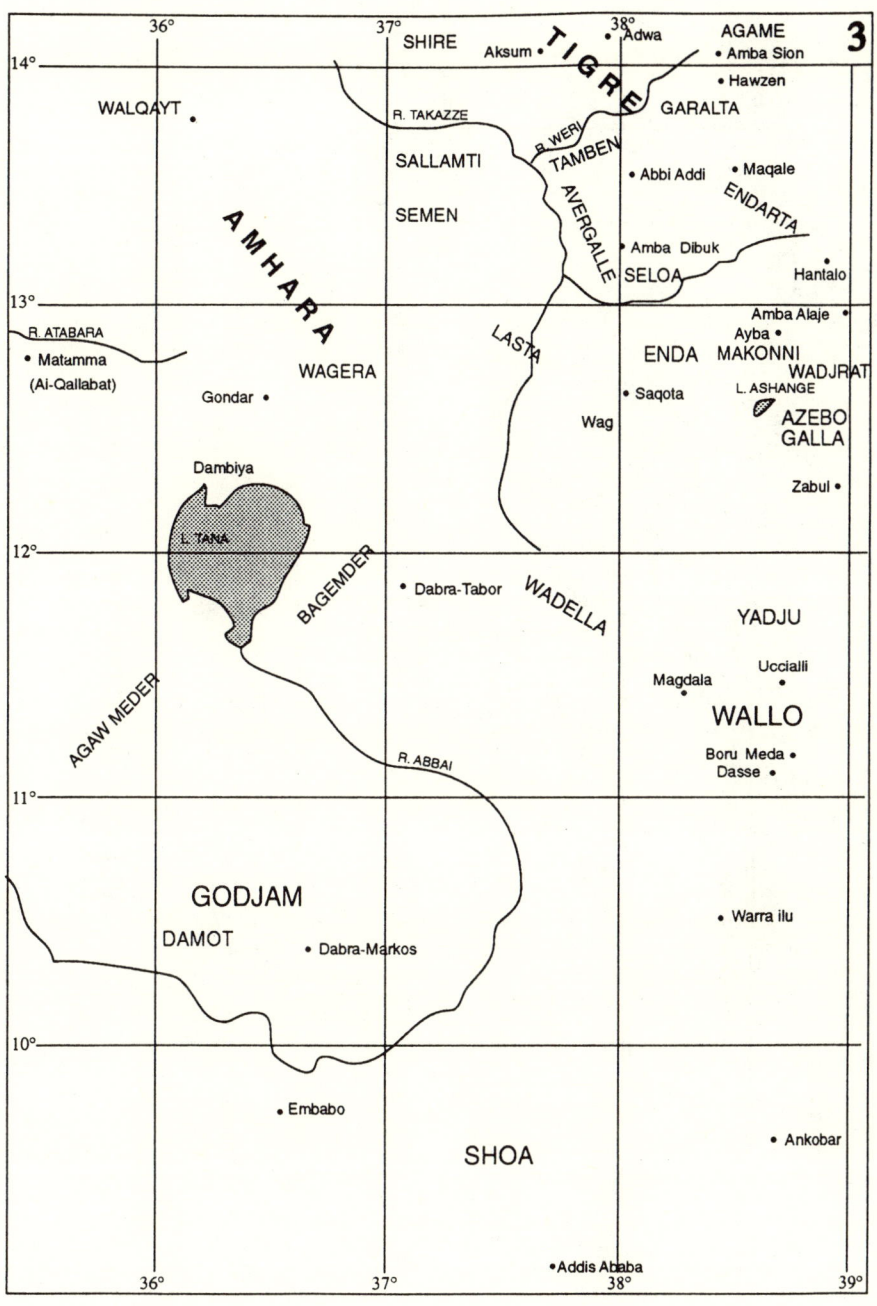

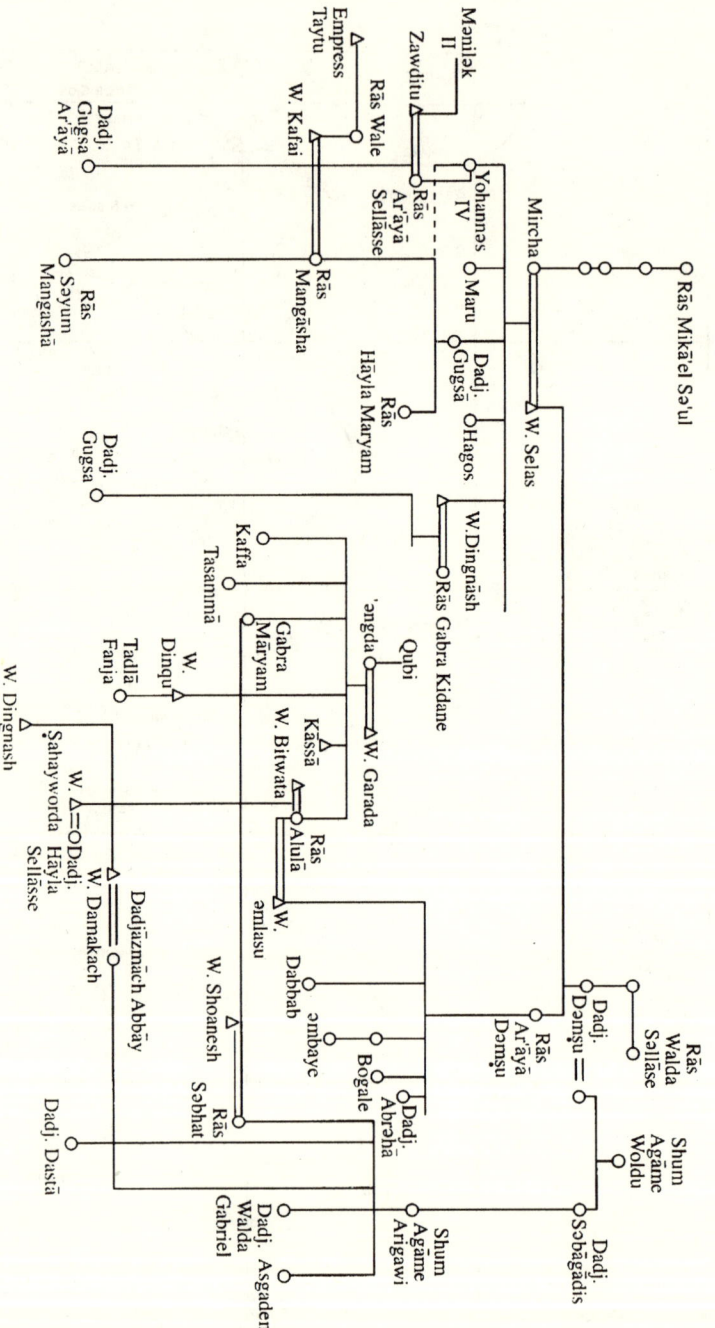

Genealogy of Alulā and the Tigrean Elite

Index

Abbarrā, *Azmāch* 190, 191.
Abba Takla-Māriām, 113.
Abbāy, *Dadjāzmāch*, 181, 182.
Abbāy Aragāwi, *Dadjāzmāch*, 172, 181, 182.
'Abdallāh, *Khalīfa*, 65, 78, 127, 136.
'Abd al-Qādir, *Shaykh*, 59, 60, 61, 64, 65, 66, 67.
Abrehā Ar'āyā, *Dadjāzmāch*, 203.
Abrehā Gabru, *Ledj*, 147.
Abrehā Hagos, *Dadjāzmāch*, 203.
Adāl, *Rās* (later *Negus* Takla-Hāymānot), 2, 10, 20, 21, 23, 35, 127.
Ad-Tamāriām, tribe, 35, 54, 59, 61.
Adwā, Battle of, 3, 191-193.
Agaw Negussē, 1.
Ahmad b. Ibrāhīm, *Imām*, 1.
'Alā' ad-Dīn, *Pasha*, 22.
'Alāmayhu Gabru, 143.
'Alī Bakhīt, *Shaykh*, 54.
'Alī Nūrīn, *Shaykh*, 62, 71, 101.
'Amda-Ṣiyon, Emperor, 4.
Andārgāchawu, *Dadjāzmāch*, 190.
Antanewos, *Abuna*, 12.
Antonelli, Count Augusto, 94, 106, 108, 129, 153, 162.
'Arāqīl Bey, 10.
Arāy, *Shaykh*, 65, 70, 71, 101, 102.
Ar'āyā, *Shālaqā*, 60, 84, 87, 94, 107, 108, 122, 132, 143.
Ar'āyā Demṣu, *Rās*, 1, 9, 18, 22, 24, 26, 35, 39, 55, 100, 118 dies in battle 135, 140, 142, 166, 203.

Ar'āyā-Sellāssē, *Rās* (Yohannes's son), 24, 36, 47, 90, 101, 117, 121, dies (1888) 129, 144, 203.
Ashinov, Nikolai, 92.
Asmē Giorgis, 148.
Assam River, Battle of, 9.
Assāwurta, tribe, 53, 92, 93, 98, 110, 111, 112, 114, 146, 147, 166.

Bāhtā Hagos, *Dadjāzmāch*, 25, 33, 34, 48, 53, 149, 150, 165, 189, 198.
Baker, General V, 43, 44, 45.
Bakrī al-Mīrghanī, *Shaykh*, 64.
Baldissera, General Antonio, 121, 131, 134, 143, 146, 147, 148, 149, 150.
Banū 'Āmir, tribe, 51, 54, 59, 61, 64, 66, 67, 69, 71, 85, 100, 102, 112, 131.
Baraka, tribe, 64.
Baratieri, General Oreste, 173, 174, 179, 180, 181, 183, 186, 187, 189.
Baria, tribe, 64, 65, 70, 71, 101-102, 104.
Bāriāu Gabra-Ṣadeq, *Rās*, 13, 21, 22.
Baring, Evelyn, 53, 114, 115.
Bayyana, *Ledj*, 173, 174, 180.
Belcredi G., 60.
Bent T.J., 182.
Berkeley G., 191, 203.
Beru, *Wāgshum*, 144, 148, 149, 190.
Bitwatā Gabra-Masqal (Alulā's first wife), 9, 22.
Borgnini, 168.
Britain, British, help Yohannes to power (1868), 2, 24, 25, continue to avoid

217

direct relations with Yohannes (1879), 31-32, 34, 41, sign a treaty with Yohannes (1884), 43-48, push Yohannes fight the Mahdists, let the Italians occupy Massawa (1885), 51-74, 82, 92, 95, mediate between Yohannes and Italians (1886), 98-99, mediate after Dogali (1887), 111-116, desert Yohannes, 117, 121, 131, 134. 197.

Cagni, General, 117.
Capucci (an Italian agent), 188.
Chermside, Colonel H., 51, 54, 59, 60, 61-67, 72.
Clapham C., 4.
Colaci (an Italian journalist), 60.
Conti Rossini, Carlo, 140.
Corazzini N., 161.
Coulbeaux J.B., 50, 89, 112.
Crispi, Francesco, 114, 146, 176.

Dabbab Ar'āyā, *Fitāwrāri* (later *Dadjāzmāch*), 9, 22, 35, 39-40, 41, 42, 43, 48, 53, 66, 88, 92, 93, 98, 107, 110, 112, 114, 118-119, 121, occupies Asmara from Alula's men, transfers it to the Italians (1889), 131-134, 140, 141-2, 143, imprisoned by Alula and Mangashā, 145-146, 148, 161, killed by Alulā, 165, 170, 194, 203.
Dammaqach (Alula's daughter), 9, 172.
Dārgē Sāhla-Sellāssē, *Rās*, 186.
Dastā Abba-Ga'i, *Bāshā* (later *Fitāwrāri*), 105, 133, 181.
Dastā Sebhat, 161, 162, 203.
De Martino (Italian resident at Adwā), 167, 170, 174, 179, 180, 181.
Dinqnash (Alulā's daughter), 9.
Dinqnash (Yohannes's sister), 146.
Dogali, Battle of, 40, 98-106, 110-111, 119, 154, 171.
Doflos (French missionary), 24.

Egerton, Sir Charles, 73.
Egypt, Egyptians, 2, threaten Yohannes and defeated (1875-6), 10-12, border relations in Eritrea (1876-1882), 17, 22, 24, 25, 30-35, deterioration towards war with Yohannes (1883), 39-42, collapse in Sudan and treaty with Yohannes (1884), 43-48, 51-55, Sudanese garrisons besieged, rescued (1885), 58, 59, 60, 61, 67, 73, 98, 99, 106, 127, 202.
Embābo, Battle of, 35.
Embāyē, *Dadjāzmāch*, 145, 148, 165, 180, 182.
Emlasu Ar'āyā (Alulā's wife), 22, 39-40, 121.
Enda Abuna-Pantaleun, Battle of, 149.
Engdā *Dadjāzmāch*, 84.
Engdā Qubi (Alulā's father), 5.

Fanjā, *Bāshā*, 105.
Fanjā Tasammā, *Ledj*, 105.
Fantā Wudā'ēl, *Ledj*, 51, 84, 87, 132.
Ferrari, Vicenzo, 58, 60.
France, French, 25, 33-34, 44, 89, 91-92, 94, 103, 104, 106, 108, 111, 112.

Gabra-Egziabhēr, *Bāshā*, 196.
Gabraesgi, *Bāshā*, 145.
Gabra-Kidānē, *Rās*, 36, 55.
Gabra-Mahden, Bāriāu, *Dadjāzmāch*, 22, 33.
Gabra-Masqal, *Rās Bitwaddad*, 36, 50.
Gabra-Māriām, *Bāshā*, 131.
Gabra-Māriām, *Bāshā* (Alulā's brother), 10, 12, 172.
Gabra-Sellāssē Bariyā-Gaber, *Dadjāzmāch*, 202, 203.
Gabrē, *Bāshā*, 50.
Gabre'et, *Bāshā*, 101, 102.
Gabru, *Dadjāzmāch*, (ruler of Hamāsēn), 10.
Gabru, *Belāttā*, 16, 27, character sketch

by Wylde, 33, 39, 59, 66, 67, 68, 69, 70, 71, 84, 87, 143, 147.
Galla — See Oromo.
Gandolfi, General Antonio, 162, 163, 167, 170, 171, 172, 173.
Genè, General Carlo, 90, 91, 93, 94, 103-105, 110, 111, 112, 117.
Ghabriyyāl Jārallāh, 72.
Gobazē, *Wāgshum* (later Emperor Takla-Giorgis), 2.
Gobazē, *Wāgshum*, 189.
Gordon, Colonel Charles, 17, 18, 22, 24, 30, 31, 32.
Graham W., 45.
Gugsa Ar'āyā-Sellāssē, *Dadjāzmāch*, 203.
Gundat, Battle of, 11.
Gurā, Battle of, 11-12, 16, 19, 40, 119.

Habbāb, tribe, 34, 35, 51, 53, 54, 59, 60, 61, 62, 67, 72, 85, protection agreement with Italians (1885), 90-91, 93, 94, 99, 100, 103, 112, 114, 131, 143.
Haddād, *Shaykh*, 54.
Hadendawa, tribe, 64.
Hadgu, *Dadjāzmāch*, 194.
Halāniqa, tribe, 64, 70, 71.
Hagos, Mirtcha, *Dadjāzmāch* (later *Rās*), 10, 50, 55, 90, 99, 111, 117, 118, 121, 130, 143, 145, 150, 162, 166, 171, 172, 173, 180, 181, 183, 186, 192, 194, 196, 198, 203.
Hagos Tafari, *Rās*, 194.
Ḥamdān Abū 'Anja, 119, 127, 130, 133, 134.
Hamīd, *Kantibā*, 51, 54, 59, 61, 62, 72, 90, 91, 93.
Ḥasan Bāshā, 17, 18.
Hāyla-Malakot Walda-Mikā'ēl, *Ledj*, 25, 142, 165.
Hāyla-Māryām, *Dadjāzmāch*, 190.
Hāyla-Māryām, *Kagnāzmāch*, 190.
Hāyla-Māryām Gugsa, *Rās* (Yohannes's nephew), 117, 130, 131, 133, 134-135, 137.
Hāyla-Sellāssē, *Dadjāzmāch*, 84, 130, 131-132, 134, 137, 169.
Haylu, *Kantibā*, 25.
Haylu, *Ledj*, 163.
Haylu Habal, *Dadjāzmāch*, 12, 13.
Heruy Walda-Sellāssē, 201.
Hewett, Sir William, Mission, Treaty, 43-48, 50, 52, 58, 60, 74, 82, 93, 95, 100, 106, 110, 114, 120, 121, 127.
Hicks Pasha, 43.
Holt, P.M., 127.

'Iffat Bey (*Mudīr* of Kassala), 59, 60, 62, 64, 72.
Ismā'īl, Khedive, 10.
Ismā'īl b. 'Abd al-Qādir, 127.
Italy, Italians, 2, landing at Massawa (1885), 58, establish first contact with Alulā, 60, build relations with Eritrean tribes, 61, 62, occupy Sahāti, 62, "cold war" with Alulā, 72, relations with Ethiopia and border problems (1885-1886), 88-95, encroachment, deterioration of relations with Alulā (1886), defeated at Dogali (1887), 98-106, punitive mission (of 1887-1888), 110-122, occupy Karan, 143, occupy Asmara, 146,148, help Menilek dominate Tigre (1890), 150-155, first rupture with Menilek (1891), 165, pro-Tigrean policy (1891), 168—172, return to "Shoan Policy" (1892), 172—174, renewed rupture with Menilek (1893), 182, defeated at Adwā, 191-193, 202, 203.
Iyāsu, *Ledj*, 203.
'Izzat Bey, 63.

Al-Jadīn, tribe, 64, 65, 70. 71.

Kafāi, *Wayzarit*, 193.

220 INDEX

Kāssā Mirtcha, *Dadjāzmāch* (late Emperor Yohannes IV), 2, 9.
Kefḻē Iyāsus, *Bālāmbārās*, 25, 48, 53, 60, 90, 104, 110, 111, 131, 132, 133, 134, 142, 143.
Koʻatit, Battle of, 189.
Kūfīt, Battle of, 61, 65, 67-72, 78, 89, 90, 99, 119.
Kunama, tribe, 101.

Lamlam, *Alaqā*, 19, 118, 129, 133.
Lawṭē, *Badjerond* (later *Fitāwrāri*), 50, 53, 100, 131.
Lazzarist, missionaries, 24, 33.
Levine, D., 4.

Mahdiyya, Mahdists, 2, emergence and Yohannes's undertaking to fight it (1884), 43, 45, 47, 48, struggle with Alulā over Eritrea and Eritrean tribes (1885), 51-80, 90, 91, 95, renewed conflict in western Eritrea and Gondar (1886), 100, 101, invasion of Amhara (1888), 117-120, 127-129, final clash with Yohannes (1889), 132-136, 141, 147, 170, 189, 202, 203.
Makonnen, *Rās*, 173, 187, 188, 191, 196, 203.
Mangashā Yohannes, *Dadjāzmāch* (Yohannes's nephew, later adopted son and *Rās*), 117, 125, 131, 133, 134, adopted by the dying Yohannes as son and heir (1889), 135, 138, avoids proclaiming emperorship (1889), 140-142, 143, 144, 145, 146, 147, saved by Alulā (1889), 148-151, submits to Menilek (1890), 152-155, and Alulā's anti-Shoan and pro-Italian policy (1890-1892), 161-174, returns to a Shoan policy, fights Alulā (1892-1894), 179-183, submits to Menilek (1894), 186-188, fights the Italians (1895), 189, 190, and Menilek after Adwā (1896), 193-196, 202, dies (1906), 203.
Mansa, tribe, 16, 17, 33, 34, 53, 54, 93.
Macropoli Bey, 63, 64, 66, 67, 70, 71.
Maria, tribe, 85.
Marshā, *Bāshā*, 105.
Masfen Walda-Mikā'ēl, *Dadjāzmāch*, 13, 25, 142, 143.
Mashashā Warqē, *Dadjāzmāch*, 153, 154, 160, 161, 163, 163, 165.
Mason Bey, 44, 45, 46, 47, 51, 52, 54.
Massaja, G., 20.
Matammā (Al-Qallābāt), Battle of, 134-136, 141.
Mātēwos, *Abuna*, 180.
Menilek, *Negus*, later Emperor, 1, 2, role in the "scramble", 3, 4, relations with Egypt 10, 16, relations with Yohannes (1877-1878), 18-20, 23, and Yohannes (1882), 35-36, 41, 94, 110, 117, revolts against Yohannes (1888), 118, friendly relations with the Italians (1888), 121, revolts gainst Yohannes (1888-1889), 127-130, 132-133, and Mahdiyya (1888), 137, 140, signs treaty of Uccialli, sends his devotees to control Tigre (1889), 144, 147, 148, crowned emperor (1889), 149, his subsequent Italian policy, 151, policy in Tigre (1890), 152-155, 161, rupture with Italians (1891), 165, pressing Mangashā to resubmit (1892-1894), 179-180, saves Alulā (1893), 183, obtains submission of the Tigrean chiefs, defeats the Italians at Adwā (1894-1896), 186-196.
Mercatelli L., 163, 164, 165, 166, 167, 170, 175.
Mikā'ēl, *Rās*, 2, 20, 36, 41, 47, 50, 117, 118, 119, 120, 125, 133, 139, transfers loyalty to Menilek following death of Yohannes (1889), 140, 144, 186, 189, 190, 203.

Mikā'ēl Sehul, *Rās*, 1, 2, 140.
Mīrghanī, family, Mīrghaniyya, 54, 57, 60, 64.
Mitchel, H.L., 16, 17.
Muḥammad b. 'Awad, *Shaykh*, 71.
Muḥammad 'Alī, *Imām* (later *Rās* Mikā'ēl), 2, 20, 21.
Mukhtār Pasha, 40, 41, 43.
Mulazzani (Italian officer), 95, 194.
Munzinger W., 10.
Musā al-Fīl, *Shaykh*, 62, 69, 71, 101.
Musā Sadīq, *Shaykh*, 64.
Muslims, Islam, 10, Yohannes's policy, 23, 31, 33, 35, 43, and Eritrean tribes during 1885 conflicts 51-74, and Alulā's regime in Eritrea 82-83, 85, 90, 95, 102, 112, 118, and Mahdist approach to Ethiopian affairs, 64-65, 127-128, 133.
Musṭafā Hadal, 64. 68.

Nadel S.F., 81.
Nāfi' al-Halāniqī, *Shaykh*, 71.
Nā'ib of Harkiku, 40, 88, 93.
Napier, General Robert, 2, 10, 95.
Naretti, Giacomo, 58.
Negus, *Fitāwrāri*, 190.
Nerazzini, Cesare, 58, 60, 94, 170.

Orero, General Baldassare, 151, 169.
Oromo (Gāllā), 1, 2, 23, 32, 50, 90, 92, 98, 102, 117, 118, 189.

Paillard, Father, 112.
Perini, R., 85.
Petros, *Abuna*, 180.
Picard, Father, 113.
Piano, Major F., 111, 134, 147.
Pollera A., 81, 101, 102.
Portal G. (mediation mission), 114-116, 117, 120, 121.
Pozzolini, General Giorgio, 93, 94.

INDEX 221

Raffray A., 24, 25, 30, 33.
Rashīd Pasha, 34, 35.
Robilant, Count Carlo, 91, 92.
Rohlfs G., 82.
Rolfe, Ernest, 45. 52.
Rubenson S., 3.

Sabāgādis, *Dadjāzmāch*, 1, 2, 141, 166.
Sabdrāt, tribe, 64, 65.
Sa'd Rif'at, Major, 56, 59.
Sadur, *Grāzmāch*, 153.
Sahāywarada (Alulā's daughter), 9.
Sahāti, Battle of (1883), 41, 43.
Sahlē, *Kantibā*, 147.
Saletta, Colonel, later General Tancredi, 59, 60, 61, 67, 72, 88, 89, 90, 91, 94, 112, 113, 114.
Salimbeni, Count Augusto, 104, 110, 111, 154, 155, 162.
Salisburi, Marquess of, 73, 115.
Salsa, Major T., 193.
San-Marzano, General Alessandro, 117, 120, 122.
Savoiroux T., 111, 112.
Sebhat Aragāwi, *Dadjāzmāch*, later *Rās*, 141, 149, 151, 153, 161-162, 163, 165, 168, 169, 171, 179, 181, 192, 194, 203.
Seyum Gabra-Kidān, *Dadjāzmāch*, 132, 141, 144, 146, 147, 148-151, 153, 161, 179.
Seyum Mangashā, *Dadjāzmāch*, 203.
Shāwīsh, *Kantibā*, 25.
Shoanesh, *Wayzaro*, 172.
Smith, Harrison, 71, 91, 98, 99, 111, 114.
Soumagne, François, 44, 50, 90, 92, 104, 111.
Speedy, Captain, 46, 51, 52, 53.
Swedish missionaries, 33.

Tadlā Abbāguben, *Dadjāzmāch*, 194.

222 INDEX

Tadlā Aybā, *Dadjāzmāch*, 90, 100, 101, 141, 142, 143, 148, 149, 150, 198.
Tadlā Fanjā, *Bāshā*, later *Dadjāzmāch*, 84, 130, 148, 181, 182.
Tadlā Wahid, *Dadjāzmāch*, 165, 168, 191.
Tagagnā, *Dadjāzmāch*, 166.
Takla-Giorgis, Emperor, 2, 9.
Takla-Hāymānot, *Dadjāzmāch*, 181.
Takla-Hāymānot, *Negus* (see also Rās Adāl), 35, 36, 41, 101, 117, 127, revolts against Yohannes (1888), 128-132, 133, 140, 144, 189.
Talā Addi Mallālē, *Bāshā*, 105.
Talā Waddi, *Bāshā*, 105.
Tasammā, *Bāshā*, later *Balāmbārās*, later *Dadjāzmāch* (Alulā's brother), 11, 104, 107, 121, 130, 143.
Tasfāyē Hantalo, *Belāttā*, 179, 180, 190, 194, 203.
Taytu, Empress, 187, 189, 191, 193.
Tēwodros II, *Emperor*, 1, 2, 5, 9, 23, 203.
Tēwoflos, *Echagē*, 19, 27, 47, 134, 135, 172, 174, 179, 180, 182, 183.

Uccialli, Treaty of, 141, 144, 151, 164, 169.
'Umar, *Shaykh*, 54, 59.
Umberto, King of Italy, 144, 162, 169-170.
'Uthmān Diqna, *Amīr*, 43, 54, 59, 61-73, 89, 90, 102, 128, 143.

'Uthmān al-Mīrghanī, *Sayyid*, 54, 59, 63, 64.
'Uthmān Pasha, 16, 17.

Victoria, Queen, 47, 73, 99, 106, 115, 116, 195.

Walda-Gabre'ēl, *Dadjāzmāch*, 101.
Walda-Giorgis, *Mamher*, 5.

Walda-Giorgis, *Mamher* later *Nebura-'ed*, 194.
Walda-Giorgis, *Nebura-'ed*, 142, 143.
Walda-Mikā'ēl Solomon, *Ledj*, later *Rās*, 10-26, 48, 82, 83, 84, 99, 132, 142, 146, 165, 166, 167, 171, 186, 201.
Walda-Samāyāt, *Mamher*, 90, 112.
Walda-Sellāssē, *Rās*, 1, 2, 140
Waldē, *Dadjāzmāch*, 161.
Walē, *Rās* (Italian-Oliè), 186, 187, 189, 190, 193.
Warqu, *Bālāmbārās*, 104.
Webē, *Dadjāzmāch*, 1.
Winstanley, W., 24, 31.
Wokidba, Battle of, 13.
Wylde A.B., 18, 31-32, 44, 62, 63, 74, 83, 187, 192, 194, 195.

Yohannes IV, Emperor, 1, his regime, nationalist concept and role in the "Scramble", 2, 4, 6, obtaining the emperorship, 9, his relations with Egypt, 10, 11, 12, 113, and Menilek (1877-1878), 18-20, his regime and nationalist concept 23, religious policy 24, 25, 26, 30, religious policy 33, and Menilek (1882) 35-36, 40, preparing to fight Egypt (1883) 41-43, and the Hewett mission, attitude to British and French policies (1884) 44-48, 50, 53, 55, 58, 59, 61, and the battle of Kūfīt, 73, 81, religious policy, 83, Alulā's influence on him (1885), 88, restrains Alulā's anti-Italian tendencies (1885), 89, entrusts Alulā with border relations, 90, 92, his concept of the Italians, 93, 94, 98, trusts British mediation, 99, 100, authorises Alulā to confront the Italians at Massawa (late 1886), 102, 103, 104, and Alulā's responsibility for Dogali 105-106, 110-112 and British mediation with the Italians 111-116, persuaded by Alulā to fight the Italians (1888) 117-120 decides to remove Alulā from Eritrea, 121, challenged by the Italians and the Mahdists, betrayed by Menilek and Takla-Hāymānot, killed in battle, 127-136, 154, 166, 169, 187, 188, 194, 202, 203.

Zabān Cha'ā, Battle of, 149-151.
Zākī 'Abd ar-Raḥmān, 39.
Az-Zākī Ṭamal, 134, 136.
Zawditu (Menilek's daughter, later Empress, 1916-1930), 36, 129, 144, 187.